THE ARTS OF READING

Ralph Ross, John Berryman, and Allen Tate

UNIVERSITY OF MINNESOTA

The Arts of Reading

THOMAS Y. CROWELL COMPANY

New York · Established 1834

Designed by Laurel Wagner

Library of Congress Catalog Card Number: 60-7127

Manufactured in the United States of America
Apollo Edition 1966

ACKNOWLEDGMENTS

Acknowledgment is gratefully made as follows (on pp. iv–vii) to reprint copyrighted material:

Aristotle, *Nicomachean Ethics:* Translation by Richard McKeon in *The Basic Works of Aristotle* reprinted by permission of the Clarendon Press, Oxford.

Isaak Babel, "In Odessa": Reprinted from *Benya Krik, the Gangster,* by Isaak Babel, by permission of Schocken Books, New York, copyright 1948 by Schocken Books, New York.

Arnold Bennett, from *The Old Wives' Tale:* Reprinted from *The Old Wives' Tale* by Arnold Bennett, by permission of Doubleday & Company, Inc., the owner of the copyright in Arnold Bennett's *The Old Wives' Tale,* and A. P. Watt & Son.

Jacob Burkhardt: From *Judgments on History and Historians* (Boston: Beacon Press, 1958) reprinted by permission of the publisher. From *Force and Freedom* (Pantheon Books, Inc.) reprinted by permission of the publisher.

Anton Chekhov, *A Marriage Proposal:* Reprinted from Theodore Hoffman's translation of *A Marriage Proposal* from *The Brute and Other Farces* (copyright 1958) by permission of Grove Press, Inc.

Stephen Crane, "The Open Boat": Reprinted from *Stephen Crane: An Omnibus,* edited by Robert Wooster Stallman, by permission of Alfred A. Knopf, Inc. Copyright 1952 by Alfred A. Knopf, Inc.

John Dewey, from *Liberalism and Social Action:* Reprinted from *Liberalism and Social Action* (1935) by John Dewey, by permission of G. P. Putnam's Sons.

T. S. Eliot, "The Love Song of J. Alfred Prufrock": From *Collected Poems 1909–1962* by T. S. Eliot, copyright, 1936, by Harcourt, Brace & World, Inc.; copyright © 1963, 1964 by T. S. Eliot; reprinted by permission of the publishers.

Friedrich Engels, from *Anti-Dühring:* Reprinted from *Anti-Düring,* by Friedrich Engels, as quoted by V. I. Lenin, *State and Revolution,* by permission of International Publishers, publishers of both books.

Epictetus, from *The Manual:* Reprinted from the P. E. Matheson translation by permission of the Clarendon Press, Oxford.

E. M. Forster, "The Machine Stops": From *The Eternal Moment and Other Stories* by E. M. Forster, copyright 1928 by Harcourt, Brace & World, Inc., renewed 1956 by E. M. Forster, by permission of the publishers.

Sigmund Freud, *Civilization and Its Discontents:* translated from the German and edited by James Strachey; copyright © 1961 by James Strachey and reprinted by permission from the publisher, W. W. Norton & Company, Inc.

Ernest Hemingway, "A Clean, Well-Lighted Place": Copyright 1933 Charles Scribner's Sons, renewal copyright © 1961 by Ernest Hemingway. Reprinted by permission of Charles Scribner's Sons from *Winner Take Nothing* by Ernest Hemingway.

O. Henry, "The Gift of the Magi": From: *The Four Million,* by O. Henry. Copyright 1905 by Doubleday & Company, Inc. Reprinted by permission.

Adolf Hitler, from *Hitler's Secret Conversations:* From *Hitler's Secret Conversations,* translated by Norman Cameron and R. H. Stevens, with an introduction by H. R. Trevor-Roper, copyright 1953 by Farrar, Straus and Young, Inc. Used by permission of the publishers, Farrar, Straus and Cudahy, Inc. and George Weidenfeld & Nicolson Ltd.

Oliver Wendell Holmes, Jr., from *Collected Legal Papers:* From *Collected Legal Papers,* by Oliver Wendell Holmes, copyright, 1920, by Harcourt, Brace and Company, Inc.; renewed, 1948, by Edward J. Holmes. Reprinted by permission of the publishers.

Henry James, from Preface to "Lady Barbarina": Copyright 1908 Charles

Scribner's Sons; renewal copyright 1936 Henry James. Reprinted from *The Art of the Novel* by Henry James by permission of the publisher.

William James: From "The Moral Equivalent of War": From *Memories and Studies* (1911) by William James. Permission to reprint granted by Paul R. Reynolds & Son, 599 Fifth Avenue, New York 17, New York. From *The Principles of Psychology:* Reprinted from *The Principles of Psychology,* by William James, by permission of Henry Holt and Company.

James Joyce, "Araby": From *Dubliners* by James Joyce, Compass books edition. Reprinted by permission of The Viking Press, Inc.

Franz Kafka: Reprinted from *The Trial,* by Franz Kafka; translated from the German by Willa and Edwin Muir; Revised and with additional material translated by E. M. Butler; illustrated by George Salter, by permission of Alfred A. Knopf, Inc. Copyright 1937, 1956 by Alfred A. Knopf, Inc. "Imperial Message" and "A Fratricide" reprinted from *Penal Colony* by Franz Kafka, by permission of Schocken Books, New York, copyright 1948, Schocken Books, New York; "Couriers" reprinted from *Parables* by Franz Kafka, by permission of Schocken Books, New York, copyright 1946, Schocken Books, New York.

Alun Lewis, "A Song": Reprinted from *Ha! Ha! Among the Trumpets,* by Alun Lewis, by permission of the publishers, George Allen & Unwin Ltd.

Karl Mannheim, from *Ideology and Utopia:* Reprinted from *Ideology and Utopia* by Karl Mannheim, by permission of Harcourt, Brace and Company, Inc. and Routledge & Kegan Paul Ltd.

Walter de la Mare, "Song of the Mad Prince": Reprinted by permission of the Literary Trustees of Walter de la Mare and the Society of Authors as their representative.

Quotation from the Minneapolis *Tribune:* Reprinted by permission from the Minneapolis *Tribune.*

José Ortega y Gasset: Reprinted from *History as a System* and other essays toward a Philosophy of History by José Ortega y Gasset, by permission of W. W. Norton & Company, Inc. Copyright 1941 ⓒ 1961 by W. W. Norton & Company, Inc. Reprinted from *The Revolt of the Masses* by José Ortega y Gasset by permission of W. W. Norton & Company, Inc. Copyright 1932 by W. W. Norton & Company, Inc., copyright ⓒ 1960 by Teresa Carey.

George Orwell, from "Politics and the English Language": From *Shooting an Elephant and Other Essays* by George Orwell, copyright, 1945, 1946, 1949, 1950, by Sonia Brownell Orwell. Reprinted by permission of Harcourt, Brace and Company, Inc., and Martin Secker & Warburg Ltd.

Blaise Pascal, from *Thoughts:* Reprinted from *Pascal's Pensées* by permission of E. P. Dutton & Co., Inc., from the Dutton Everyman Paperbacks edition, and by J. M. Dent & Sons Ltd.

Karl Popper, *The Open Society and Its Enemies:* Reprinted from *The Open Society and Its Enemies,* by Karl Popper, by permission of the Princeton University Press.

John Crowe Ransom: "The Equilibrists": Reprinted from *Selected Poems* by John Crowe Ransom, by permission of Alfred A. Knopf, Inc. Copyright 1927 by Alfred A. Knopf, Inc.; renewed 1955 by John Crowe Ransom. From "A Poem Nearly Anonymous": Copyright 1933 Bookman Publishing Company, Inc. Reprinted with the permission of Charles Scribner's Sons from *The World's Body* by John Crowe Ransom.

Bertrand Russell, from *Why Men Fight:* Reprinted from *Why Men Fight,* originally published as *Principles of Social Reconstruction,* by Bertrand Russell, by permission of the publishers, George Allen & Unwin Ltd.

George Sand and Gustave Flaubert, Correspondence: From: *The George Sand-Gustave Flaubert Letters.* Translated by Aimee L. McKensie, Copyright (R) 1949. By permission of Liveright, Publishers, New York, N.Y.

George Santayana: From "Classic Liberty" and from "German Freedom": Reprinted from *Soliloquies in England and Later Soliloquies,* by George Santayana, by permission of Constable and Company, Ltd. Published in the United States by Charles Scribner's Sons. From "Tragic Philosophy": Copyright 1936 *Scrutiny.* Reprinted with the permission of Charles Scribner's Sons.

Dylan Thomas, "A Refusal to Mourn the Death, by Fire, of a Child in London": Reprinted from *The Collected Poems of Dylan Thomas.* Copyright 1939, 1942, 1946 by New Directions. Copyright 1952, 1953 by Dylan Thomas. Reprinted by permission of New Directions and J. M. Dent & Sons Ltd.

Heinrich von Treitschke, from *Politics:* Selection reprinted by permission of Mr. Michael Dugdale and Constable and Company, Ltd.

G. M. Trevelyan, *History of England:* From *History of England,* by G. M. Trevelyan, (3rd edition, 1945), by permission of Longmans, Green & Co., Inc.

Ernst Troeltsch, from "The German Idea of Freedom": From *Modern Political Thought* by William Ebenstein. Translated by William Ebenstein from Ernst Troeltsch, "The German Idea of Freedom" (1916), reprinted in *Deutscher Geist und Westeuropa* (J. C. B. Mohr, 1925). Reprinted by permission of the publisher, Rinehart & Company, Inc.

"The Twa Corbies": Reprinted from *The Oxford Book of Ballads* by permission of the Clarendon Press, Oxford.

W. B. Yeats: "Sailing to Byzantium" reprinted from *Collected Poems* by W. B. Yeats, by permission of The Macmillan Company, Mrs. W. B. Yeats, the Macmillan Company of Canada Ltd., and A. P. Watt & Son. Selection from *Autobiographies* reprinted by permission of The Macmillan Company, Mrs. W. B. Yeats, the Macmillan Company of Canada Ltd., and A. P. Watt & Son.

The authors do not, individually, want credit for anything the reader likes. They have talked to each other and helped each other very much over the years. But they are not unwilling to accept individual responsibility for what the reader dislikes. Mr. Ross admits the original conception of the book and his primary responsibility for Part I. Mr. Berryman accepts his primary responsibility for Part II, with the exception of the analyses of the Marvell, Donne, Carew, and Ransom poems, for which Mr. Tate accepts responsibility.

Contents

(Indented selections are Exercises)

✒ PART II

IMAGINATIVE WRITING 195

Section Two: Poetry   298

Section Three: Drama   358

THE ARTS OF READING

Introduction

Readers may be divided into four classes:

    1. <u>Sponges</u>, who absorb all they read and return it nearly in the same state, only a little dirtied.

    2. <u>Sand-glasses</u>, who retain nothing and are content to get through a book for the sake of getting through the time.

    3. <u>Strain-bags</u>, who retain merely the dregs of what they read.

    4. <u>Mogul diamonds</u>, equally rare and valuable, who profit by what they read, and enable others to profit by it also.

Samuel Taylor Coleridge, Notebooks

I

How can we explain this book? We don't believe reading well can be taught all by itself. But then we don't believe writing well can be taught, or thinking well, each by itself. If any of them is basic and a little independent of the others, it is thinking, but thinking without the arts of language is rudimentary. <u>To be fluent in thinking, reading, and writing, one must be fluent in them all</u>.

So we try, in this book, to teach them all. We teach them on the basis of reading, because this is after all a book, and there is no way to learn from a book except by reading it. But you cannot learn to read, write, and think well only by studying principles or only by doing exercises. If you are just told the principles, you will just know the principles; but you will not know how to use them. If you are just told to practice, without learning the principles, you will not

1

Limitations of mere literacy —

know what to practice; you may pick up one or two principles on the way, but you will be confirmed in many errors. So you can best learn these skills by doing them and learning the principles at the same time.

If you only study logic, you do not become logical; you become a logician. If you only study writing, you don't become a writer; you become a grammarian or a windbag. And if you only study reading, you become a sponge, a sand-glass, or a strain-bag.

We assume that anyone using this book is able to read the words on a page, to know more or less what each word means and in general what the page is about. This skill, uninformed by the intellectual disciplines that make up education, may be called *mere* literacy. If one acquires it, he can write laundry lists, follow simple printed directions, and vote. But "mere" literacy serves neither life nor civilization. The merely literate man can enjoy at best only the prefabricated stories and articles of the slick magazines. His intellectual fodder is pap, good enough to sustain life at the child's level. His knowledge of life and the world is a homogenized mess of stereotypes and delusions. His motto is: I get by. And so he does when the machines of society grind smoothly. But in catastrophe and crisis, he becomes bewildered. For the world is more than the moment he knows, and he has never been prepared for disaster.

Like a little knowledge, a little literacy is a dangerous thing. Some awe of the printed word goes with incapacity for thinking about it. Those who can read but not read well usually believe all they read (or they become churlish and cynical, and believe nothing of it). Before World War II, Japan boasted that its rate of literacy was the highest in the world. Germany's was certainly very high. Yet the peoples of those nations believed in the divine Mikado or the Führer, in kamikaze warfare and brutal concentration camps, in racial supremacy and genocide. They accepted as gospel a shoddy propaganda telling them that the United States could not fight because race riots would paralyze it, that Jews were inferior beings, that Negroes were almost apes. They believed all these things partly because they read them. The curse of mere literacy is inability to criticize or discriminate, and a paralysis of the will to resist the author.

A comment much made in Europe today is that when Americans meet Communists (as happens in Europe), they are astonished at how persuasive the Communists are, and can answer them only in clichés. The reason is clear: most Americans don't know their own case, and have never heard any other. The predigested accounts of

Communist doctrine that come before the eyes of the merely literate in the United States wouldn't even be recognized as his own beliefs by an intelligent Communist.

Of course, our book cannot cure all these disorders. It cannot even make a merely literate man educated. But it offers some elementary tools necessary to education, and much practice in their use. It is not only for those without college degrees; the rate of mere literacy among college graduates is staggering. Nor is it just for those who need it. Our book is for all who can use it or enjoy it.

Since we are concerned with the arts of reading, the book contains readings and our discussions of them. Since the readings must be about something, and be good or bad, we have not selected readings only as exercises, but we have chosen what we thought could help immunize the reader against the ills we have just mentioned, develop his taste, and offer a few standards by which to judge prose and verse.

We are concerned with thinking, too, so we not only provide models, as best we can, by our discussions, but we ask the reader questions that require thought, not just information. As for speaking and writing, his answers will give him practice. We offer a good deal of help with the questions we ask, especially at first, and we repeat ourselves deliberately, usually in other words, as a teacher should. We even repeat our questions on other levels and in different terms.* Within the limitations of print, we attempt an exchange with the reader, a continuing dialogue. In questions and discussion we try to show how conclusions should be reached, and how we reached ours, for we believe with Edmund Burke, who said:

I am convinced that the method of teaching which approaches most nearly to the method of investigation is incomparably the best; since, not content with serving up a few barren and lifeless truths, it leads to the stock on which they grew; it tends to set the reader himself in the track of invention, and to direct him into those paths in which the author has made his own discoveries . . .

Our plan is simple. Part I deals with intellectual discourse: chiefly argument and exposition, which we call, briefly, expository prose. Part II deals with other literary forms as well: stories, verse, and plays, which we include under the heading, imaginative literature. Only a few of the same principles are used in understanding both expository prose and imaginative literature, and they are sometimes used differently. We will return to these differences later.

* Sometimes we repeat a definition. The reader, after all, may have skipped.

In each of the two Parts, we proceed from the simple to the relatively difficult. We reprint a sentence, a paragraph, a letter, an essay or a poem, a play, a story. We then analyze it, explaining the terms and principles * needed for the analysis. These are used again and again as new ones are added, so the reader becomes increasingly familiar with them. Between our analyses, or Commentaries, are Exercises. These are questions about still other selections. The questions require knowledge only of the terms and principles that have already been introduced.

The reader may answer the questions under his breath. He will do better if he writes the answers. When the book is used in the classroom, it will be easier to vary this. Some of the questions can be answered on the spot, and the answer discussed and criticized by class and teacher. Others may be used as the subjects of written papers, to be corrected and returned by the teacher. Still others may be occasions for short talks by students.† We have given no indications which questions should be used for which purposes. The teacher may decide as he likes, and would anyhow. But thinking, reading, writing, and speaking should, ideally, all be involved as this book is read.

II

A book—in this case, the readings in our book—is itself used to test ideas about it: anything said about a book should be supported by evidence in the book. Of course, much has to be brought to a book in order to understand what is in it. We must know the meanings of words and the structure of sentences, recognize allusions, and be able to follow arguments; above all, we must bring attention and thoughtfulness to our reading. A book is to the reader what a man's experience is to his knowledge of life: the materials of his learning. But he has to do the learning himself; and how much he learns is due not only to the variety and types of his experience or reading, but also to his attentiveness and the quality of his reflection. A man may travel around the world, and be the same fool who started: Immanuel Kant never left Königsberg. A man may read voraciously,

---

* As these are introduced, they are numbered. The number appears again after the Commentary, with a definition. Terms and Principles may also follow an Exercise.

† Speaking should be part of the same study as reading, writing, and thinking. It has not been mentioned until now, because the reader will have little chance to practice it, unless he is in a classroom. There, discussion of our materials and talks in answer to questions can be the basis for practice in speaking to the point. Oratory is an art, like poetry, and we do not pretend to help with it. Nor do we help with salesmanship, or with the use of words. to hide meanings.

and be clear about nothing; men of intellectual distinction have been raised largely on the Bible and Shakespeare. Thomas Hobbes once said, "If I had read as much as other men, I should be as foolish as they." So it is *how* one reads that counts. Still, whatever you bring to it, each book contains the evidence for what you think about it, as nature contains the evidence for what the scientist thinks about it.

You can deal with expository prose, to begin with, as a scientist deals with a problem, formulating questions precisely, making hypotheses that may answer them, testing the hypotheses by reference to the material. But you must also treat expository prose as a philosopher treats a problem, analyzing meanings and relationships, discovering what is presupposed by an idea, seeking the key principle in any argument.

Imaginative literature is not easier to understand than exposition, as the man thinks who says, "It's only a story." The procedures of logic and science bear on serious exposition, as does the ability to discriminate the focal from the peripheral, and the relevant from the irrelevant. All that seems necessary to understand imaginative literature is cultivated taste. But it is not so. Or if it is, *cultivated* taste requires knowledge, discipline, very close reading, and a grasp of literary forms. In addition, the reader must proceed on another set of principles from those that guide him through exposition.

In exposition, a word should have one meaning, and that clear. In poetry, a word may be used richly in a variety of meanings. The structure of argument must square with logic; that of literature with rhetoric. The chief ideas in exposition require explicit and precise statement; in literature, they are often properly implicit. One can go on and on stating the differences between the two kinds of writing. In the text, many of them should become clear. So should the differences in the questions the reader asks of a text. The reader of imaginative literature should not ask, in the same way, the questions about meaning, relationships, and presuppositions, that the reader of expository prose asks. In exposition, if the author says something and then contradicts himself, he is wrong. But in a play or story if a character says something and then contradicts himself, or if another character contradicts him, the author is neither right nor wrong. For the author of the play or story to contradict *himself* would be a very different thing, and discoverable in different ways, than contradiction in a scientific article.

An introduction of great length may lead the reader to suppose that the text that follows is not finished and self-contained. That may be the case with this book, but we do not want the reader to think so at this point. So we stop.

and be doctrinaire, publishes moral analysis. A claim that you have raised largely on the Bible and Shakespeare. Thoreau, I believe, once said, "I'd rather read... teaches than I should be as foolish as they." Sometimes how one... Socrates, I believe? why ever you have the facts and theories contain the evidence for whatever little about it. As nature confines their course to what the scientist understands if you can deal with expository prose; to begin with, as a student deals with a problem, formulating questions, proposing hypotheses by... to the material. But you treat the literary experiences as a philosopher treats a problem, question, meaning, and enterprises discovery; or what is the purpose of a sane ideal as clarify the key thought in any argument.

Imaginative literature is not easier to understand than exposition, as the man thinks who says, "It's only a story". The procedures
of logic and science bear on serious exposition, as does the ability
to discriminate the focal from the peripheral, and the relevant from
the irrelevant. All that genius of whatever, and varied imaginative
literature is cultivated taste. But it is not to. Or it is a matter and
taste requires knowledge; disturbance very close reading, and in map
of literary terms. In addition, the reader must proceed on another set
of immediacy from those that guide him through exposition.

In poetry, a word should have one meaning, and that clear.
In poetry, a word may be used richly in a variety of meanings. The
structure of argument must square with logic, that of literature with
rhetoric. The chief ideas in exposition require explicit and precise
statement; in literature, they are often properly implicit. One can go
on and on stating the differences between the two kinds of writing. In
the text, many of them should become clear. So should the differences
in the questions the reader asks of a text. The reader of imaginative
literature should not ask, in the same way, the questions about
meaning, relationships, and presuppositions, that the reader of expository prose asks. In exposition, if the author says something and
then contradicts himself, he is wrong. But in a play or story, if a
character says something and then contradicts himself, or if another
character contradicts him, the author is neither right nor wrong. For
the author of the play or story to contradict himself would be a very
different thing; and discoverable in different ways, that contradiction
in a scientific article.

An introduction of great length may lead the reader to suppose
that the text that follows is not finished and self-contained. That may
be the case with this book, but we do not want the reader to think
so at this point. So we stop.

PART I

Exposition and Argument

Writing, Good and Bad

Our discussion will be adequate if it has as much clearness as the subject-matter admits of, for precision is not to be sought for alike in all discussions, any more than in all the products of the crafts . . . . it is the mark of an educated man to look for precision in each class of things just so far as the nature of the subject admits; it is evidently equally foolish to accept probable reasoning from a mathematician and to demand from a rhetorician scientific proofs.

Aristotle, *Nicomachean Ethics*

We will start by analyzing a paragraph.

RALPH WALDO EMERSON

From "Self-Reliance"

A foolish consistency is the hobgoblin of little minds, adored by little statesmen and philosophers and divines. With consistency a great soul has simply nothing to do. He may as well concern himself with his shadow on the wall. Speak what you think now in hard words and to-morrow speak what to-morrow thinks in hard words again, though it contradict every thing you said to-day. —"Ah, so you shall be sure to be misunderstood." Is it so bad then to be misunderstood? Pythagoras was misunderstood, and Socrates, and Jesus, and Luther, and Copernicus, and Galileo, and Newton, and every pure and wise spirit that ever took flesh. To be great is to be misunderstood.

COMMENTARY

Is Emerson against consistency? But first, what is consistency? One definition is that it is noncontradiction; you are consistent when your remarks do not contradict each other.[1] For example: Suppose you said, "This animal is a cat" and then, pointing to the same animal, added, "This animal is not a cat." That is inconsistent; it is like saying, "That cat is not a cat," which is obviously absurd. Does Emerson support such inconsistency? "No," a reader might answer, "he isn't opposed to consistency, but to 'a foolish consistency.' "

But what is "a foolish consistency"? "Foolish" might mark a distinction between kinds of consistency. (So if we ask for a *red* rose, we do so because some roses are white and others yellow.) Then at least one kind of consistency is foolish, and others are not. They may even be wise. Or "foolish" may be an adjective which, for Emerson, would always qualify "consistency" (as when we speak of the *vast* ocean without meaning to distinguish it from small oceans). Then consistency is always foolish. Which does Emerson mean?

If he means that "a foolish consistency" is only one kind of consistency, then there must be a difference between kinds of consistency, on the basis of which he distinguishes the foolish kind from others. For distinctions should be made only where there are differences.[2] (We cannot properly distinguish quantitatively between twelve and a dozen, or twenty and a score, because there is no difference.) And we find no difference mentioned here. How, then, can we proceed?

A principle of scientific method may be helpful. Whenever two or more hypotheses account for all the facts that are at hand, find out whether one will account better than the others for facts (equally relevant) that are not at hand. As applied to alternative interpretations of the meaning of a passage, the principle is: Continue to read, looking for a statement that fits one interpretation, but not the others.[3]

As we do that with this passage, we find a sentence that permits us to test both our alternatives. The sentence is: "Speak what you think now in hard words and to-morrow speak what to-morrow

thinks in hard words again, though it contradict every thing you said
to-day." In thus defending contradiction, Emerson is opposing consistency. But the sentence shows what *kind* of contradiction he defends, and so what kind of inconsistency. Actually, he is using two
words, "contradiction" and "consistency," in a special sense which
is not usually given them. For when we are warned by logicians
against inconsistency, it is inconsistency in a single argument that is
meant. And Emerson only urges you to say what you think even if
it contradicts something *else* you said *at another time.* But if you
never did this, you wouldn't be able to grow intellectually, or to
change your mind because of new evidence and argument.

Consistency, like the single meaning of a word, is logically important in any *one* argument or statement. If you contradict yourself,
or use the same word to mean different things, you will not make
sense in any one exposition or piece of reasoning. But you may change
your mind or the meaning of your words in another exposition or
argument, which is what Emerson is urging.

So we conclude that neither of our alternative readings was
quite correct. By "foolish consistency," Emerson does mean that
consistency is foolish, which was our second alternative. But he does
not use the word in an ordinary sense, as we did. Emerson means
by "consistency," noncontradiction over a period of time. A man
who is consistent from his earliest utterance would either never have
been wrong or never learned anything new. The former is absurd, the
latter pathetic, but impossible except for the subnormal. And Emerson thinks of great men as always learning and having new ideas.

Now we can understand the analogy [4] in the third sentence of
Emerson's paragraph. A great soul may as well concern himself with
his shadow on the wall as with consistency. What a great man has
said is always with him, like his shadow; it is what he has believed.
But it is also intangible and dim, like a shadow, in contrast with his
living words and beliefs of the moment.

A final comment. If you say one thing today and another tomorrow, you will be misunderstood.* But don't care, Emerson says, because great men are always misunderstood. "To be great is to be
misunderstood." Suppose he is right. Does it follow that to be misunderstood is to be great? Of course not, or there would be more
great men than grains of sand on the shore.

* But that is no reason for being misunderstood in each separate utterance.
It is only a reason for being misunderstood if your hearer or reader foolishly
combines what you say today with what you say tomorrow.

TERMS AND PRINCIPLES

1. *Consistency:* The logical agreement of the parts of any statement, the absence of contradiction in a single argument, or at any one time.
2. Distinctions between meanings should be made when, and only when, there is a real difference in the things meant.
3. Whenever two or more hypotheses account equally well for all the known facts, find out whether one will account better for facts not now at hand. If so, choose that one throughout. If the hypotheses are interpretations of a passage, read on and see which interpretation best suits the sentences that follow.
4. *Analogy:* A comparison of one thing with another in respect to some element which is identical, or alike, in both. Analogies may clarify or persuade; they are not proof.

EXERCISE

KARL POPPER

From *The Open Society and Its Enemies*

The so-called *paradox of freedom* is the well-known idea that freedom in the sense of absence of any restraining control must lead to very great restraint, since it makes the bully free to enslave the meek.

Less well known is the *paradox of tolerance:* Unlimited tolerance must lead to the disappearance of tolerance. If we extend unlimited tolerance even to those who are intolerant, if we are not prepared to defend a tolerant society against the onslaught of the intolerant, then the tolerant will be destroyed, and tolerance with them. —In this formulation, I do not imply, for instance, that we should always suppress the utterance of intolerant philosophies; as long as we can counter them by rational argument and keep them in check by public opinion, suppression would certainly be most unwise. But we should claim the *right* even to suppress them, for it may easily turn out that they are not prepared to meet us on the level of rational argument, but begin by denouncing all argument; they may forbid their followers to listen to anything as deceptive as rational argument, and teach them to answer arguments by the use of their fists. We should therefore claim, in the name of tolerance, the right not to tolerate the intolerant. We should claim that any movement preaching intolerance places itself outside the law, and we should consider incitement to intolerance and persecution as criminal, exactly as we should consider incitement to murder, or to kidnapping; or as we should consider incitement to the revival of the slave trade. Another of the less well-known paradoxes is the *paradox of democracy,* or more precisely, of majority rule; i.e. the possibility that the majority may decide that a tyrant should rule.

All these paradoxes can be easily avoided if we frame our political demands in some such manner as this. We demand a government that rules according to the principles of equalitarianism and protectionism; that tolerates all who are prepared to reciprocate, i.e. who are tolerant; that is controlled by, and accountable to, the public. And we may add that some form of majority vote, together with institutions for keeping the public well informed, is the best, though not infallible, means of controlling such a government. (No infallible means exist.)

COMMENTARY

The word "paradox" has several meanings, two of which concern us here.[1] One meaning is seeming, or apparent, contradiction as opposed to real contradiction. A contradiction is what it seems and cannot be resolved. A paradox, in this sense, can.

In Gilbert and Sullivan's light opera *The Pirates of Penzance,* Frederic is apprenticed as a boy to a pirate band, with which he must remain until he has reached his twenty-first birthday. When he is twenty-one years old he leaves them and leads the police against them. The question of his age is all-important. The pirates force Frederic to return to them by pointing out that he was born on February twenty-ninth, a date that occurs only once in four years. So, although he has lived twenty-one years, he has had only five birthdays.

As the pirate king tells him, ". . . going by birthdays, you are as yet only five and a quarter."

Obviously, the formal phrase "on his twenty-first birthday" most likely means "twenty-one years old." Still, "to be twenty-one years old" could be defined as "having reached the twenty-first birthday." So Frederic is both twenty-one years old and five-and-a-quarter years old at the same time. This *seems* like a contradiction (to be twenty-one years old and at the same time not twenty-one years old), but it is not, for Frederic is not "both twenty-one and not twenty-one" *in the same sense.*

A basic principle of discourse is that a word must be used in one and the same sense throughout any one argument or statement.[2] "Age" has, in this case, been used in two senses, calculated in two different ways. As soon as we specify the two senses, we resolve the paradox. Frederic is twenty-one by years, and five and a quarter by birthdays.

Another meaning of "paradox" is a statement whose logical implications seem to contradict it. If someone says "I never tell the truth," we may ask whether that statement is itself true. If we argue that it cannot itself be true, for the reason that the speaker *never* tells the truth, the reason we give is itself an assumption that the statement is true. But if it *is* true, we are back where we started. For if "I never tell the truth" is true, then "I never tell the truth" is false.

Paradoxes of this kind are not so easily resolved as are paradoxes of the first kind, but the way to resolve them is the same: specify exactly what is meant.[3] In our last instance, we should ask the speaker precisely what he means. He may, for example, mean that all his *other* statements are false; then this one, which says that his other statements are false, may itself be true.

SOME QUESTIONS

1. Which of the two types of paradox just discussed is found in Popper's examples?

2. At the beginning of his last paragraph, Popper says, "All these paradoxes can be easily avoided," and he tries to show how. Now, is he *resolving* the paradoxes, that is, distinguishing different meanings that had been compressed into one or specifying more clearly what is meant, or is he actually *avoiding* them? If he is avoiding them—as he says he is—how does he do it? Does he restate the principles of freedom, tolerance, and democracy so they are no longer paradoxical? If so, do we still get what we want in his restatement,

or do we lose it? After all, if we want freedom, tolerance, and democracy, we don't want the words defined so they mean something different. For then, even if we get what the words now mean, we may lose what we originally wanted. But perhaps we will lose them altogether, or have more chance of doing so, if they are not restated as Popper does. Which do you think is more likely?

TERMS AND PRINCIPLES

1. *Paradox:* (1) A statement which seems to be self-contradictory, but turns out on analysis not to be; (2) a statement whose logical implication seems to contradict it, but actually does not.
2. A word should be used in one and the same sense throughout any single argument or statement.
3. Paradoxes can be resolved by specifying exactly what is meant.

EXERCISE

GEORGE SANTAYANA

From "Classic Liberty"

When ancient peoples defined what they called their liberty, the word stood for a plain and urgent interest of theirs: that their cities should not be destroyed, their territory pillaged, and they themselves sold into slavery. For the Greeks in particular liberty meant even more than this. Perhaps the deepest assumption of classic philosophy is that nature and the gods on the one hand and man on the other, both have a fixed character; that there is consequently a necessary piety, a true philosophy, a standard happiness, a normal art. The Greeks believed, not without reason, that they had grasped these permanent principles better than other peoples. They had largely dispelled superstition, experimented in government, and turned life into a rational art. Therefore when they defended their liberty what they defended was not merely freedom to live. It was freedom to live well, to live as other nations did not, in the public experimental study of the world and of human nature. This liberty to discover and pursue a natural happiness, this liberty to grow wise and to live in friendship with the gods and with one another, was the liberty vindicated at Thermopylae by martyrdom and at Salamis by victory.

GEORGE SANTAYANA

From "German Freedom"

There is a fine theory of Hegel's that the universe exists in order to realize freedom. In Oriental despotisms, he tells us, only one man was free. In ancient republican cities a minority, the aristocracy of citizens, obtained freedom.

Now at last freedom has extended to all; not, however, as we might fondly suppose, in free and casual America, but under the perfect organization of the Prussian monarchy. For freedom in the mouth of German philosophers has a very special meaning. It does not refer to any possibility of choice nor to any private initiative. It means rather that sense of freedom which we acquire when we do gladly and well what we should have to do anyhow, as when in passing from a close room into the open air we say we breathe freely at last. German freedom is like the freedom of the angels in heaven who see the face of God and cannot sin. It lies in such a deep love and understanding of what is actually established that you would not have it otherwise; you appropriate and bless it all and feel it to be the providential expression of your own spirit. You are enlarged by sympathy with your work, your country, and the universe, until you are no longer conscious of the least distinction between the Creator, the state, and yourself. Your compulsory service then becomes perfect freedom.

COMMENTARY

It may seem that Santayana is caricaturing the German idea of freedom. As proof he is not, we include an explanation of the idea by a distinguished German thinker.

Liberty as creative participation in the formation of state authority means to us, not the bringing forth of governmental will out of individual wills, not control of the mandatory by the principal, but the free, conscious and dutiful dedication of oneself to the whole, as it has been molded by history, state and nation. The whole as the expression and incarnation of collectivity is to be willed freely and always re-created anew in personal activity. Thus, prince and officials consider themselves as the first servants of the state, and citizens think of themselves as members of the state. They are all organs of the one sovereign whole which they bring forth anew in ceaseless self-devotion. Liberty consists more in duties than in rights, or, rather, in rights which are simultaneously duties. The individuals do not compose the whole, but identify themselves with it. Liberty is not equality, but service of the individual in his station organically due to him. In this, lie the dignity and active participation of the individual, but also his restraint, and all modern achievements of national unity, equality before the law, parliaments and universal military service, are molded by this spirit. . . . This spirit has created all that is great in the past German century, it characterizes two expressions of life so contrary to one another as the German army and the socialist party.

Ernst Troeltsch, *The German Idea of Freedom*

SOME QUESTIONS

1. Would we today think of what ancient peoples "called their liberty," as Santayana describes it, as liberty or as autonomy (self-government), and perhaps successful defense in war? Liberty may be opposed to slavery—part of what Santayana says—but is it opposed to destruction of one's city or pillage of one's territory? For that matter can it be opposed to death on the battlefield? To be sure, a man is no longer free when he is dead, but neither is he enslaved.

Can a man be free in a country ruled by another nation and enslaved in a nation ruled by his own countrymen? If so, autonomy is not necessary for freedom.

2. If, for the Greeks, liberty was freedom to live well, and they made mistakes in their free decisions so that, in fact, they did not live well, would we say that such mistakes made them unfree by their own criterion? Wouldn't we rather conclude that one was free so long as he could try unhampered to live well (as he understood living well), whether or not he succeeded?

3. In the first sentence of the second passage above, does Hegel's theory, as Santayana states it, involve either a belief that the universe is conscious or, perhaps, that it is guided by God's decrees? Does the phrase "in order to" imply purpose? And does purpose imply consciousness or, at least, mind?

4. Is a theory in which "compulsory service" becomes "perfect freedom" either contradictory or paradoxical? For Hegel it might

seem just a paradox; is it really a contradiction? When the slave loves his chains, is he free? If you agree that when you want to do what you have to do, or are ordered to do, you are free, does it follow that that is the *only* time you can be free? For example, if you are not stopped from doing what you want to do, although nobody has ordered it, are you not also free?

Is the difficulty with the German philosophers' use of "freedom" perhaps this: they use the word in a special sense of their own and *also,* at the same time, in its ordinary sense? If so, they are using the same word in more than one meaning in a single argument. But why not use another word and let "freedom" mean what it does ordinarily? Then they could say they are against freedom and for X (defined as wanting to do what you are told to do). Perhaps they use "freedom" because it is an honorific word, a slogan widely accepted. It is easier to redefine it than to oppose it openly. And of course one can redefine any word so that it means its opposite. Try the same trick with "virtue," "good," "right." Everybody is against "sin," but if we all define the word differently, we are all against different things.

EXERCISE

The following is quoted in its entirety from the Minneapolis *Tribune* of July 8, 1958:

Q. A NEIGHBOR said it was unlawful to give a haircut to a member of one's own family.

A. THE LAW SAYS that a person must be licensed to perform any of the acts in barbering, but the definition of "barbering" is a judicial question which, apparently, awaits a test case in regard to the point you raise.

A letter was written to the Minneapolis *Tribune* on July 22, 1958, which is quoted in part:

A FIRST COUSIN says it's unlawful to give myself a haircut. I've been doing it five years and have the head to prove it. I guess I've swindled barbers and beauty parlors out of about $500. I see where you say (July 8) that one must be licensed to perform the act of barbering but the definition of "barbering" is a judicial question which awaits a test case. Perhaps I'm just the case.

SOME QUESTIONS

1. Suppose you were empowered to straighten out this difficulty. To do justice to barbers and to ensure their ability, you want to continue giving licenses only to those who have at least minimal skill. But you also want to permit men to shave themselves without breaking the law (or give themselves haircuts, for that matter). Your problem is to define "barber" in such a way that both your wishes are attained. Try a few definitions of "barber" to see how they work.

2. Suppose your definition were: "A barber is someone who shaves those men who do not shave themselves." (For the sake of brevity, we will omit haircuts, singes, shampoos, etc.) At first glance, the definition seems to be all right. Men may shave themselves, while those who shave others can be licensed. But, after a moment's thought, you realize you have said too much and too little. If you stroke your beard as you ponder the definition, you may suddenly realize that you do not shave yourself, nor does a barber shave you. So the definition is inadequate since it does not include men with beards. But does it include men with no hair growing on their faces? And what about men who need two shaves a day, who shave themselves every morning and are shaved by a barber every evening?

3. Another problem in our definition is: what of the barber who shaves himself? If he shaves himself, he is not a barber, because barbers shave "only those men who do not shave themselves." Is this a contradiction or a paradox?

4. Assume that "a barber who shaves himself" is a paradox. How would you resolve it? Remember to make a distinction between two meanings the same word can have.

KARL MANNHEIM

From *Ideology and Utopia*

The first point which we now have to emphasize is that the approach of the sociology of knowledge intentionally does not start with the single individual and his thinking in order then to proceed directly in the manner of the philosopher to the abstract heights of "thought as such." Rather, the sociology of knowledge seeks to comprehend thought in the concrete setting of an historical-social situation out of which individually differentiated thought only very gradually emerges. Thus, it is not men in general who think, or even isolated individuals who do the thinking, but men in certain groups who have developed a particular style of thought in an endless series of responses to certain typical situations characterizing their common position.

Strictly speaking it is incorrect to say that the single individual thinks. Rather it is more correct to insist that he participates in thinking further what other men have thought before him. He finds himself in an inherited situation with patterns of thought which are appropriate to this situation and attempts to elaborate further the inherited modes of response or to substitute others for them in order to deal more adequately with the new challenges which have arisen out of the shifts and changes in his situation. Every individual is therefore in a two-fold sense predetermined by the fact of growing up in a society: On the one hand he finds a ready-made situation and on the other he finds in that situation preformed patterns of thought and of conduct.

COMMENTARY

This is a statement about the method of a relatively new intellectual discipline, made by its most eminent practitioner. It is very badly written. Let us see why.

Consider the first sentence. Would anything be lost if the first fourteen words were omitted, and the sentence began: "The sociology of knowledge . . ."? On the contrary, much would be gained. Excess verbiage would be pruned, and we would be spared the statement that an "approach" to a particular study does not "intentionally" do something. Still, even eliminating fourteen words leaves us with the "sociology of knowledge" *intentionally* avoiding something. Since things are done and avoided "intentionally" only by thinking creatures, Mannheim might better have started: "The sociologist of knowledge intentionally . . ." Wordiness obscures meaning and gives a misleading impression of profundity.[1] It can also—as it does here—hide fantastic and false statements.

Note the jargon, the unnecessary technical language,[2] as "seeks to comprehend thought in the concrete setting of an historical-social situation out of which individually differentiated thought only very gradually emerges." Is "the concrete setting of an historical-social situation" different from "a social situation"? Aren't all social situations "concrete"? Could they be anything but "historical"? Doesn't "social conditions" carry the whole meaning of "concrete . . . situation"? Isn't "studies" adequate for "seeks to comprehend thought . . ."? Mannheim may mean only that a man's ideas should be studied in the context of his particular social situation. That would be true for some purposes, and not for others (not for their value as art or their logical consistency). But Mannheim would have to write differently for us to be clear that that was his meaning.

This kind of prose style allows Mannheim to write: "Strictly speaking it is incorrect to say that the single individual thinks." Doesn't a moment's reflection make it clear that, because men inherit so many of their ideas and so many of their ways of thinking, we are entitled to say *metaphorically* that no man's thought is *entirely* his own. But that *speaking strictly,* it is incorrect to say that any thinking goes on anywhere except in the minds of individual men? Can Mannheim really be denying this? Unfortunately, he doesn't even make that clear.

"Rather it is more correct to insist," Mannheim continues, "that he participates in thinking further what other men have thought before him." That sounds like a bad translation of bad German, which is just what it is. But does the sentence support his belief that the "single individual" does not think? No; it just befogs the issue. When he talks of "thinking further what other men have thought before him," is he suggesting that if one thinks something that was thought before, he doesn't really think it? And as for saying "participates in thinking," is he suggesting that when someone is thinking about the same thing as others, they all only "participate" in what is either a joint or group thought, floating somewhere above them, perhaps? He seems to be suggesting both without saying either explicitly.

If I participate in thinking, I *do* think, just as I play tennis if I participate in a game of tennis. Mannheim is entitled to a metaphor, as we said: little of our thinking is ever original. But he is surely not entitled to say that, "strictly speaking," individual men do not think. Also, do we—or does Mannheim—really "think *further*" what Socrates or St. Paul thought? There may be a silly implication of inevitable progress concealed here.

Words and thoughts go together. We cannot think, except in a rudimentary way, without words. Equally, we cannot use words lucidly and exactly unless our thought is clear. So we can help our thinking by learning to use words well, as we can help our writing and speaking by learning to think clearly.

Mannheim provides an excellent example of the breach of these principles. One does not know if he is intellectually confused and, perhaps, pretentious; or if his muddy prose has discolored his thought; or both. When he says: ". . . it is not men in general who think, or even isolated individuals who do the thinking, but men in certain groups who have developed a particular style of thought . . . ," he raises more questions than one can easily follow. For example, what is meant by "men in general"? How isolated must one be to be an "isolated individual" (Robinson Crusoe without Friday)? He does not even say that "men in certain groups" think, but that they "have *developed* a particular style of thought." Does that mean they think only about how to develop a style of thought, or that they develop that style somehow without thinking?

Mannheim seems to be making distinctions throughout, without basing them on real differences. ". . . the concrete setting of an historical-social situation . . ." *seems* to be distinguished from mere "social conditions," but on examination we find no difference between them. After all, when one qualifies a substantive by an adjective, his readers should be able to assume that there is normally a distinction in meaning between the substantive alone and the substantive with the adjective.* "A *rich* man" means something different from "a man." But in Mannheim's writing, "the concrete setting" is the same as "the setting," and "an historical-social situation" the same as "a social situation." If he meant something else, or something simple, he should have said it.

TERMS AND PRINCIPLES

1. Excess verbiage hides thought. It is to be avoided.
2. *Jargon:* Unnecessary technical language. It hides thought and gives a false impression of profundity. It is to be avoided. When jargon is encountered by the reader, he should try to translate it into ordinary English.

* Except, of course, when an adjective is used as an epithet. We gave an instance of this in "vast ocean," when we discussed Emerson. But Mannheim is not writing the sort of rhetoric which allows this.

EXERCISE

Mannheim is a scholar and a man of ideas. Much that one reads today is even poorer in style, as it is poorer in ideas. The following is, unfortunately, not utterly untypical of contemporary writing in sociology. Its authors will not be named, but their article, published in 1959, graces a technical sociological journal.

The community-centered individuals also tend not to have young children at home, which allows freedom for outside activity.

In contrast, the people who enjoy the home-centered style of leisure engage in most of it around their residence.

At the end of the article, the authors summarize their findings, under the heading, "Conclusions." One especially striking conclusion is worth quoting:

An individual with a large family of children is more likely to be home-centered.

SOME QUESTIONS

1. In the second sentence above, what is meant by "people who enjoy the home-centered style of leisure"? Would it be reasonable to say that they are those who engage in most of their leisure activities at home? If so, we can substitute the meaning of the first phrase for the phrase itself. The sentence now becomes: "Those who engage in most of their leisure activities at home engage in most of their leisure activities at home." Is it fair to rewrite the sentence in this way?

2. In the "conclusion" quoted above, what do you make of the phrase, "a large family of children"? What other kind of family is likely?

3. Does the sentence mean that people with many children at home are likely to spend more time at home than they would otherwise? Does it mean that they are likely to spend more time at home than people with no children or few children? How can you tell which is meant? (The rest of the paragraph, which is not quoted, casts no light on the matter, so the question is fair.) What words in the sentence create the difficulty?

4. Does this conclusion seem true? Is it startling?

5. Is there any jargon in the sentences quoted? If so, can you translate it into ordinary English?

EXERCISE

ARISTOTLE

From *Nicomachean Ethics*

To judge from the lives that men lead, most men, and men of the most vulgar type, seem (not without some ground) to identify the good, or happiness, with pleasure; which is the reason why they love the life of enjoyment. For there are, we may say, three prominent types of life—that just mentioned, the political, and thirdly the contemplative life. Now the mass of mankind are evidently quite slavish in their tastes, preferring a life suitable to beasts, but they get some ground for their view from the fact that many of those in high places share the tastes of Sardanapalus.* A consideration of the prominent types of life shows that people of superior refinement and of active disposition identify happiness with honour; for this is, roughly speaking, the end of the political life. But it seems too superficial to be what we are looking for, since it is thought to depend on those who bestow honour rather than on him who receives it, but the good we divine to be something proper to a man and not easily taken from him. Further, men seem to pursue honour in order that they may be assured of their goodness; at least it is by men of practical wisdom that they seek to be honoured, and among those who know them, and on the ground of their virtue; clearly, then, according to them, at any rate, virtue is better. And perhaps one might even suppose this to be, rather than honour, the end of the political life. But even this appears somewhat incomplete; for possession of virtue seems actually compatible with being asleep, or with lifelong inactivity, and, further, with the greatest sufferings and misfortunes; but a man who was living so, no one would call happy, unless he were maintaining a thesis at all costs. But enough of this; for the subject has been sufficiently treated even in the current discussions. Third comes the contemplative life, which we shall consider later.

The life of money-making is one undertaken under compulsion,

* [Legendary king of Assyria, whose tastes were sybaritic.]

and wealth is evidently not the good we are seeking; for it is merely useful and for the sake of something else. And so one might rather take the aforenamed objects to be ends; for they are loved for themselves. But it is evident that not even these are ends; yet many arguments have been thrown away in support of them. Let us leave this subject, then.

Let us again return to the good we are seeking, and ask what it can be. It seems different in different actions and arts; it is different in medicine, in strategy, and in the other arts likewise. What then is the good of each? Surely that for whose sake everything else is done. In medicine this is health, in strategy victory, in architecture a house, in any other sphere something else, and in every action and pursuit the end; for it is for the sake of this that all men do whatever else they do. Therefore, if there is an end for all that we do, this will be the good achievable by action, and if there are more than one, these will be the goods achievable by action.

So the argument has by a different course reached the same point; but we must try to state this even more clearly. Since there are evidently more than one end, and we choose some of these (e.g. wealth, flutes, and, in general, instruments) for the sake of something else, clearly not all ends are final ends; but the chief good is evidently something final. Therefore, if there is only one final end this will be what we are seeking, and if there are more than one, the most final of these will be what we are seeking. Now we call that which is in itself worthy of pursuit more final than that which is worthy of pursuit for the sake of something else, and that which is never desirable for the sake of something else more final than the things that are desirable both in themselves and for the sake of that other thing, and therefore we call final without qualification that which is always desirable in itself and never for the sake of something else.

Now such a thing happiness, above all else, is held to be; for this we choose always for itself and never for the sake of something else, but honour, pleasure, reason, and every virtue we choose indeed for themselves (for if nothing resulted from them we should still choose each of them), but we choose them also for the sake of happiness, judging that by means of them we shall be happy. Happiness, on the other hand, no one chooses for the sake of these, nor, in general, for anything other than itself.

From the point of view of self-sufficiency the same result seems to follow; for the final good is thought to be self-sufficient. Now by self-sufficient we do not mean that which is sufficient for a man by himself, for one who lives a solitary life, but also for parents, children, wife, and in general for his friends and fellow citizens, since man is born for citizenship. But some limit must be set to this; for if we extend our requirement to ancestors and descendants and friend's friends we are in for an infinite series. Let us examine this question, however, on another occasion; the self-sufficient we now define as that which, when isolated, makes life desirable and lacking in nothing; and such we think happiness to be; and further we think it most desirable of all things, without being counted as one good thing among others—if it were so counted it would clearly be made more desirable by the addition of even the least of goods; for that which is added becomes an excess of goods, and of goods the greater is always more desirable. Happiness, then, is something final and self-sufficient, and is the end of action.

Presumably, however, to say that happiness is the chief good seems a platitude, and a clearer account of what it is is still desired. This might perhaps be given, if we could first ascertain the function of man. For just as for a flute-player, a sculptor, or any artist, and, in general, for all things that have a function or an activity, the good and the "well" is thought to reside in the function, so would it seem to be for a man, if he has a function. Have the carpenter, then, and the tanner certain functions or activities, and has man none? Is he born without a function? Or as an eye, hand, foot, and in general each of the parts evidently has a function, may one lay it down that man similarly has a function apart from all these? What then can this be? Life seems to be common even to plants, but we are seeking what is peculiar to man. Let us exclude, therefore, the life of nutrition and growth. Next there would be a life of perception, but *it* also seems to be common even to the horse, the ox, and every animal. There remains, then, an active life of the element that has a rational principle. . . . And, as "life of the rational element" also has two meanings, we must state that life in the sense of activity is what we mean, for this seems to be the more proper sense of the term. Now if the function of man is an activity of soul which follows or implies a rational principle, and if we say "a so-and-so" and "a good so-and-so" have a function which is the same in kind, e.g. a lyre-player and a good lyre-player, and so without qualification in all cases, eminence in respect of goodness being added to the name of the function (for the function of a lyre-player is to play the lyre, and that of a good lyre-player is to do so well); if this is the case, (and we state the function of man to be a certain kind of life, and this to be an activity or actions of the soul implying a rational principle, and the function of a good man to be the good and noble performance of these, and if any action is well performed when it is performed in accordance with the appropriate excellence: if this is the case) human good turns out to be activity of soul in accordance with virtue, and if there are more than one virtue, in accordance with the best and most complete.

But we must add "in a complete life." For one swallow does not make a summer, nor does one day; and so too one day, or a short time, does not make a man blessed and happy.

SOME QUESTIONS

We do not know which of Aristotle's extant writings were finished by him, which were lecture notes, and which were notes taken by his students. But again and again we find passages so clear in exposition, and so organized in argument, that they can serve as models. How different from the writing of Mannheim!

1. Aristotle says: ". . . possession of virtue seems actually compatible with being asleep . . ." What idea of virtue must one have, in order that Aristotle's comment be correct? What other idea of virtue would make it incorrect?

2. Aristotle argues that wealth is not the kind of good he seeks, because it is merely useful, and not an end in itself. And he says: "The life of money-making is one undertaken under compulsion . . ." Who or what compels us to undertake such a life? What circumstance would remove the compulsion?

3. Aristotle says that "the good" is different in different activities. The good in medicine is health, in strategy it is victory, in architecture a house. What word or words would we more commonly use for what he calls "the good" in that passage?

4. What does Aristotle mean when he says ". . . for all things that have a function or an activity, the good and the 'well' is thought to reside in the function . . ."?

5. What does Aristotle mean by "self-sufficient" in the statement, ". . . the final good is thought to be self-sufficient." What, explicitly, does he not mean?

6. What point is made by the phrase, ". . . one swallow does not make a summer . . ."?

7. Summarize the argument of the next to last paragraph. Show how Aristotle argues from step to step. Number each step. Note the connections between them.

Note that in answer to questions 1 and 2, you had to find something that was not explicitly stated in the text, but was *presupposed* by it. Yet if you could not find it, you would not understand the text. We will deal with presupposition in Section Two.

EXERCISE

EPICTETUS

From *Encheiridion* (*The Manual*)

1. Of all existing things some are in our power, and others are not in our power. In our power are thought, impulse, will to get and will to avoid, and, in a word, everything which is our own doing. Things not in our power include the body, property, reputation, office, and, in a word, everything which is not our own doing. Things in our power are by nature free, unhindered, untrammeled; things not in our power are weak, servile, subject to hindrance, dependent on others. Remember then that if you imagine that what is naturally slavish is free, and what is naturally another's is your own, you will be hampered, you will mourn, you will be put to confusion, you will blame gods and men; but if you think that only your own belongs to you, and that what is another's is indeed another's, no one will ever put compulsion or hindrance on you, you will blame none, you will

accuse none, you will do nothing against your will, no one will harm you, you will have no enemy, for no harm can touch you.

Aiming then at these high matters, you must remember that to attain them requires more than ordinary effort; you will have to give up some things entirely, and put off others for the moment. And if you would have these also—office and wealth—it may be that you will fail to get them, just because your desire is set on the former, and you will certainly fail to attain those things which alone bring freedom and happiness.

Make it your study then to confront every harsh impression with the words, "You are but an impression, and not at all what you seem to be." Then test it by those rules that you possess; and first by this—the chief test of all—"Is it concerned with what is in our power or with what is not in our power?" And if it is concerned with what is not in our power, be ready with the answer that it is nothing to you.

2. Remember that the will to get promises attainment of what you will, and the will to avoid promises escape from what you avoid; and he who fails to get what he wills is unfortunate, and he who does not escape what he wills to avoid is miserable. If then you try to avoid only what is unnatural in the region within your control, you will escape from all that you avoid; but if you try to avoid disease or death or poverty you will be miserable.

Therefore let your will to avoid have no concern with what is not in man's power; direct it only to things in man's power that are contrary to nature. But for the moment you must utterly remove the will to get; for if you will to get something not in man's power you are bound to be unfortunate; while none of the things in man's power that you could honorably will to get is yet within your reach. Impulse to act and not to act, these are your concern; yet exercise them gently and without strain, and provisionally.

3. When anything, from the meanest thing upwards, is attractive or serviceable or an object of affection, remember always to say to yourself, "What is its nature?" If you are fond of a jug, say you are fond of a jug; then you will not be disturbed if it be broken. If you kiss your child or your wife, say to yourself that you are kissing

a human being, for then if death strikes it you will not be disturbed.

4. When you are about to take something in hand, remind yourself what manner of thing it is. If you are going to bathe put before your mind what happens in the bath—water pouring over someone, others being jostled, some reviling, others stealing; and you will set to work more securely if you say to yourself at once: "I want to bathe, and I want to keep my will in harmony with nature," and so in each thing you do; for in this way, if anything turns up to hinder you in your bathing, you will be ready to say, "I did not want only to bathe, but to keep my will in harmony with nature, and I shall not so keep it, if I lose my temper at what happens."

5. What disturbs men's minds is not events but their judgments on events. For instance, death is nothing dreadful, or else Socrates would have thought it so. No, the only dreadful thing about it is men's judgment that it is dreadful. And so when we are hindered, or disturbed, or distressed, let us never lay the blame on others, but on ourselves, that is, on our own judgments. To accuse others for one's own misfortunes is a sign of want of education; to accuse oneself shows that one's education has begun; to accuse neither oneself nor others shows that one's education is complete.

6. Be not elated at an excellence which is not your own. If the horse in his pride were to say, "I am handsome," we could bear with it. But when you say with pride, "I have a handsome horse," know that the horse is the ground of your pride. You ask then what you call your own. The answer is—the way you deal with your impressions. Therefore when you deal with your impressions in accord with nature, then you may be proud indeed, for your pride will be in a good which is your own.

7. When you are on a voyage, and your ship is at anchorage, and you disembark to get fresh water, you may pick up a small shellfish or a truffle by the way, but you must keep your attention fixed on the ship, and keep looking towards it constantly, to see if the helmsman calls you; and if he does, you have to leave everything, or be bundled on board with your legs tied like a sheep. So it is in life. If you have a dear wife or child given you, they are like the shellfish or the truffle, they are very well in their way. Only, if the

Helmsman call, run back to your ship, leave all else, and do not look behind you. And if you are old, never go far from the ship so that when you are called you may not fail to appear.

8. Ask not that events should happen as you will, but let your will be that events should happen as they do, and you shall have peace.

9. Sickness is a hindrance to the body, but not to the will, unless the will consent. Lameness is a hindrance to the leg, but not to the will. Say this to yourself at each event that happens, for you shall find that though it hinders something else it will not hinder you.

10. When anything happens to you, always remember to turn to yourself and ask what faculty you have to deal with it. If you see a beautiful boy or a beautiful woman, you will find continence the faculty to exercise there; if trouble is laid on you, you will find endurance; if ribaldry, you will find patience. And if you train yourself in this habit your impressions will not carry you away.

11. Never say of anything, "I lost it," but say, "I gave it back." Has your child died? It was given back. Has your wife died? She was given back. Has your estate been taken from you? Was not this also given back? But you say, "He who took it from me is wicked." What does it matter to you through whom the Giver asked it back? As long as He gives it to you, take care of it, but not as your own; treat it as passersby treat an inn.

12. If you wish to make progress, abandon reasonings of this sort: "If I neglect my affairs I shall have nothing to live on"; "If I do not punish my son, he will be wicked." For it is better to die of hunger, so that you be free from pain and free from fear, than to live in plenty and be troubled in mind. It is better for your son to be wicked than for you to be miserable. Wherefore begin with little things. Is your drop of oil spilt? Is your sup of wine stolen? Say to yourself, "This is the price paid for freedom from passion, this is the price of a quiet mind." Nothing can be had without a price. When you call your slave-boy, reflect that he may not be able to do anything you want. But he is not so well off that it rests with him to give you peace of mind.

13. If you wish to make progress, you must be content in

external matters to seem a fool and a simpleton; do not wish men to think you know anything, and if any should think you to be somebody, distrust youself. For know that it is not easy to keep your will in accord with nature and at the same time keep outward things; if you attend to one you must needs neglect the other.

14. It is silly to want your children and your wife and your friends to live for ever, for that means that you want what is not in your control to be in your control, and what is not your own to be yours. In the same way if you want your servant to make no mistakes, you are a fool, for you want vice not to be vice but something different. But if you want not to be disappointed in your will to get, you can attain to that.

Exercise yourself then in what lies in your power. Each man's master is the man who has authority over what he wishes or does not wish, to secure the one or to take away the other. Let him then who wishes to be free not wish for anything or avoid anything that depends on others; or else he is bound to be a slave.

15. Remember that you must behave in life as you would at a banquet. A dish is handed round and comes to you; put out your hand and take it politely. It passes you; do not stop it. It has not reached you; do not be impatient to get it, but wait till your turn comes. Bear yourself thus towards children, wife, office, wealth, and one day you will be worthy to banquet with the gods. But if when they are set before you, you do not take them but despise them, then you shall not only share the gods' banquet, but shall share their rule. For by doing so Diogenes and Heraclitus and men like them were called divine and deserved the name.

16. When you see a man shedding tears in sorrow for a child abroad or dead, or for loss of property, beware that you are not carried away by the impression that it is outward ills that make him miserable. Keep this thought by you: "What distresses him is not the event, for that does not distress another, but his judgment on the event." Therefore do not hesitate to sympathize with him so far as words go, and if it so chance, even to groan with him; but take heed that you do not also groan in your inner being.

17. Remember that you are an actor in a play, and the Play-

wright chooses the manner of it: if he wants it short, it is short; if long, it is long. If he wants you to act a poor man you must act the part with all your powers; and so if your part be a cripple or a magistrate or a plain man. For your business is to act the character that is given you and act it well; the choice of the cast is Another's.

18. When a raven croaks with evil omen, let not the impression carry you away, but straightway distinguish in your own mind and say, "These portents mean nothing to me; but only to my bit of a body or my bit of property or name, or my children, or my wife. But for me all omens are favorable if I will, for, whatever the issue may be, it is in my power to get benefit therefrom."

19. You can be invincible, if you never enter on a contest where victory is not in your power. Beware then that when you see a man raised to honour or great power or high repute you do not let your impression carry you away. For if the reality of good lies in what is in our power, there is no room for envy or jealousy. And you will not wish to be praetor, or prefect or consul, but to be free; and there is but one way to freedom—to despise what is not in our power.

SOME QUESTIONS

1. Epictetus talks much of "impressions." What does he mean by the word? One way to go about answering the question is to ask yourself what else there is in the world besides impressions. That is, with what can you contrast them?

Here is a story that may help. A man and his wife were dining gaily on their wedding anniversary, when they received a telegram that their only son had been killed in an accident. They were distraught for they loved him dearly. They rushed home; the mother sobbed hysterically all night, while her equally distressed husband tried to console her. With the dawn came a second telegram. The first had been a mistake. Their boy was elsewhere when the accident took place, and was in excellent health.

Now, what upset the parents so dreadfully? Their son's death? But he had not died. Their belief in his death, perhaps? Is that what Epictetus would call an impression?

But suppose the boy had been killed. What would then have been the cause of parental grief? The fact, or reality, of his death, or their judgment of what it meant? Would Epictetus have called the latter an impression, too? Is his use of the word a way of showing that whatever disturbs us is never an actual occurrence or situation, but only our judgment of it? If so, does it follow that if we train ourselves as he advises, we can judge things differently, and live in peace?

2. In his first statement, Epictetus tells us what is in our power and what isn't. He says: "Things not in our power include the body, property, reputation, office, and, in a word, everything which is not our own doing." Is it possible that I have no power over the care of my body and property (and getting and losing property), or over my reputation, or the position I attain in life? Or does Epictetus mean that I don't have *complete* power over them?

Taking the two interpretations just stated as alternative possibilities, can you find sentences of Epictetus farther along in his text that show which one he intends?

Let us look at some of the consequences of each interpretation, so we can know which one accords better with the rest of his text. If he means that I have *no power at all* over my body, etc., we know immediately that he is wrong. But was he wrong when he wrote it, sometime about 100 A.D.? He was a Greek slave of a Roman master. He may, indeed, have been right about himself, and even about his society. If this interpretation is correct, he might, later in the text, mention conditions of oppression and servitude.

But if Epictetus means that I have *incomplete* power over my body, etc.—which is true even today—what follows? Well, since he urges us not to be concerned with such things, but only with those that *are* in our power, it follows that he assumes we have *complete* power over the latter. He lists some of them as "thought, impulse, will to get and will to avoid." So he is taking no chances at all, but concentrating on what depends *entirely* on our discipline and fortitude, and is not subject to chance and fortune. If this interpretation is correct, he might, later in the text, show that he wants to remove us from concern with anything that can be altered by the world outside us.

3. In his third statement, Epictetus urges us always to remember the nature of whatever we are fond of, or find useful. "If you kiss your child or your wife, say to yourself that you are kissing a human being, for then if death strikes it you will not be disturbed." Why will you not be disturbed? Because you know human beings are mortal? Is the principle the same with the jug in the sentence before? That is, are you not disturbed when it is broken because you always bore in mind that it was a jug, and you know jugs are breakable? Or is it that you know it is *only* a jug, hence not really important?

Even if Epictetus means the former—that jugs are breakable—doesn't it (when you think of it as an abstract class) lose much of the quality that made you fond of it? Does the same thing happen when you think of your wife as *a* human being, not *the* person who shares your life?

Epictetus's principle seems to be: always remember that any individual thing is a member of a species, and subject to the things that happen to that species. One can go farther: every species is in a genus, and subject to what happens to that genus. I am a man (species), and men are animals (genus), and animals are, to jump a few steps, natural objects. Where are we to stop? Or shouldn't we stop? Is it wisdom for my wife to think of me as an object in the universe? It may save her pain when I die, but what other, less fortunate consequences may it have?

4. In the nineteenth statement, Epictetus tells us we can be invincible by competing only when we are sure to win. That is true—is it not?—by the definition of "invincible." But what consolation is it? If you marry the girl, or man, you know you can have, instead of trying for one you want, is that all to the good?

EXERCISE

WILLIAM JAMES

From *Principles of Psychology*

You reach the Mephistophelian point of view as well as the point of view of justice by treating cases as if they belonged rigorously to abstract classes. Pure rationalism, complete immunity from prejudice, consists in refusing to see that the case before one is absolutely unique. It is always possible to treat the country of one's nativity, the house of one's fathers, the bed in which one's mother died, nay, the mother herself if need be, on a naked equality with all other specimens of so many respective genera. It shows the world in a clear frosty light from which all fuliginous mists of affection, all swamp-lights of sentimentality, are absent. Straight and immediate action becomes easy then—witness a Napoleon's or a Frederick's career. But the question always remains, "Are not the mists and vapors *worth* retaining?" The illogical refusal to treat certain concretes by the mere law of their genus has made the drama of human history. The obstinate insisting that tweedledum is *not* tweedledee is the bone and marrow of life. Look at the Jews and the Scots, with their miserable factions and sectarian disputes, their loyalties and patriotisms and exclusions—their annals now become a classic heritage, because men of genius took part and sang in them. A thing is important if any one *think* it important. The process of history consists in certain folks becoming possessed of the mania that certain special things are important infinitely, whilst other folks cannot agree in the belief. The Shah of Persia refused to be taken to the Derby Day, saying "It is already known to me that one horse can run faster than another." He made the question *"which* horse?" immaterial. Any question can be made immaterial by subsuming all its answers under a common head. Imagine what college ball-games and races would be if the teams were to forget the absolute distinctness of Harvard from Yale and think of both as One in the higher genus College. The sovereign road to indifference, whether to evils or to goods, lies in the thought of the higher genus. "When we have meat before us," says Marcus Aurelius, seeking indifference to *that* kind of good, "we must receive the impression that this is the dead body of a fish, and this is the dead body of a bird or of a pig; and again that this Falernian * is only a little grape-juice, and this purple robe some sheep's wool dyed with the blood of a shell-fish. Such, then, are these impressions, and they reach the things themselves and penetrate them, and we see what kind of things they are. Just in the same way ought we to act through life, and where there are things which appear most worthy of our approbation, we ought to lay them bare and look at their worthlessness and strip them of all the words by which they are exalted."

SOME QUESTIONS

1. How is James's criticism of Marcus Aurelius related to question 3 about Epictetus? †

* [A famous Roman wine.]

† Marcus Aurelius and Epictetus were both Stoics, so both, in general, had the same philosophy.

2. Why does James identify "the point of view of justice" with "the Mephistophelean point of view" (i.e. the devil's point of view)? Is he implying that justice isn't enough? But what more could anyone want than justice? A suggestion: James seems to mean by "justice," treating every member of a class in the same way. Then, if all residents of the United States are treated alike by American courts, any resident accused of a crime may hire the best legal counsel available. But the rich have the money to do so; the poor don't. When the judge sentences the defendant to a $30 fine or 30 days in jail, any defendant may take his choice. But what if he doesn't have $30? James wants more than justice. He wants consideration for each person, in all his differences from others. This may be thought of as equity, or even mercy, but, whatever one calls it, it goes beyond justice. Even the devil would be just, if he punished sinners only, and treated each one like all others who have committed the same sin.

3. Expand on James's sentence: "A thing is important if any one *think* it important."

Section Two

Politics

. . . it is clear that the decline of a language must ultimately have political and economic causes: it is not due simply to the bad influence of this or that individual writer. But an effect can become a cause, reinforcing the original cause and producing the same effect in an intensified form, and so on indefinitely. A man may take to drink because he feels himself to be a failure, and then fail all the more completely because he drinks. It is rather the same thing that is happening to the English language. It becomes ugly and inaccurate because our thoughts are foolish, but the slovenliness of our language makes it easier for us to have foolish thoughts. The point is that the process is reversible. Modern English, especially written English, is full of bad habits which spread by imitation and which can be avoided if one is willing to take the necessary trouble. If one gets rid of these habits one can think more clearly, and to think clearly is a necessary first step toward political regeneration: so that the fight against bad English is not frivolous and is not the exclusive concern of professional writers.

George Orwell:
"Politics and the English Language"

Ours is an age of ideology, of opposed and irreconcilable political systems. We have come through two world wars and several smaller, but equally bitter, wars. Millions of men have fought, suffered, and died, and the end is not yet. We cannot help the situation without knowledge, and if we find we cannot help it even with knowledge, we can at least know why we fight, and what we risk our lives for.

That is a partial excuse, or explanation, for the content of a whole section in a book like this. The texts are concerned with political ideas. Any subject and any ideas will do for our exercises in language and thought; any one subject for our attempt to show how ideas are related. A fairly long section with a single subject matter is best to gain familiarity with something, to move with ease through an intellectual landscape, and note changes and developments. Political thought serves those purposes as well as anything else, and has the added advantage that we can start with the very familiar, the heritage of every schoolboy.

In this section, we expand our commentaries, make them more exact, and introduce many more principles. In addition, we define terms, like "contradiction," which were used casually throughout Section One. Close attention is required, as it is for any intellectual endeavor. The sooner one learns that, the sooner the excitement of the life of mind becomes a part of life.

THOMAS JEFFERSON, ET AL.

Declaration of Independence

We hold these truths to be self-evident—that all men are created equal; that they are endowed by their Creator with certain inalienable rights; that among these are life, liberty, and the pursuit of happiness. That, to secure these rights, governments are instituted among men, deriving their just powers from the consent of the governed; that, whenever any form of government becomes destructive of these ends, it is the right of the people to alter or abolish it, and to institute new government, laying its foundation on such principles, and organizing its powers in such form, as to them shall seem most likely to effect their safety and happiness.

I

What is the meaning of "We hold these truths to be self-evident"? Is it different from a more ordinary assertion, "We hold these statements to be true"? It is different, and we can start to analyze the meaning of the Declaration's words by pointing out that difference.

1. The sentence we just invented *asserts* explicitly that the sentences to come are true. The Declaration *assumes* that they are true.

2. Our sentence contains no other assertion. The Declaration adds that the statements to follow are self-evident.

Now what does it mean for a statement to be self-evident? It means that the statement itself contains evidence that it is true; that is, the very meaning of the statement is such that the statement *must* be true. How can this be? Don't we always need facts as proof of truth? No; there are statements which need no observation of fact to prove them true. Let us distinguish them from statements of fact.

Statements of fact are not self-evident, they do not carry their own evidence with them, but are called true only if evidence outside themselves is forthcoming. And *all* statements about matters of fact are of this kind. If I say, "The grass on my lawn is green," no one can know whether that statement is true unless he *looks* at the grass on my lawn. That observation provides the evidence by which we determine whether the statement is true or false. After all, if one sees that the grass is withered and brown, it is false to think it green.

How about a statement that is self-evident? Can the evidence that the statement itself offers be evidence that it is false? Yes. But only if the evidence is a contradiction. Thus, the statement, "Men who are taller than I are shorter than I" is self-evidently false if the words are used throughout in a simple unequivocal way. The principle on which we decide this is: All self-contradictions are false.[1]

Can a statement be, in the same way, self-evidently true? Yes, if it is tautological, the opposite of self-contradictory. The statement, "I am shorter than men who are taller than I" is self-evidently true. In a self-contradiction, the predicate contradicts the subject. In a tautology, the predicate merely restates the subject, or to put it another way, the meaning of the subject includes the meaning of the predicate.[2]

Any conclusion of an argument that is derived by logic alone is self-evident.[3] No truth has been added from the outside, no observation of fact is required. If the premises (the statements in the argument) are true—and they may require observation to prove them true—then the conclusion drawn from them *must* be true. If all men are mortal and Socrates is a man, then it must follow that Socrates is mortal. For in drawing a conclusion by logic alone we only analyze and manipulate the meanings of the premises. The meaning of the conclusion is already logically contained in the premises, although we may not see that until we think about it, that is, draw the conclusion.

II

Are the statements which the Declaration calls self-evident, then, all tautologies? Let us examine the first one, "All men are created equal." If it is a tautology, the meaning of "men" would have to include the meaning of "equality," as the meaning of "I am shorter" includes the meaning "others are taller." Is there anything about the idea, "men," which includes the idea that men are equal? There does not seem to be. Now for the second statement, that all men are endowed by their Creator with certain inalienable rights. It is surely not self-evident that men have a Creator, so it cannot be self-evident that He has endowed them with rights. And the rest of the statements are based on the assumption that these two are true, so they can be no more self-evident than the first two.

Suppose, then, that these are not self-evident truths. Are they truths for which we can readily find evidence, as we can for the statement, "The grass is green"? No. Even if we grant that there is a Creator and He has given man rights, how can we discover just what rights they are? How could we ever be sure that our God-given rights are just those detailed in the Declaration?

To make things worse, aren't some of the statements in the Declaration almost obviously false, by any evidence or standards? We know that men are unequal in health, strength, intelligence, sensitivity, moral behavior. What could lead us to believe that they were created equal? Are they, perhaps, equal at birth but unequal later as a result of environing conditions? No, not even that. For babies are unequal in size, health, strength, and, we think, intelligence. If people are not equal at birth, then they are not equal at the moment they are created.*

Next, the Declaration holds that there are certain inalienable rights, which include life, liberty, and the pursuit of happiness. What does "inalienable" mean? It means that which cannot be surrendered,

---

* That statement is itself a tautology, if we are using "the moment they are created" to mean "at birth," rather than "at conception."

transferred, or taken away. But these "rights" have been taken away all through history. People have been, and are being, deprived of their liberty and their pursuit of happiness, to say nothing of their lives. Even the freest of societies have jails and, for the most part, capital punishment. So these statements, too, are false.

Consider the next statement, that "to secure these rights, governments are instituted among men." Surely, governments have been instituted for all kinds of reasons, including sheer desire for power. If governments were instituted "to secure these rights" it would be very strange that so few governments have ever secured them, and even stranger that so many of them have officially accepted slavery, which is the very opposite of "these rights." (We might even ask what the signers of the Declaration thought they were signing, since ours was a slave society, and those signers did not change it when they came to power.) Clearly, this statement, too, is false.

Shall we say, then, that the Declaration is a tissue of falsehood and unproved conclusions? That is what it seems. But there is still one way of understanding it, that we haven't taken. To get to that way indirectly: could the statement that men are created equal refer only to rights, which is the only equality talked about thereafter? That is the context of the statement and should guide us in understanding it.[4] So let us re-examine the words of the Declaration in the context of human rights and values.

". . . all men are created equal." Does that mean they are equal in all their qualities? Of course not. No one would deny that some men are brown-eyed and some blue-eyed, and that brown eyes are different from blue eyes. Yet there is a sense in which brown eyes are equal to blue eyes: equally valuable for the purpose of seeing. Men, too, may be unequal in all their particular qualities, but equal in value as men. Don't we, in fact, speak that way all the time? "In our club, everyone is equal" doesn't mean the members are all of one size or intelligence; it means they are equal as members, and so are given identical rights as members.

". . . they are endowed by their Creator with certain inalienable rights." Since they are equal in value, insofar as they are men, they must, like the club members above, have identical rights. They have these rights, not as Mr. Snodgrass or Miss Piccalilly, who are unique persons, but insofar as they are, equally, human beings. Now, my rights as a lawyer may be taken away if I am disbarred, and I may be deprived of my rights as a citizen if I am disfranchised, but I cannot lose my rights as a man so long as I live, unless some Circe changes me into a pig. If I cannot lose my rights, they are properly said to be inalienable. But didn't we see that governments do take away men's rights? Not quite, not as we are using language here. Governments may refuse to let men *act* on any particular right, but they are wrong to do so. Men have the right, inalienably, to freedom of speech, even if the government does not let them speak freely. It is not your right the government takes away, but your power to act on it.

So being a man means being possessed of certain rights. Still, how do we know that "among these are life, liberty, and the pursuit of happiness"? Well, what is the one possession that all men have, and that they have equally? Each man possesses his own life. It is his, and his alone. And what follows? Why, that he can use his life as he chooses, at least within legal limits; what else could "possession" mean? But what about the pursuit of happiness? Well, if we assume that every man wants to be happy in his own way, he will use his liberty to bring himself happiness, if he can. Of course, he may not be able to attain happiness, but that is another matter. He has the right to *pursue* happiness; he cannot have a right *to be happy*.

Now, suppose a reader objects that the Declaration assumes a Creator Who has made man what he is, a Creator *in whose eyes* men are equally valuable and have equal rights. Could we come to the same conclusions, this reader asks, if we assume a different sort of Creator, or no Creator at all? Won't we then have to start from the facts alone? If we do, we see that some men are born free and some slave; some inherit thrones and others only debts; surely they are not equal in rights. We must agree that is, indeed, the case. But is it relevant? Men may be *born* into slavery, but the Declaration says nothing about that. It says men were *created* equal. Can we interpret "created" without, for the moment, any reference to a Creator, and still make the same sense of the Declaration?

The answer is that "created" may refer to man *as a natural creature,* not as a *social* being. When Genesis says "Male and female created he them," it refers to a time before there was human society. So, whether or not we think of man as made by a Creator, we may concern ourselves with his natural, as distinct from his social, status. And whether or not we think of nature as created by God, we know it was not created by man. But society was. Children are born to their parents and their parents' society, but they are also natural creatures in a natural world.

As members of society from birth, some babies are princes and some slaves, some babies are rich and some poor, but all that depends on their parents and the laws of society. As natural creatures—considered for the moment apart from society—one baby may be healthier than another, but he cannot be richer; one baby may be brighter, but he cannot be freer. The reason is that health and intelligence are natural traits, but wealth and freedom are social traits. One cannot have the social *right* to be strong and intelligent (natural traits), for no earthly power can secure it. One *can* have the *right* to be free (a social trait), for it can be secured. As a natural creature, no one comes into the world with the *right* to enslave others, for slavery is a social institution. In fact, as natural creatures we are equal in having no social rights; we have only powers.

Still—there could be another objection—if some people have greater *powers* than others, isn't it only *natural* that they should rule over them? This is a notion to which many people readily assent. After all, they say, the strong beast preys on the weak one, the intelligent outwits the stupid. But are we beasts or are we men? To say that we are classified, for purposes of biological taxonomy, as animals doesn't change the issue. We have much in common with animals, but not everything. We are distinguished from them by many things, including language, culture, and morals.

Now, what follows for human conduct from the fact that some men have greater natural powers than others? Nothing. The strong may enslave the weak. They may be indifferent to them. They may protect and care for them. They may devote all their energies to serving them. Which choice they make cannot, obviously, depend on the sheer physical fact of difference. What, then, does it depend on? It depends on morality, whether explicit or implicit. I may believe that the weak should serve the powerful or that the powerful should serve the weak, but my belief can be defended only on moral principle.

III

The Declaration now takes on a different aspect. If the section we have quoted from it is a moral statement, it means that since men are not *naturally* *un*equal in rights, they *ought* socially to be treated as equal. Since the Declaration deals with men as natural creatures, it deals with all men. When it tells how they *ought* to be treated, it refers to society and governments. Rights ought to be utterly inalienable.*

* Note that when a right is inalienable by law, not only is no one permitted to take it away from you, but you are not permitted to give it away, sell it, or transfer it in any fashion. If the liberty of Americans is inalienable, they do not have the right to rid themselves of it.

Then what about the idea that governments are instituted to secure these rights? That, too, is not factual, but moral. Here the difference between the two kinds of statements is best expressed by distinguishing between an explanation of the way governments do come
into existence, factually, and a justification for that existence, morally.
It does not matter how in fact any government started, if we are
concerned with justifying it. It only matters how it behaves.

And what can justify some men ruling over others? That depends on your other moral principles. If you believe that the strong
ought to rule, then a particular government is justified to you only
if it is made up of the strongest men.

But if you believe in the moral principles of the Declaration,
then a government can be justified only if it secures the inalienable
rights of its citizens. Still, you may object, the Declaration says that
is why governments were instituted, and it surely sounds like a statement about their origin. Not at all. It is a statement about the purpose
of governments, the *legitimate* purpose of *any* government, not the
actual purposes of those men who started *a* government. If the government has not that legitimate purpose in fact, as exhibited in its
conduct, people have the right "to alter or to abolish it." Why? Because it ought to have that purpose, and it loses its legitimacy if it
does not. In fact, such a purpose becomes an implicit definition of
legitimacy.*

IV

The Declaration, then, makes sense, and excellent sense. We
see that when we know what kinds of statements it contains. Those
statements are not self-evident—today the word would be "analytic"
—nor are they factual—today often called "synthetic," or "empirical."
They are evaluative or "normative" statements, judgments of what is
good or bad.[5] (The "normative" also includes judgments of beauty
and ugliness.)

There are still two puzzles left: why did Jefferson call the statements "self-evident" when they so obviously are not? And how can
one tell whether a moral statement is true or false? Perhaps we can
answer the first of these questions by attending to the second.

There is enormous controversy over whether we can prove a
moral statement. The difficulty is to prove ultimate, or basic, moral
belief, not other moral judgments that depend on it. Thus it may be

* The signers, by the way, knew that their principles implied opposition
to slavery. Jefferson had originally included an antislavery section, but it was
deleted for reasons of politics. Yet it was still implied.

difficult or impossible to prove that no one should ever take a human life. But if I believe that no one ever should, and I am not raising the question of proof at the moment, it is easy to answer the question whether I should kill you when I am angry at you. For of course I should not. Indeed, it can be said to be *self-evident* that I should not. You are, after all, a person, and it follows logically from the meaning of my moral principle that I should not kill you. And that, we saw, is one meaning of "self-evident."

Perhaps, then, if one knew the ultimate beliefs of Jefferson and his colleagues, it would be obvious that all the theoretical statements of the Declaration followed from them self-evidently.

Here we are driven to another stage in our investigation of meaning, and must introduce another principle. Whenever the statement we read was made in another place or time, we must find out how the words and phrases were used there or then.[6] Even an understanding of words and phrases may not be sufficient to understand what an author intended. We may have to know many things he believed that he simply took for granted *in his readers* as the common intellectual currency of his time. The Declaration bears witness of this. It was written as a document to the world in justification of an important action. The signers could scarcely have based their words on a set of beliefs that they had in common but few other people knew about—at least, not without some explanation of those beliefs.

So we must look to the time and place of the Declaration. The intellectual climate of writers and presumed readers is that of eighteenth-century Europe and America. The beliefs common to many educated men of the time, which could be, and probably are, a basis for the Declaration, are these: There is an order of nature, or natural law, which man can discover by the exercise of his reason. Human laws should be based on natural law. Man issues from the hands of his Maker naked and helpless, with but one possession, himself. Society has often taken that property from him, but it is not entitled to. Since man was created with it, it is his. And that property includes his life, liberty, and estate.*

The doctrines of the Declaration follow logically. They are restatements of, or deductions from, the pervasive ideas of the eighteenth century, and in that sense are "self-evident."

You may be interested in Lincoln's comment on the Declaration:

* The phrase "life, liberty, and estate" came from John Locke. Jefferson substituted "the pursuit of happiness" for the last word in the phrase.

I think the authors of that notable instrument [the Declaration of Independence] intended to include all men, but they did not intend to declare *all* men equal *in all respects.* They did not mean to say all were equal in color, size, intellect, moral developments, or social capacity. They defined with tolerable distinctness in what respects they did consider all men created equal—equal with "certain inalienable rights, among which are life, liberty, and the pursuit of happiness." This they said, and this they meant. They did not mean to assert the obvious untruth that all men were then actually enjoying that equality, nor yet that they were about to confer it immediately upon them. In fact, they had no power to confer such a boon. They meant simply to declare the right, so that enforcement of it might follow as fast as circumstances should permit.

Abraham Lincoln, Address of June 26, 1857

TERMS AND PRINCIPLES

1. *Self-contradiction:* A proposition whose subject and predicate contradict each other. All self-contradictions are logically false.
2. *Tautology:* A proposition the meaning of whose predicate is contained in the meaning of its subject. All tautologies are logically true.
3. *Analytic truth:* All propositions that are true analytically are themselves tautologies, or are part of an argument or a system that is formally or logically true. When a conclusion is derived logically from premises, its meaning is contained in those premises. The conclusion is true if the premises are, and is said to be analytic of the premises.
4. *Textual context:* Meaning is not entirely in isolated words but is provided by their context as well. (This will be expanded later.)
5. There are three kinds of proposition:
   (a) *Analytic:* Their truth-value (truth or falsehood) depends on whether they are tautologies or self-contradictions. In either event, no evidence outside the propositions is relevant. Analysis of meaning is all that counts.
   (b) *Empirical:* Their truth-value is determined in the end by reference to observation. Evidence comes ultimately from outside the propositions.
   (c) *Normative:* These are judgments of value, moral and aesthetic. They assert that something is good or bad, beautiful or ugly, better or worse.
6. *Historical context:* The meaning of statements uttered in other

times and places can be discovered only by learning how the words were used then or there and by finding the assumptions and beliefs relevant to the passage that were common to the writer and his probable audience.

EXERCISE

DANIEL WEBSTER

From Speech on the Conscription Bill House of Representatives, December 9, 1814

This, sir, is a bill for calling out the militia, not according to its existing organization, but by draft from new created classes;—not merely for the purpose of "repelling invasion, suppressing insurrection, or executing the laws," but for the general objects of war—for defending ourselves, or invading others, as may be thought expedient; —not for a sudden emergency, or for a short time, but for long stated periods; for two years, if the proposition of the Senate should finally prevail; for one year, if the amendment of the House should be adopted. What is this, sir, but raising a standing army out of the militia by draft, and to be recruited by draft, in like manner, as often as occasion may require?

. . . That measures of this nature should be debated at all, in the councils of a free government, is cause of dismay. The question is nothing less than whether the most essential rights of personal liberty shall be surrendered, and despotism embraced in its worst form.

The Secretary of War has favored us with an argument on the constitutionality of this power . . .

Congress having, by the Constitution, a power to raise armies, the secretary contends that no restraint is to be imposed on the exercise of this power, except such as is expressly stated in the written letter of the instrument. In other words, that Congress may execute its powers, by any means it chooses, unless such means are particularly prohibited. But the general nature and object of the Constitution impose as rigid a restriction on the means of exercising power as could be done by the most explicit injunctions. It is the first principle applicable to such a case, that no construction shall be admitted which impairs the general nature and character of the instrument. A free constitution of government is to be construed upon free principles, and every branch of its provisions is to receive such an interpretation as is full of its general spirit. No means are to be taken by implication which would strike us absurdly if expressed. And what would have been more absurd than for this Constitution to have said that to secure the great blessings of liberty it gave to government an uncontrolled power of military conscription? Yet such is the absurdity which it is made to exhibit, under the commentary of the Secretary of War.

But it is said that it might happen that an army could not be raised by voluntary enlistment, in which case the power to raise armies would be granted in vain, unless they might be raised by compulsion. If this reasoning could prove anything, it would equally show, that whenever the legitimate power of the Constitution should be so badly administered as to cease to answer the great ends intended by them, such new powers may be assumed or usurped, as any existing administration may deem expedient. This is the result of his own reasoning, to which the secretary does not profess to go. But it is a true result. For if it is to be assumed, that all powers were granted, which might by possibility become necessary, and that government itself is the judge of this possible necessity, then the powers of government are precisely what it chooses they should be. Apply the same reasoning to any other power granted to Congress, and test its accuracy by the result. Congress has power to borrow money. How is it to exercise this power? Is it confined to voluntary loans? There is no express limitation to that effect, and in the language of the secretary, it might happen, indeed it has happened, that persons could not be found willing to lend. Money might be borrowed then in any other mode. In other words, Congress might resort to a *forced* loan. It might take the money of any man by force, and give him in exchange exchequer notes or certificates of stock. Would this be quite constitutional, sir? It is entirely within the reasoning of the secretary, and it is a result of his argument, outraging the rights of individuals in a far less degree than the practical consequences which he himself draws from it. A compulsory loan is not to be compared, in point of enormity, with a compulsory military service.

If the Secretary of War has proved the right of Congress to enact a law enforcing a draft of men out of the militia into the regular army, he will at any time be able to prove, quite as clearly, that Congress has power to create a Dictator. The arguments which have helped him in one case, will equally aid him in the other, the same reason of a supposed or possible state necessity, which is urged now, may be repeated then, with equal pertinency and effect.

Sir, in granting Congress the power to raise armies, the people have granted all the means which are ordinary and usual, and which are consistent with the liberties and security of the people themselves, and they have granted no others. To talk about the unlimited power of the Government over the means to execute its authority, is to hold a language which is true only in regard to despotism. The tyranny of arbitrary governments consists as much in its means as in its ends; and it would be a ridiculous and absurd constitution which should be less cautious to guard against abuses in the one case than in the other. All the mean and instruments which a free government exercises, as well as ends and objects which it pursues, are to partake of its own essential character, and to be conformed to its genuine spirit. A free government with arbitrary means to administer it is a contradiction; a free government without adequate provision for personal security is an absurdity; a free government, with an uncontrolled power of military conscription, is a solecism, at once the most ridiculous and abominable that ever entered into the head of man.

SOME QUESTIONS

1. According to Webster, the Secretary of War argued that where the Constitution grants Congress a specific power, Congress must (unless the Constitution expressly limits it) have power also to

use whatever means it deems fit. That sounds like an analytic statement, but it is not.

If Congress is granted a power, it must have some means to carry it out. If it has not means to do so, it does not, in fact, have the power. For example, Congress may be granted the *right* to print money, but if it can never control a printing press, it never has the *power* to print money. So it is an analytic statement that to have the power to bring about an end, one must control *some* means to do so. (Indeed, that one controls some means is the meaning of "one has power to bring about an end.")

To repeat: if I am granted a *power* to effect an end, I must be permitted *some means*. But does it follow that I must be permitted *any* means I desire? Of course not. To urge it is to urge a normative proposition, and a foolish one. There are many ways to skin a cat, and many means to bring about an end. Each means has other consequences, beyond that particular consequence I desire and call my "end." The police are empowered to keep order. One way of doing so is to censor all speech. But another consequence of that means is to interfere with, and perhaps eliminate, political parties. The police are not empowered to do that. So, granted the police must have some means of keeping order, that means has to accord with the other duties of the police and with the principles of democratic government.

Suppose we discover three possible means for attaining an end, and each means has other consequences, as follows:

Means No. 1 . . .	Consequence A
	Consequence B (the end)
	Consequence C
Means No. 2 . . .	Consequence B (the end)
	Consequence D
	Consequence E
	Consequence F
Means No. 3 . . .	Consequence B (the end)
	Consequence G

We should ask such questions as (1) Do the other consequences of the means contradict, or destroy, the end? (2) Do the other consequences of the means interfere with something else (still another end, or a principle) to which we cling? If consequences A, C, D, E, and F are opposed to other principles or ends, or harmful somehow to B, which is our end at the moment, we should reject means 1 and

2. If consequence G does none of these things, we should choose means 3.

Explain Webster's opposition to conscription, using the scheme outlined above.

2. If I desire an end (as the Secretary of War desired a standing army), but find no *possible* means I could approve, does that mean I must, in all consistency, give up the end? If there are no *present* acceptable means at my command, but I can envisage such means as possible, is it sensible to continue to hold the end? If I continue to hold an end when I know there are no possible means to attain it, would you call me utopian?

3. Webster, in the fourth paragraph, characterizes the Secretary's belief as "absurd." Is an argument wrong because it is "absurd"? Today "absurd" is often used as a synonym of "foolish," "silly," "preposterous." But "absurd" used to mean "self-contradictory." Is Webster asserting that the Secretary's statement is self-contradictory, that is, logically false?

4. Is Webster's answer, in his own opinion, analytic and true? That is, does Webster's belief about the sort of means Congress should use derive logically from the nature of the Constitution as he understands it? Is he saying that the nature of the means it empowers is thus-and-so?

Webster thinks his argument against conscription also holds of forced borrowing of money by the government. Does it, then, hold equally of the income tax?

5. Examine the argument by which Webster shows that, on the Secretary's reasoning, Congress might force people to lend the government money. Is it a good argument? Examine the argument by which Webster shows that, on the Secretary's reasoning, "Congress has power to create a Dictator." Are the arguments identical? Is one more persuasive than the other?

6. At the end of the quotation, Webster states three ideas about free government. He calls the first a contradiction, the second an absurdity, the third a solecism. Does he mean by "absurdity" here something different from "contradiction," or is he using the two words as synonyms so that he will not have to repeat himself? A solecism is an ungrammatical combination of words. Is the Secretary of War's statement ungrammatical? Is it rather illogical, in the sense of contradictory (and, thus, "ungrammatical" only as a concession to his rhetoric)?

ABRAHAM LINCOLN

From the Gettysburg Address

. . . we here highly resolve that these dead shall not have died in vain, that this nation under God shall have a new birth of freedom, and that government of the people, by the people, for the people, shall not perish from the earth.

COMMENTARY

How many people ask what this means? Familiarity breeds assurance. And these phrases are so misread that their meaning is often obscured or confused.

I

The first puzzle is this: "government of the people, by the people, for the people" seems meaningful, because it is so familiar, but as you think about it, you may find it repetitious. A government *of* the people, presumably, is a government composed of the people themselves. But isn't that exactly what government *by* the people is? Of course, government *for* the people is government in the interests of the people. So government of the people, by the people, for the people would be government composed of the people themselves acting in their own interests. The governors and the governed would be identical, both being the people, even if the governors were a minority representing the people.

What does Lincoln mean by "the people"? That is our second puzzle. He cannot simply mean human beings. If he did, he would say "people," not "*the* people." And his statement would be so fatuous that there would be no need to discuss it. Again, we need the historical context.

The Romans spoke of *Senatus populusque Romanus* as the sources of political authority. The Senate and the people of Rome! "The people" were a class distinguished from the Senate, men of great family, usually of wealth and social position. Feudal society also treated "the people" as a class or (the feudal term) "estate." In earlier feudal councils, only the nobility and clergy had a voice, but from the thirteenth century on some attention was paid to three estates: nobility, clergy, and commons. The latter were "the people." It was to them, when it was not more narrowly to peasants or workers, that revolutionary movements in the modern world appealed.

Lincoln is probably, then, talking of the people as those who are not aristocrats or hereditary rulers; in fact, in our egalitarian society, a single group of political equals, who have dispensed with an inherited ruling class. Our government, he is saying, is of, by, and for this one group which, in the United States, is constituted by all citizens.

So far so good. But our first puzzle is still with us. In so careful an address, it seems unlikely that Lincoln merely repeated himself for rhetorical effect.* And if he did, wouldn't it have been better to keep the same preposition? Yet "government of the people" and "government by the people" are usually taken to mean the same thing.

Let us have a fresh look at Lincoln's words. The phrase, after all, is "government of the people, by the people, for the people." Yet it is always read aloud with a pause between "government" and "of," as though there were a comma between the words. And in consequence, "of" is emphasized. Read it aloud now as it is written, with a pause only where there are commas, and with no emphasis on "of." It becomes "government of the people (pause) by the people (pause) for the people." That is, it is government *over* the people. "Government of the people" is the same as "the governing of the people."

Lincoln is asking victory so that the kind of government that (he assumes) only his nation has, "shall not perish from the earth." That kind of government he characterizes, or defines, as rule over a nation of politically equal citizens by those citizens themselves in their own interest.

II

Did Lincoln offer his great phrase as a definition of democracy? It would seem so, for if he merely meant to characterize or describe democracy, he would probably have used the word. We may *describe* an apple as juicy, but not if we don't use the word "apple." If we have *defined* a thing, however, we may substitute the definition for the name: [1] we may say "male sovereign" instead of "king."

---

* Lincoln's reputation is not thus. A complaint has been registered in a stunning epigram about other prose styles:

> The State of the Union is this, chiefly:
> No one since Lincoln says things briefly.
> *The Commonweal,* March 15, 1946

The Gettysburg Address contains neither "democracy" nor "republic." * It is about "this nation," which is described at the beginning as "conceived in liberty, and dedicated to the proposition that all men are created equal." And it states a resolution at the end "that this nation, under God, shall have a new birth of freedom, and that government of the people, by the people, for the people shall not perish from the earth." "A new birth of freedom" may be emancipation of slaves, something this nation did not have before the war. But "government of the people, by the people, for the people" must be preserved; so it already existed and is different from the nation's new freedom. It is, indeed, our form of government.

Let us suppose, then that Lincoln intended a definition of democracy here. There are two more questions: Is it, actually, a definition? If so, is it a satisfactory definition? An answer to the first question requires some knowledge of what a definition is. We shall take this occasion to discuss it.

A definition tells the meaning of a word.[2] In a sense, the choice of a word is arbitrary, or the result of convention.[3] If people agree to use it to stand for some meaning, that is sufficient. But what the word means, its definition, is rarely arbitrary. It is a meaning that we need for some purpose, and it characterizes all objects to which the word refers. Those objects may be things (e.g. "horse") or ideas (e.g. "infinity"). The things may be real (e.g. men) or imaginary (e.g. centaurs).

"*All* objects to which a word refers" is ordinarily called "a class," and *each* of the objects "a member of the class." [4] Definitions, then, characterize classes; [5] they do not describe individual members, for definitions hold of each member equally. They tell what characteristics objects must have in order to be called by the same name. The definition of "horse" states the characteristics which entitle any object to be called "a horse," and whose absence means that it is not "a horse." So the definition of a word must include all objects to which the word refers and exclude all other objects.[6]

Aristotle defined man as "a rational animal." Obviously, "animal" alone is not enough to define man, although all men are animals, for it includes apes, rabbits, and pigs. The word "rational"

---

* External evidence, in which Lincoln used the names for this form of government, also makes it seem that he intended his phrase as a definition. Lincoln convened a special session of Congress on July 4, 1861 (the date itself is a reminder of his belief) to plead the cause of union. In his message, he said: ". . . this issue . . . presents . . . the question whether a constitutional republic, or democracy—a government of the people, by the same people—can preserve its territorial integrity . . ."

excludes all non-human animals, however, because it is—or was, then—understood to mean the ability to do such things as make a logical argument or learn grammar. And if Aristotle had defined man as "a rational being," it would not distinguish man from the angels.

Of course, we do not state every common characteristic of members of a class in our definition. We select some and reject others. The principle of selection is usefulness.[7] The information that a whale is a mammal, and not a fish, seems strange since a fish is a creature whose natural habitat is water, and mammals are creatures with mammary glands, who bear children and nurse them. These are not contradictory: a mammal can live in the water, and whales do.* Whales are called mammals because biologists, who made the definition, are interested in child-bearing, suckling, and so on, not in natural habitat. So they chose these, from all the characteristics of whales, to define them.

If others have different purposes, they may define "whale" differently. Indeed, for dietary purposes, the Roman Catholic Church implicitly defines whales as fish, for meat may not be eaten on Fridays, but whale may. Whatever the medical definition of "insanity" may be, its legal definition is "inability to manage one's own affairs and perform one's social duties." That is what the law is interested in, but not what medicine is interested in. And think of the difference between a chemist's and a chef's definitions of "sugar."

Although we select defining characteristics for our own purposes, we select them from the common characteristics of the members of a class.[8] We are entitled to select characteristics that serve our purposes; we are not entitled to define in terms of characteristics that the objects do not have. If we do, our definition is false. We may define a newly coined word as we please, for it does not yet refer to any object. But we are wrong if we define "horse" (using the word to refer to the familiar four-footed beast) as an animal with wings and beak.

III

Let us examine Lincoln's definition with its referent, democracy, in mind. But first, a caution. The inadequacies, abuses, and follies of particular democratic governments cannot be part of a definition of democracy. For they are not common characteristics of all democratic governments. Still, suppose some abuse has existed in every known

---

* It is more precise to say that the natural habitat of whales is water, than that they live *in* the water. For, in one sense, they live *on* the water, surfacing to breathe. Fish live *in* the water, and can breathe in it.

democracy? Even that does not mean that it must be included in a definition. For "democracy" stands for all democracies, past, present, and future—indeed, for all possible democracies. An abuse, by definition, is not a necessary part of the meaning. And all that *must* be included in the meaning of "democracy" is what is *necessary* for a government to have in order to be called by the name; in other words, those characteristics in the absence of which no government would properly be called democratic.

In a sense every definition states the ideal type. That you are blind, and I am lame, and Socrates was snub-nosed, is irrelevant to the definition of "man." Defects in individual members of a class are left for the description of those members; they do not enter the definition of the class.

Now if we do not think that "government of the people, by the people, for the people" is a definition, we can start to criticize it by pointing out that the people never really govern themselves, but at the very least have bureaucrats, administrators, and parties or factions, whether or not they are representatives; and that these, not the people, make up a governing class. Yet, even if that is true, the "governing class" in a democracy, like representatives, is responsible *to* the people. If the people do not use their power, or do not use it effectively, that does not mean they do not have it.

Another way of criticizing Lincoln's "definition" is by arguing that "government for the people" neither *includes* all democratic governments nor *excludes* all other kinds. After all, most governments would maintain that they were "for the people," and insofar as the welfare of the people is concerned, non-democratic governments may, and often do, serve that welfare better than democratic governments (unless, of course, self-government is thought of as part of that welfare). Democratic governments, like all governments, can be foolish or venal. Often they do not serve the welfare of the people they govern. Even in our personal lives, on occasions when there is nothing to interfere with free choice, we often make bad choices. How else could one account for the divorce rate, or the number of people in jail?

Yet there are two reasons why this criticism is not effective. In the first place, "government for the people" need not, and probably should not, be thought of as government which *actually* serves the welfare of the people. Surely it should not be thought of as government which *always* serves that welfare. Such government could never be expected of mere men. A governor would have to be perfectly good, all-wise and all-powerful. And that is a definition of God, not of man. It is enough if the *aim* of government is the welfare of the

people. Even that is not always true of every action of every democratic government. Special interests may be served; powerful groups,
on occasion, bring great pressure on government. But it is true *in
general* of democratic government in a way in which it is not true
of non-democratic government. Democratic government has only
one political class, the people. Non-democratic governments always
have more than one political class, even though they sometimes try
to hide that fact. There may be an aristocracy or a church with special
privileges. There may be a group with special political powers, as was
true of England when the House of Lords was more than the cere-
monial institution it is now. For then Parliament was composed of
two houses, both with political power, and one, the House of Commons, represented an "estate," the people, which made up the vast
majority of subjects, while the other, the House of Lords, represented
the small minority of nobles.

In our day, when the old aristocracy has no especial political
power, non-democratic governments have a new élite which gets
political consideration that the people do not get. In the totalitarian-
isms of the twentieth century *the* Party (communist, fascist, Nazi)
has been an implicit organ of government. The Party has not been
responsible to the people, and no matter what the ideals of some of
its members, it has ruled to a considerable extent *for* the Party.
Democratic government is the only government devoid of such
groups, the only government in which the people can, *if they want to*
and will expend the time and energy, keep all political groups
strictly accountable.

The second reason that this criticism does no violence to the
idea that Lincoln's words constitute a successful definition is that,
even if the phrase "government for the people" did not exclude non-
democratic governments, that makes no difference. For it is only
part of the definition, not the whole. And while a definition as a whole
must exclude everything that the word defined does not stand for,
that is not true of a mere part of the definition. If men are "rational
animals," that definition excludes chipmunks. But one part of it,
namely, "animals," does not exclude them at all. What is necessary
is that "government for the people" does include democratic governments. And we have seen that in general, or as a matter of theory,
it does.

We may probably conclude that Lincoln's words are a definition
of democracy, and not a bad one.

TERMS AND PRINCIPLES

1. A definition may be substituted for the word it defines. The two are equivalent.
2. *Definition:* The meaning of a word.
3. Words themselves are conventional symbols.
4. *Class of objects:* All objects referred to by the same word when it has a single meaning.
5. Definitions characterize classes.
6. A definition of a word properly includes all objects to which the word refers and excludes all others.
7. Defining characteristics are chosen because they are useful for some interest or purpose.
8. Defining characteristics are chosen from the totality of actual characteristics.

EXERCISE

JAMES MADISON (PUBLIUS)

From *The Federalist,* No. X

By a faction, I understand a number of citizens, whether amounting to a majority or minority of the whole, who are united and actuated by some common impulse of passion, or of interest, adverse to the rights of other citizens or to the permanent and aggregate interests of the community.

There are two methods of curing the mischiefs of faction: the one, by removing its causes; the other, by controlling its effects.

There are again two methods of removing the causes of faction: the one, by destroying the liberty which is essential to its existence; the other, by giving to every citizen the same opinions, the same passions, and the same interests.

It could never be more truly said than of the first remedy, that it was worse than the disease. Liberty is to faction what air is to fire, an ailment without which it instantly expires. But it could not be less folly to abolish liberty, which is essential to political life, because it nourishes faction, than it would be to wish the annihilation of air, which is essential to animal life, because it imparts to fire its destructive agency.

The second expedient is as impracticable as the first would be unwise. As long as the reason of man continues fallible, and he is at liberty to exercise it, different opinions will be formed. As long as the connection subsists between his reason and his self-love, his opinions and his passions will have a reciprocal influence on each other; and the former will be objects to which the latter will attach themselves. The diversity in the faculties of men, from which the rights of property originate, is not less an insuperable obstacle to a uniformity, of interests. The protection of these faculties is the first object of government. From the protection of different and unequal faculties of acquiring property, the possession of different degrees and kinds of property immediately results; and from the influence of these on the sentiments and views of the respective proprietors, ensues a division of the society into different interests and parties. . . .

The inference to which we are brought is that the causes of faction cannot be removed, and that relief is only to be sought in the means of controlling its effects.

If a faction consists of less than a majority, relief is supplied by the republican principle, which enables the majority to defeat its sinister views by regular vote. It may clog the administration, it may convulse the society; but it will be unable to execute and mask its violence under the forms of the Constitution. When a majority is included in a faction, the form of popular government, on the other hand, enables it to sacrifice to its ruling passion or interest both the public good and the rights of other citizens. To secure the public good, and private rights, against the danger of such a faction, and at the same time to preserve the spirit and the form of popular government, is then the great object to which our inquiries are directed. Let me add that it is the great *desideratum,* by which alone this form of government can be rescued from the opprobrium under which it has so long labored, and be recommended to the esteem and adoption of mankind. . . .*

---

* [Note that here Madison is solving this problem by distinguishing between republican and democratic government.]

A point of difference is, the greater number of citizens and extent of territory which may be brought within the compass of republican than of democratic government; and it is this circumstance principally which renders factious combinations less to be dreaded in the former, than in the latter. The smaller the society, the fewer probably will be the distinct parties and interests composing it; the fewer the distinct parties and interests, the more frequently will a majority be found of the same party; and the smaller the number of individuals composing a majority, and the smaller the compass within which they are placed, the more easily will they concert and execute their plans of oppression. Extend the sphere, and you take in a greater variety of parties and interests; you make it less probable that a majority of the whole will have a common motive to invade the rights of other citizens; or if such a common motive exists, it will be more difficult for all who feel it to discover their own strength, and to act in unison with each other. Besides other impediments, it may be remarked that where there is a consciousness of unjust or dishonorable purposes, communication is always checked by distrust, in proportion to the number whose concurrence is necessary.

Hence it clearly appears that the same advantage which a republic has over a democracy, in controlling the effects of faction, is enjoyed by a large over a small republic—is enjoyed by the Union over the States composing it. Does the advantage consist in the substitution of representatives, whose enlightened views and virtuous sentiments render them superior to local prejudices, and to schemes of injustice? It will not be denied that the representation of the Union will be most likely to possess these requisite endowments. Does it consist in the greater security afforded by a greater variety of parties, against the event of any one party being able to outnumber and oppress the rest? In an equal degree does the increased variety of parties, comprised within the Union, increase this security. Does it, in fine, consist in the greater obstacles opposed to the concert and accomplishment of the secret wishes of an unjust and interested majority? Here, again, the extent of the Union gives it the most palpable advantage.

The influence of factious leaders may kindle a flame within their particular States, but will be unable to spread a general conflagration through the other States. A religious sect may degenerate into a political faction in a part of the confederacy; but the variety of sects dispersed over the entire face of it must secure the national councils against any danger from that source. A rage for paper money, for an abolition of debts, for an equal division of property, or for any other improper or wicked project will be less apt to pervade the whole body of the Union than a particular member of it; in the same proportion as such a malady is more likely to taint a particular county or district than an entire State.

In the extent and proper structure of the Union, therefore, we behold a republican remedy for the diseases most incident to republican government. And according to the degree of pleasure and pride we feel in being republicans, ought to be our zeal in cherishing the spirit and supporting the character of federalists.

SOME QUESTIONS

1. Two terms often employed in political studies are "direct democracy" and "indirect democracy" (or "representative government"). With what terms of Madison's can these be equated?

2. Is Madison's argument an attack (implicit or explicit) on a two-party system? To what extent, if any, are "factions" to be identified with "political parties"?

3. In the first paragraph quoted, Madison allows a faction to be either a majority or a minority. In which case, according to Madison, is it a greater danger? Is Madison persuasive in his proposed cure? What, exactly, is it?

4. It is believed by many that the people are allowed, in a democracy, to choose their own ends and to get what they want, within the limits of possibility. But Madison, in his penultimate paragraph, states a number of examples of things that are "improper or wicked." Does he urge that such things be banned by law, or merely that they are less likely in the Union than in states, less likely in a large republic than a small one? How does he defend or explain his belief?

EXERCISE

HEINRICH VON TREITSCHKE

From *Politics*

On close examination then, it becomes clear that if the State is power, only that State which has power realizes its own idea, and this accounts for the undeniably ridiculous element which we discern in the existence of a small state. Weakness is not itself ridiculous, except when masquerading as strength. In small States that puling spirit is hatched, which judges the State by the taxes it levies, and does not perceive that if the State may not enclose and repress like an egg-shell, neither can it protect. Such thinkers fail to understand that the moral benefits for which we are indebted to the State are above all price. It is by generating this form of materialism that small States have so deleterious an effect upon their citizens.

Moreover, they are totally lacking in that capacity for justice which characterizes their greater neighbors. Any person who has plenty of relations and is not a perfect fool is soon provided for in a small country, while in a large one, although justice tends to become stereotyped, it is not possible to be so much influenced by personal and local circumstances as in the narrower sphere. . . .

Everything considered, therefore, we reach the conclusion that the large State is the nobler type. This is more especially true of its fundamental functions such as wielding the sword in defence of the hearth and of justice. Both are better protected by a large State than a small one. The latter cannot wage war with any prospect of success.

SOME QUESTIONS

1. Madison preferred, under certain conditions, a large state to a small one. What are those conditions? Treitschke, too, has that preference. Does he also hold to the same conditions as Madison?

2. When Treitschke says "the State is power," he may mean that it is the only legitimate user of power within a nation, or that it has ultimate coercive authority over those within its jurisdiction.

These are reasonable definitions of the state. Does it follow, as Treitschke asserts, that a small state is therefore ridiculous? May not a small state have as much authority over its citizens as a large state?

3. If a small state may have as much power over its citizens as a large state, Treitschke is either using the word "power" in more than one sense, or his definition, "the State is power," means something different from what we suggested above. Does he mean by "power," "ability to defeat other nations in war"? He says later, "if the State may not enclose and repress like an egg-shell, neither can it protect." So he may be thinking of internal power. Still, "protect" may be protection from foreign enemies as well as protection from internal disorder. Conceivably, Treitschke identifies the state's power to repress its own citizens with its external power. But the two surely need not go together. Tiny Latin-American despotisms have often repressed their citizens and yet had almost no external power. What do you make of this tangle? In the last paragraph, Treitschke writes of the state's "fundamental functions." Do the two he chooses cast any light on our problem?

EXERCISE

JOHN ADAMS

From Letter to J. H. Tiffany
March 31, 1819

". . . custom is said to be the standard of the meaning of words; and for the purposes of common parlance it may answer well enough but when science is concerned, something more technical must be introduced. The customary meanings of the words *republic* and *commonwealth* have been infinite. They have been applied to every government under heaven; that of Turkey and that of Spain, as well as that of Athens and of Rome, of Geneva and San Marino. The strict definition of a republic is, that in which the sovereignty resides in more than one man. A democracy, then, is a republic, as well as an aristocracy, or any mixture of both.

"The Federalist is a valuable work, and Mr. Madison's part in it as respectable as any other. But his distinction between a republic and a democracy cannot be justified. A democracy is as really a republic as an oak is a tree, or a temple a building. There are, in strictness of speech and in the soundest technical language, democratical and aristocratical republics, as well as an infinite variety of mixtures of both."

SOME QUESTIONS

1. What, according to Adams, is the relation of a democracy to a republic?
2. Does Adams's definition of "republic" differ from Madison's? If so, how?
3. If we use Madison's definition of "republic" from the exercise before last, what is then the relation of "democracy" and "republic"?

OLIVER WENDELL HOLMES, JR.

From For the court, *Schenck* vs. *United States*, 1919

The question in every case is whether the words used are used in such circumstances and are of such a nature as to create a clear and present danger that they will bring about the substantial evils that Congress has a right to prevent. It is a question of proximity and degree. When a nation is at war many things that might be said in time of peace are such a hindrance to its effort that their utterance will not be endured so long as men fight and that no court could regard them as protected by any constitutional right.

FIRST COMMENTARY

I

Oliver Wendell Holmes, Jr. wrote these words as the opinion of the United States Supreme Court. The theoretical issue involved in the trial of Schenck was: under what conditions can the state punish a man for his words? Neither slander nor libel was involved. The question was about words that in some way tend to cause unlawful acts or, as Holmes put it, "substantial evils that Congress has a right to prevent."

The First Amendment to the Constitution reads in part: "Congress shall make no law . . . abridging the freedom of speech . . ." We *might* argue, therefore, that if Congress has abided by the Constitution, there are no laws abridging free speech, and no one can if punished for what he says. But if a man can be punished for what he says, it follows that Congress has violated the Constitution by making a law that curtails free speech.

Now, apart from the Schenck case, can a man in fact be punished, under the laws of the United States, for something he says? We all know that we can be punished for speaking or writing falsehoods that damage another person, for that violates the laws of slander and libel. Don't these laws actually abridge free speech, although not perhaps explicitly? And what about Mr. Justice Holmes's statement (also in his decision on the Schenck case) that the right of free speech does not allow a man to shout "Fire!" in a crowded theater?

Apparently these cases are not thought of as matters of free speech; the laws covering them are not thought of as abridging free speech. Obviously, then, "free speech" does not simply mean freedom to say anything, at any time, or in any place. If you start to deliver a speech from the floor of a public hall, while the official speaker is talking, you are guilty of disturbing the peace. If you use foul language in print, you may be guilty of obscenity. And if you violate the Supreme Court's decision about "clear and present danger" you may be guilty of incitement to murder, espionage, or treason. What, then, is meant by freedom of speech? What kind of law is Congress forbidden to pass? We will return to this problem in our second commentary. In this one, we will try to establish a basis for our answer.

II

Let us begin our inquiry by attending to the phrase, "clear and present danger." First, what is a clear danger?

Perhaps we can tell what a *clear* danger is by asking if there is any other kind. If "danger" and "clear danger" mean the same thing, the word "clear" is sheer waste. One way to find out whether "clear" modifies "danger" in any way, is to ask if there can be an unclear danger. The reason for this question is a simple rule of discourse (we may call it the *principle of significant assertion* [1]) that a statement or phrase has meaning only if its contradictory has meaning. "A high place," then, would be meaningless if "a low place" had no meaning.

Now, an unclear danger is the opposite of a clear danger. What can it mean? One guess might be that there is a danger, but it is unclear that it is a danger. What does "unclear" mean in this sentence? Probably that the danger is not fully *understood* to be such. A wolf in sheep's clothing is a real danger, but if we believe he really is a sheep we do not know that he is dangerous. "Unclear," on this interpretation, means not understood, or not understood sufficiently. "Clear," then, would mean understood, or understood sufficiently (i.e. clearly). And a clear danger would be a danger understood to be such.

Still, there are three further questions about the meaning of "clear danger."

A. Is it the same thing to say (as we have, implicitly) that (1) a clear danger exists when (a) a situation is, in fact, dangerous, and (b) it is understood to be dangerous; and to say that (2) a clear danger exists when (a) a situation is, in fact, dangerous, and (b) it is understood what that situation is? The answer is "No." To consider the wolf again: suppose that while he was in sheep's clothing, we didn't know he was dangerous, nor that he was a wolf. If we learned later that he was a wolf, does it follow that we would know he was dangerous? Possibly, even probably; but not surely. For that would depend on another piece of knowledge: namely, that wolves are dangerous. And there may be people who do not know that. Hence to know what a situation is does not always mean to know whether it is dangerous.

B. Now one may ask the opposite question: can we ever know that a situation is dangerous without knowing clearly what the situation is? To this, the answer is "yes," although often we may have to know both in order to be clear about either. Suppose we don't know that the presumed sheep is really a wolf, but we see him attack and eat other sheep. We might regard him as a brand-new phenomenon —a carnivorous sheep. We would be quite wrong about the situation, but quite right in believing it dangerous.

C. Do we have to know in what way a situation is dangerous in order to know *that* it is dangerous? Do we have to know that this one "sheep" will try to kill and eat other sheep in order to know that he is dangerous? To some extent, the answer is "Yes." We may know the beast to be dangerous without knowing that he intends to eat the sheep, but not without knowing at least that, given the chance, he will try to do them bodily harm. We can know that a human enemy is dangerous, because he has sworn to murder us, without knowing that, in fact, he intends to poison us. It is important to know: shall we examine our food or wear steel vests? Still, we do not have to know *exactly* what the danger is, in order to know that there is danger; but we do have to know the general nature of the danger.

Here a caution may be necessary. We have been considering Holmes's much-quoted phrase all by itself. Not only is the textual context [2] important, but the historical context is indispensable. Holmes was writing a Supreme Court decision which would be the law of the land. Action would follow his words, so his concern was more than speculative. Holmes accepted the awful responsibility of stating conditions for forbidding a man to speak his mind.

How does the historical context bear on our understanding of Holmes's phrase? If action is to be taken, then it is not enough to know that we are in danger. We must know *how* a situation is dangerous, and *what* the danger is. If we know less, how can we decide whom to act against, and what action to take? Our conduct will be uninformed. Indeed, we must know *to whom* or *to what* there is danger. Clearly, nothing can be dangerous in itself, without possible harm to anything in the world. And what is a danger to one man may be a blessing to another. The cobra is a deadly snake, but what would professional snake-charmers do without him?

Words, too, are never in themselves dangerous. (Here we use the textual context.) As Holmes puts it in his first sentence, the question (of the Court) is, in every case, whether the nature of the words are such, and the circumstances in which they are used are such, that they create a clear and present danger. (I may shout "Fire!" in isolation, but not in a crowded theater.) The danger is that the words "will bring about the substantial evils that Congress has a right to prevent." No other evils, note. Just evils like treason and riot.

Is there a precise way in which the Court can determine that there is such danger? Apparently not: "It is a question of proximity and degree." "Proximity and degree" obviously refer to nearness (present-ness) and clearness. How near? We will consider that in a moment. How clear? Holmes doesn't say, but our interpretation would lead us to conclude: very clear.

III

Now, what is a present danger? We know what a danger is. What difference does the adjective "present" make? If nothing that is not present can be dangerous in any way, the word makes no difference.

Would you regard an absent tiger as dangerous to you? Assume that he is prowling the Indian jungle, looking for prey, and you are warm in bed in Paducah, Kentucky. Clearly, you are safe from the tiger, as safe as you are from the lamb he seeks. Yet, though tiger and lamb are both in India, and you safe, surely there is some difference in the danger they represent. It is this: *if* the tiger were present, he would be dangerous; but *if* the lamb were present, he would not be dangerous. The difference between the two can be rendered by saying that the tiger is a potential danger, and the lamb is not. And, in general, we can distinguish between a present danger and a danger that is not present by calling the latter "potential."

So all actual dangers are present dangers, and other dangers are potential. It is not just the nature of the words uttered that makes a danger, according to Holmes, but also the circumstances of their use. A hungry, man-eating tiger must not only exist but be present, free, and able to get at me before I need take action against him. War is a circumstance in which actions that in times of peace are normal, or at worst a nuisance, become dangerous. To tell a friend where I am, when he has a message for me, is a helpful act. But to tell the enemy where I am, when I am with my regiment, proceeding against him, is an act of treason, at least if you are a fellow countryman.

Still, just as we asked how clear a danger must be before we act, we can now ask about its proximity. How close must it be? If the tiger is not in India, but in the next room, we may still call the danger potential, but then we must admit that there are degrees of potentiality. The closeness to actual danger depends on how many conditions have to be satisfied, and how likely it is that they will be satisfied, to make the potential danger actual. A great many conditions would have to be satisfied before the tiger in India became an actual danger. But as for the tiger in the next room, all one need do is open the door.

So it is difficult to know under what circumstances legal action should be taken to avert a danger. In terms of "proximity and degree" one must decide whether the danger is clear and present. But what about a potential danger which is very likely to become actual if somebody does one thing rather than another (e.g. if he is about to open the door to the tiger's room)? Should he be prevented? How far back can one go (there is the man who brought the tiger into the room)? It all depends on the number of conditions under which a potential danger becomes actual, and the likelihood that those conditions will be realized.

In a more practical instance, if you urge A to murder B, and it is learned by the authorities that you did so, must they wait until murder is done before they intervene? Perhaps A will not do as you wanted. Then there will be no crime. Perhaps he will. Shall authority wait on the outcome?

Holmes is deciding, in effect, that you are legally guilty if it is likely that A will do as you asked, and not guilty if he is unlikely to do so. "It is a question of proximity and degree." Does what you say create "a clear and present danger" that a man will be murdered? That depends on the character and circumstances of A, on your persuasiveness and your relations to him, and on the conditions under which you incited him.

Of course, it was not murder the court was concerned with in the Schenck case. But the principle is the same whether the case involves murder, or treason, or revolution. If there is a murder, there will be a corpse, and if the corpse is not in evidence it will be difficult, or impossible, to get a conviction. But when the issue is one of speech, there will be a time lag between incitement to the crime and its commission. We cannot always wait to see what happens. A man may be killed if we do, or we may all be killed. So Holmes lays down a rule that makes legal guilt and punishment depend on the likelihood, the degree of probability, that there will be a corpse, or its equivalent, as a result of what was said. And can we even test the correctness of our decision by learning in the future that the murder did or did not take place? We want to prevent it, and if we act effectively enough, we may. So we have to be content with a rational estimate that the situation was such that there *would* have been a crime but for our intervention.

How can we possibly make such an estimate? Actually, we do it all the time, when we act to prevent occurrences we do not want. We keep baby from crossing the street, chain the dog, lock our doors. We know what may happen if we don't do these things. And in the case of speech that urges criminal action, we must know enough history and politics to tell what sort of situations can be transformed into action by speech of this nature. Then, if the situation in which a speech is uttered is a situation of that sort, we can decide that the speech creates a clear and present danger that the action will take place.

Still, a rational estimate is only an estimate, subject to the blindness and prejudice of men, as well as to their insight and wisdom. How precisely can we apply the principle of "clear and present danger"? If I meet the man-eating tiger face to face, is danger "present," or must I wait for him to spring before I pull my trigger? After all, he *might* not be hungry at the moment. Yet—is it true that *no* tiger kills unprovoked unless he is hungry?

Holmes's phrase is, perhaps, a wise one. But it often takes wisdom to apply a wise principle.

TERMS AND PRINCIPLES

1. *The principle of significant assertion:* A statement or phrase has meaning only if its contradictory has meaning.
2. *Textual context:* The statement, argument, and purpose of a sentence bears on the meaning of the words and phrases in it; the meaning of a sentence depends in part on the paragraph in which it occurs; and so on.

SECOND COMMENTARY

Some interesting problems arise from reflection on the passage by Mr. Justice Holmes which we have just analyzed. We shall consider two logical points, and a legal or political one.

Holmes treats words as able, in some circumstances, to create a danger. Presumably, he presupposes [1] that words alone cannot constitute a danger. It is like

> Sticks and stones can break my bones
> But words can never hurt me.

Of course, words can wound emotionally, but Holmes is concerned with "substantial evils," and words cannot in themselves bring about changes in material things.

But words can bring change about *indirectly,* by influencing conduct. The decision in the Schenck case had to do with the man who influences by his words, not with the man who is influenced and performs a criminal act. We all know that he is guilty and liable to punishment. What is most difficult to establish, though, is that the man who acted, and who heard the words intended to instigate that action, did in fact act *because* he heard those words.

To argue that A is the cause of B just because it preceded B in time is to commit the fallacy of *post hoc ergo propter hoc* [2]—after that, therefore because of that. If it rains (as it seems to) just after I put my umbrella away, I can scarcely conclude that it rains because I put my umbrella away. Suppose you are on a jury. Mr. A is on trial for persuading Mr. B to perform a criminal act. Mr. B's guilt has already been established. The prosecuting attorney now proves to your satisfaction that, prior to B's action, A had talked to him at length, urging him to do it. How can you tell that B would not have done it anyway? Perhaps he was impelled to the act by something that happened after his conversation with A, or before it.

Because of these difficulties, we might think it best simply to make laws forbidding some statements. Then, if the laws were violated, the culprits could be punished. We would not have to prove that they influenced others to perform criminal acts.

Would such laws be an intolerable "abridgement" of free speech? They need not be. Here we are ready to consider the issue of free speech, with which we started the commentary on Holmes's decision. Isn't it like any other liberty in this respect, that if it is guaranteed equally to everyone, there is a necessary limit to its use in each case? If we are all guaranteed equal freedom of action, your freedom to act must stop at the point where it takes some one else's away. You cannot, when the freedom of all is guaranteed, justify enslaving others on the grounds that you were free to act as you chose. Free speech, too, is limited by being guaranteed to all of us; it is not permissible to use your freedom of speech to deprive others of theirs. And there is another limit on free speech. It is, after all, only *one* of the liberties guaranteed to Americans. It must not be used in such a way that it interferes with the use of those other liberties.

An example may clarify the distinction between legitimate freedom of speech and criminal action in speech. Every citizen may oppose any law he chooses by urging its repeal. He may, for example, urge the repeal of laws against theft. He may speak publicly to this effect or publish his views in writing. No matter how addlepated his views, he is allowed to try to convince a majority of voters that he is right. But while the law he opposes still exists as law, he may not urge that it be broken: he may not try to persuade *me* to rob *you,* or *you* to rob *me.* All he may urge is that laws against theft be repealed, so that we are free to rob each other if we want to.

Freedom of speech, then, is essentially the right of the people to self-government. They must be able to say what they believe, in order to make the laws they want, and to repeal the laws they don't want. But *if* we agree that violation of existing laws is criminal action, and *if* we agree that men can be influenced by words, then we must agree further that *advocacy* of law-breaking in any particular instance aids and abets a crime, and does not find protection under the First Amendment.

Once this theoretical point is established, we can see that slander, libel, obscenity, and the like are not protected by the First Amendment either. The Bill of Rights grants those rights which make us free men. To do so it must protect us from each other as well as from Congress; and it can only accomplish this by a restraint on some actions—verbal as well as physical.

Within this theoretical framework, Holmes's problem becomes one of application, of practice and expediency. Perhaps a man should not say certain things. Yet is he always to be punished for saying them, even when there is not the remotest chance that anyone will act on them? Theoretically, it may be wrong to say them. But will we punish him in the same way, no matter what the probable consequences of his speech? Perhaps you think we should, for his guilt is the same in any case. Let us see if you hold that view consistently.

If a man plans to commit a murder and, after careful preparation, has his intended victim in the sights of his rifle, then squeezes the trigger, and misses entirely because his victim trips and falls, is he guilty of murder? He scarcely can be, for no one has been injured, let alone killed. Still, morally, he is just as guilty as if he committed the murder, since it was none of his doing that the victim is alive. Very well, but is he *legally* as guilty? No. For there was, in fact, no murder to be guilty of. He may, indeed, be guilty of something else, but not of murder.

Our highways too often have drunken and careless drivers on them. If one of them runs over and kills a child, the law treats him harshly. But many of the other drunken and careless drivers might have had no better control of their cars than he of his. Had they been in the exact situation that he was, they would probably have killed the child, too. Morally, then, all such drivers may be equally guilty. But legally, one killed a child and the others did not.

The law recognizes moral as well as legal responsibility. If A kills B, it will make a great deal of difference in his punishment whether or not he *intended* to kill him. But if he does not injure B at all, his intent is irrelevant, for there has been no crime. The essential difference between moral guilt and legal guilt, then, is the difference between intent and fact. The law can punish you only if you are legally guilty. But if you kill with intent to do so (moral guilt) you will be charged with a greater crime than if you killed accidentally.

If you agree to this, will you not have to agree to something like it with respect to speech? If you urge A to murder B, and he does, you are at least an accomplice to his crime. But if he does not, there is no crime to which you are an accomplice. Morally, you may be as guilty, but legally, you are not. And if it becomes illegal to urge murder, you may be punished for urging it, but you will not be punished as an accomplice to a murder that did not take place.

TERMS AND PRINCIPLES

1. *Presupposition:* An unstated assumption. Its truth gives our argument logical validity. If it is false, our conclusion *may*

yet be true, but that is accidental and not the result of the argument's logic.

2. *Post hoc ergo propter hoc* (after this, therefore because of this): The fallacy of assuming that A caused B just because A preceded B.

EXERCISE

JOHN STUART MILL

From *On Liberty*

Let us suppose, . . . that the government is entirely at one with the people, and never thinks of exerting any power of coercion unless in agreement with what it conceives to be their voice. But I deny the right of the people to exercise such coercion, either by themselves or by their government. The power itself is illegitimate. The best government has no more title to it than the worst. It is as noxious, or more noxious, when exerted in accordance with public opinion than when in opposition to it. If all mankind minus one were of one opinion, mankind would be no more justified in silencing that one person than he, if he had the power, would be justified in silencing mankind. Were an opinion a personal possession of no value except to the owner, if to be obstructed in the enjoyment of it were simply a private injury, it would make some difference whether the injury was inflicted only on a few persons or on many. But the peculiar evil of silencing the expression of an opinion is that it is robbing the human race, posterity as well as the existing generation—those who dissent from the opinion, still more than those who hold it. If the opinion is right, they are deprived of the opportunity of exchanging error for truth; if wrong, they lose, what is almost as great a benefit, the clearer perception and livelier impression of truth produced by its collision with error.

It is necessary to consider separately these two hypotheses, each of which has a distinct branch of the argument corresponding to it. We can never be sure that the opinion we are endeavoring to stifle is a false opinion; and if we were sure, stifling it would be an evil still.

SOME QUESTIONS

1. Why are the government, the people, all mankind minus one, not justified, for Mill, in silencing that one man?

2. Could Mill, on the strength of this quotation, possibly accept Holmes's doctrine of "clear and present danger"? Isn't that doctrine a limitation of free speech? But consider this: if I urge you to murder some one, to overthrow the government, or to blow up bridges, how can Mill's argument defend my freedom to do so? Because what I say may be true? It cannot. Because what I say may be false, and falsehood "is almost as great a benefit" as truth? But it cannot be false, either. Why? Because I have neither asserted nor denied anything. I have not uttered a proposition capable of being true or false; I have tried to instigate action. (If I say: "Open the window," that is neither true nor false.) Holmes was writing about words that in particular circumstances might constitute a danger, presumably by leading to action. Is that the same as, or different from, what Mill means by opinion?

3. Why can we never be sure that the opinion we stifle is false?

4. Yet if we can never be sure an opinion is false, does Mill need the second part of his argument: namely, that if the opinion is wrong, we still have no right to suppress its utterance?

5. Why do those who dissent from an opinion lose more if it is suppressed than those who accept it?

6. Does the introduction of "posterity" cause a problem for democratic society? If the majority is to enact laws, why are those laws binding on their descendants, who had no voice in making them?

7. Does Mill, like Madison, hold there are some things the majority has no right to do? Isn't that anti-democratic? Doesn't this belief imply a puzzle? Liberals often defend the right of the majority against all minorities, holding that majority rule is the basic principle of democracy. Liberals also defend individual liberties and rights: freedom of religion, of speech, of assembly, of the press, etc. Then whose side is the liberal on if the majority decides to suppress those individual liberties? After all, to say "Congress shall not . . . ," which is the language of the Bill of Rights, is to limit majority rule.

8. Let us assume that the proposition, "Men should be allowed legally to murder their enemies" is what Mill would call "opinion." And let us assume that the exhortation, "Let's assassinate the president," uttered to a howling and angry mob, constitutes, for Holmes, "a clear and present danger."

Now, if someone argued that acceptance of the proposition by the majority of citizens would bring repeal of the law against murder, he might conclude that the exhortation would then no longer be illegal. So, he could continue, no one should be allowed to utter the proposition as an opinion because it might lead to the exhortation which is dangerous. How could this argument be answered so as to defend both Mill and Holmes?

EXERCISE

JOSÉ ORTEGA Y GASSET

From *Toward A Philosophy of History*

When, proceeding through the century, we reach the great theorists of liberalism—John Stuart Mill and Spencer—we are surprised to find that their supposed defense of the individual is based not on the question of whether liberty is of profit or advantage to the individual, but, on the contrary, on whether it is of profit or advantage to society. The aggressive-looking title that Spencer chose for his book —*The Man versus the State*—has caused a good deal of willful misunderstanding among those who go no farther in a book than the title. Actually, as used in this title, the terms "man" and "state" mean simply two organs of the same subject—society—and the matter of discussion is whether certain social needs are best served by one organ or the other. That is all. Spencer's famous "individualism" is continually at odds with the collectivist atmosphere of his sociology. Fundamentally both he and John Stuart Mill treat the individual with the same socializing cruelty that termites display towards certain of their fellow beings, fattening them in order later to suck out their substance. For both, the collective was the real basis, the platform for the ingenuous dance of their ideas.

SOME QUESTIONS

1. Is what Ortega says of Mill justified by the passage from Mill in the last exercise?

2. Suppose one were to base a "defense of the individual" on

"the question of whether liberty is of profit or advantage to the individual." Should we consider only whether A's liberty is of advantage to A, and B's liberty to B; or should we also ask whether A's liberty is of advantage to B, and B's liberty to A? If we do the latter, don't we have to include other individuals until we ask whether A's liberty is of advantage to society?

EXERCISE

JOHN QUINCY ADAMS

From Letter to the Citizens of Bangor, Maine
July 4, 1843

It is only as immortal beings that all mankind can in any sense be said to be born equal; and when the Declaration of Independence affirms as a self-evident truth that all men are born equal, it is precisely the same as if the affirmation had been that all men are born with immortal souls; for, take away from man his soul, the immortal spirit that is within him, and he would be a mere tameable beast of the field, and, like others of his kind, would become the property of his tamer. Hence it is, too, that, by the law of nature and of God, man can never be made the property of man. And herein consists the fallacy with which the holders of slaves often delude themselves, by assuming that the test of property is human law. The soul of one man cannot by human law be made the property of another. The owner of a slave is the owner of a living corpse; but he is not the owner of a man. . . .

SOME QUESTIONS

1. If Adams's last two sentences were accepted as true by everyone, and as a basis for laws concerning slavery, what practical difference would that make in a slave-holding country? Could a slaveowner argue effectively that he didn't want the souls of slaves, nor could he do anything with them if they were granted him legally; all he wanted was the strict obedience of their bodies?

2. Is Adams claiming that the statement ". . . man can never

be made the property of man . . ." is self-evident, in the sense in which the Declaration uses that term? Is Adams's statement really an analytic one, is it empirical, or is it normative?

JOHN ADAMS

From Letter to J. H. Tiffany
March 31, 1819

I would define liberty to be a power to do as we would be done by. The definition of liberty to be the power of doing whatever the laws permit, meaning the civil laws, does not appear to be satisfactory.

COMMENTARY

I

It is interesting, indeed, that Adams thinks of liberty as power to act according to the Golden Rule. If the Golden Rule is the fundamental law of moral conduct, then liberty would be, simply, power to be good. Liberty must have meant a great deal to Adams, to be defined that way.

But is there any virtue in defining liberty in moral terms rather than political or legal terms? There is at least one important connection between liberty and morality. If one is forced to do something, he cannot be held morally responsible for it. If I am pushed out the window and fall on a person below, I cannot be held responsible for his injuries. A moral choice is a *free* choice, and a moral act is a *free* act, although not all free choices and free acts are in the realm of morals.

Liberty, then, is a necessary condition for moral conduct. A *necessary condition* for an event is whatever *has* to be present in order that the event occur. If you want to build a fire, what must you have? A piece of inflammable material. And what else must be present? Oxygen. So both of those are necessary conditions for fire: *in their absence there will be no fire* (a negative statement like this is the usual way of talking about a necessary condition). All right, you may say, but surely I must also apply a lighted match. Isn't that a necessary condition, too? No, because you do not have to use a match to start a fire. It's convenient, but it's not necessary. A cigarette lighter will do. So will rubbing two sticks together (if you're lucky). Or a bolt of lightning (if you're not lucky). There are a number of things *any one of which* will ignite that material. But there must, of course, be at least one of them present. We call these *sufficient conditions,* for one of them must be present if the event is to occur, but not any particular one. No one of them is a necessary condition, for the event *can* occur in its absence.

Now, more formally (to conform to textbook definitions): A necessary condition for an event is that condition in the absence of which the event does not occur. A is a necessary condition for B, if not-A implies not-B.[1] A sufficient condition for an event is that condition in whose presence the event does occur. A is a sufficient condition for B, if A implies B.[2] (Or D might also imply B.)

When both necessary and sufficient conditions for an event are present, the event occurs. This is a traditional definition of cause.[3] However this traditional definition is regarded in contemporary science, it is immensely valuable in ordinary discourse.

We have said that liberty is a necessary condition for moral choice or action. But liberty is not a sufficient condition for either. A man may be free to choose, and still choose immorally or not choose at all; he may be free to act, and act immorally or not at all. So liberty does not cause moral conduct. It takes good and wise men to act well and wisely. And freedom is no guarantee of goodness and wisdom. Still, since liberty is a necessary condition for morality, we must provide a certain amount of liberty if we want people to be moral agents. So liberty is justifiable on moral, not only on political, grounds. But Adams is defining liberty, not justifying it.

II

Adams thinks of liberty as a power. Is it? If a man is free to do something, does it follow that he has the power to do it? Not as we ordinarily use the words "liberty" and "power." Does Adams's use give greater clarity? We do not think so.

When a man is in no way prohibited by law from doing something, we usually say he is free to do it. Suppose Leander is about to swim the Hellespont to seek his love, Hero. Suppose, further, there are no laws to prevent his trying and no men to bar his way. He is free to swim. But can he? Well, he must be a strong swimmer to do it, and of great endurance. Even if he is, is it a stormy night? Are the tides too treacherous? If so, shall we say he was prohibited by nature from swimming the Hellespont that night, and so was not free to do so? Surely that is strained, and blurs the distinction between liberty and power. A storm does not take away a man's liberty; it may destroy his power.

Politically, then, Leander is free to swim the Hellespont if nobody may legally stop him. But it is not always true that a man can, in fact, do what he is free to do. You are free to become President (if you are a native-born American citizen over 35 years of age), but can you? It is most unlikely, not because you are not free, but because you do not have the power. You are free to state your opinions in public, but you cannot if you are dumb. You need the *power* of speech as well as *freedom* of speech, if you are to talk. So freedom and power are better thought of as distinct.

III

Now, what of the particular power with which Adams equates liberty, "a power to do as we would be done by"? If liberty is to be treated as a power, isn't it the power to do as we please? Indeed, why is it not power to do as we would *not* be done by? We have already argued that liberty is a necessary condition for morality, and that means we must be free to choose to be immoral, for otherwise we are not free at all. (We can scarcely say that people are free to be members of the Mohammedan Church if it turns out that they have to be church members but are not free to join any other.) Freedom of choice in moral matters is freedom to choose *between* good and evil. If we are "free" only to choose good, we have neither choice nor responsibility, and we cease to be moral agents.

In answer, Adams might say he agreed. He was defining liberty, after all, not advocating it. To choose freedom rather than bondage is an intellectual and moral decision, though one may not have the power to get the freedom he desires. Adams might point out that he had once fought in a war to increase freedom, and the limits of freedom were normally defined by law. Still, one may choose to live under the rule of law, even a special kind of law, although of course he is seldom able to do much about it. Politically, man is free to do whatever the law does not forbid.

Here two ways of treating "freedom" become clear. We may say that freedom is the absence of external restraint, and argue that a man is usually free to commit murder, although he may have to suffer the legal consequences. Or we may say that freedom is the absence of legal prohibition, so a man is never free to commit murder because the law forbids it. Let us call the latter political liberty.

Now Adams does not think it "satisfactory" to define liberty in terms of law, but he defines liberty in the same way as what we called "political liberty," except that he substitutes morality for law. The law may be unjust, but morality as summed up in the Golden Rule is, he assumes, a proper guide to conduct. A man ought to be free, then, only to do what morality does not forbid. Adams, by using the Golden Rule, chose a positive statement of morality, thou shalt, rather than thou shalt not. That is like saying that since we are not free to do what the moral law forbids, we are free to do only what it enjoins. People may, of course, do immoral things; it happens all the time. But Adams would not say they were at "liberty" to do them. He would probably use another word, like "license."

The use of morals instead of law in the definition of liberty suggests that a man might oppose a government in the name of liberty, and feel that he was choosing God instead of Caesar. After all, we judge governments and laws by moral standards. To reverse that judgment would be to deify the state and to accept, as just, anything it did.

Two brief criticisms. To repeat one: liberty should not be defined as a power. We may be *free* to do as we would be done by, even when we don't have the *power* to act on our liberty. If it is not wrong to pull you out of a well, I am *free* to do so, even if I do not have the strength. But if there is a law against it, or for Adams a moral law, I am not free to pull you out, even if I am strong enough.

Then there is the use of the Golden Rule as though it were a complete guide to moral conduct. Admirable as the Golden Rule is, other moral precepts must be added or there will be some areas in which we are permitted more than the author of the Golden Rule would allow. After all, I may want to be beaten or enslaved. Does that mean I should have the liberty to beat or enslave you? If you answer that I would not do so anyway because *I* want to be beaten, etc., I might answer that I *also* want to beat and enslave others. Hence I am only doing as I would be done by. Or I might like to fight, just for the sake of fighting. Adams's definition of liberty would allow me then to attack you, for I would also welcome an attack by you.

Still, we can assume that Adams regarded the Golden Rule as an adequate principle of morality. So, if we are to have liberty under the law, then, at least for Adams, the law should not forbid moral acts or enjoin immoral acts. This is an ideal of liberty in the state. We have precious little liberty if laws are oppressive. We want the laws to suit our ideal of liberty; we do not want merely to define liberty as obedience to law.

But should a definition be a statement of the ideal? Of course.

We have seen that it always is. A definition states qualities that, ideally, characterize all members of a class. The individual members of the class share those qualities, but are often *in fact* defective or impaired in them. A horse is defined as a four-legged beast, but if a particular horse should lose a leg, he is still a horse. The definition states the characteristics without the blemishes that are found in individual members. In that sense, it is always a statement of the ideal of a class, or type.[4] And Adams's statement of the idea of liberty is, whatever its shortcomings, properly conceived as an ideal of liberty.

TERMS AND PRINCIPLES

1. *Necessary condition:* Something in the absence of which an event does not occur.
2. *Sufficient condition:* Something, granted the necessary conditions, in the presence of which an event does occur.
3. *The cause of an event:* Traditionally, the necessary *and* sufficient conditions for that event.
4. The idea of anything (thought of as a definition) is also the ideal of that thing, for the idea is a *conception* of a class or type, and so does not include the blemishes in any of its individual members.

LORD ACTON

From "The History of Freedom in Antiquity"

It is bad to be oppressed by a minority, but it is worse to be oppressed by a majority. For there is a reserve of latent power in the masses which, if it is called into play, the minority can seldom resist. But from the absolute will of an entire people there is no appeal, no redemption, no refuge but treason.

COMMENTARY

I

We tend to think of the French and American Revolutions as struggles for liberty and democracy in which the majority of the people freed themselves from an oppressive minority. And we tend to think of the majority either quasi-mystically (*vox populi, vox Dei,* the voice of the people is the voice of God), or as somehow representing the will of all. But to the extent that democratic government really expresses the will of the majority, it is curious that we have constructed safeguards against it, as in the Bill of Rights. And it was Jefferson, the great exponent of democracy, who insisted most strongly that there be a Bill of Rights, without which he would probably have opposed ratification of the Constitution.

We have encountered this question earlier; it is time to meet it directly. Rather than stick closely to the text, let us try, this time, to see how much thought may be involved in grasping a single idea, particularly if it runs counter to our assumptions.

Acton's first sentence leads us at once to the idea we shall analyze. Who can be oppressed by a minority? Any number of people, up to a majority. Who can be oppressed by a majority? No more than a minority. But isn't it all right, indeed proper, for the majority to have its way, rather than a minority? Many—perhaps most—believers in democracy think so. Then what is Acton objecting to? Not to the majority having its way, in the ordinary political sense of deciding the laws, but to oppression. For oppression is, by definition, unfair and bad.

Yet many people would argue that since majority rule defines democracy, oppression cannot exist under democratic government. Isn't it government by the people? And how can the people oppress themselves? If, indeed—a most unlikely thing—they wanted to treat themselves badly, wouldn't that be their prerogative under democratic government? This puzzle turns out to be more verbal than real.[1] If we deny that people in a democracy can be oppressed, we are either factually wrong or are committing several logical fallacies.

If we define oppression in some way that allows us to recognize it when we see it, and then look around in a democracy to discover whether there are instances of it, we'll find it. A democratic United States cheated, lied to, and murdered Indians. It hounded Mormons. A democratic France was responsible for the Reign of Terror. There may be a question as to what brings oppression in a democracy, but there is no doubt that it can exist.

On the other hand, if we define oppression in terms of the presumed conditions for its existence, or of some philosophical principles,[2] we may never recognize the fact of oppression even if we trip over it. For we will have to deny that it exists except under those conditions, or according to those principles. Suppose a man who thought that democracy would cure all ills (of course a man who doesn't live in a democracy), defined oppression as exploitation of the masses by aristocrats. Obviously, when there were no more aristocrats, or aristocrats had no political power, he would have to deny there was oppression, *no matter what he saw.*

If you think that this is so extreme a case as to be unlikely, the evidence should convince you that you are wrong. Tom Paine often argued that way, and Communists do it all the time. To stick to Paine (and democracy) for the moment, he could write of democracy: "Where there are no distinctions, there can be no superiority; perfect equality affords no temptation." It follows that, since equality of rank obtains in a democracy—for it has no ranks—no one will try to be superior to anyone else. Happily, then, we can define "struggle for pre-eminence" as something that takes place only in an aristocratic or monarchical state! Now, as a matter of fact, that struggle is nowhere more evident than in the United States, where there is no rank and all citizens are equal before the law. But if we believed Paine to be defining democracy, we could no longer admit the truth before our eyes, for our definition makes it impossible that it is what it is. We would either have to find another name for the struggle, pretending it is something else, or we would have to deny that this is a democracy.

II

Now, if there is oppression by the majority in a democracy, it is oppression of a minority. *All* the people, the entire citizenry, cannot be expected to be in unanimous agreement on any one question. So in popular assemblies or democratic parliaments of representatives, some portion of the whole is allowed to outvote other portions. It might be a specified plurality. It is usually a majority. And what happens to the minority in consequence may be ordinary democratic process, or it may be oppression.

If absolute majority rule were the only (or the basic) principle of democratic government, the majority could decide to take away the property of the minority, to deny them civil liberties, to make them into slaves. And those measures, surely, are oppressive. But if the majority decided to deny suffrage to the minority, democracy itself would be at an end. And that could happen any time a majority preferred to stay in power undemocratically rather than continue the democratic process with its virtual certainty that they would get voted out at some time.

And what is it that restrains majorities in this country from such action? The Constitution? But isn't that the dead hand of the past, as we are told every so often, blighting the aspirations of the living? Not at all. The Constitution defines democracy (and does other things). Its basic principle, as definition, is that new majorities must be allowed to form freely, as the people decide what they believe. And each new majority must limit its own actions in the same way, if it is to continue our form of government.*

III

Acton goes on to say that minorities cannot oppress majorities as terribly as majorities can oppress minorities because in the former case the pressure of the majority is difficult for the minority to resist, and limits their oppression, but in the latter there is "no refuge but treason." This is easy enough to understand, but is it true?

Through ages of history, minorities oppressed majorities—as we see it. But was it felt as oppression by those majorities? No doubt the ancient Egyptians oppressed the Israelites. We know, because the Israelites revolted and fled. No doubt the Romans oppressed their slaves and gladiators. We know, because under Spartacus they revolted, and fought to the death. But Israelites, slaves, and gladiators were a minority, often a tiny minority. And the majority of Egyptians, even the majority of Romans, were treated very badly, by our standards. Did they think so? It is very hard to know, but it is at least probable that for many of them their treatment seemed the way of the world, right and proper. Oppression is relative to expectation. If one expects to be a slave, he does not feel oppressed if he is one. He may prefer to be free, and even scheme to be so. But that might be like scheming to be a millionaire today. One wants it, and is delighted if he attains it, but he scarcely feels oppressed if he doesn't.

In the sense of being treated badly—as judged by other, and alien, standards—oppression of majorities by minorities was the rule for centuries, and still is in many parts of the world. But in the sense of being treated unfairly, in ways in which they think they shouldn't be treated, majorities have been oppressed very much less and in fewer places. Because expectation is fashioned by experience or belief. One has to have experienced something better to expect it; or one has at least to believe in a different order of things, as the medieval serf, learning from the church that all souls were equal, may have felt actual inequalities on earth to be wrong.

---

* The people who wrote the Constitution represented, one would suppose, a majority. In any event, our Constitution was ratified by a majority. Yet they limited *their own* action by guaranteeing both democratic process and individual rights.

Under *some* conditions—Acton is too dogmatic—pressure on the oppressive minority was great. England yielded to it, considerably, in the Glorious Revolution of 1688. American pressure on England before 1776 had come from a minority of Englishmen abroad; and when England did not yield sufficiently, the colonists revolted, though conditions in the colonies were better than in most of Europe, and were superb by medieval or Roman standards. The French middle class and peasantry had a harder time, before the French Revolution, but still there had been many concessions. Revolution came when the pressure didn't bring enough reform; and not just because people were treated badly, oppressed, but because of the gap between reality and belief. The *threat* of revolution has often, but not always, been the greatest pressure the majority could bring.

Revolution, of course, is always treason from the official standpoint. Yet people felt driven to it, when "pressures" were insufficient to gain their ends, including men of great wealth and possessions like George Washington, who could scarcely be thought of as "oppressed." Sir John Harington * wrote:

> Treason doth never prosper; what's the reason?
> Why, if it prosper, none dare call it treason.

IV

What sort of oppression *by a majority* can exist? In answer, there is the history of Negroes in the United States, or of Jews in Nazi Germany. These are minorities oppressed by majorities. And again and again, of course, single persons are oppressed. Theirs is a long history, which includes great names, like Socrates and Galileo. But when is there "no refuge but treason"? Which of us would applaud treason? Many doubtless, but only under special circumstances. Germans who opposed Hitler were guilty of treason to the Nazi state, but they won the world's gratitude, as have the Russians who oppose Communism. There may be no "absolute will of an entire people" in these cases, but there is an approximation of it. That approximation today exists most nearly in the totalitarian nations. The Germans—a majority of them—supported Hitler, and a majority of Russians probably support Communism. But is there "no refuge" from totalitarianism "but treason"? Clearly not, for there are no *legal* ways to get your beliefs heard, to persuade a majority to alter the law. In a way, the point was made long before Acton. The Declaration of Independence states: ". . . whenever any form of government becomes destructive of these ends [the rights of man], it is the right of the

---

* An English writer of the Elizabethan Age.

people to alter or to abolish it . . ." The order of words in that
sentence should be the order of events. Oppressive government should
be altered. If it cannot be altered, it must be abolished.

There are two chief reasons that governments sometimes cannot
be altered. First, that despite the existence and use of channels of
expression, a dissenter cannot persuade the majority of what he
believes. What should he do then? Continue to try. If he attempts
more—to abolish or overthrow the government and seize power himself—he is attempting to substitute his own tyranny for the orderly
process of free government. He is a tyrant in intent even before he
is one in fact, and he should be treated as such. But, secondly, there
may be no channels of expression, no ways to alter the government,
even if a majority wanted to do so. What is more important, there
may be no peaceful way for a minority to become a majority. That
means there is no democracy, nor any way of getting one within the
limits of the law. At this point, and this point only, is one morally
justified in "treason," in rebellious action outside the law.

Now, can a democratic state ever have this second situation?
In one sense, no; for by definition the situation is undemocratic. But
a democratic state can, by violating the words and spirit of its
Constitution, cease to be democratic. And it can do this by majority
vote. Louis Napoleon was *elected* Emperor of France. On one
occasion, the ancient Athenians, about to vote on a motion, first
mustered a majority for the proposal that all who voted against the
motion should be put to death.* When things like these occur, democracy is at an end. Opposition that one moment before was democratic and proper, becomes "treason." So sheer persistence in democratic action becomes treasonable and invokes the most extreme
penalties of the law.

SOME QUESTIONS

Let us consider some questions that might be pondered with
profit, on the basis of Lord Acton's statement and this analysis of it:

1. Is democracy a necessary condition for altering the law in
accordance with majority will and without violence? Are there not
occasions when an absolute ruler or a ruling group are responsive to
the pressures of the people?

2. If democracy is not a necessary condition for altering the law
in such ways, is it the best condition for it? What would "best" mean
in the question? As suggestions: responsiveness to expressed opinion;

* See Xenophon, *Hellenica*, 1:7:15.

freedom to express opinion; responsibility of representatives to their electors.

3. How, if at all, is oppression relative to expectation and belief?

4. Do you know the word "plebiscite"? What meaning would you give to the term "plebiscitary dictatorship"? Can you see how readily it could masquerade as democracy?

TERMS AND PRINCIPLES

1. *Verbal problems and real problems:* A verbal problem is actually a problem about the meaning of a question or proposition, although it often seems, erroneously, to be a question of truth. A real problem is a question of truth, and cannot be resolved, as a verbal problem can, by stating clearly what is meant.

2. One should not express a belief or hypothesis about the conditions under which an event takes place as if it were a definition, or part of a definition, of that type of event. (This does occur sometimes in science, but it is safe only when the hypothesis has been validated over and over by rigorous scientific methods.) This will be explained in detail later.

EXERCISE

KARL MARX

From *The Poverty of Philosophy*

In the course of its development, the working class will replace the old bourgeois society by an association which excludes classes and their antagonism, and there will no longer be any real political power, for political power is precisely the official expression of the class antagonism within bourgeois society.

SOME QUESTIONS

1. Consider Marx's definition of "political power," in relation to our discussion of Lord Acton. Is it acceptable as a definition or is it a hypothesis about the conditions under which political power is expressed? Remember that such a hypothesis is not a definition. As a way of deciding your answer, suppose someone were to say, "That's

not what political power is, for I can point to instances of it in non-bourgeois society." Couldn't Marx answer, "That is impossible because, by my definition, what you point out cannot be political power"? Who would be right, Marx or his critic? Why?

2. Notice the word "association." As Marx uses it, does it suggest that when "the old bourgeois society" is replaced, it will not be by another form of "society," but by something else? Is that suggestion, if it is there, justified, or is it imparted by verbal sleight-of-hand? Is "association," here, just a euphemism for "society," which is treated as bad?

3. Marx says that bourgeois society is to be replaced by an "association." Does that suggest that, unless the social order is bourgeois, it is not to be called a society? Does the use of "bourgeois" as an adjective imply that there were societies before bourgeois society (feudal society, for example), even if after the working class replaces the bourgeoisie, there never will be a "society" again?

EXERCISE

NIKOLAI LENIN

From *Selected Works,* Vol. VII

To recognize defense of one's fatherland means recognizing the legitimacy and justice of war. Legitimacy and justice from what point of view? Only from the point of view of the socialist proletariat and its struggle for emancipation. We do not recognize any other point of view. If war is waged by the proletariat after it has conquered the bourgeoisie in its own country, and is waged with the object of strengthening and extending socialism, such a war is legitimate and "holy."

SOME QUESTIONS

1. Lenin's first sentence probably means that if we recognize defense of one's fatherland as legitimate, that is the same as recognizing the legitimacy of war. Doesn't the mere existence of sovereign states imply that it is legitimate to make war?

2. Does a nation at war normally recognize the legitimacy of its opponent's war-making? Were the Nuremberg Trials an exception in modern history, or the ordinary aftermath of war?

3. Is there a distinction between the legitimacy of making war and being right in a particular war? If all states may legitimately make war, it cannot follow that their cause is always right, especially since they fight each other. Is Lenin confusing the legitimate power to make war with having a good cause?

4. Is Lenin operating on a double standard of judgment? Is he assuming that it is only legitimate to make war when you are in the right? Is he assuming, further, that only the proletariat can ever be right? And that it can never be wrong?

5. If he is assuming these things, what if an opponent assumed equivalent things and said that only his side was right and so it was never legitimate for the proletariat to go to war? What practical difference would it make in a war if both sides felt that way? Would it mean that the conquerors would not treat the conquered simply as a defeated nation—which had the right to make war, but lost—but rather as a gang of criminals? What was the opinion on these questions presupposed by American, English, French, and Russian action in the Nuremberg Trials? Did it differ from Lenin's?

EXERCISE

MAXIMILIAN ROBESPIERRE

From Speech to the National Convention
February 5, 1794

They say that terrorism is the resort of despotic government. Is our government then like despotism? Yes, as the sword that flashes in the hand of the hero of liberty is like that with which the satellites of tyranny are armed. . . . The government of the Revolution is the despotism of liberty against tyranny.

JOHN ADAMS

From Letter to Thomas Jefferson
November 13, 1815

The fundamental article of my political creed is that despotism, or unlimited sovereignty, or absolute power, is the same in a majority of a popular assembly, an aristocratical council, an oligarchical junto, and a single emperor. Equally arbitrary, cruel, bloody, and in every respect diabolical.

SOME QUESTIONS

1. What do you think Adams would say about Robespierre's phrase, "the depotism of liberty against tyranny"?
2. How do you think Robespierre would answer "the fundamental article" of Adams's "political creed"?
3. Which of the two, Robespierre or Adams, sounds like Lenin, as quoted in the last exercise?
4. Do you believe that it makes all the difference *who* acts tyrannically? Do you believe it makes *no* difference? Do you hold a belief in between? If so, what is it? Argue your case.
5. Use the analysis of means and ends in the first question of the Webster exercise as a basis for criticism of Robespierre.

🦜

FRIEDRICH ENGELS

From *Anti-Dühring*

The proletariat seizes state power, and then transforms the means of production into state property. But in doing this, it puts an end to itself as the proletariat, it puts an end to all class differences and class antagonisms, it puts an end also to the state as the state. Former society, moving in class antagonisms, had need of the state, that is, an organisation of the exploiting class at each period for the maintenance of its external conditions of production; therefore, in particular, for the forcible holding down of the exploited class in the conditions of oppression (slavery, bondage or serfdom, wage labour) determined by the existing mode of production. The state was the official representative of society as a whole, its embodiment in a visible corporate body; but it was this only in so far as it was the state of that class which itself, in its epoch, represented society as a whole: in ancient times, the state of the slave-owning citizens; in the

Middle Ages, of the feudal nobility; in our epoch, of the bourgeoisie. When ultimately it becomes really representative of society as a whole it makes itself superfluous. As soon as there is no longer any class of society to be held in subjection; as soon as, along with class domination and the struggle for individual existence based on the former anarchy of production, the collisions and excesses arising from these have also been abolished, there is nothing more to be repressed, and a special repressive force, a state, is no longer necessary. The first act in which the state really comes forward as the representative of society as a whole—the seizure of the means of production in the name of society—is at the same time its last independent act. The interference of a state power in social relations becomes superfluous in one sphere after another, and then becomes dormant of itself. Government over persons is replaced by the administration of things and the direction of the processes of production. The state is not "abolished," *it withers away*. It is from this standpoint that we must appraise the phrase "people's free state"—both its justification at times for agitational purposes, and its ultimate scientific inadequacy—and also the demand of the so-called Anarchists that the state should be abolished overnight.

FIRST COMMENTARY

In the analysis that follows, we will try not only to discover Engels's meaning, but also to probe his points. After all, when we read anything, we want to know both what it means and whether it is true. Our discussion will illustrate some ways of establishing what logicians call the "truth-value" of propositions.

I

Engels's passage is a very dense one, with ideas packed in so tight they jostle each other. Yet it is crucial to Marxian theory, and Lenin made much of it in his *State and Revolution*. Let us see if we can separate the ideas, understand them, put them together systematically, and appraise them.

We start with the social revolution, for the proletariat, it is assumed, has just revolted successfully and seized control of the state. Apparently its first action is to take the factories, mines, farms, etc. —the "means of production"—away from the former owners and give them to the state. That act, says the second sentence, abolishes both the proletariat and the state. How? By ending, Engels continues, any need for a state. A state is an organization of the exploiting class for the repression of the exploited class. When there are no such classes, it is assumed, there can be no state, just as there can be no hats if there are no heads.

Let us examine what we have so far, before continuing with Engels's statement. The state is, in Marxist language, the executive committee of the ruling class. That class, in our time the bourgeoisie, is the one that owns the means of production. The state pretends to be above classes, it claims every one's allegiance, but its real task is to keep down the oppressed class.

When the proletariat seize the state, they use it to dispossess the owners of the means of production of their wealth. The state takes it all. Then there is no longer a bourgeois class, for that is defined entirely in economic terms, as owning the means of production in a capitalist economy: and there are no longer any bourgeois, for they are defined as owners. Next, what of the proletariat? They are, by definition, those who work for the bourgeoisie in return for a wage, yet themselves do not own any of the means of production. Now that the bourgeoisie has disappeared, the proletariat can no longer work for them and, far from owning none of the means of production, they own them all, not privately, but through the state. So the proletariat, too, ceases to exist.

And what happens to the state? By taking all wealth, it has ended all classes. Yet the state itself was only a class organ. Hence the state, too, is gone. And obviously, if there are no classes, there can be no "class differences and class antagonisms." *

All that is needed for this to be the gateway to Eden is the belief that almost every social ill comes from the struggle for profit. Marx and Engels believed just that.

Delightful as it would be to contemplate so many wonderful things taking place virtually at once, we may be a little suspicious of the truth of the account. Of course, we cannot decide the truth of

---

* The whole argument may be thought of as a series of definitions and what follows from them logically:
    1. Ruling class ("exploiters")—those who own the means of production.
    2. Ruled class ("exploited")—those who work for the ruling class in return for a wage.
    3. State—An organ of the ruling class for the repression of the ruled class.
    Then, if the means of production are taken from their owners there is no more ruling class. Also, there is no ruled class, for there is no class to work for. And there is no state, for there is no class for it to represent or to repress.

factual matters just by analyzing meanings. But we can discover contradictions, fallacies, and ambiguities. We can learn at least what is logically true and logically false.[1]

II

Let us look first at the names "bourgeoisie," "proletariat," and "state." Apparently they stand for things in *our* society, but do not stand for anything after the means of production are taken over by the state, after the proletariat wins power. At this point we must know something about names. All names have (a) meanings or definitions of the sort we find in dictionaries, the defining characteristics of a class; and (b) reference to a group of objects, the actual or possible members of the class—the things the word "stands for." We can call (a) the meanings, by the name "intension," or "intensional meaning," [2] and (b) the things, by the name "extension," or "extensional meaning." [3]

There is another set of terms that corresponds, in part, to intension and extension. They are "connotation" and "denotation." Unhappily, to the logician, "connotation" means "intension," and "denotation" means "extension." But to the grammarian, "denotation" means "intension," [4] and "connotation" does not mean "extension" at all. It refers to the meanings associated with a word, but not part of its precise definition.[5] Thus "home" is where one dwells, usually with his family, but the connotation of the word, in the grammarian's sense, is "privacy, comfort, relaxation, etc."

To confuse matters more, the logician uses the word "imply," or "implication," to mean whatever follows deductively, or by logical reasoning alone, from a statement. So "No Frenchmen are Americans" implies "No Americans are Frenchmen." But the grammarian is likely to use "imply" or "implication" to mean whatever is associated with an idea. So "home" implies its connotations—privacy, comfort, and so on.[6]

In order to talk about the two sorts of meaning we have noted here, we will use "intension" and "extension" only, because their meanings remain unequivocal. (Perhaps it would be best if this procedure were generally adopted, and if the word "connotation" were used to mean "associations." Then the word "denotation" could be dropped altogether.)

The intension of "bourgeoisie" is, for Marxists, "owners of the means of production in a capitalist economy." * That is, logically, a class, and the extension is its members: a number of people doing

---

* As the intension of "aristocracy" is, for Marxists, "owners of the means of production in a feudal society."

certain things. The intension of "proletariat" is "those who work for the bourgeoisie in return for a wage." But the extension is a number of other people doing other things. When the proletarian state takes all the means of production, and classes "disappear," what has really happened? The intension of the words, of course, remains the same. And as for the extension: the people, presumably, still live. Then what has changed? Perhaps the things they did, which identified them as bourgeois and proletarian, have changed. But to what extent, if at all? Some people used to manage and direct industry. And some people, though perhaps not the same ones, still do. Others used to work with their hands. And many people, including (one would think) most of those who did before, still do.

Now where are we? Something must have changed. And this, at least, did: the managers and directors are rewarded in wages, not profits; the workers, still paid wages, are paid *by* the state or a public organization, not by individual owners. The class "bourgeoisie" now has no members, no extension, since no one is an owner. That is not so much change as one might have expected. Perhaps there is also a change in the relations between the former bourgeoisie and the former proletariat. The former bourgeoisie no longer employ and pay the proletariat. Since they, too, receive wages, they are now what would formerly have been "proletarians." But even that turns out to be less than it seems. For the managers do have something to say about employment and must sign and dispense pay checks. Still, the money they pay is not their own, but the state's.

One more possibility. If people's conduct *before* the revolution was determined considerably by class affiliation, so that the interests of owners and workers were mutually exclusive, then *after* the social revolution their conduct might be quite different. The elimination of "class differences" and "class antagonisms" would be an important social change, not simply verbal. Doubtless, that is what Engels meant. Further, we must grant the logic of such an argument, given Engels's assumptions. What we can doubt seriously is how far behavior is determined by economic class alone, and how *much* the interests of owners and workers differ. We need not deny that economic class influences behavior, and that owners and workers do not have absolutely identical economic interests, in order to make our point. And we must ask whether the effects of economic class membership *in our society* are substantially greater than that of membership in other groups * of managers and of workers *after the revolu-*

---

* Marxists refuse to call such groups "classes," because class is, for them, only an economic designation.

tion. Today we can answer that question much better than when Engels lived. For in the Soviet Union the differences between managers and workers are in many ways greater than the differences between owners and workers in, say, England and the United States.

III

But if we did not have this fact about the Soviet Union at our disposal, if we had simply to criticize Engels's argument, our question about differences after the revolution would still carry weight. Why, after all, should membership in a class that makes profit influence us more than any other social membership? Yet this question would not shake a Marxist at all, because he must presuppose something that allows him to think that "class differences and class antagonisms" can be wiped out at a stroke and, presumably, *not* be replaced by equivalent differences and antagonisms, or *not* continue what they are, but under a different name. For if equivalent differences were to exist after the revolution, there would be very little sense, if any, in supporting the revolution. What can that presupposition be? It is: The direct consequence of private ownership of the means of production, namely, profit, causes the antagonisms, hatreds, and differences among men. It follows that if the possibility of profit were eliminated, antagonism, hatred, difference, would vanish, or nearly so.

If this presupposition is true, what Engels is saying has logical warrant.* If it is false, Engels's argument loses its logical force. What, then can we say of its truth?

Our first problem is: what would be evidence for or against the truth of the presupposition? That there are such antagonisms, etc., in bourgeois society we all grant. Is that evidence? Perhaps, but quite insufficient, for it may be irrelevant to the profit motive. What we would need to find is not only: (1) whenever there is private ownership of the means of production, there are such antagonisms, etc.; but also (2) whenever there is not private ownership, all other institutions being the same, there are no such antagonisms, etc.

To test the first point, we must examine other societies with private ownership (Engels speaks of "the state of the slave-owning citizens . . . of the feudal nobility . . . of the bourgeoise") and see if there were strifes and hatreds, as there are today. (Of course there were, although they may have been expressed differently.) Then for the second point, we must examine societies without private ownership, but with the other institutions found in our society, and look for the same thing. (Again, we find strife and hatred.)

---

* There are other difficulties, as we shall see.

Marxists must accept what was just said about the kinds of evidence necessary for their presupposition, or be convicted of making no sense. What they will deny is the facts themselves, namely that strife and hatred exist in societies without private ownership. But facts are facts, and hard to dispute.

IV

There are two ways of getting around our argument. Marxists may maintain, first, that no societies without private ownership have existed; second, that what we thought were antagonisms and hatreds were really something else. After all, they can say, the facts cannot really be what you think they are, because where there is no profit motive there is no antagonism or hatred.

A. Here the first way out leads Marxists to a curious difficulty. If there have been no societies without private ownership, how can it be proven that when private ownership is eliminated strife and hatred will cease? For in claiming that private ownership caused these ills, they were implicitly stating that it was both a sufficient and necessary condition for them.

To show that whenever there is private ownership there are these ills, does not fully establish that it is even a *sufficient* condition for them. For private ownership, though present, might be irrelevant. If fifteen men on a polar exploration are later found dead and there is a puzzle about what killed them, the fact that they all had blue eyes might not be very helpful. If they died of the same cause, one would expect, properly, to find some common element in all the corpses. But there would be innumerable common elements, since they were all men. The only ones that would be of any use in learning what killed them would have to be relevant, directly or indirectly, to dying.

Private ownership coexists with many things. It is relevant to the existence of some of them but not others—not hunger, thirst, and sex, for example, which are found wherever there are animals. Private ownership may affect the *expression* of these drives, as it may affect the *expression* of antagonism and hatred. But our question is whether it created them. If antagonism and hatred are merely expressed differently in societies without private ownership (and perhaps even more virulently), then the Marxists are wrong.

A cause must not only be sufficient, but necessary. The reason is that any number of other conditions may also be sufficient. A knife across my throat is a sufficient condition for my death. But so is hanging, drowning, poison, decapitation, and countless other sorry possibilities. Any one of them is sufficient for *a* death, but no one of them is *the* cause of death. To discover that, we would have to know what is common to all of them, including diseases, old age, and so on.

That is why, when we said it had to be shown that whenever there is not private ownership, there are also no antagonisms and hatreds, we added, "all other institutions being the same." [7] We had to allow for the possibility that some other institution or institutions might be the cause of antagonisms and hatreds. If the struggle for prestige, let us say, were in fact the cause, and we found a society without antagonism and hatred, and without private ownership and prestige, we would have no right to conclude that the absence of private ownership was responsible for the absence of antagonisms and hatred. In order to establish private ownership as a necessary condition, we would have to find a society without it and without antagonism and hatred, but with prestige and with all other things that might turn out to be relevant.

So if a Marxist denies that there have ever been societies without private ownership, he rules out the possibility of evidence for his thesis. He cannot show that private ownership is a necessary condition for the existence of antagonisms. He cannot even show it is a sufficient condition, for it might be irrelevant. All he can show is that private ownership can coexist with antagonisms and hatreds, which everybody knows in the first place.

B. Now, as for the Marxist's second way out, that of denying that we identify hatred and antagonism correctly in societies without private ownership, because they cannot exist in such societies: this is the fallacy of arguing in a circle, or begging the question. [8] We beg the question when we try to prove A, and yet offer A as part of the evidence, or all of it. When I try to borrow money from the bank and am asked for references, I may say that John will vouch for me. But if the banker never heard of John, I don't help matters by saying, "He's all right. I vouch for him." To say that the conduct I call antagonism and hatred in a society without private ownership cannot be such, because that conduct is the result only of private ownership, is to beg the question. The assertion that it *is* the result of private ownership is the very one whose truth we were examining. How, then, can it enter, as presumably true, into the discussion of its own truth-value?

V

If it is dubious that private ownership and the profit motive are chiefly responsible for human strife, can we say anything helpful about the problem? What is responsible? Actually, that is not our task, for it takes us both outside the text and the question whether Engels is right, but it is helpful to show how one could go about it. Section V, then, is an excursus, to see if we can find the kind of answer Engels's question requires.

We asserted that there are often many possible sufficient conditions for an event, and that to find a single sufficient condition for that *type* of event, we would have to discover what all the particular conditions had in common. *The* cause for death, remember, is different from *a* cause or condition for *a* death. Now, there is little doubt that the forms and expressions of struggle in our society are influenced by our high evaluation of monetary success. We struggle for wealth and the reputation of wealth. Is it true that without private ownership and the possibility of profit, that particular struggle would vanish? Not very likely. It could exist whenever differences in monetary reward existed.* Could it exist if the possession of wealth were no longer prized or evaluated highly? No, then it would disappear.

So the two sure ways to end the struggle for wealth are: (1) to have no possible inequality in wealth; (2) to eradicate the high value we place on having and acquiring money. But if either or both of these alternatives existed, and the struggle for wealth ceased, does that mean no other struggle so widespread and so intense would replace it? Probably one would.

Isn't it possible, even likely, that a struggle for wealth is only one form of a common human competition? Or that the possibility of different incomes and the high value placed on money is only one of the many sufficient conditions for the human struggle? If so, what are some other sufficient conditions? Probably the existence of and desire for political or military power, prowess at arms or at hunting, genius in the arts or sciences, success in attracting the opposite sex, or any of a number of such things. The man of wealth belonged to a lower class in the middle ages, and his achievement was little regarded. But the man of might was at the top of the social hill, and his achievement was treated with awe and reverence. So the political and military struggle was intense. It was probably as intense, but less widespread, than competition for money today; most people not born in the upper class were excluded from commanding positions. But they often performed military service and could compete for lower ranks.

We can at least see what such instances have in common that is relevant to human competition. Perhaps pre-eminence, or power,

---

* Note that although there is private ownership, and so profit, in England today, but not in the Soviet Union, the differences in wealth are greater in the latter.

prestige, or reputation, is our common denominator in these matters. One or more of these could be *the* cause of the social struggle.

It is much easier to eliminate profit than to eliminate pre-eminence or prestige, power or reputation, if that could be done at all. But do we want to? Probably not. The issue, anyhow, is not one of eliminating the source or sources of man's struggle against man, but of controlling the nature and violence of that struggle.

Even if a basic human competition of some sort cannot be eliminated, and even if it is actually valuable, the different ways in which it is manifested may be better and worse. Perhaps the violence of the struggle is too great under some conditions, or too widespread, or too costly.

Here we are pushed back to something most fundamental. Those things we cherish dearly, prize highly, and sacrifice for—in short, our values—are probably what decide how harmful or beneficial human competition can be. Pre-eminence in one's community *could* derive from what one did for others, from nobility of soul, or from artistic, philosophical, and scientific achievement. The struggle for pre-eminence, then, would be more beneficial and less harmful, especially if reputation depended, at least in part, on our treatment of others. What nonsense it seems, from this point of view, to believe that eliminating one possible condition for the strife of men eliminates that strife! Or that human happiness and social welfare depend on eliminating all forms of it! *

VI

Now we are ready to tackle the question of the disappearance of the state after the means of production are taken from private hands. Engels defines "state" as "an organization of the exploiting class at each period for the maintenance of its external conditions of production; therefore, in particular, for the forcible holding down of the exploited class in the conditions of oppression (slavery, bondage or serfdom, wage-labor) determined by the existing mode of production." In other words, the state exists only in class societies, for the purpose of maintaining the external conditions of production. What conditions are external as opposed, presumably, to internal? If, "in particular," the state does its job by keeping the exploited class oppressed, we might suppose that the internal conditions are purely

---

* To be fair to Engels, he might be willing to distinguish between good and bad forms of competition, although he would probably insist on calling good competition by another name. And he would still claim that profit is a necessary condition of bad competition. So our criticisms would still hold.

economic and technological: production, distribution, pricing, etc.; and that the external conditions are social and political: there would have to be a labor supply, workers would have to be present at their jobs, there must not be rioting, violence, or perpetual strikes, etc.

We have already discussed "oppression" in writing about Lord Acton, and we need add nothing here beyond the comment that what Engels calls oppression might be called "order" by others. Anyhow, we must be careful to keep the meanings of Engels's words—their intension—free from the association of good and bad that Marxist terminology has acquired over the years, or we will never get the argument straight. Remember that in the Second World War those people in the conquered nations who collaborated with the Nazis were contemptuously called "collaborationists." Madison collaborated with Jefferson, and "collaborator" is still a good word. But the connotations of "collaborate" (in the grammarian's sense of connotation) have not been so happy since Quisling. We must put all such connotations to one side in analyzing Marxist arguments.

To continue with Engels. The state, he says, has always really represented only one class. When the state represents "society as a whole" it is unnecessary, for there are no more classes. "The first act in which the state really comes forward as the representative of society as a whole—the seizure of the means of production in the name of society—is at the same time its last independent act as a state." If this is the last "independent" act of the state, we may assume there will be other acts, but "dependent" ones. Dependent on whom? The proletariat, perhaps? Yet the state was always, in a sense, dependent, because it represented the ruling class. What is this change from "independent" action to some other kind? And can there even be a change? Engels's second sentence says that when the means of production become state property, that "puts an end to the state as the state." If there is no state, its actions cannot change. But Engels did not say there is no state. He said there is no state "as the state." Does it, in some way, continue to exist, but under another form or another name?

These puzzles can be solved. But they shouldn't exist, and Engels's definition of the state is to blame. He should have defined it in some normal way, so that actual states can be identified when we encounter their workings. Then he could have formulated as hypotheses whatever he thought was true of all states, and we could test those hypotheses. Instead, he defined "state" entirely in terms of his chief hypothesis about states, that they come into existence and continue only when there are economic classes in a society, and one class tries to oppress another. We have already discussed this methodological error. Let us call it "definition by hypothesis," in order to refer to it more readily.[9]

As with all definition by hypothesis, if the hypothesis is false, we cannot identify the extension of the term defined. Even if the hypothesis is true, it may interfere with identification. If Engels were right, how difficult it would still be to identify particular national states! How much easier if we were to define "state" as, let us say, "the ultimate sovereign power over all territory within its jurisdiction." At least, abstract as that definition seems, we could use it as a test of social actions, to discover whether or not they were the state's.

The puzzle about the disappearance of the state is aggravated by Engels's definition, and requires him to write about the end of "the state as the state." Because, in terms of its ordinary operations— printing of money, regulation of shipping, control of the courts, etc. —it remains, whether or not the proletariat has seized power. The functions of state must be performed and, in a large and complex society, require some central co-ordination. If you cease to call that central authority the state, you had better give it another name. But if you say the state has disappeared, and something else, brand new and with an entirely new name, functions in most overt ways just as the state did, people will be rightly suspicious of your argument.

VII

As Engels uses the phrase "the state as the state," the word "state" may have different meanings each time it is used. Perhaps thus: "It puts an end to the state (as we ordinarily define it), but only insofar as it is the 'state' of the Marxist definition." If this is what Engels intends, he tacitly admits that there is another meaning to "state," which he does not reject even when he uses his own definition. So the state, in its ordinary functions, persists, but the state, in its "deeper" meaning of "representative of the exploiting class," disappears. If Engels had not accepted a definition by hypothesis of the state, he could have said simply that the state (ordinarily defined) did, in his opinion, always act as an executive committee of the ruling class. But that, he could add, ceased (of course) when a society was reconstituted so there was no longer a ruling class.

A note on clarity of language: had Marx and Engels talked in the manner just suggested, endless controversy about the "withering away of the state," the "people's free state," and "people's democracy" could have been avoided. As it is, because of this definition by hypothesis, even the U.N. is a forum for fruitless debate about democracy: are England, France, and the United States really democracies, or are the "people's democracies" of the Balkans and the Baltic the "real" democracies?

A word of caution. Whenever the word "real" or "really" qualifies a word, so that there seems to be a distinction between its ordinary, garden-variety meaning and a more profound one, be suspicious. This distinction between the apparent and the real usually masks a refusal to base one's judgments on experience, or marks insistence on a definition by hypothesis. And those alternatives are by no means exclusive. There are not only those who offer you "real democracy," in which, of course, the governed have no voice, but others who offer "real love," in which there is probably no concern for your welfare; "real truth," which is undoubtedly false; or "real happiness," in which you are miserable.

TERMS AND PRINCIPLES

1. The truth or falsehood of factual matters cannot be decided by the use of logical analysis alone. It requires observation. Analysis can yield formal truth (as in tautology) and formal falsehood (as in self-contradiction).

2. *Intension:* The meaning or definition of a word, in the dictionary sense. It characterizes a class, not a particular object.

3. *Extension:* The meaning of a word in the sense of the things it refers to, or stands for; the *members* of a class, not the class itself.

4. *Denotation:* To the grammarian, "denotation" is a synonym for "intension." To the logician, it is a synonym for "extension." One must make sure of the context—grammatical or logical—before deciding how it is used.

5. *Connotation:* To the logician, "connotation" is a synonym for "intension." To the grammarian it means the associations that cluster around a word, rather than its precise definition.

6. *Implication* (or *imply*): Logicians use this term to mean whatever follows deductively, or by reason alone, from a statement. Grammarians often use the word to mean whatever we associate with a word, its connotations (in their sense).

7. When we try to learn whether A is a necessary condition for B, we must see whether or not B exists in the absence of A. (If it does, A is *not a necessary condition.*) We must make sure, if B has occurred in the presence of A and of other pos-

sibly relevant circumstances, that when we eliminate A to see
if B, too, is eliminated, all of the other circumstances remain.

8. *Begging the question,* or *arguing in a circle:* A logical fallacy.
It occurs when we try to prove A and offer as evidence a
statement that assumes the truth of A.

9. *Definition by hypothesis:* The use of a hypothesis about an
event as though it were a definition of that event.

SECOND COMMENTARY

We have not quite finished discussing Engels's passage. There is
still the "withering away" of the state to consider. Let us make some
points about it, and then treat the entire passage and our analysis of
it as the basis for an exercise.

What has perplexed many honest readers of Engels's passage is
easy enough to resolve now that we know what he has done with the
word "state." Their difficulty has been that in the second sentence,
the state vanishes all at once, like a ghost, but in the penultimate
sentence "the state is not abolished, *it withers away.*" That is, it then
disappears like the Cheshire Cat, slowly, a bit at a time, until nothing
remains but its grin.

Lenin himself, an astute and surely a deeply concerned reader,
explains this seeming contradiction by writing of "the state as the
state" that "As a matter of fact, Engels speaks here of the destruction
of the bourgeois state by the proletarian revolution . . ." (*State and
Revolution*). He continues, ". . . the words about its withering away
refer to the remains of *proletarian* statehood *after* the Socialist revolution." The word "remains" is confusing because the proletarian state
didn't exist at all until after the revolution. Lenin makes some amends
in a later sentence, "What withers away after the revolution is the
proletarian state or semi-state."

Lenin isn't entirely wrong about Engels's meaning, but he is
ensnared by the determination that "state" shall have a special
Marxist definition. Then he, too, has to use strange phrases about
what, in fact, happens, or what he thinks will happen. So he speaks of
the "remains" of a state which is just beginning, and then of a "semi-
state." Here you might ask whether any serious damage is done by this
intellectual and verbal confusion. What, after all, is the difference, if
one knows what he means?

The answer is that Engels and Lenin did not know clearly what
they meant. Their definition by hypothesis obscured the meaning of
"state." However much they admitted the ordinary meaning tacitly,

they could not rest content with it. But what harm was done? We shall see.

Consider the word "semi-state." What can Lenin mean by it? He knows that a state exists after the revolution, and he knows, too, that it is in the hands of the proletariat, or former proletariat.* But because he accepts the Marxist definition of the state, Lenin sees that the very essence of the state, its character as an instrument of a class, is gone. What is left? The state itself, in its ordinary sense. All the facts of behavior which we usually call "the state." What shall he call them? There is no other name by which they are known. So he continues to call them "the state," implicitly admitting ordinary definition, but insists that the real "state," the state as Marx conceived it, is gone. What remains is a "semi-state."

But "semi-state" misled Lenin and his followers, as the whole idea had misled Marx and Engels. They expected much of the state to be gone immediately the revolution was won. Since the state was *really* "a special repressive force," it expressed that character through the organs of government by which others might define "state." When the repressive, class character of the state came to an end, so, too, they thought, should the organs through which the state exerted its chief repressive powers. Hence they believed that immediately after the revolution a number of those organs would be "abolished." Both Marx and Engels listed them. They are the standing army, the police, bureaucracy, clergy, and judiciary. Imagine even a "semi-state" without police, government officials, and courts. (For Lenin, these were all to exist, but transformed. Judges would be replaced by people utterly untrained in law, government officials by ordinary workingmen at workingmen's salaries.) This is obviously folly when stated clearly. But millions of men saw nothing wrong with it because its meaning was hidden under elaborate Marxist clothing.

Engels goes on to assert that what is left of the state *gradually* disappears. All its organs are connected, in some way, with repression and, finally, none are needed any longer. This is the famous "withering away" of the state, and it is in this way that he asks appraisal of such phrases as "people's free state"—in our day supplanted by "people's democracy." He intends these phrases to characterize the truncated

* A slight change in wording had to be made after the Russian Revolution. The erstwhile bourgeoisie was still bourgeois at heart, the proletariat still proletarian. So the government was openly called "the dictatorship of the proletariat" and admitted to be a class instrument, a special repressive force to hold down the bourgeoisie. The bourgeoisie, at this point, could scarcely be "owners of the means of production." So they must have been redefined, implicitly, as "those loyal to their *former* class," and, after a time, as "those opposed to the Soviet government."

state after the revolution, but not the society that ultimately replaces it. For these are the states that wither away. So, as slogans, such phrases may be excellent propaganda, but they should not be thought of seriously, or as ultimate goals.

SOME QUESTIONS

Now let us ask some questions on the basis of the quotation from Engels and our analysis of it.

1. The Marxist reason that the state, after the Socialist revolution, can be called a "people's democracy," is that for the first time in history that state supposedly represents the vast majority of the people, instead of repressing them. "We all know," wrote Lenin, "that the political form of the 'state' at that time is complete democracy." It is "complete democracy," because it governs on behalf of the majority. Compare this with Lincoln's definition of democracy. What is missing? Much later, Lenin could write: "The Soviet Socialist Democracy is in no way inconsistent with the rule and dictatorship of one person: . . . the will of a class is at times best realized by a dictator . . ." Is that inconsistent with the earlier view?

2. Lenin opposed devotion to the phrase "people's free state," by saying: ". . . every state is a 'special repressive force' for the suppression of the oppressed class. Consequently, *no* state is either 'free' or a 'people's state.' " Is that consistent with Engels? Suppose we find a nation in which the state does not in fact suppress a class. How would Lenin greet our discovery? Show how his answer might both beg the question and use definition by hypothesis.

3. If the intensional meaning of "democracy" is "rule in the interest of the majority," not "by the majority," see if you can state some part of its extension. What are some of the connotative (in the grammarian's sense) advantages to communist propaganda in labeling such states "democracies"?

EXERCISE

SIGMUND FREUD

From *Civilization and Its Discontents*

The time comes when every one of us has to abandon the illusory anticipations with which in our youth we regarded our fellow-men, and when we realize how much hardship and suffering we have been caused in life through their ill-will. It would be unfair, however, to reproach culture with trying to eliminate all disputes and competition from human concerns. These things are undoubtedly indispensable; but opposition is not necessarily enmity, only it may be misused to make an opening for it.

The Communists believe they have found a way of delivering us from this evil. Man is whole-heartedly good and friendly to his neighbour, they say, but the system of private property has corrupted his nature. The possession of private property gives power to the individual and thence the temptation arises to ill-treat his neighbour; the man who is excluded from the possession of property is obliged to rebel in hostility against the oppressor. If private property were abolished, all valuables held in common, and all allowed to share in the enjoyment of them, ill-will and enmity would disappear from among men. Since all needs would be satisfied, none would have any reason to regard another as an enemy; all would willingly undertake the work which is necessary. I have no concern with any economic criticisms of the communistic system; I cannot enquire into whether the abolition of private property is advantageous and expedient. But I am able to recognize that psychologically it is founded on an untenable illusion. By abolishing private property one deprives the human love of aggression of one of its instruments, a strong one undoubtedly, but assuredly not the strongest. It in no way alters the individual differences in power and influence which are turned by aggressiveness to its own use, nor does it change the nature of the instinct in any way. This instinct did not arise as the result of property; it reigned almost supreme in primitive times when possessions were still extremely scanty; it shows itself already in the nursery when possessions have hardly grown out of their original . . . shape; it is at the bottom of all the relations of affection and love between human beings—possibly with the single exception of that of a mother to her male child.

SOME QUESTIONS

1. At the beginning of his second paragraph, Freud suggests that the communists have a view of human nature that underlies their conclusions. It is that man is natively good but can be, and has been, corrupted by one social institution. If man is natively good, where did the corrupting institution come from? How could good men create a bad institution? Is it perhaps that they didn't know its consequences, and so didn't know it was evil? To say man is naturally good is not to say he is naturally bright.

2. Is it perhaps that such institutions are not created deliberately at all, but arise out of responses to the environment and changing social conditions? Yet if man never creates his institutions deliberately, is it reasonable to ask him to abolish them deliberately, as communists seem to do?

3. Has your reading of Marx, Engels, and Lenin led you to believe that Freud is right in attributing this view of human nature to them?

4. Freud seems to believe in an aggressive instinct. What kinds of evidence could show that he is right or wrong? That is, how could one go about proving that he is right or wrong?

5. If there is such an instinct, what sort of human institutions would make its manifestations relatively beneficial and what sort would make them harmful?

6. After answering question 5, make up a list of the values presupposed by your answer. Explain how you know that the values you list are presupposed by the answer.

EXERCISE

KARL MARX AND FRIEDRICH ENGELS

From The Communist Manifesto

The history of all hitherto existing society is the history of class struggles.

Freeman and slave, patrician and plebeian, lord and serf, guildmaster and journeyman, in a word, oppressor and oppressed, stood in constant opposition to one another, carried on uninterrupted, now hidden, now open fight, a fight that each time ended, either in a revolutionary re-constitution of society at large, or in the common ruin of the contending classes.

In the earlier epochs of history we find almost everywhere a complicated arrangement of society into various orders, a manifold gradation of social rank. In ancient Rome we have patricians, knights, plebeians, slaves; in the Middle Ages, feudal lords, vassals, guild-masters, journeymen, apprentices, serfs; in almost all of these classes, again, subordinate gradations.

The modern bourgeois society that has sprouted from the ruins of feudal society, has not done away with class antagonisms. It has but established new classes, new conditions of oppression, new forms of struggle in place of the old ones.

Our epoch, the epoch of the bourgeoisie, possesses, however, this distinctive feature; it has simplified the class antagonisms. Society as a whole is more and more splitting up into two great hostile camps, into two great classes directly facing each other; Bourgeoisie and Proletariat.

From the serfs of the Middle Ages sprang the chartered burghers of the earliest towns. From these burgesses the first elements of the bourgeoisie were developed.

The discovery of America, the rounding of the Cape, opened up fresh ground for the rising bourgeoisie. The East Indian and Chinese markets, the colonization of America, trade with the colonies, the increase in the means of exchange and in commodities generally, gave to commerce, to navigation, to industry, an impulse never before known, and thereby, to the revolutionary element in the tottering feudal society, a rapid development.

The feudal system of industry, under which industrial production was monopolized by closed guilds, now no longer sufficed for the growing wants of the new market. The manufacturing system took its place. The guild-masters were pushed on one side by the manufacturing middle-class: division of labor between the different corporate guilds vanished in the face of division of labor in each single workshop.

Meantime the markets kept ever growing, the demand ever rising. Even manufacture no longer sufficed. Thereupon, steam and machinery revolutionized industrial production. The place of manufacture was taken by the giant, Modern Industry, the place of the industrial middle-class, by industrial millionaires, the leaders of whole industrial armies, the modern bourgeois.

Modern industry has established the world market, for which the discovery of America paved the way. This market has given an immense development to commerce, to navigation, to communication by land. This development has, in its turn, reacted on the extension of industry; and in proportion as industry, commerce, navigation, railways extended, in the same proportion the bourgeoisie developed, increased its capital, and pushed into the background every class handed down from the Middle Ages.

We see, therefore, how the modern bourgeoisie is itself the product of a long course of development, of a series of revolutions in the modes of production and of exchange.

Each step in the development of the bourgeoisie was accompanied by a corresponding political advance of that class. An oppressed class under the sway of the feudal nobility, an armed and self-governing association in the mediaeval commune, here independent urban republic (as in Italy and Germany), there taxable "third estate" of the monarch (as in France), afterwards, in the period of manufacture proper, serving either the semifeudal or the absolute monarch as a counterpoise against nobility, and, in fact, corner stone of the great monarchies in general, the bourgeoisie has at last, since the establishment of Modern Industry and of the world-market, conquered for itself, in the modern representative State, exclusive political sway. The executive of the modern State is but a committee for managing the common affairs of the whole bourgeoisie.

The bourgeoisie, historically, has played a most revolutionary part.

The bourgeoisie, wherever it has got the upper hand, has put an end to all feudal, patriarchal, idyllic relations. It has pitilessly torn asunder the motley feudal ties that bound man to his "natural superiors," and has left no other nexus between man and man than naked self-interest, than callous "cash payment." It has drowned the most heavenly ecstasies of religious fervor, of chivalrous enthusiasm, of

Philistine sentimentalism, in the icy water of egotistical calculation. It has resolved personal worth into exchange value, and in place of the numberless indefeasible chartered freedoms, has set up that single, unconscionable freedom—Free Trade. In one word, for exploitation, veiled by religious and political illusions, it has substituted naked, shameless, direct, brutal exploitation.

The bourgeoisie has stripped of its halo every occupation hitherto honored and looked up to with reverent awe. It has converted the physician, the lawyer, the priest, the poet, the man of science, into its paid wage laborers.

The bourgeoisie has torn away from the family its sentimental veil, and has reduced the family relation to a mere money relation.

The bourgeoisie has disclosed how it came to pass that the brutal display of vigor in the Middle Ages, which reactionists so much admire, found its fitting complement in the most slothful indolence. It has been the first to show what man's activity can bring about. It has accomplished wonders far surpassing Egyptian pyramids, Roman aqueducts and Gothic cathedrals; it has conducted expeditions that put in the shade all former Exoduses of nations and crusades.

The bourgeoisie cannot exist without constantly revolutionizing the instruments of production, and thereby the relations of production, and with them the whole relations of society. Conservation of the old modes of production in unaltered form was, on the contrary, the first condition of existence for all earlier industrial classes. Constant revolutionizing of production, uninterrupted disturbance of all social conditions, everlasting uncertainty and agitation distinguish the bourgeois epoch from all earlier ones. All fixed, fast frozen relations, with their train of ancient and venerable prejudices and opinions, are swept away, all new formed ones become antiquated before they can ossify. All that is solid melts into the air, all that is holy is profaned, and man is at last compelled to face with sober senses, his real conditions of life, and his relations with this kind.

The need of a constantly expanding market for its products chases the bourgeoisie over the whole surface of the globe. It must nestle everywhere, settle everywhere, establish connections everywhere.

The bourgeoisie, during its rule of scarce one hundred years, has created more massive and more colossal productive forces than have all preceding generations together. Subjection of Nature's force to man, machinery, application of chemistry to industry and agriculture, steam-navigation, railways, electric telegraphs, clearing of whole continents for cultivation, canalization of rivers, whole populations conjured out of the ground—what earlier century had even a presentiment that such productive forces slumbered in the lap of social labor?

We see then: the means of production and of exchange on whose foundation the bourgeoisie built itself up, were generated in feudal society. At a certain stage in the development of these means of production and of exchange, the conditions under which feudal society produced and exchanged, the feudal organization of agriculture and manufacturing industry, in one word, the feudal relations of property became no longer compatible with the already developed productive forces; they became so many fetters. They had to burst asunder; they were burst asunder.

Into their places stepped free competition, accompanied by a social and political constitution adapted to it, and by economical and political sway of the bourgeois class.

A similar movement is going on before our own eyes. Modern bourgeois society with its relations of production, of exchange and of property, a society that has conjured up such gigantic means of production and of exchange, is like the sorcerer, who is no longer able to control the powers of the nether world whom he has called up by his spells. For many a decade past, the history of industry and commerce is but the history of the revolt of modern productive forces against modern conditions of production, against the property relations that are the conditions for the existence of the bourgeoisie and of its rule. It is enough to mention the commercial crises that by their periodical return put on its trial, each time more threateningly, the existence of the entire bourgeois society. In these crises a great part not only of the existing products, but also of the previously created productive forces are periodically destroyed. In these crises there breaks out an epidemic that, in all earlier epochs, would have seemed an absurdity—the epidemic of overproduction. Society suddenly finds itself put back into a state of momentary barbarism; it appears as if a famine, a universal war of devastation, had cut off the supply of every means of subsistence; industry and commerce seem to be destroyed; and why? Because there is too much civilization, too much means of subsistence, too much industry, too much commerce. The productive forces at the disposal of society no longer tend to further the development of the conditions of the bourgeois property; on the contrary, they have become too powerful for these conditions by which they are fettered, and as soon as they overcome these fetters they bring disorder into the whole of bourgeois society, endanger the existence of bourgeois property. The conditions of bourgeois society are too narrow to comprise the wealth created by them. And how does the bourgeoisie get over these crises? On the one hand by enforced destruction of a mass of productive forces; on the other, by the conquest of new markets, and by the more thorough exploitation of the old ones. That is to say, by paving the way for more extensive and more destructive crises, and by diminishing the means whereby crises are prevented.

The weapons with which the bourgeoisie felled feudalism to the ground are now turned against the bourgeoisie itself.

But not only has the bourgeoisie forged the weapons that bring death to itself; it has also called into existence the men who are to wield those weapons—the modern working-class—the proletarians.

In proportion as the bourgeoisie, i. e., capital, is developed, in the same proportion is the proletariat, the modern working-class, developed, a class of laborers who live only so long as they find work, and who find work only so long as their labor increases capital. These laborers, who must sell themselves piecemeal, are a commodity, like every other article of commerce, and are consequently exposed to all the vicissitudes of competition, to all the fluctuations of the market.

Owing to the extensive use of machinery and to division of labor, the work of the proletarians has lost all individual character, and, consequently, all charm for the workman. He becomes an appendage of the machine, and it is only the most simple, most monotonous and most easily acquired knack that is required of him. Hence, the cost of production of a workman is restricted almost entirely to the means of subsistence that he requires for his maintenance, and for the propagation of his race. But the price of a commodity, and also of labor, is equal to its cost of production. In proportion, therefore, as the repulsiveness of the work increases, the wage decreases. Nay more, in proportion as the use of machinery and division of labor increases, in the same proportion the burden of toil increases, whether by prolongation of the working hours, by increase of the work enacted in a given time, or by increased speed of the machinery, etc.

Modern industry has converted the little workshop of the patriarchal master into the great factory of the industrial capitalist. Masses of laborers, crowded into factories, are organized like soldiers. As privates of the industrial army they are placed under the command of a perfect hierarchy of officers and sergeants. Not only are they the slaves of the bourgeois class and of the bourgeois state, they are daily and hourly enslaved by the machine, by the overlooker, and, above all, by the individual bourgeois manufacturer himself. The more openly this despotism proclaims gain to be its end and aim, the more petty, the more hateful and the more embittering it is.

The less the skill and exertion or strength implied in manual labor, in other words, the more modern industry becomes developed, the more is the labor of men superseded by that of women. Differences of age and sex have no longer any distinctive social validity for the working class. All are instruments of labor, more or less expensive to use, according to their age and sex.

Hitherto every form of society has been based, as we have already seen, on the antagonism of oppressing and oppressed classes. But in order to oppress a class, certain conditions must be assured to it under which it can, at least, continue its slavish existence. The serf, in the period of serfdom, raised himself to membership in the commune, just as the petty bourgeois, under the yoke of feudal absolutism, managed to develop into a bourgeois. The modern laborer, on the contrary, instead of rising with the progress of industry, sinks deeper and deeper below the conditions of existence of his own class. He becomes a pauper, and pauperism develops more rapidly than population and wealth. And here it becomes evident that the bourgeoisie is unfit any longer to be the ruling class in society, and to impose its conditions of existence upon society as an overriding law. It is unfit to rule, because it is incompetent to assure an existence to its slave within his slavery, because it cannot help letting him sink into such a state that it has to feed him, instead of being fed by him. Society can no longer live under this bourgeoisie; in other words, its existence is no longer compatible with society.

The essential condition for the existence, and for the sway of the bourgeois class, is the formation and augmentation of capital; the condition for capital is wage labor. Wage labor rests exclusively on competition between the laborers. The advance of industry, whose involuntary promoter is the bourgeoisie, replaces the isolation of the laborers, due to competition, by their involuntary combination, due to association. The development of Modern Industry, therefore, cuts from under its feet the very foundation on which the bourgeoisie produces and appropriates products. What the bourgeoisie therefore produces, above all, are its own grave diggers. Its fall and the victory of the proletariat are equally inevitable.

JOHN DEWEY

From *Liberalism and Social Action*

The crisis in democracy demands the substitution of the intelligence that is exemplified in scientific procedure for the kind of intelligence that is now accepted. The need for this change is not exhausted in the demand for greater honesty and impartiality, even though these qualities be now corrupted by discussion carried on mainly for purposes of party supremacy and for imposition of some special but concealed interest. These qualities need to be restored. But the need goes further. The social use of intelligence continued to be identified simply with discussion and persuasion, necessary as are these things. Approximation to use of scientific method in investigation and of the engineering mind in the invention and projection of far-reaching social plans is demanded. The habit of considering social realities in terms of cause and effect and social policies in terms of means and consequences is still inchoate. The contrast between the state of intelligence in politics and in the physical control of nature is to be taken literally. What has happened in this latter is the outstanding demonstration of the meaning of organized intelligence. The combined effect of science and technology has released more productive energies in a bare hundred years than stands to the credit of prior human history in its entirety. Productively it has multiplied nine million times in the last generation alone. The prophetic vision of Francis Bacon of subjugation of the energies of nature through change in methods of inquiry has well-nigh been realized. The stationary engine, the locomotive, the dynamo, the motor car, turbine, telegraph, telephone, radio and moving picture are not the products of either isolated individual minds nor of the particular economic régime called capitalism. They are the fruit of methods that first penetrated to the working causalities of nature and then utilized the resulting knowledge in bold imaginative ventures of invention and construction.

We hear a great deal in these days about class conflict. The past history of man is held up to us as almost exclusively a record of struggles between classes, ending in the victory of a class that had been oppressed and the transfer of power to it. It is difficult to avoid reading the past in terms of the contemporary scene. Indeed, fundamentally it is impossible to avoid this course. With a certain proviso, it is highly important that we are compelled to follow this path. For the past as past is gone, save for esthetic enjoyment and refreshment, while the present is with us. Knowledge of the past is significant only as it deepens and extends our understanding of the present. Yet there is a proviso. We must grasp the things that are most important in the present when we turn to the past and not allow ourselves to be misled by secondary phenomena no matter how intense and immediately urgent they are. Viewed from this standpoint, the rise of scientific method and of technology based upon it is the genuinely active force in producing the vast complex of changes the world is now undergoing, not the class struggle whose spirit and method are opposed to science. If we lay hold upon the causal force exercised by this embodiment of intelligence we shall know where to turn for the means of directing further change.

When I say that scientific method and technology have been the active force in producing the revolutionary transformations society is undergoing, I do not imply no other forces have been at work to arrest, deflect and corrupt their operation. Rather this fact is positively implied. At this point, indeed, is located the conflict that underlies the confusions and uncertainties of the present scene. The conflict is between institutions and habits originating in the pre-scientific and pre-technological age and the new forces generated by science and technology. The application of science, to a considerable degree, even its own growth, has been conditioned by the system to which the name of capitalism is given, a rough designation of a complex of political and legal arrangements centering about a particular mode of economic relations. Because of the conditioning of science and technology by this setting, the second and humanly most important part of Bacon's prediction has so far largely missed realization. The conquest of natural energies has not accrued to the betterment of the common human estate in anything like the degree he anticipated.

Because of conditions that were set by the legal institutions and the moral ideas existing when the scientific and industrial revolutions came into being, the chief usufruct of the latter has been appropriated by a relatively small class. Industrial entrepreneurs have reaped out of all proportion to what they sowed. By obtaining private ownership of the means of production and exchange they deflected a considerable share of the results of increased productivtiy to their private pockets. This appropriation was not the fruit of criminal conspiracy or of sinister intent. It was sanctioned not only by legal institutions of age-long standing but by the entire prevailing moral code. The institution of private property long antedated feudal times. It is the institution with which men have lived, with few exceptions, since the dawn of civilization. Its existence has deeply impressed itself upon mankind's moral conceptions. Moreover, the new industrial forces tended to break down many of the rigid class barriers that had been in force, and to give to millions a new outlook and inspire a new hope;—especially in this country with no feudal background and no fixed class system.

Since the legal institutions and the patterns of mind characteristic of ages of civilization still endure, there exists the conflict that brings confusion into every phase of present life. The problem of bringing into being a new social orientation and organization is, when reduced to its ultimates, the problem of using the new resources of production, made possible by the advance of physical science, for social ends, for what Bentham called the greatest good of the greatest number. Institutional relationships fixed in the pre-scientific age stand in the way of accomplishing this great transformation. Lag in mental and moral patterns provides the bulwark of the older institutions; in expressing the past they still express present beliefs, outlooks and purposes. Here is the place where the problem of liberalism centers today.

The argument drawn from past history that radical change must be effected by means of class struggle, culminating in open war, fails to discriminate between the two forces, one active, the other resistant and deflecting, that have produced the social scene in which we live. The active force is, as I have said, scientific method and technological application. The opposite force is that of older institutions and the habits that have grown up around them. Instead of discrimination between forces and distribution of their consequences, we find the two things lumped together. The compound is labeled the capitalistic or the bourgeois class, and to this class as a class is imputed all the important features of present industrialized society—much as the defenders of the régime of economic liberty exercised for private property are accustomed to attribute every improvement made in the last century and a half to the same capitalistic régime. Thus in orthodox communist literature, from the Communist Manifesto of 1848 to the present day, we are told that the bourgeoisie, the name for a distinctive class, has done this and that. It has, so it is said, given a cosmopolitan character to production and consumption; has destroyed the national basis of industry; has agglomerated population in urban centers; has transferred power from the country to the city, in the process of creating colossal productive force, its chief achievement. In addition, it has created crises of ever renewed intensity; has created imperialism of a new type in frantic effort to control raw materials and markets. Finally, it has created a new class, the proletariat, and has created it as a class having a common interest opposed to that of the bourgeoisie, and is giving an irresistible stimulus to its organization, first as a class and then as a political power. According to the economic version of the Hegelian dialectic,* the bourgeois class is thus creating its own complete and polar opposite, and this in time will end the old power and rule. The class struggle of veiled civil war will finally burst into open revolution and the result will be either the common ruin of the contending parties or a revolutionary reconstitution of society at large through a transfer of power from one class to another.

The position thus sketched unites vast sweep with great simplicity. I am concerned with it here only as far as it emphasizes the idea of a struggle between classes, culminating in open and violent warfare as being the method for production of radical social change. For, be it noted, the issue is not whether some amount of violence will accompany the effectuation of radical change of institutions. The question is whether force or intelligence is to be the method upon which we consistently rely and to whose promotion we devote our energies. Insistence that the use of violent force is *inevitable* limits the use of available intelligence, for wherever the inevitable reigns intelligence cannot be used. Commitment to inevitability is always the fruit of dogma; intelligence does not pretend to *know* save as a result of experimentation, the opposite of preconceived dogma. Moreover, acceptance in advance of the inevitability of violence tends to produce the use of violence in cases where peaceful methods might otherwise avail. The curious fact is that while it is generally admitted that this and that particular social problem, say of the family, or railroads or banking, must be solved, if at all, by the method of intelligence, yet there is supposed to be some one all-inclusive social problem which can be solved only by the use of violence. This fact would be inexplicable were it not a conclusion from dogma as its premise.

It is frequently asserted that the method of experimental intelligence can be applied to physical facts because physical nature does not present conflicts of class interests, while it is inapplicable to

* [Marx based his philosophical theory in part on that of Hegel. Both believed that development or progress is "dialectical," i.e. that conditions create their opposites, and that these in time come to a new synthesis.]

society because the latter is so deeply marked by incompatible interests. It is then assumed that the "experimentalist" is one who has chosen to ignore the uncomfortable fact of conflicting interests. Of course, there *are* conflicting interests; otherwise there would be no social problems. The problem under discussion is precisely *how* conflicting claims are to be settled in the interest of the widest possible contribution to the interests of all—or at least of the great majority. The method of democracy—inasfar as it is that of organized intelligence—is to bring these conflicts out into the open where their special claims can be seen and appraised, where they can be discussed and judged in the light of more inclusive interests than are represented by either of them separately. There is, for example, a clash of interests between munition manufacturers and most of the rest of the population. The more the respective claims of the two are publicly and scientifically weighed, the more likely it is that the public interest will be disclosed and be made effective. There is an undoubted objective clash of interests between finance-capitalism that controls the means of production and whose profit is served by maintaining relative scarcity, and idle workers and hungry consumers. But what generates violent strife is failure to bring the conflict into the light of intelligence where the conflicting interests can be adjudicated in behalf of the interest of the great majority. Those most committed to the dogma of inevitable force recognize the need for intelligently discovering and expressing the dominant social interest up to a certain point and then draw back. The "experimentalist" is one who would see to it that the method depended upon by all in some degree in every democratic community be followed through to completion.

In spite of the existence of class conflicts, amounting at times to veiled civil war, any one habituated to the use of the method of science will view with considerable suspicion the erection of actual human beings into fixed entities called classes, having no overlapping interests and so internally unified and externally separated that they are made the protagonists of history—itself hypothetical. Such an idea of classes is a survival of a rigid logic that once prevailed in the sciences of nature, but that no longer has any place there. This conversion of abstractions into entities smells more of a dialectic of con-

cepts than of a realistic examination of facts, even though it makes
more of an emotional appeal to many than do the results of the
latter. To say that all past historic social progress has been the result
of coöperation and not of conflict would be also an exaggeration. But
exaggeration against exaggeration, it is the more reasonable of the
two. And it is no exaggeration to say that the measure of civilization
is the degree in which the method of coöperative intelligence replaces
the method of brute conflict.

But the point I am especially concerned with just here is the
indiscriminate lumping together as a single force of two different
things—the results of scientific technology and of a legal system of
property relations. It is science and technology that have had the
revolutionary social effect while the legal system has been the relatively static element. According to the Marxians themselves, the economic foundations of society consist of two things, the forces of
production on one side and, on the other side, the social relations of
production, that is, the legal property system under which the former
operates. The latter lags behind, and "revolutions" are produced by
the power of the forces of production to change the system of institutional relations. But what are the modern forces of production save
those of scientific technology? And what is scientific technology save
a large-scale demonstration of organized intelligence in action?

It is quite true that what is happening socially is the result of
the combination of the two factors, one dynamic, the other relatively
static. If we choose to call the combination by the name of capitalism,
then it is true, or a truism, that capitalism is the "cause" of all the
important social changes that have occurred—an argument that the
representatives of capitalism are eager to put forward whenever the
increase of productivity is in question. But if we want to *understand,*
and not just to paste labels, unfavorable or favorable as the case may
be, we shall certainly begin and end with discrimination. Colossal
increase in productivity, the bringing of men together in cities and
large factories, the elimination of distance, the accumulation of capital, fixed and liquid—these things would have come about, at a
certain stage, no matter what the established institutional system.
They are the consequence of the new means of technological produc-

tion. Certain other things have happened because of inherited institutions and the habits of belief and character that accompany and support them. If we begin at this point, we shall see that the release of productivity is the product of coöperatively organized intelligence, and shall also see that the institutional framework is precisely that which is not subjected as yet, in any considerable measure, to the impact of inventive and constructive intelligence. That coercion and oppression on a large scale exist, no honest person can deny. But these things are not the product of science and technology but of the perpetuation of old institutions and patterns untouched by scientific method. The inference to be drawn is clear.

The argument, drawn from history, that great social changes have been effected only by violent means, needs considerable qualification, in view of the vast scope of changes that are taking place without the use of violence. But even if it be admitted to hold of the past, the conclusion that violence is the method now to be depended upon does not follow—unless one is committed to a dogmatic philosophy of history. The radical who insists that the future method of change must be like that of the past has much in common with the hide-bound reactionary who holds to the past as an ultimate fact. Both overlook the *fact that history in being a process of change generates change not only in details but also in the method of directing social change.* I recur to what I said at the beginning of this chapter. It is true that the social order is largely conditioned by the use of coercive force, bursting at times into open violence. But what is also true is that mankind now has in its possession a new method, that of coöperative and experimental science which expresses the method of intelligence. I should be meeting dogmatism with dogmatism if I asserted that the existence of this historically new factor completely invalidates all arguments drawn from the effect of force in the past. But it is within the bounds of reason to assert that the presence of this social factor demands that the present situation be analyzed on its own terms, and not be rigidly subsumed under fixed conceptions drawn from the past.

SOME QUESTIONS

1. Summarize the argument of this portion of the *Communist Manifesto,* point by point.

2. At what points does Dewey contradict Marx and Engels? Make up a list of statements from the *Communist Manifesto* that Dewey discusses, and then a second list of opposed or contradictory statements from Dewey.

3. What is the meaning of the "class struggle," according to the *Communist Manifesto?* What is the theory of the class struggle supposed to explain?

4. Dewey offers an alternative explanation. What is it?

5. Dewey proposes the use of intelligence, not force. Does he mean by "intelligence" more than free discussion and parliamentary procedure? What does his "method of intelligence" involve?

6. Is Dewey's distinction between intelligence and force persuasive? Why (or why not)? Is the way left open for what might be called "an intelligent use of force"?

7. Dewey suggests that belief in the inevitability of violent revolution is harmful. How? Is he persuasive?

8. There is an error of thought that has been called hypostatizing, or reifying, an abstraction. It consists in treating an abstraction as if it were a real or living thing. Thus one is hypostatizing an abstraction, the state, when one argues: "What difference if you're unhappy, so long as your action makes the state happy." But the state cannot be happy or unhappy, because it is not a living creature.

Dewey thinks the Marxists are hypostatizing "classes" and talking about them as if they behaved like individual people. Explain his argument. Is he right or wrong? Why?

🎵 *Section Three*

Reflections

"Beware of first-hand ideas!" exclaimed one of the most advanced of them. "First-hand ideas do not really exist. They are but the physical impressions produced by love and fear, and on this gross foundation who could erect a philosophy? Let your ideas be second-hand, and if possible tenth-hand, for then they will be far removed from the disturbing element—direct observation. Do not learn anything about this subject of mine—the French Revolution. Learn instead what I think that Enicharmon thought Urizen thought Gutch thought Ho-Yung thought Chi-Bo-Sing thought Lafcadio Hearn thought Carlyle thought Mirabeau said about the French Revolution. Through the medium of these eight great minds, the blood that was shed at Paris and the windows that were broken at Versailles will be clarified to an idea which you may employ most profitably in your daily lives. But be sure that the intermediates are many and varied, for in history one authority exists to counteract another. Urizen must counteract the scepticism of Ho-Yung and Enicharmon, I must myself counteract the impetuosity of Gutch. You who listen to me are in a better position to judge about the French Revolution than I am. Your descendants will even in a better position than you, for they will learn what you think I think, and yet another intermediate will be added to the chain. And in time"—his voice rose—"there will come a

generation that has got beyond facts, beyond impressions,
a generation absolutely colourless, a generation

'seraphically free
From taint of personality,'

which will see the French Revolution not as it happened,
nor as they would like it to have happened, but as it would
have happened, had it taken place in the days of the Machine."

E. M. Forster, "The Machine Stops"

We continue our discussions, commentaries, and exercises as
they were in Section Two, but with different subjects. There we stayed
sufficiently within a single subject in our texts so that we could see
relationships among various arguments and beliefs, and discover
some of the virtues of thinking systematically. Here our subjects vary
from the question of God's existence to the problems of human
failure. But there are still connections among the ideas considered;
and there are contradictions and corrections.

One must not only know something about good books. He must
also know something about bad ones, at least why they are bad. And
there are some bad books and mediocre books that must be read as
carefully as great ones, because they have an importance in the world
that makes their study indispensable. In our day, Hitler's *Mein
Kampf* (My Struggle) was such a book. We have selected passages
from Hitler's conversation to discuss. They serve the same purpose
as passages from *Mein Kampf,* and are perhaps more revealing.

The other texts are from mathematicians, philosophers, judges,
psychologists, and statesmen. Some of the authors were several of
these things at once. Pascal was a great mathematician, scientist, and
religious thinker. James was the most eminent American philosopher
of his time and one of the two founders of modern psychology.
Holmes was judge, soldier, legal philosopher. Jefferson did so many
things so well that he makes us humble. First-rate minds and first-
rate writers make a startling contrast to the perceptive, muddy, and
arrogant world-conqueror.

We proceed with our principles of analysis here, listing them as
we use them, though not always numbering them in the text. But
later in Section Four we often use them without comment. By the
time you read that section, you should be ready to recognize the
principles as they are employed.

ADOLF HITLER

From *Hitler's Secret Conversations*
October 10, 1941

Christianity is a rebellion against natural law, a protest against nature. Taken to its logical extreme, Christianity would mean the systematic cultivation of the human failure.

COMMENTARY

I

". . . a rebellion against natural law, a protest against nature." We have discussed natural law briefly, in writing about the Declaration of Independence. This raises further questions. Remember that we have here an utterance of one of the most powerful men who ever lived. That alone gives it importance. Yet more highly acclaimed thinkers, although with less worldly power, have talked in the same way. What can they mean?

Natural law has usually been understood as the set of principles inherent in nature which should guide human conduct. For the signers of the Declaration, natural law contained such principles as justice, the essential equality of men, living in accordance with reason, and every man's right to property in himself. A philosopher of natural law today, Jacques Maritain, following Thomas Aquinas, argues that natural law, in its application to conduct, is the law of the nature of man, human nature itself. His reason is that each thing in the natural world has a nature of its own, and so "its own natural law, that is, the normality of its functioning." If it functions normally, it achieves "fulness of being either in its growth or in its behavior." If it does not function normally it is thwarted, misguided, distorted. Maritain writes: "Any given situation, for instance the situation of Cain with regard to Abel, implies a relation to the essence of man, and the possible murder of the one by the other is incompatible with the general ends and innermost dynamic structure of that rational essence. It is rejected by it. Hence the prohibition of murder is grounded on or required by the essence of man. The precept: thou shalt do no murder, is a precept of natural law."

It might take a lengthy analysis to find out all that Maritain is saying. But one thing is clear. What he means by "natural law" and what Hitler means are worlds apart, as are what Hitler means and what Jefferson means.

And what does Hitler mean? The one clue he gives is his description of Christianity as opposed to natural law, and in its logical extreme as "the systematic cultivation of the human failure." Now the extreme of a protest, a rebellion, an opposition, should be the contradictory of what is opposed. And if we can understand what Hitler means by his description of Christianity, we can understand what he means by natural law, for that will be the contradictory (or something a bit like it, if Hitler's logic is loose) of the description of Christianity.

The first problem in Hitler's phrase about Christianity is what he means by "the human failure." If Cain were stronger than Abel, and could kill him in a fight, would that make Abel a failure? Yes, in one sense. He would be a failure in a fight with Cain. But he might be far less a failure than Cain in other things. Is anyone a failure altogether? It is hard to believe he can be. Yet is that what Hitler means: namely, a man who is a complete failure in everything? Perhaps, or perhaps he means what we colloquially call "*a* failure"—rather unthinkingly—a person who does not make a success at a job or profession, who does not earn a living, who perhaps stands on street corners and begs.

Clearly, Hitler has not said enough to give an adequate context for understanding the word "failure." On the day these words were recorded stenographically, he said no more on the subject. "A failure" at life in general, by and large, is a vague idea. Who is such a failure, and who isn't? Which of us has the temerity to call himself a success?

II

It is worth stopping our analysis to make clear that the difficulty we just found is vagueness. Words like "failure" need greater specification than words like "horse," as we shall see. When a word is used so that it is not clear what is meant, the sentence in which it is contained is vague; just as the sentence is vague when its structure makes the meaning misty.

Ambiguity is sometimes confused with vagueness. But a vague sentence is one whose meaning cannot be specified *at all,* and an ambiguous sentence is one which has more than one specifiable meaning, but no clear indication which meaning is intended. So "The king yet lives that Henry shall depose" is ambiguous. It has two meanings, and it is not clear which is intended. "The world is will," with no explanatory comment, is vague: we cannot state *one* clear meaning for it.

A few questions can show how the use of "failure," with no explanation of what is failed, makes a sentence vague. Can a man fail at a task he did not undertake? Can there be failure if one neither wanted nor tried to succeed? Does a man fail if he tries to fail? (This could be a paradox. Suppose every young man had to take a test to get into the army. Would those who tried to fail, and managed to, be successes or failures?)

III

We can probably still guess what Hitler means if we see how Christianity as "the systematic cultivation of the human failure" is opposed to "natural law." Surely Christianity cannot be thought of as "a rebellion against natural law" if natural law includes human equality, justice, and liberty, as eighteenth-century thinkers conceived it. But if "Christianity" here means chiefly (this is our guess, based on the word "failure") moral precepts like Love your neighbor, The meek shall inherit the earth, and If you are slapped on one cheek, turn the other, then it *is* "a protest against nature" if nature is thought of as opposed to these. "Nature red in fang and claw," the battleground of the struggle for survival, dog eat dog! Nature is thus conceived as a struggle to the death of all against all, and natural law as the survival of the fittest. That would be opposed to the Christianity of the Gospels. And surely Hitler, from what the world knows of him, worshipped strength and abhorred weakness. Failures, in his mind, would be the weak.

Then natural law would be Darwinism: the survival of the fittest. And, since Darwin was not talking of human society, but of animal species outside society, natural law as applied to man would be Social Darwinism, the belief that the principle of natural selection should be allowed to rule society as it rules nature. The opposite of "failure" is "success" and if Christianity cultivates "human failure" then presumably natural law favors "human success." What is a "success" in this sense? The fit, who survive.

IV

Here there is an immediate difficulty. We are told that the fittest survive. If we ask, "What are they fittest for?" the answer is, quite obviously, "For survival." But that begs the question. It means that whoever survives is called the fittest. And we know no more than when we started.

Suppose, though, one answered that the fittest for survival are the strongest. That sounds good, especially when said very quickly, but the evidence is all against it. The strongest beasts in the history of earth, except the whales, are now extinct. Where is the dinosaur? Where is Tyrannosaurus? And if one says that they were only strong in a brute, physical sense but not in a total sense, he returns to question-begging. For he would be implicitly defining "the fittest" as the "totally strongest" and defining "totally strongest" as "the fittest." Then any powerful creature that did not survive could be called "not totally strong" or, perhaps, not *really* strong (that misleading "really" again).

Further, if one thinks of the great predators (lions, tigers, leopards), they cannot survive if their prey does not survive, for they have nothing to eat. So the mighty lion survives *because* the weak deer survives. The size of the owl population depends, in fact, on the size of the mouse population. What sense, then, would it make to say that lions and owls survive because they are fierce and strong? Do mice survive because they are weak? Are we even helped by saying that it is "natural" for lions to catch and kill deer? It is equally natural for deer to get away.

If we take a different tack altogether and say that those creatures survive who are most adaptable, we have gone a little farther. But that means—and it is true—that the amoeba, an extraordinarily adaptable organism, outlasts mastodons and saber-tooth tigers. Yet, unless we are to beg the question again, it will be useless to call the amoeba "strong." The amoeba may be fittest for survival, but what else can it adapt itself to, how else can we call it strong? The amoeba can outlast the philosopher, but can it adapt to the study or the classroom? Remember that we are talking about Social Darwinism, not about animal species alone. Adaptability, rather than strength, may explain the physical survival of species or even of individuals. But in society "adaptability" may mean conformity to social values. And if a society greatly values the mystics, as many American Indian societies do, then adaptation is at its best when one becomes a mystic. If a society honors the sage, however weak or ill, he will survive if his health permits. What we have to adapt to in society depends on the social environment we, as a society, create, and the moral values we accept.

Hitler could still argue that whatever the combination of qualities, mental and physical, which ensure survival, those creatures that have them succeed, and the others fail. That seems unobjectionable. It is either analytic or a decision: This is how I propose to use the words "succeed" and "fail." But would he cling to that use? A simple argument should make him give it up.

There is one quality that aids survival enormously, and probably always has. That is the ability and willingness to co-operate. The most successful predators in the jungle are perhaps not the great cats, but the hunting dogs. They run in a pack, single out one creature from the herd of their prey, and pursue him. As the lead dogs get exhausted, they fall back, and others replace them. They continue this indefinitely, allowing the hunted creature no rest, until one dog closes merciless jaws on his throat. Then they all dine. Tiny ants, moving in a large army, are invincible. And defense, too, is best when co-operative.

When we discussed the Declaration of Independence, we argued that one cannot draw conclusions about human conduct from observing the conduct of other animals. That is true. But evidence is equally direct that among men as among animals, co-operation aids survival. An army is superior to a mob in fighting power, and not only when it is better armed. Would Hitler, in the face of what we have just said, maintain his use of "succeed" and "fail"? He scarcely could, for he would then have to admit that people can succeed by co-operating and fail by refusing to co-operate. And he could not admit that, after what he said, because co-operative groups of men usually do care for the aged, the infirm, and the weak, even for reasons of individual survival.

If you are a great warrior and hunter in a primitive tribe, you may suggest, thoughtlessly, that since the weak eat too much and move too slowly, they should be killed. But that principle, if adopted, would one day apply to you. You may not even have a number of years to wait; you might break a leg. Of course, you can regard your proposal as meaning a single action, not a principle to remain in effect after one slaughter. But if you think systematically, you will know that another brawny man might propose the same remedy when you are old. You had better have a principle in force, and an opposite one, so his proposal will not be accepted. The more you urge now that the aged and infirm be cared for, the safer you will be later.

Indeed, there may once have been many societies in which the aged and weak were killed, and some Eskimoes are found even today to behave this way, so bitter is their struggle against nature. There may be societies of the same kind in the future even if they can afford to care for the infirm, because they have accepted a belief like Hitler's. But unless the people are conditioned to an invincible stoicism or fanaticism, the fear of growing old or being sick might very well be great enough to being about desertion to more humane societies, or revolution, or inability to accomplish very much in the face of constant terrors. The formula for survival may thus bring destruction.

TERMS AND PRINCIPLES

1. *Vagueness:* Inexactness of meaning of a sentence, phrase, or word.
2. *Ambiguity:* Inexactness about which one of several clear meanings the sentence, phrase, or word actually has.
3. If a word or phrase has two or more possible meanings, and one or more of these meanings is vague, it is probably clearer to call the word or phrase vague rather than ambiguous.
4. Ambiguity is resolved by deciding which meaning to assign, or by making a separate statement for each meaning.
5. Vagueness is often the result of using ideas that have their meanings only in a relation to other ideas, without including a statement of that relation. So if we use a comparative form without specification, we are vague. "That hill is higher" makes sense only if we have been talking of another hill, or some object. Otherwise it is hopelessly vague.
6. Vagueness can be resolved by specifying the relations that have been omitted, or by qualifying a vague word or phrase.

EXERCISE

ADOLF HITLER

From *Hitler's Secret Conversations*
July 11, 1941

The heaviest blow that ever struck humanity was the coming of Christianity. Bolshevism is Christianity's illegitimate child. Both are inventions of the Jew. The deliberate lie in the matter of religion was introduced into the world by Christianity. Bolshevism practices a lie of the same nature, when it claims to bring liberty to men, whereas in reality it seeks only to enslave them. In the ancient world, the relations between men and gods were founded on an instinctive respect. It was a world enlightened by the idea of tolerance. Christianity was the first creed in the world to exterminate its adversaries in the name of love. Its key-note is intolerance.

SOME QUESTIONS

1. Why is Bolshevism Christianity's illegitimate child? Because the Jew invented both? Or because Bolshevism lies like Christianity? Or both?

2. "Both are inventions of the Jew." Does "inventions" imply deliberation or consciousness? Are there unconscious inventions? If the Jews invented Christianity, why didn't all Jews become Christians? Since so many Jews did not accept the new religion, can one say "the Jew" invented it? Or did the Jews invent Christianity because they wanted to be persecuted by the Christians? Is Hitler clear about what he is saying? Is the word "invention" vague?

3. In the ancient world, people of each nation were expected to have their own gods and their own religion; it was believed that other people's gods, like one's own, existed and cared for their worshippers. What does Hitler mean when he says "the relations between men and gods were founded on an instinctive respect"? That men respected the gods and the gods respected them? Or perhaps that men respected even other people's gods? Can we know what he means? If he means respect for other people's gods, is that an instance of being "enlightened by the idea of tolerance"? Or were people unconcerned, or ignorant, or respectful because of superstitious fear? Could Hitler mean something else?

Does "tolerance" of another religion mean, or at least include, not trying to destroy it? After all, it was common in the ancient world to destroy the shrines and relics of another religion, so that the gods who presided over them could not again help their now-defeated worshippers. Sometimes the captured shrines and statues were incorporated into one's own religion so that the hitherto alien gods would help out, too. Can this behavior be explained as "tolerance" in any sense? Is Hitler's use of "tolerance" vague, or ambiguous, or neither?

4. Consider the word "enlightened" in the phrase we have been analyzing. Isn't it a laudatory word? Doesn't it mean Hitler was in favor of what follows it? If so, he was devoted to what he calls "the idea of tolerance." At the time he said this, he had already closed the Catholic monasteries and convents in Germany, put Protestant ministers, like Niemoeller, in concentration camps, and was well on his

way to gas and burn six million Jews. What could he possibly mean? Could he be trying to keep all the "good" or honorific words for himself and his cause?

5. Is Hitler using emotion-laden words and phrases without any attempt to make his meaning clear? Does he use ambiguities which gain persuasive strength from having more than one meaning? Is "illegitimate" one of them? Can you pick out such words, phrases, and ambiguities?

EXERCISE

WILLIAM JAMES

From *Principles of Psychology*

I am often confronted by the necessity of standing by one of my empirical selves and relinquishing the rest. Not that I would not, if I could, be both handsome and fat and well dressed, and a great athlete, and make a million a year, be a wit, a bon-vivant, a lady-killer, as well as a philosopher; a philanthropist, statesman, warrior, and African explorer, as well as a "tone-poet" and saint. But the thing is simply impossible. The millionaire's work would run counter to the saint's; the bon-vivant and the philanthropist would trip each other up; the philosopher and the lady-killer could not well keep house in the same tenement of clay. Such different characters may conceivably at the outset of life be alike possible to a man. But to make any one of them actual, the rest must more or less be suppressed. So the seeker of his truest, strongest, deepest self must review the list carefully, and pick out the one on which to stake his salvation. All other selves thereupon become unreal, but the fortunes of this self are real. Its failures are real failures, its triumphs real triumphs, carrying shame and gladness with them . . . Our thought, incessantly deciding, among many things of a kind, which ones for it shall be realities, here chooses one of many possible selves or characters, and forthwith reckons it no shame to fail in any of those not adopted expressly as its own.

I, who for the time have staked my all on being a psychologist, am mortified if others know much more psychology than I. But I am contented to wallow in the grossest ignorance of Greek. My deficiencies there give me no sense of personal humiliation at all. Had I "pretensions" to be a linguist, it would have been just the reverse. So we have the paradox of a man shamed to death because he is only the second pugilist or the second oarsman in the world. That he is able to beat the whole population of the globe minus one is nothing; he has "pitted" himself to beat that one; and as long as he doesn't do that nothing else counts. He is to his own regard as if he were not, indeed he is not.

Yonder puny fellow, however, whom everyone can beat, suffers no chagrin about it, for he has long ago abandoned the attempt to "carry that line," as the merchants say, of self at all. With no attempt there can be no failure; with no failure no humiliation. So our self-feeling in this world depends entirely on what we back ourselves to be and do. It is determined by the ratio of our actualities to our supposed potentialities; a fraction of which our pretensions are the denominator and the numerator our success: thus,

$$\text{Self-esteem} = \frac{\text{Success}}{\text{Pretensions}}$$

Such a fraction may be increased as well by diminishing the denominator as by increasing the numerator. To give up pretensions is as blessed a relief as to get them gratified; and where disappointment is incessant and the struggle unending, this is what men will always do. The history of evangelical theology, with its conviction of sin, its self-despair, and its abandonment of salvation by works, is the deepest of possible examples, but we meet others in every walk of life. There is the strangest lightness about the heart when one's nothingness in a particular line is once accepted in good faith.

SOME QUESTIONS

1. Discuss James's use of "failure" in contrast to Hitler's. Is James vague, as Hitler was? Show how James did or did not relate "failure" to other ideas.

2. Explain why, in James's equation, "such a fraction may be

increased as well by diminishing the denominator as by increasing the numerator."

3. What instances are there in your own life that justify James's last sentence? What instances are there in which you should have followed his advice?

4. Look at James's second sentence. Does the word "fat" come as a bit of a shock? Can you explain why James used it here? (In case you think it relevant, James was quite thin.) Does it help to apply the principle of historical context?

EXERCISE

BERTRAND RUSSELL

From *Why Men Fight*

The essential merit of the State is that it prevents the internal use of force by private persons. Its essential demerits are that it promotes the external use of force, and that, by its great size, it makes each individual feel unimportant even in a democracy . . . The prevention of the sense of individual impotence cannot be achieved by a return to the small City State, which would be as reactionary as a return to the days before machinery. It must be achieved by a method which is in the direction of present tendencies. Such a method would be the increasing devolution of positive political initiative to bodies formed voluntarily for specific purposes, leaving the State rather in the position of a federal authority or a court arbitration. The State will then confine itself to insisting upon *some* settlement of rival interests: its only principle in deciding what is the right settlement will be an attempt to find the measures most acceptable, on the whole, to all the parties concerned. This is the direction in which democratic States naturally tend, except in so far as they are turned aside by war or the fear of war. So long as war remains a daily imminent danger, the State will remain a Moloch, sacrificing sometimes the life of the individual, and always his unfettered development, to the barren struggle for mastery in the competition with other States. In internal as in external affairs, the worst enemy of freedom is war.

OLIVER WENDELL HOLMES, JR.

From Memorial Day Speech
May 30, 1895

Who of us could endure a world, although cut up into five-acre lots and having no man upon it who was not well fed and well housed, without the divine folly of honor, without the senseless passion for knowledge outreaching the flaming bounds of the possible, without ideals the essence of which is that they never can be achieved? I do not know what is true. I do not know the meaning of the universe. But in the midst of doubt, in the collapse of creeds, there is one thing I do not doubt, that no man who lives in the same world with most of us can doubt, and that is that the faith is true and adorable which leads a soldier to throw away his life in obedience to a blindly accepted duty, in a cause which he little understands, in a plan of campaign of which he has no notion, under tactics of which he does not see the use.

SOME QUESTIONS

1. Who is essentially right about war—Bertrand Russell or Oliver Wendell Holmes?

2. "If Holmes is basically right, Russell is a rationalistic utopian." "If Russell is basically right, Holmes is a chauvinist and militarist." What do you think about those sentences?

3. Anatole France once said that to die for an ideal is to pay a high price for a conjecture. Does his comment apply to Holmes? Does Holmes imply dying for an ideal? If so, what ideal? If not, what does he ask one to die for?

4. Why, according to Russell, is war "the worst enemy of freedom"?

5. Should we be free to choose war, whether or not it is "the worst enemy of freedom"? That is, is it a limitation on our freedom if we are not allowed to go to war, even if we want to?

6. Holmes says, "I do not know what is true. I do not know the meaning of the universe." He goes on to say that, "in the collapse of creeds," he does know that it is right for "a soldier to throw away his life" for something he does not understand. Does Holmes presuppose

that if he did know what was true, and what the meaning of the universe was, he might not believe what he does about soldiers? Is his a faith in the absence of a larger faith, the faith of a man who has no other faith but knows he must make choices and live in this world?

7. Why does Holmes bring in the "passion for knowledge" and "ideals" that "never can be achieved"? Does he think that they are like the soldier's dedication to "a blindly accepted duty"? Do you think Holmes believes that if men were incapable of the soldier's dedication, they would be incapable of the other two? How far do you think all three are similar?

8. Do Russell and Holmes flatly contradict each other? If so, one of them must be right and one wrong. If they do not contradict each other, what can be said for and against each belief? Would it be possible somehow to reconcile the two? If so, how? After answering this question, read the next selection, by William James.

EXERCISE

WILLIAM JAMES

From "The Moral Equivalent of War"

Modern war is so expensive that we feel trade to be a better avenue to plunder; but modern man inherits all the innate pugnacity and all the love of glory of his ancestors. Showing war's irrationality and horror is of no effect upon him. The horrors make the fascination. War is the *strong* life; it is life *in extremis;* war-taxes are the only ones men never hesitate to pay, as the budgets of all nations show us.

Reflective apologists for war at the present day all take it religiously. It is a sort of sacrament. Its profits are to the vanquished as well as to the victor; and quite apart from any question of profit, it is an absolute good, we are told, for it is human nature at its highest dynamic. Its "horrors" are a cheap price to pay for rescue from the only alternative supposed, of a world of clerks and teachers, of co-education and zoophily, of "consumer's leagues" and "associated charities," of industrialism unlimited, and feminism unabashed. No scorn, no hardness, no valor any more! Fie upon such a cattleyard of a planet!

. . . pacifism makes no converts from the military party. The military party denies neither the bestiality nor the horror, nor the expense; it only says that these things tell but half the story. It only says that war is *worth* them; that, taking human nature as a whole, its wars are its best protection against its weaker and more cowardly self, and that mankind cannot *afford* to adopt a peace-economy.

Pacifists ought to enter more deeply into the aesthetical and ethical point of view of their opponents. . . . So long as antimilitarists propose no substitute for war's disciplinary function, no *moral equivalent* of war, analogous, as one might say, to the mechanical equivalent of heat, so long they fail to realize the full inwardness of the situation. And as a rule they do fail. The duties, penalties, and sanctions pictured in the utopias they paint are all too weak and tame to touch the military-minded. Tolstoi's pacifism is the only exception to this rule, for it is profoundly pessimistic as regards all this world's values, and makes the fear of the Lord furnish the moral spur provided elsewhere by the fear of the enemy. But our socialistic peace-advocates all believe absolutely in this world's values; and instead of the fear of the Lord and the fear of the enemy, the only fear they reckon with is the fear of poverty if one be lazy. This weakness pervades all the socialistic literature with which I am acquainted. . . . Meanwhile men at large still live as they always have lived, under a pain-and-fear economy—for those of us who live in an ease-economy are but an island in the stormy ocean—and the whole atmosphere of present-day utopian literature tastes mawkish and dishwatery to people who still keep a sense for life's more bitter flavors. It suggests, in truth, ubiquitous inferiority.

Having said thus much in preparation, I will now confess my own utopia. I devoutly believe in the reign of peace and in the gradual advent of some sort of socialistic equilibrium. The fatalistic view of the war-function is to me nonsense, for I know that war-making is due to definite motives and subject to prudential checks and reasonable criticisms, just like any other form of enterprise. And when whole nations are the armies, and the science of destruction vies in intellectual refinement with the sciences of production, I see that war becomes absurd and impossible from its own monstrosity. Extravagant ambitions will have to be replaced by reasonable claims, and nations must make common cause against them. I see no reason why all this should not apply to yellow as well as to white countries, and I look forward to a future when acts of war shall be formally outlawed as between civilized peoples.

All these beliefs of mine put me squarely into the antimilitarist party. But I do not believe that peace either ought to be or will be permanent on this globe, unless the states pacifically organized preserve some of the old elements of army-discipline. A permanently successful peace-economy cannot be a simple pleasure-economy. In the more or less socialistic future towards which mankind seems drifting we must still subject ourselves collectively to those severities which answer to our real position upon this only partly hospitable globe. We must make new energies and hardihood continue the manliness to which the military mind so faithfully clings. Martial virtues must be the enduring cement; intrepidity, contempt of softness, surrender of private interest, obedience to command, must still remain the rock upon which states are built—unless, indeed, we wish for dangerous reactions against commonwealths fit only for contempt, and liable to invite attack whenever a center of crystallization for military-minded enterprise gets formed anywhere in their neighborhood.

Let me illustrate my idea more concretely. There is nothing to make one indignant in the mere fact that life is hard, that men should toil and suffer pain. The planetary conditions once for all are such, and we can stand it. But that so many men, by mere accidents of birth and opportunity, should have a life of *nothing else* but toil and pain and hardness and inferiority imposed upon them, should have *no* vacation, while others natively no more deserving never get any taste of this campaigning life at all,—*this* is capable of arousing indignation in reflective minds. It may end by seeming shameful to all of us that some of us have nothing but campaigning, and others nothing but unmanly ease. If now—and this is my idea—

there were, instead of military conscription a conscription of the whole youthful population to form for a certain number of years a part of the army enlisted against *Nature,* the injustice would tend to be evened out, and numerous other goods to the commonwealth would follow. The military ideals of hardihood and discipline would be wrought into the growing fiber of the people; no one would remain blind as the luxurious classes now are blind, to man's relations to the globe he lives on, and to the permanently sour and hard foundations of his higher life. To coal and iron mines, to freight trains, to fishing fleets in December, to dish-washing, clothes-washing, and window-washing, to road-building, and tunnel-making, to foundries and stokeholes, and to the frames of sky-scrapers, would our gilded youths be drafted off, according to their choice, to get the childishness knocked out of them, and to come back into society with healthier sympathies and soberer ideas. They would have paid their blood-tax, done their own part in the immemorial human warfare against nature; they would tread the earth more proudly, the women would value them more highly, they would be better fathers and teachers of the following generation.

We should get toughness without callousness, authority with as little criminal cruelty as possible, and painful work done cheerily because the duty is temporary, and threatens not, as now, to degrade the whole remainder of one's life. I spoke of the "moral equivalent" of war. So far, war has been the only force that can discipline a whole community, and until an equivalent discipline is organized, I believe that war must have its way. But I have no serious doubt that the ordinary prides and shames of social man, once developed to a certain intensity, are capable of organizing such a moral equivalent as I have sketched, or some other just as effective for preserving manliness of type. It is but a question of time, of skillful propagandism, and of opinion-making men seizing historic opportunities.

The amount of alteration in public opinion which my utopia postulates is vastly less than the difference between the mentality of black warriors who pursued Stanley's party on the Congo with their cannibal war-cry of "Meat! Meat!" and that of the "general-staff" of any civilized nation. History has seen the latter interval bridged over; the former one can be bridged over much more easily.

SOME QUESTIONS

1. Does James reconcile the beliefs of Russell and Holmes in the preceding exercise? If so, how? If not, why not?

2. Why, according to James, is it of no effect to show the horror of war, and its senselessness? Would Holmes accept the answer?

3. James says that "reflective apologists for war" treat it as a religious sacrament. Does this suggest that most advocates of peace argue their case chiefly in non-religious and material terms? Of what kind of pacifist is this especially true? Of people like Bertrand Russell?

4. William Jennings Bryan once said: "I know of no real peace that can come in this world that will not be merely a larger manifestation of that inward peace that Christ came to bring to all who would have it. He was called the Prince of Peace." Does Bryan sound like the sort of pacifist referred to in question 3? Does he sound like a religious pacifist? Does he sound like a man who is religious and pacific, but who has little or nothing to say on the issues of war and peace? Did James mention a type of pacifist like Bryan?

5. What, essentially, does James mean by the phrase, "the moral equivalent of war"? Why must there be an equivalent at all? If there must be one, how can we be sure it will not, like war, be "the worst enemy of freedom"?

6. What of James's own proposal, the army against nature? Is it offered as an example of a moral equivalent of war, or as *the* moral equivalent of war? Do you think it could work? Do you think it needs to be part of a larger program? Is it on the wrong track altogether?

JOSÉ ORTEGA Y GASSET

From *The Revolt of the Masses*

Both Bolshevism and Fascism are two false dawns;* they do not bring the morning of a new day, but of some archaic day, spent over and over again: they are mere primitivism. And such will all

* [Note the confusion caused by bad writing—in this case, perhaps bad translating. Either "both" or "two" should be deleted. As it is, it sounds like four false dawns.]

movements be which fall into the stupidity of starting a boxing-match with some portion or other of the past, instead of proceeding to digest it. No doubt an advance must be made on the liberalism of the XIXth century. But this is precisely what cannot be done by any movement such as Fascism, which declares itself anti-liberal. Because it was that fact—the being anti-liberal or non-liberal—which constituted man previous to liberalism. And as the latter triumphed over its opposite, it will either repeat its victory time and again, or else everything—liberalism and anti-liberalism—will be annihilated in the destruction of Europe. There is an inexorable chronology of life. In it liberalism is posterior to anti-liberalism, or what comes to the same, is more vital than it, just as the gun is more of a weapon than the lance.

COMMENTARY

We will use this passage to make a few points, and will then ask some questions about it.

Bolshevism and Fascism, Ortega says, "are mere primitivism." Does Ortega mean that literally? He also says, "they do not bring the morning of a new day, but of some archaic day." If literal, the passage means that Bolshevism and Fascism return us to an earlier time, archaic and primitive, through which mankind has already lived.

But note the second sentence. Bolshevism and Fascism are among the movements that start a boxing-match with some portion or other of the past. Let us take "boxing-match" to mean, among other things, oppose, fight against. Bolshevism and Fascism can scarcely be fighting against that portion of the past to which they return us. So we will have to assume that they fight against some other portion of the past. But then Ortega would be saying that all movements which oppose some portion of the past other than primitivism, return us to primitivism. That sounds like nonsense.

Let us assume, sensibly then, that Ortega is writing figuratively, not literally. Bolshevism and Fascism bring a time that is like the archaic or primitive in some respect. They are movements which oppose some portion of the past. What, in particular, they oppose is liberalism. But surely the respect in which Bolshevism and Fascism are primitive cannot be that they oppose something in the past. Primitive and archaic peoples ordinarily cling to the past as they understand it, and try not to change.

Perhaps Ortega does not specify the respect in which Bolshevism and Fascism are primitive, but makes another point. In opposing liberalism, those movements implicitly adopt the attitudes of times before liberalism, which also opposed it, but in the sense of trying to keep it from coming into existence. Further, if liberalism has been the civilizing influence in western civilization and has had a very long history, of which nineteenth-century liberalism is only a special form, then the ages before the first liberal elements entered civilization were "archaic" or "primitive." It is these to which Bolshevism and Fascism return man, not in all their detail, but in the one respect in which they are all alike: opposition to and exclusion of liberalism.

II

The literary device that Ortega employs when he writes, "Bolshevism and Fascism . . . are mere primitivism" is metaphor. And metaphor is not just ornament but a necessary and vastly useful form of thought and expression.

As Ortega writes of "some archaic day," it is evident that we cannot live in it unless we can go backward in time, for it is an earlier time that he means. All we can do is reproduce some of its aspects in the present. What is the advantage of the way he puts it?

There are large contexts of thought (sometimes called "universes of discourse"),[1] in each of which a number of terms are meaningful that are literally meaningless in other contexts. Consider the physical universe—the world of matter, space, and time—as one such context. In talking about the things it contains, physical objects, we can say they have one location or another, they are larger and smaller than each other, to the right and the left, higher and lower. We can say that these things move or are at rest, that they move faster and slower, that they have direction.

Then consider another context: the world of emotions. We can say that the things in this context, our emotions, are static or changeable, are strong or feeble, controllable or uncontrollable. We can also say that they are happy or painful (and sometimes both at once), serene or troubled, steadfast or mercurial.

Now try to apply the words of one context to things in the other. Can you say that your love for your mother is to the right of your hatred of injustice, that your admiration for efficiency moves faster than your disdain of laziness? On the other hand, can you say that atoms are serene, but molecules are troubled, or that rocks are happy, but trees are in pain? Not if you want to make sense.

Some of the words meaningful in one of these contexts are also meaningful in the other. Emotions may change; so may physical objects. But few of the terms we choose are applicable, literally, in more than one context. And now, if we think of a third context, that of ideas, we see that several terms obviously apply to the things in it, our ideas, that do not apply literally to other contexts: true and false, for example.

We all know that a metaphor [2] is a comparison without the use of "like" or "as." In what way, then, is it metaphoric to speak of Bolshevism and Fascism as "mere primitivism"? It could be a way of saying that Bolshevism and Fascism are as antiliberal as primitivism.* That statement is a simile, but whenever you expand a metaphor you get a simile, which is a comparison using "like" or "as." Our real point, though, is that metaphors usually compare things in one universe of discourse to things in another. And to carry out this comparison, we may use terms that are *literally* meaningful only in Context A to apply *metaphorically* to things in Context B.

Instead of saying that I understand something, I may say that I grasp it or see it. Both are literally meaningless but metaphorically meaningful in the universe of ideas. If I say that the moon is serene, a word from the context of emotions, you know there are no storm clouds crossing it. What I refer to, in talking of ideas, as "point of view," or "perspective," is a metaphor that would be rendered more technically as "frame of reference," for *literally* it has nothing to do with vision.

What do such metaphors accomplish? They make clear a relation in one context by comparing it to a relation in another context. It is harder, for example, to write literally about ideas and emotions than about sensuous experience. So one can clarify a relation among ideas or emotions by showing its similarity to a relation among experienced objects. And sometimes we can explain relations among the latter by comparing them with relations among the former. It is as if we were solving for X in an equation like "A is to X as B is to C," where A, B, and C are known.

III

SOME QUESTIONS

1. Ortega says, "There is an inexorable chronology of life. In it liberalism is posterior to anti-liberalism . . . ." He also says that liberalism "will either repeat its victory time and again, or else every-

* Then "archaic" refers to the ages in the history of man that can be characterized as "primitive."

thing—liberalism and anti-liberalism—will be annihilated in the destruction of Europe." Can you reconcile these two statements or are they in flat contradiction?

2. What is the simile in Ortega's last sentence? Restate the sentence so the simile becomes a metaphor.

3. Explain what Ortega means when he says that it comes to the same thing to call liberalism posterior to antiliberalism or more vital than it. Does this idea presuppose a theory that in history if B succeeds A, B is "more vital" than A?

4. How good is the image of a boxing-match as illustrative of Ortega's meaning? In a boxing-match, one's opponent hits back. Does a portion of the past in any way hit back at some present movements?

5. Note the phrase, "proceeding to digest it." Is "digest" better for Ortega's meaning than "devour" would be?

TERMS AND PRINCIPLES

1. *Universe of discourse:* A context that includes everything meant by a given term and its contradictory. So the universe of color is the context including everything meant by "red" and "non-red" (which amounts to all colors). A universe of discourse contains some terms that are literally applicable only to the things in that context. The term "criminal" for example, applies literally to actions only in a legal and political context; "sin" in a religious and moral one.

2. *Metaphor:* Usually understood as a comparison without the use of "like" or "as," it normally applies terms from one context to things in another. This clarifies the meaning of relationships.

OLIVER WENDELL HOLMES, JR.

From *Collected Legal Papers*

Certitude is not the test of certainty. We have been cocksure of many things that were not so. . . . property, friendship, and truth have a common root in time. One cannot be wrenched from the rocky crevices into which one has grown for many years without feeling that one is attacked in one's life. What we most love and revere generally is determined by early associations. I love granite rocks and barberry bushes, no doubt because with them were my earliest joys that reach back through the past eternity of my life. But while one's experience thus makes certain preferences dogmatic for oneself, recognition of how they came to be so leaves one able to see that others, poor souls, may be equally dogmatic about something else. And this . . . means scepticism. Not that one's belief or love does not remain. Not that we would not fight and die for it if important—we all, whether we know it or not, are fighting to make the kind of a world that we should like—but that we have learned to recognize that others will fight and die to make a different world, with equal sincerity or belief. Deep-seated preferences cannot be argued about—you cannot argue a man into liking a glass of beer—and therefore, when differences are sufficiently far-reaching, we try to kill the other man rather than let him have his way. But that is perfectly consistent with admitting that, so far as appears, his grounds are just as good as ours.

COMMENTARY

I

Why isn't "certitude" the test of "certainty"? Holmes's second sentence makes it clear what difference Holmes ascribes to the two words. We often *feel* sure (certitude) of things that aren't so (not certain, indeed not true). "Certitude" is psychological; "certainty" logical. And our feelings are no test of certainty.

Holmes, of course, is right. But we can go a step farther, to get the principle straight.* Logical certainty can be attributed to analytic statements alone; empirical statements are only probable. Analytic statements are true only because of their meanings. They yield no new truth, and no truth about fact. We call them formal truth as distinct from empirical truth. But we are often startled by a purely analytic conclusion, like one in plane geometry, which says something we didn't know. And if we didn't know it, isn't it a new truth? It is new, to be sure, but only *psychologically. Logically,* the truth was al-

---

* This follows directly from the treatment of analytic and empirical propositions in our discussion of the Declaration of Independence.

ready contained in the premises. It is just that we didn't recognize it until it was restated in the conclusion. So we can distinguish between psychological novelty and logical novelty, as we just distinguished between psychological assurance and logical certainty.

Psychological assurance doesn't guarantee logical certainty. Does it guarantee empirical truth, which is about fact, and may be logically novel? Of course not. We feel sure of many statements about fact that turn out to be false. So our principle becomes: *psychological assurance is not a test of truth.* Only evidence or analysis is, and which of the two is the test depends on the kind of proposition we are testing, empirical or analytic.

II

Now for Holmes's third sentence: how do property, friendship, and truth have "a common root in time"? Holmes's examples indicate that our feelings about love and reverence depend on our associations, especially early ones. That may be so, and it constitutes an analogy among them. But Holmes points out that other people have their preferences, too, and on grounds as good as ours. Is he right? Or are some things more lovable than others? How can we find out whether anything is lovable at all? Let us pursue the question briefly.

Is there an analogy between finding something lovable and finding something true? In one respect, there is. If you hold a belief that is actually false, you *ought* to give it up. And if you value (to use a larger term than "love," and a more technical one) something that is valueless perhaps you *ought* to give *it* up. If a woman loves a man who turns out to be entirely different from what she thought him, and is most unlovable indeed, it is a misfortune for her if she cannot change her feelings. If a man values self-sufficiency enough to remain a bachelor, and then finds it makes him miserable, he should marry (and, of course, change his value).

What has just been said *presupposes* a connection between valuing and knowing such that learning something new and different about what one values would make him alter his evaluation. Indeed, many people are capable of changing their minds in this way, and all of us do it to some extent. But changing one's mind is not the same as changing one's heart. Here is the important distinction. *Valuing* something may be the same as loving it. But *thinking it valuable* is not. If I find something valuable, I have a belief about it: I think it good. But I may not love it. I may even dislike it. I may think a life of hard labor is good, and still hate to work.

So emotions and reflective values (those we find valuable) do not always go hand in hand. Perhaps they would in an ideally rational man. But if so, our ideal of a rational man, as implied in the last sentence, does not necessarily include his having a better mind than others, but rather controlling his emotions better, so that they accord with rational decision. Still, in a larger sense, it may be unreasonable to be rational in that way. As Santayana put it, "It is not wisdom always to be wise."

But it is often important to follow the head, not the heart. If a young man loves and is about to propose marriage to a beautiful and fascinating girl, and then learns that she is greedy, untruthful, and dishonest, what shall he do? Well, his evaluation of her has changed because of what he learned. Have his feelings changed? Is he still breathless and excited when he sees her? Is she as fascinating as ever? It may be. And it would be folly to say he should not love her, as though that were only a matter of decision. But it would also be folly to say that he should marry her, for that *is* a matter of decision.

We cannot legislate, even for ourselves, about feelings. We can and must legislate about actions. New knowledge can, and should, change our judgments. To a considerable extent (but not entirely), our judgments should guide our conduct. But they have far less to do with emotions than with conduct. Our presupposition was more or less right about thought, but not about feeling.

So we must qualify Holmes's analogy, although we need blame him for nothing, since we do not know how far he would go with it. There is "a common root in time" for property (but surely personal and intimate things chiefly, not so much stocks and bonds), friendship, and belief (what we think is true, rather than what is actually true). And there is also an analogy among our intellectual evaluations (of property, friendship, and all else), for new knowledge ought to affect them all. But there is often less of an analogy between our love of things (our "values" in one sense), and our intellectual decision that they are lovable, or ought to be pursued, or are good (our evaluations, or "values" in another sense).

What about the last two sentences in the quotation? "Deep-seated preferences cannot be argued about." Is the example of liking beer a good one? Yes, because Holmes is not talking about what is valuable, but about what we like or, in fact, value. Yet it is perhaps not so good an example as it might be. Is a taste for beer a "deep-seated" preference? Would we fight and die for it? That is extremely doubtful. So Holmes is perhaps offering it as a metaphor, not as an example. Expanded into a simile, it says: "Deep-seated preferences cannot be argued about, as a taste for beer cannot be argued about."

". . . when differences are sufficiently far-reaching, we try to kill the other man rather than let him have his way." It is because reason is inapplicable, and we cannot argue about our preferences, that there is nothing left to do but fight. Of course, there are two other obvious possibilities he does not mention (and one less obvious, with which we shall conclude): we may surrender, or we may tolerate each other. What would tolerance mean here? You like whatever you like, and I will not bother you; in return you allow me my preferences. Why not tolerance rather than fighting? The answer is that tolerance can work *if* what I tolerate in you doesn't interfere with what I expect you to tolerate in me. But if you love command and I love freedom, we cannot tolerate each other, for you will want me to obey your orders, and I will want to make my own decisions. This interference is what Holmes has in mind, for he speaks of a world "that we should like," and that involves other people. So if we get a world that I should like, you are still free, for I believe in freedom, but if we get your sort of world, I am enslaved. Even this statement needs a qualification in order to be true. My love of freedom must be a love for a world that is free, for if it is only a love of my own freedom, I may try to enslave you.

There remains the possibility of surrender. Holmes believes that we are all, "whether we know it or not," fighting for the kind of world we want, and that does away, in his mind, with the possibility of surrender. But are we all willing literally to fight, to the death if need be? What about pacifists and cowards? One might say that even they will fight if a preference is at stake that is deep-seated enough. How deep-seated is "deep-seated enough"? Or, put differently, what is the meaning of "enough" in that sentence? We must ask, enough for what? And the only answer can be, enough so that we will fight. And that is question-begging, for we have assumed the truth of the statement that there are some preferences for which any man will fight, while the question itself was *whether* there are.

Either we decide, then, that Holmes is talking of most men, not all men, or we do not construe the word "fight" literally. Both alternatives make perfect sense of what he is saying, but the latter is probably correct. Pacifists are often willing to die so that they will not have to kill others. And that is a "fight" for peace. Cowards are rarely so cowardly that nothing makes them fight. And they may act bravely out of an excess of fear; every general knows that about his troops. There is still another cowardly response. Guy de Maupassant wrote a revealing story called "The Coward," in which a man was so afraid of his opponent's pistol in a duel, that he shot himself. Thus cowards often bring about what they fear.

The less obvious possibility in interpreting Holmes is a conclusion from our earlier discussion. Holmes's final statement removes
preference from reason and argument. And in our analysis, we have
agreed with him. What *is* subject to reason and argument? Questions
of truth and questions of value. Here the rational man, as we described
him before, is of service to humanity, for he allows himself to love
only what is valuable. Then, when there is a clash of "preferences,"
he can argue the point, because he gives up his preference and
adopts what he thinks ought to be valued. He need not admit that
his opponent's grounds are just as good as his. Nor need he fight, or
surrender—although he might still tolerate. Of course, this will do
no good unless his opponent, too, is a rational man, and the heart
sinks at the improbability of two rational men at once.

A final point. Even for those of us who are not rational men,
whose preferences are not what we think valuable, it is not *literally*
true that other people's grounds are as good as ours. There are no
grounds at all—in the sense of evidence or argument—for anyone's
preferences. That is perhaps what Holmes means. Other "grounds"
are as good as yours, or as bad as yours, in that they are only
emotional or biographical, but they are not grounds for proof.

TERMS AND PRINCIPLES

1. *Psychological novelty in ideas:* Discovery of the meaning of
   a conclusion that was already contained in its premises, but
   not recognized.
2. *Logical novelty in ideas:* Meaning in a statement that was
   not contained in immediately prior statements or arguments.
3. Analytic statements are certain because they are tautological.
   But they give no new knowledge, and no knowledge about
   fact.
4. Empirical statements can only be probable. But they do give
   new knowledge, and knowledge about fact.

EXERCISE

BLAISE PASCAL

From *Thoughts*

. . . "God is, or He is not." But to which side shall we incline?
Reason can decide nothing here. There is an infinite chaos which

separates us. A game is being played at the extremity of this infinite distance where heads or tails will turn up. What will you wager? According to reason, you can do neither the one thing nor the other; according to reason, you can defend neither of the propositions.

Do not then reprove for error those who have made a choice; for you know nothing about it. "No, but I blame them for having made, not this choice, but a choice; for again both he who chooses heads and he who chooses tails are equally at fault, they are both in the wrong. The true course is not to wager at all."

—Yes; but you must wager. It is not optional. You are embarked. Which will you choose then? Let us see. Since you must choose, let us see which interests you least. You have two things to lose, the true and the good; and two things to stake, your reason and your will, your knowledge and your happiness; and your nature has two things to shun, error and misery. Your reason is no more shocked in choosing one rather than the other, since you must of necessity choose. This is one point settled. But your happiness? Let us weigh the gain and the loss in wagering that God is. Let us estimate these two chances. If you gain, you will gain all; if you lose, you lose nothing. Wager then without hesitation that He is.

SOME QUESTIONS

Note that this is a dialogue. Pascal is arguing with an imaginary antagonist, who may be within himself. The antagonist's words are in quotation marks.

1. Our argument in discussing the Holmes selection was that reason and evidence were logically relevant to truth and value, but not to emotions. On the question whether God is, or is not, Pascal says "Reason can decide nothing here." Is that because it is a matter of emotion, a predilection for God's existence or non-existence? Or is it something entirely different, namely, that though this is a question of truth, man cannot arrive at decisive proof? How can you justify your choice between these two possibilities, by using Pascal's text?

The antagonist says: ". . . he who chooses heads and he who chooses tails are equally at fault, they are both in the wrong." What can he mean by saying ". . . they are both in the wrong"? If I toss a coin and you call "heads," are you more likely to be right than if you had called "tails"? No; the probability of either is the same, exactly 50 per cent. You are wrong to wager, *except as a sheer gamble,* because there is no more *reason* for the coin to fall heads than tails. Does that help you decide Pascal's meaning?

2. Why, in the first place, *must* you wager? And what does it mean, in terms of belief in God's existence, *not* to wager? Does it mean you are an agnostic, one who neither accepts nor denies God's existence? If so, Pascal must be arguing that you cannot be an agnostic. Since you must wager, saying God exists or God does not exist, you must be either a believer or an atheist. Or does Pascal, when he says you *must* wager, mean "ought to"? If so, would he prefer that you be an atheist rather than an agnostic? Yet is that a necessary conclusion? Does he prefer, perhaps, that you decide for or against God's existence, because then you might choose His existence? As a mathematician, is he perhaps thinking that if all agnostics were to choose, there is a high probability that *some*— perhaps half, in the absence of evidence—would choose for God? Thus, for a devout man like Pascal, many souls would be saved.

If, however, Pascal does not mean "ought to" by "must," and you must wager, in the sense of "have to," it would imply that, in fact, it is impossible for you to be an agnostic. Yet Pascal must have known that there were agnostics. Indeed, his antagonist in this debate is one. What else, then, can he mean? Does he believe, perhaps, that an agnostic is actually an atheist? How could he believe that? Well, he could, if he presupposed, for example, that if you do not accept God's existence, you have rejected God, for you have rejected His love and His grace. The agnostic, who is not affirmative about God's existence, hence cuts himself off from God, with all that that implies. What good does it do, then, for him to say that he has not rejected God but merely refused to accept Him? Might not Pascal, if he has such a presupposition, argue that acceptance and rejection of God are contradictories; therefore, one or the other must be chosen, for there are no other alternatives possible?

Note that the antagonist does not take the usual agnostic position, which is to choose neither acceptance nor rejection, but doubt. He wants to refuse to wager, or choose, perhaps because he, too, admits that there are only two possible choices. Then, if our last suggestion is correct, Pascal is urging that to reject choice is to choose rejection.

Which of the two alternatives, based on the meaning of "must," do you accept? Can Pascal have meant both, or do they exclude each other? If you accept neither, can you offer another possibility?

3. "If you gain, you will gain all; if you lose, you lose nothing." Let us list the implied possibilities of choice, truth, and gain. (1) If

you choose God's existence and are right, you gain eternal life. (2) If you choose God's existence and are wrong, you gain and lose nothing. (3) If you reject God's existence and are right, you gain and lose nothing. (4) If you reject God's existence and are wrong, you lose eternal life.

Would you agree with Pascal about the consequences of each in terms of gain and loss? The first seems to be a true statement, at least within some religions. But is it true that you gain and lose as stipulated in the other three choices? If (2) you choose God's existence, you may go to church, keep certain observances, pray, and meditate. What time you have lost, to speak of nothing else, if you are wrong! If (3) you reject God's existence correctly, you have gained truth, saved time, kept yourself from folly and what would, if you are right, be superstition. Do you agree with this? And if you acccpt the first as a true statement, would you have to accept the fourth as true, too?

4. Is it possible that when Pascal says, "If you lose, you lose nothing," he is contrasting "nothing" with "all" in the first part of the sentence? "All" probably means, or includes, salvation. And compared with salvation, whatever you might lose—like time wasted or superstition accepted—is nothing. Is this a likely interpretation?

5. Suppose you choose God's existence on the basis of Pascal's argument. You have chosen as you did because of a careful weighing of personal advantage. Pascal apparently thinks that is a good thing to do, but would God (as ordinarily conceived in Christian thought) think so? List all the points in favor of your answer.

6. Would Pascal agree with Holmes that "certitude is not the test of certainty"?

EXERCISE

THOMAS JEFFERSON

From Letter to John Adams
October 28, 1813

. . . . I agree with you that there is a natural aristocracy among men. The grounds of this are virtue and talents. Formerly, bodily powers gave place among the aristoi. But since the invention of gunpowder has armed the weak as well as the strong with missile death, bodily strength, like beauty, good humor, politeness and other accomplishments, has become but an auxiliary ground of distinction. There is also an artificial aristocracy, founded on wealth and birth, without either virtue or talents; for with these it would belong to the first class. The natural aristocracy I consider as the most precious gift of nature, for the instruction, the trusts, and government of society. And indeed, it would have been inconsistent in creation to have formed man for the social state, and not to have provided virtue and wisdom enough to manage the concerns of the society. May we not even say, that that form of government is the best, which provides the most effectually for a pure selection of these natural aristoi into the offices of government?

The artificial aristocracy is a mischievous ingredient in government, and provision should be made to prevent its ascendancy. On the question, what is the best provision, you and I differ; but we differ as rational friends, using the free exercise of our own reason, and mutually indulging its errors. You think it best to put the pseudo-aristoi into a separate chamber of legislation, where they may be hindered from doing mischief by their co-ordinate branches, and where, also, they may be a protection to wealth against the agrarian and plundering enterprises of the majority of the people. I think that to give them power on order to prevent them from doing mischief, is arming them for it, and increasing instead of remedying the evil. For if the co-ordinate branches can arrest their action, so may they that of the co-ordinates. Mischief may be done negatively as well as positively. Of this, a cabal in the Senate of the United States has furnished many proofs. Nor do I believe them necessary to protect the wealthy; because enough of these will find their way into every branch of the legislation, to protect themselves. From fifteen to twenty legislatures of our own, in action for thirty years past, have proved that no fears of an equalization of property are to be apprehended from them. I think the best remedy is exactly that provided by all our constitutions, to leave to the citizens the free election and separation of the aristoi from the pseudo-aristoi, of the wheat from the chaff. In general they will elect the really good and wise. In some instances, wealth may corrupt, and birth blind them; but not in sufficient degree to endanger the society.

It is probable that our difference of opinion may, in some measure, be produced by a difference of character in those among whom
we live. From what I have seen of Massachusetts and Connecticut
myself, and still more from what I have heard, and the character
given of the former by yourself, who know them so much better, there
seems to be in those two states a traditionary reverence for certain
families, which has rendered the offices of the government nearly
hereditary in those families. I presume that from an early period
of your history, members of those families happening to possess
virtue and talents, have honestly exercised them for the good of the
people, and by their services have endeared their names to them. In
coupling Connecticut with you, I mean it politically only, not morally.
For having made the Bible the common law of their land, they seemed
to have modeled their morality on the story of Jacob and Laban.
But although this hereditary succession to office with you, may, in
some degree, be founded in real family merit, yet in a much higher
degree, it has proceeded from your strict alliance of Church and
State. These families are canonised in the eyes of the people on
common principles, "you tickle me, and I will tickle you." In Vir-
ginia we have nothing of this. Our clergy before the Revolution,
having been secured against rivalship by fixed salaries, did not give
themselves the trouble of acquiring influence over the people. Of
wealth, there were great accumulations in particular families, handed
down from generation to generation, under the English law of entails.
But the only object of ambition for the wealthy was a seat in the
King's Council. All their court then was paid to the crown and its
creatures; and they Philipised in all collisions between the King and
the people. Hence they were unpopular; and that unpopularity continues attached to their names. A Randolph, a Carter, or a Burwell
must have great personal superiority over a common competitor to be
elected by the people even at this day.

At the first session of our legislature after the Declaration of
Independence, we passed a law abolishing the privilege of
primogeniture, and dividing the lands of intestates equally among all
their children, or other representatives. These laws, drawn by myself, laid the axe to the foot of pseudo-aristocracy. And had an-

other which I prepared been adopted by the legislature, our work would have been complete. It was a bill for the more general diffusion of learning. This proposed to divide every county into wards of five or six miles square, like your townships; to establish in each ward a free school for reading, writing, and common arithmetic; to provide for the annual selection of the best subjects from these schools, who might receive, at the public expense, a higher degree of education at a district school; and from these district schools to select a certain number of the most promising subjects, to be completed at an University, where all the most useful sciences should be taught. Worth and genius would thus have been sought out from every condition of life, and completely prepared by education for defeating the competition of wealth and birth for public trusts. My proposition had, for a further object, to impart to these wards those portions of self-government for which they are best qualified, by confiding to them the care of their poor, their roads, police, elections, the nomination of jurors, administration of justice in small cases, elementary exercises of militia; in short, to have made them little republics, with a warden at the head of each, for all those concerns which, being under their eye, they would better manage than the larger republics of the county or state. A general call of ward meetings by their wardens on the same day through the state, would at any time produce the genuine sense of the people on any required point, and would enable the state to act in mass, as your people have so often done, and with so much effect by their town meetings. The law for religious freedom, which made a part of this system, having put down the aristocracy of the clergy, and restored to the citizen the freedom of the mind, and those of entails and descents nurturing an equality of condition among them, this on education would have raised the mass of the people to the high ground of moral respectability necessary to their own safety, and to orderly government, to the exclusion of the pseudalists.

I have thus stated my opinion on a point on which we differ, not with a view to controversy, for we are both too old to change opinions which are the result of a long life of inquiry and reflection; but on the suggestions of a former letter of yours, that we ought not to die before we have explained ourselves to each other. We acted in perfect harmony, through a long and perilous contest for our liberty and independence. A constitution has been acquired, which, though neither of us thinks perfect, yet both consider as competent to render our fellow citizens the happiest and the securest on whom the sun has ever shone. If we do not think exactly alike as to its imperfections, it matters little to our country, which after devoting to it long lives of disinterested labor, we have delivered over to our successors in life, who will be able to take care of it and of themselves.

JOHN ADAMS

Letter to Thomas Jefferson
November 15, 1813

. . . though we are agreed in one point, in words, it is not yet certain that we are perfectly agreed in sense. Fashion has introduced an indeterminate use of the word talents. Education, wealth, strength, beauty, stature, birth, marriage, graceful attitudes and motions, gait, air, complexion, physiognomy, are talents, as well as genius, science, and learning. Any one of these talents that in fact commands or influences two votes in society gives to the man who possesses it the character of an aristocrat, in my sense of the word. Pick up the first hundred men you meet, and make a republic. Every man will have an equal vote; but when deliberations and discussions are opened, it will be found that twenty-five, by their talents, virtues being equal, will be able to carry fifty votes. Every one of these twenty-five is an aristocrat in my sense of the word; whether he obtains one vote in addition to his own, by his birth, fortune, figure, eloquence, science, learning, craft, cunning, or even his character for good fellowship, and a *bon vivant*.

What gave Sir William Wallace his amazing aristocratical superiority? His strength. What gave Mrs. Clarke her aristocratical influence—to create generals, admirals and bishops? Her beauty. What gave Pompadour and DuBarry the power of making cardinals and popes? And I have lived for years in the Hotel de Valentinois, with Franklin, who had as many virtues as any of them. In the investigation of the meaning of the word "talents," I could write 630 pages as pertinent as John Taylor's of Hazlewood; but I will select a single example; for female aristocrats are nearly as formidable as males. A daughter of a greengrocer walks the streets in London daily, with a basket of cabbage sprouts, dandelions, and spinach, on her head. She is observed by the painters to have a beautiful face, an elegant figure, a graceful step, and a *debonair*. They hire her to sit. She complies, and is painted by forty artists in a circle around her. The scientific Dr. William Hamilton outbids the painters, sends her to school for a genteel education, and marries her. This lady not only causes the triumphs of the Nile, Copenhagen, and Trafalgar, but separates Naples from France, and finally banishes the king and queen from Sicily. Such is the aristocracy of the natural talent of beauty. Millions of examples might be quoted from history, sacred and profane, from Eve, Hannah, Deborah, Susanna, Abigail, Judith, Ruth, down to Helen, Mrs. de Mainbenor, and Mrs. Fitzherbert. For mercy's sake do not compel me to look to our chaste States and territories to find women, one of whom let go would in the words of Holophernes's guards, deceive the whole earth. . . .

. . . Your distinction between natural and artificial aristocracy, does not appear to me founded. Birth and wealth are conferred upon some men as imperiously by nature as genius, strength, or beauty. The heir to honors, and riches, and power, has often no more merit in procuring these advantages than he has in obtaining a handsome face, or an elegant figure. When aristocracies are established by human laws, and honor, wealth and power are made hereditary by municipal laws and political institutions, then I acknowledge artificial aristocracy to commence; but this never commences till corruption in elections become dominant and uncontrollable. But this artificial aristocracy can never last. The everlasting envies, jealousies, rivalries, and quarrels among them; their cruel rapacity among the poor, ignorant people, their followers, compel them to set up Caesar, a demagogue, to be a monarch, a master; *pour mettre chacun à sa place*.* Here you have the origin of all artificial aristocracy, which is the origin of all monarchies. And both artificial aristocracy and

* [In order to put every one in his place.]

monarchy, and civil, military, political, and hierarchical despotism, have grown out of the natural aristocracy of virtues and talents. . . .

SOME QUESTIONS

1. Do Jefferson and Adams agree on the definition of "natural aristocracy"? What does Adams mean by saying that he and Jefferson are agreed in "words," but perhaps not perfectly agreed in "sense"? If they do not agree, what is the difference between their definitions? Do both equally observe the rules for definition?

2. Adams rejects Jefferson's distinction between natural and artifical aristocracies, saying that birth and wealth (part of Jefferson's criteria for artificial aristocracy) are as natural as genius or beauty. The man who writes great poetry, one might say, has a native gift, and is no more responsible for his genius than a man born to great wealth is responsible for his fortune. Does this argument refute Jefferson's distinction. Is it relevant?

3. Adams does admit the existence of artificial aristocracy when such things as wealth and power "are made hereditary by municipal laws and public institutions." Is this different from Jefferson's idea? Is any one born to wealth and power except by human laws? Is anyone born to genius and beauty except by nature? Can wealth and power belong to any man at birth through nature alone? Can genius and beauty be conferred by society?

4. Is Adams right that artificial aristocracy has grown out of natural aristocracy? And what does he mean? Is the first artificial aristocrat in any family line also a natural aristocrat? If so, does it make any difference that he was a natural aristocrat when we consider his descendants, who inherit his artificial titles, wealth, and power?

5. Is Jefferson using "natural" and "artificial" as a distinction that might be made in the Declaration of Independence?

6. If the natural aristocrat is elected to high office, as Jefferson hoped, is he likely, by virtue of his greater talents, to exploit the citizenry more than an ordinary man in the same position would?

7. What are the advantages, in Jefferson's opinion, of the free public education he wanted to offer, and of his system of scholarships? Does he expect too much of education?

8. Consider the first sentence in Jefferson's second paragraph. Is being "without either virtue or talents" a necessary condition for the artificial aristocracy? Does Jefferson imply that all men of wealth and birth are without virtue and talent? Does he imply that some men belong to both aristocracies?

monarchy, and civil, military, political, and hierarchical despotism,

🎵 *Section Four*

Literary Criticism

> I took them [the poets] some of the most elaborate passages in their own writings, and asked what was the meaning of them—thinking that they would teach me something. Will you believe me? I am almost ashamed to confess the truth, but I must say that there is hardly a person present who would not have talked better about their poetry than they did themselves. Then I knew that not by wisdom do poets write poetry, but by a sort of genius and inspiration . . .
>
> Socrates speaking in Plato's *Apology*

> You describe the poet as a great and wonderful man whose feet are on the ground, while his head disappears in the clouds. Of course, that is a perfectly ordinary image drawn within the intellectual framework of lower-middle-class convention. It is an illusion based on wish fulfillment, which has nothing in common with reality. In fact, the poet is always much smaller and weaker than the social average. Therefore he feels the burden of earthly existence much more intensely and strongly than other men. For him personally his song is only a scream.
>
> Franz Kafka speaking in Janouch's
> *Conversations with Kafka*

This section is a conclusion to Part I of this book, and a transition to Part II. We have so far concerned ourselves with exposition—to use that name for all prose that is not imaginative literature. And we still do, in that our texts here are expository. But their *subject* is the nature of art, and of literature as art. So we not only proceed with our analysis of exposition, but we discover differences between the principles of logical analysis and those of literary criticism. Indeed, we discuss some of the more general and pervasive principles of criticism, in preparation for Part II.

In this section, Santayana is making a general point about literature, writing half as philosopher, half as critic. Henry James is introducing a book of stories by revealing how he works as an artist. Ransom writes as a literary critic. And, in their exchange of letters, George Sand and Gustave Flaubert explain two views of art. The views are profoundly different and reflect—perhaps influence—opposed temperaments. Yet, on the human level, it is important to note that Sand and Flaubert loved each other with remarkable devotion (despite her male pseudonym, George Sand was a woman—and a lady), and each did all in his power to help the other's career.

Our procedure here differs from that of the earlier sections in two respects. We do not call attention as explicitly as before to the principles of analysis we employ. And we attend more to the relationships of the parts to the whole in an argument or statement. At this point, the reader can fill in anything we leave out.

GEORGE SANTAYANA

From "Tragic Philosophy"

In comparing a passage from *Macbeth* with one from the *Paradiso*, Mr. T. S. Eliot tells us that poetically the two are equally good, but that the philosophy in Shakespeare is inferior. By what standard, I am tempted to ask, may the poetic value of different types of poetry in different languages be declared equal? By the equal satisfaction, perhaps, that fills the critic's mind? But the total allegiance of a mature person, his total joy in anything, can hardly be independent of his developed conscience and his sense for ultimate realities. He cannot be utterly enchanted by what he feels to be trivial or false. And if he is not utterly enchanted, how should he recognize the presence of the supremely beautiful? Two passages could hardly be pronounced equal in poetic force if the ultimate suggestions of the one were felt to be inferior to those of the other.

Admitting, then, that poetry expressing an inferior philosophy would to that extent be inferior poetry, we may ask this further question: in what respect other than truth may philosophies be called inferior or superior? Perhaps in being more or less poetical or religious, more or less inspired? Sometimes a philosopher may spring up imaginatively, and in that sense may be inspired rather than strictly reasoned or observed, as the myths of Plato are inspired; but nobody would call such inspired philosophy *superior* unless he felt it to spring from the total needs and total wisdom of the heart; and in that case he would certainly believe, or at least hope, that this superior philosophy was true. How, then, should the poetic expression of this inspired philosophy not be conspicuously superior as poetry, and more utterly enchanting, than the expression of any other philosophy?

Let me postpone generalities and turn to the passages in question.

Lady Macbeth is dead. Macbeth foresees his own end. All the prophecies flattering his ambition have been fulfilled, and after the mounting horror of his triumph he stands at the brink of ruin. Surveying the whole in a supreme moment, he consents to his destiny:

> Tomorrow, and tomorrow, and tomorrow
> Creeps in this petty pace from day to day
> To the last syllable of recorded time;
> And all our yesterdays have lighted fools
> The way to dusty death. Out, out, brief candle!
> Life's but a walking shadow; a poor player
> That struts and frets his hour upon the stage,
> And then is heard no more. It is a tale
> Told by an idiot, full of sound and fury,
> Signifying nothing.

Mr. Eliot says that this philosophy is derived from Seneca; and it is certain that in Seneca's tragedies, if not in his treatises, there is a

pomp of diction, a violence of pose, and suicidal despair not unlike
the tone of this passage. But would Seneca ever have said that life
signifies nothing? It signified for him the universal reign of law, of
reason, of the will of God. Fate was inhuman, it was cruel, it excited
and crushed every finite wish; yet there was something in man that
shared that disdain for humanity, and triumphed in that ruthless
march of order and necessity. Something superior, not inferior,
Seneca would have said; something that not only raised the mind
into sympathy with the truth of nature and the decrees of heaven, but
that taught the blackest tragedy to sing in verse. The passions, in
foreseeing their defeat, became prophets, in remembering it, became
poets; and they created the noblest beauties by defying and tran-
scending death.

In Seneca this tragic philosophy, though magnificent, seems
stilted and forced; it struts rhetorically like an army of hoplites tread-
ing down the green earth. He was the last of ancient tragedians, the
most aged and withered in his titanic strength; but all his predecessors, from Homer down, had proclaimed the same tragic truths,
softened but not concealed by their richer medium. Some of them,
like Virgil, had rendered those truths even more poignant precisely
by being more sensitive to the loveliness of perishable things. After
all, the same inhuman power that crushes us breeds us and feeds
us; life and death are but two aspects of the same natural muta-
tion, the same round of seed-time and harvest. And if all human
passions must be fugitives, they need not all be unamiable: some are
merry in their prime, and even smile at their own fading. An accident of ritual led the ancients to divide tragedy sharply from comedy;
I think it has been a happy return to nature in modern dramatists
and novelists to intermingle the two. Comic episodes abound in the
most tragic experience, if only we have the wit to see them; and even
the tragic parts are in reality relieved by all sorts of compensations
that stimulate our sense of life and prompt us to high reflection. What
greater pleasure than a tear that pays homage to something beautiful
and deepens the sense of our own profundity?

Not every part of this classic philosophy re-echoes in the pes-
simism of Macbeth. Shakespeare was not expressing, like Seneca, a

settled doctrine of his own or of his times. Like an honest miscellaneous dramatist, he was putting into the mouths of his different
characters the sentiments that, for the moment, were suggested to
him by their predicaments. Macbeth, who is superstitious and un-
decided, storms excessively when he storms; there is something
feverish and wild in his starts of passion, as there is something delicate in his perceptions. Shakespeare could give rein in such a
character to his own subtle fancy in diction and byplay, as well as
in the main to the exaggerated rhetoric proper to a stage where everybody was expected to declaim, to argue, and to justify sophistically
this or that extravagant impulse. So at this point in *Macbeth,* where
Seneca would have unrolled the high maxims of orthodox Stoicism,
Shakespeare gives us the humours of his distracted hero; a hero non-
plussed, confounded, stultified in his own eyes, a dying gladiator, a
blinded lion at bay. And yet intellectually—and this is the tragedy of
it—Macbeth is divinely human, rational enough to pause and survey
his own agony, and see how brutish, how insignificant it is. He sees
no escape, no alternative; he cannot rise morally above himself; his
philosophy is that there is no philosophy, because, in fact, he is incapable of any.*

COMMENTARY

I

Note how clear Santayana's prose is, and how easy his statement
seems. Yet he is a difficult philosopher to read, although there is much
aesthetic satisfaction in doing so.

Santayana criticizes T. S. Eliot for saying that two verse passages
are equally good as poetry, but that one is inferior to the other as
philosophy. A very important principle is involved. One cannot
separate the poetic quality of a work from its content.[1] The poetic
quality is that of the poem in its entirety. Poetry is not music; its
sounds alone, however organized, do not make a work of art. Like
all literature, poetry presents something to the imagination and the
mind as well as to the ear. Since it has a content, poetry can be as

---

* [For direct comparison with these views, the reader may look at our
own analysis of *Macbeth:* Part II, Section Three.]

banal as any prose, or as profound. But its meanings are not separable from the verse in which they are embedded, as meanings are from the expository prose that states them. For the meanings of a poem are created by the verse form itself, elaborated by its images, and intensified by its rhythms. We will deal with these things in detail in Part II of this book.

In the first sentence of the second paragraph, Santayana says ". . . poetry expressing an inferior philosophy would *to that extent* be inferior poetry . . ." To that extent then, and no more, a poem expressing inferior philosophy is inferior poetry. But why "to that extent"? Because, presumably, it may not be inferior as poetry in other ways. So Santayana presupposes that there are other ways in which poems may be judged equal, superior, or inferior. Surely that is acceptable. Spinoza's *Ethics* and Kant's *Critique of Pure Reason* are great philosophy, but doggerel verse paraphrasing their arguments would not be great poetry. Yet Santayana may be slipping into a violation of the very principle we have approved, that the poetic quality of verse is inseparable from its context.

Of course, Santayana does not think for a moment that poetry is only a philosophic statement in verse. Note that he never writes that poetry "states" a philosophy, but always that it "expresses" it. The difference between statement and expression is in part the distinction between explicit verbal assertion or denial and implicit meaning, never put in so many words. A woman, by weeping over a dead child, thus expresses, but does not state, her grief. In its origin, *expression* is the act or product of pressing out. One expresses juice from grapes, and juice is an expression of grapes. Less literally, we may say that poetry expresses ideas or "philosophy" as the weeping woman expresses grief. Ideas may be, and often are, stated quite explicitly in poetry. The poet may ask, "Shall I compare thee to a summer's day?" and mean just that. But the meanings of a whole poem, not just of a line, are expressed in the images, the sounds, the cadences of the poem, as grief is expressed in the tears and visage of the stricken mother.

II

Santayana could have come to another conclusion about Eliot's meaning. Eliot believes, according to Santayana, that Shakespeare's passage and Dante's passage are equally good as poetry, and that Dante's passage is superior as philosophy. One possible conclusion— the one Santayana drew—is that Eliot was judging the two passages as poetry apart from their content. But there is another possible conclusion: that Eliot is making two judgments, one including their content, and the other about the philosophic content alone.

Here you may interpose a question. Doesn't the second alternative include the first: that is, even in the second, Eliot's procedure implies that, since Dante's passage is better as philosophy, but both are equal poetically, then *considered apart from their content,* Shakespeare's passage is better poetically than Dante's, so much better that it makes up in other ways for its philosophical inferiority? If Eliot wouldn't accept this implication, then he couldn't accept the second alternative as his own. And he would be guilty of Santayana's charge, for he would still be judging poetry apart from its content.

A simple logical principle is involved which may clarify our argument. If proposition A implies proposition B, then if A is true, B is true, but if B is false, A is false. Since "All apples are red" implies "This apple is red," then if this apple is not red, it follows that "All apples are red" is false.[2]

Can we defend Eliot? Yes, and rather simply: we can at least find things he could have meant. One cannot separate the poetic quality of a work from its content, we have said. But one cannot separate that quality from its cadences, images, and organization either. The poem is a whole. Still, that doesn't mean that one cannot talk about its parts intelligently and critically. To say a poem is a whole is, usually, to imply that it is like an organic whole rather than a mechanical whole. In an organic body, like that of a man, whatever happens to a part affects the whole, and the health or illness of the whole affects the parts. Putting it another way, suppose you were a judge at a beauty contest. The prize is to go to the most beautiful girl, not the one with the best legs or hair, but the one who is most beautiful as a whole. Couldn't you decide that Miss Pickering was prettier than Miss Trumbull, and still admit that Miss Trumbull had better legs? Of course.

Here we may qualify the implication we suggested for the second alternative of Eliot's meaning. If Miss Trumbull has better legs, but Miss Pickering is prettier, does it follow that Miss Pickering's other physiological details are so much better than Miss Trumbull's that they make up for the difference in legs? Perhaps, but not necessarily. For the total organization of the body, neck, and head, *including the legs,* may still be better in Miss Pickering's case than Miss Trumbull's. Indeed, Miss Trumbull's beautiful legs may not suit Miss Trumbull's physique as well as Miss Pickering's less beautiful legs suit her physique. So Eliot may be justified in thinking—if he does—that Shakespeare's passage as a whole is as beautiful as Dante's, but that the philosophy of Dante's passage is superior to the philosophy of Shakespeare's.

Still, how could Eliot answer Santayana's assertion that if two poems are *equal* except for their philosophies, the poem with the better philosophy is the better poem? After all, if two poems *are* equal in all other respects, the poem with the better philosophy contains one element—its philosophy—which is superior to that element of the other poem. Why does that not make it, in all, a superior poem?

The answer hinges on Santayana's question in the second paragraph: "in what respect other than truth may philosophies be called inferior or superior?" Suppose, first, it is a matter of truth. If philosophy A is *clearly* true and philosophy B *clearly* false, then a poem expressing B will probably suffer. It will *ring* false and, whatever its other virtues, it will not give the "satisfaction," the "total joy," that A might. But although single propositions in a philosophy, or particular arguments, may be true or false, valid or invalid, the philosophy as a whole, as a vision of life or perspective on the world, can scarcely be called true or false in any straightforward sense. It may be, as Santayana says, more or less religious, or poetic, or inspired. It may be more or less congenial to the reader's beliefs. But, unless it is shallow or trivial, it will be as useful for poetry as any other philosophy.

So a poem will suffer if what it expresses is clearly false, or shallow, or trivial. But if its philosophy is serious and profound, it is our own temperament and belief that brings us to like it or dislike it. The poem, then, which contains a philosophy less congenial to us is, *to that extent,* no worse a poem than one containing a more congenial philosophy, although we may like it less. If this is what Eliot meant, we would support his view. The reason he provoked Santayana's attack may have been that he called the philosophies in question "superior" and "inferior," and thus seemed to assume objective standards of judgment.

What we have said about good and important philosophies may also be said about good and important works of art. We may prefer one to another, but that does not mean it is better art. There are four possibilities: (1) A work of art is good and we like it; (2) it is good and we don't like it; (3) it is bad and we like it; (4) it is bad and we don't like it. If we are asked whether Bach's B Minor Mass is better than Beethoven's late string quartets, we can't answer. We can only tell which we prefer and, even then, when and under what circumstances we prefer it, for sometimes we may prefer the other. And we often like an inferior work for what we consider to be its charm, gaiety, or brilliance, while we dislike a superior work for its pretentiousness or bombast.[3]

IV

Despite what we have said about his use of "expression" rather than "statement," isn't Santayana thinking of the philosophy of a poem too much as "statement," and not enough as "expression"? In great poetry, as in all great art, the philosophy emerges from the whole work. It is the poem's implicit meaning, and is not found in any particular explicit statement.

Yet, if Santayana's tone gives us the feeling that he is too much concerned with explicit philosophical statement, what he says about Macbeth's great speech shows that he knows better. In the last paragraph, he says of Shakespeare: "Like an honest miscellaneous dramatist, he was putting into the mouths of his different characters the sentiments that, for the moment, were suggested to him by their predicaments." Of course! One is not entitled to conclude that Shakespeare believes what Macbeth does when, besieged by his enemies, he learns his wife is dead. Indeed, the play makes it clear that even Macbeth did not believe it at other moments in his life. Eliot may prefer the philosophy of Dante to that of Macbeth when, after a succession of murders and a brutal reign as King of Scotland, Macbeth came to his death. But who wouldn't? Even Shakespeare would, and did, as his judgment of Macbeth in the play shows. The philosophy of Shakespeare is never at issue. In that philosophy, among other things, Macbeth stands condemned. The play shows that clearly. And the philosophy of Shakespeare, at the time he wrote *Macbeth,* and so far as it was concerned with the problems in *Macbeth,* is implicit in, or expressed by, the play itself as an organized whole.[4]

Eliot does violate critical principles *if* he treats Macbeth's soliliquy as Shakespeare's belief—and Santayana thinks he does. Indeed, there is always the question whether a character in a play or fiction believes or means what he himself says. (He may be lying consciously; he may be deceiving himself.) We can determine that only by the situation in which he says what he does, by his conduct, and by reference to the entire work.[5] We would judge Macbeth's statement to be an expression of his deepest feeling at the moment, but no more than that.

TERMS AND PRINCIPLES

1. The content of a work of art is not fully separable from the form of the work. And the form, of course, has no actual existence apart from its content.
2. If one statement implies a second, then if the first is true the second is true, but if the second is false, the first is false.
3. Our preferences and likes do not determine even our own judgment of the worth of works of art. We often like what we acknowledge as mediocre and dislike what we acknowledge as great.
4. The speech or thought of a character in a play or work of fiction must not be treated as the belief of the author.
5. The speech or thought of a character may not express what he himself means. The way to find out what he means is to relate it to the situation, the conduct of the character, and the whole work.

EXERCISE

HENRY JAMES

From Preface to "Lady Barbarina"

The great truth in the whole connexion, however, is, I think, that one never really chooses one's general range of vision—the experience from which ideas and themes and suggestions spring: this proves ever what it has had to be, this is one with the very turn one's life has taken; so that whatever it "gives," whatever it makes us feel and think of, we regard very much as imposed and inevitable. The subject thus pressed upon the artist is the necessity of his case and the fruit of his consciousness; which truth makes and has ever made of any quarrel with his subject, any stupid attempts to go behind *that,* the true stultification of criticism. The author of these remarks has in any case felt it, from far back, quite his least stupid course to meet halfway, as it were, the turn taken and the perceptions engendered by the tenor of his days. Here it is that he has never pretended to "go behind"—which would have been for him a de-

plorable waste of time. The thing of profit is to *have* your experience
—to recognize and understand it, and for this almost any will do;
there being surely no absolute ideal about it beyond getting from it
all it has to give. The artist—for it is of this strange brood we speak
—has but to have his honest sense of life to find it fed at every pore
even as the birds of the air are fed; with more and more to give, in
turn, as a consequence, and, quite by the same law that governs the
responsive affection of a kindly-used animal, in proportion as more
and more is confidently asked.

SOME QUESTIONS

Henry James has a notably difficult prose style. It is defended by
his admirers as a style exquisitely adapted to the difficulty of its
content. He is a master of nuance and subtlety, of insights almost
evading language. See what you can make of his statement.

1. What is meant, in the first sentence, by "one's general range
of vision"? Is it what we called one's "philosophy" in discussing
Santayana? James gives his own explanation: "the experience from
which ideas and themes and suggestions spring." Does he mean
simply that everyone's total experience is unique, or that the way in
which each of us views the world brings "ideas and themes and
suggestions" somewhat different from those of others? Perhaps he
means "point of view," or "perspective," by his phrase. Does each
perspective on the world imply a "philosophy"?

2. Would you expect some men to be more remarkable in
"range of vision" than others, and with a perspective on the world,
or "vision," more highly individual? Would such men, if they had
the other talents needed for it, be more or less likely to be first rate
artists?

3. In what sense do we not, according to James, choose our
"general range of vision"?

4. Why is it "the true stultification of criticism" to attempt to go
behind the artist's subject? But, first, how can one go behind the
subject?

As a suggestion, from another universe of discourse: suppose
you were a law student, and your teacher asked you what law covered
a hypothetical case in which A killed B by frightening him to death.
Wouldn't you be going behind the subject by asking why A did it,
or by arguing that it was unlikely that a man could be frightened to
death? And wouldn't your remarks be beside the point? For you

were asked to assume a case and then say something particular about it, not to question the case itself.

5. Expand and comment on the article of James's artistic creed contained in the sentence: "The thing of profit is to have your experience—to recognize and understand it, and for this almost any will do; there being surely no absolute ideal about it beyond getting from it all it has to give."

First, paraphrase and explain James's meaning; second, suggest examples of his meaning; third, make a reasoned statement of agreement or disagreement.

EXERCISE

JOHN CROWE RANSOM

From "A Poem Nearly Anonymous"

Anonymity, of some real if not liberal sort, is a condition of poetry. A good poem, even if it is signed with a full and well-known name, intends as a work of art to lose the identity of the author; that is, it means to represent him not actualized, like an eye-witness testifying in court and held strictly by zealous counsel to the point at issue, but freed from his juridical or prose self and taking an ideal or fictitious personality; otherwise his evidence amounts the less to poetry. Poets may go to universities and, if they take to education, increase greatly the stock of ideal selves into which they may pass for the purpose of being poetical. If on the other hand they insist too narrowly on their own identity and their own story, inspired by a simple but mistaken theory of art, they find their little poetic fountains drying up within them. Milton set out to write a poem mourning a friend and poet who had died; in order to do it he became a Greek shepherd, mourning another one. It was not that authority attached particularly to the discourse of a Greek shepherd; the Greek shepherd in his own person would have been hopeless; but Milton as a Greek shepherd was delivered from being Milton the scrivener's son, the Master of Arts from Cambridge, the handsome and finicky young man, and that was the point. In proceeding to his Master's degree he had made studies which gave him dramatic insight into many parts foreign to his own personal experience; which was precisely the technical resource he had required the moment he determined to be a poet. Such a training was almost the regular and unremarked procedure with the poets of his time. Today young men and women, as noble as Milton, those in university circles as much as those out of them, try to become poets on another plan, and with rather less success. They write their autobiographies, following perhaps the example of Wordsworth, which on the whole may have been unfortunate for the prosperity of the art; or they write some of their intenser experiences, their loves, pities, griefs, and religious ecstasies; but too literally, faithfully, piously, ingenuously. They seem to want to do without wit and playfulness, dramatic sense, detachment, and it cuts them off from the practice of an art.

Briefly, it was Milton's intention to be always anonymous as a poet, rarely as a writer of prose. The poet must suppress the man, or the man would suppress the poet. What he wanted to say for himself, or for his principles, became eligible for poetry only when it became what the poet, the *dramatis persona* so to speak, might want to say for himself. The poet could not be directed to express faithfully and pointedly the man; nor was it for the sake of "expression" that the man abdicated in favor of the poet.

SOME QUESTIONS

1. What does Ransom mean when he says: "Anonymity . . . is a condition of poetry"? The answer requires reading the whole of the first paragraph. Let us suggest two possible meanings, and see which is supported by the text. But first we can dispose of "real" anonymity. That occurs in an unsigned poem, or perhaps, since Ransom speaks of "*some* real" anonymity, in a pseudonym. That, at least, is necessary, Ransom thinks, *if* there is no "liberal" anonymity. But the latter is more important, and is the subject of the rest of the passage.

"Liberal" anonymity, as "a condition for poetry," might mean: (1) the poet puts nothing of himself in the poem, but excludes his own temperament, values, and perspective on the world, writing entirely as someone else; or (2) the poet writes as if *he* were someone else, a shepherd, a lover, a soldier, imaginatively taking on the background and situation of the other person, but fusing his own temperament, values, etc. with those of the imaginary person.

Which of the two devices poets actually adopt may be inferred by asking about some of the consequences of each device. If poets write anonymously in the first sense, no two poems by the same writer will be recognizable as his by style, imagery, insight, etc. If poets write anonymously in the second sense, different poems by the same writer will differ because of the various persons presumably speaking, but will be recognizable as composed by the same hand.

Which alternative is that *actually* chosen by poets? Which does Ransom urge? And what evidence is there in the rest of the text to show you are right?

2. What are the advantages, according to Ransom, of writing anonymously (in his sense)? What happens if one doesn't?

3. How may education profit a poet who writes "anonymously"? Can you think of other virtues of education for a poet, beyond what Ransom suggests?

4. Explain in your own words: "The poet must suppress the man, or the man would suppress the poet."

5. What does Ransom mean by: ". . . nor was it for the sake of 'expression' that the man abdicated in favor of the poet." Does he use the word "expression," as Santayana does, to distinguish it from "statement"? Or does he intend the usage that is more common, that you "express" yourself when you utter (or act out) your deepest feelings, or your feelings at the moment? There is one way to answer this: determine which meaning of "expression" suits better what Ransom is saying about anonymity in poetry.

EXERCISE

GEORGE SAND

To Gustave Flaubert, in Paris

Nohant, 18th and 19th December, 1875

What's our next move? For you, of course, *desolation,* and, for me, *consolation.* I do not know on what our destinies depend; you see them pass, you criticise them, you abstain from a literary appreciation of them, you limit yourself to depicting them, with deliberate meticulous concealment of your personal feelings. However, one sees them very clearly through your narrative, and you make the people sadder who read you. As for me, I should like to make them less sad. I cannot forget that my personal victory over despair was the work of my will and of a new way of understanding which is entirely opposed to what I had before.

I know that you criticise the intervention of the personal doctrine in literature. Are you right? Isn't it rather a lack of conviction than a principle of esthetics? One cannot have a philosophy in one's soul without its appearing. I have no literary advice to give you, I have no judgment to formulate on the author friends of whom you speak. I, myself, have told the Goncourts all my thought; as for the others, I firmly believe that they have more education and more talent than I have. Only I think that they, and you especially, lack a definite and extended vision of life. Art is not merely painting. True painting, moreover, is full of the soul that wields the brush. Art is not merely criticism and satire: criticism and satire depict only one side of the truth.

I want to see a man as he is, he is not good or bad, he is good and bad. But he is something more . . . nuance. Nuance which is for me the purpose of art, being good and bad, he has an internal force which leads him to be very bad and slightly good,—or very good and slightly bad.

I think that your school is not concerned with the substance, and that it dwells too much on the surface. By virtue of seeking the form, it makes the substance too cheap! it addresses itself to the men of letters. But there are no men of letters, properly speaking. Before everything, one is a man. One wants to find man at the basis of every story and every deed. This was the defect of *l'Education sentimentale,** about which I have so often reflected since, asking myself why there was so general a dislike of a work that was so well done and so solid. This defect was the absence of action of the characters on themselves. They submitted to the event and never mastered it. Well, I think that the chief interest in a story is what

* [A novel by Flaubert, published in 1869. It was translated into English as *The Sentimental Education,* and published in 1898.]

you did not want to do. If I were you, I would try the opposite; you are feeding on Shakespeare just now, and you are doing well! He is the author who puts men at grips with events; observe that by them, whether for good or for ill, the event is always conquered. In his works, it is crushed underfoot.

GUSTAVE FLAUBERT

To George Sand

December, 1875

I am constantly doing all that I can to enlarge my brain, and I work in the sincerity of my heart. The rest does not depend on me.

I do not enjoy making "desolation," believe me, but I cannot change my eyes! As for my "lack of convictions," alas! I choke with convictions. I am bursting with anger and restrained indignation. But according to the ideal of art that I have, I think that the artist should not manifest anything of his own feelings, and that the artist should not appear any more in his work than God in nature. The man is nothing, the work is everything! This method, perhaps mistakenly conceived, is not easy to follow. And for me, at least, it is a sort of permanent sacrifice that I am making to good taste. It would be agreeable to me to say what I think and to relieve Mister Gustave Flaubert by words, but of what importance is the said gentleman?

I think as you do, dear master, that art is not merely criticism and satire; moreover, I have never tried to do intentionally the one nor the other. I have always tried to go into the soul of things and to stick to the greatest generalities, and I have purposely turned aside from the accidental and the dramatic. No monsters and no heroes!

You say to me: "I have no literary advice to give you; I have no judgments to formulate on the authors, your friends, etc." Well, indeed! but I implore advice, and I am waiting for your judgments. Who, pray, should give them, and who, pray, should formulate them, if not you?

Speaking of my friends, you add "my school." But I am ruining

my temperament in trying not to have a school! *A priori,* I spurn
them, every one. The people whom I see often and whom you desig-
nate cultivate all that I scorn and are indifferently disturbed about
what torments me. I regard as very secondary, technical detail, local
exactness, in short the historical and precise side of things. I am seeking above all for beauty, which my companions pursue but languidly.
I see them insensible when I am ravaged with admiration or horror.
Phrases make me swoon with pleasure which seem very ordinary to
them. Goncourt is very happy when he has seized upon a word in
the street that he can stick in a book, and I am well satisfied when I
have written a page without assonances or repetitions. I would give
all the legends of Gavarni for certain expressions and master strokes,
such as "the shade was nuptial, august and solemn!" from Victor
Hugo, or this from Montesquieu: "The vices of Alexander were
extreme like his virtues. He was terrible in his wrath. It made him
cruel."

In short, I try to think well, in order to write well. But writing
well is my aim, I do not deny it.

GEORGE SAND

To Gustave Flaubert, in Paris

Nohant, 12th January, 1876

When you feel you are on the ladder, you will mount very
quickly. You are about to enter gradually upon the happiest and most
favorable time of life: old age. It is then that art reveals itself in
its sweetness; as long as one is young, it manifests itself with anguish.
You prefer a well-turned phrase to all metaphysics. I also, I love to
see condensed into a few words what elsewhere fills volumes; but
these volumes, one must have understood them completely (either
to admit them or to reject them) in order to find the sublime résumé
which becomes literary art in its fullest expression; that is why one
should not scorn the efforts of the human mind to arrive at the
truth.

I tell you that, because you have excessive prejudices as to words. In truth, you read, you dig, you work much more than I and a crowd of others do. You have acquired learning that I shall never attain. Therefore, you are a hundred times richer than all of us; you are a rich man, and you complain like a poor man. Be charitable to a beggar who has his mattress full of gold, but who wants to be nourished only on well-turned phrases and choice words. But brute, ransack your own mattress and eat your gold. Nourish yourself with the ideas and feelings accumulated in your head and your heart; the words and the phrases, the form to which you attach so much importance, will issue by itself from your digestion. You consider it as an end, it is only an effect. Happy manifestations proceed only from an emotion, and an emotion proceeds only from a conviction. One is not moved at all by the things that one does not believe with all one's heart.

I do not say that you do not believe: on the contrary, all your life of affection, of protection, and of charming and simple goodness, proves that you are the most convinced individual in the world. But, as soon as you handle literature, you want, I don't know why, to be another man, one who should disappear, one who destroys himself, who does not exist! What an absurd mania! what a false rule of good taste! Our work is worth only what we are worth.

Who is talking about putting yourself on the stage? That, in truth, is of no use, unless it is done frankly by way of a chronicle. But to withdraw one's soul from what one does, what is that unhealthy fancy? To hide one's own opinion about the characters that one puts on the stage, to leave the reader therefore uncertain about the opinion that he should have of them, that is to desire not to be understood, and from that moment, the reader leaves you; for if he wants to understand the story that you are telling him it is on the condition that you should show him plainly that this one is a strong character and that one weak.

L'Education sentimentale has been a misunderstood book, as I have told you repeatedly, but you have not listened to me. There should have been a short preface, or, at a good opportunity, an expression of blame, even if only a happy epithet to condemn the evil, to characterize the defect, to signalize the effort. All the characters in that book are feeble and come to nothing, except those with bad instincts; that is what you are reproached with, because people did not understand that you wanted precisely to depict a deplorable state of society that encourages these bad instincts and ruins noble efforts; when people do not understand us it is always our fault. What the reader wants, first of all, is to penetrate into our thought, and that is what you deny him, arrogantly. He thinks that you scorn him and that you want to ridicule him. For my part, I understood you, for I knew you. If anyone had brought me your book without its being signed, I should have thought it beautiful, but strange, and I should have asked myself if you were immoral, skeptical, indifferent or heartbroken. You say that it ought to be like that, and that M. Flaubert will violate the rules of good taste if he shows his thought and the aim of his literary enterprise. It is false in the highest degree. When M. Flaubert writes well and seriously, one attaches oneself to his personality. One wants to sink or swim with him. If he leaves you in doubt, you lose interest in his work, you neglect it, or you give it up.

I have already combated your favorite heresy, which is that one writes for twenty intelligent people and does not care a fig for the rest. It is not true, since the lack of success irritates you and troubles you. Besides, there have not been twenty critics favorable to this book which was so well written and so important. So one must not write for twenty persons any more than for three, or for a hundred thousand.

One must write for all those who have a thirst to read and who can profit by good reading. Then one must go straight to the most elevated morality within oneself, and not make a mystery of the moral and profitable meaning of one's book. People found that with *Madame Bovary*.* If one part of the public cried scandal, the healthiest and the broadest part saw in it a severe and striking lesson given to a woman without conscience and without faith, to vanity, to ambition, to irrationality. They pitied her; art required that, but the lesson was clear, and it would have been more so, it would have been so for everybody, if you had wished it, if you had shown more clearly the

* [Flaubert's most famous novel.]

opinion that you had, and that the public ought to have had, about the heroine, her husband, and her lovers.

That desire to depict things as they are, the adventures of life as they present themselves to the eye, is not well thought out, in my opinion. Depict inert things as a realist, as a poet, it's all the same to me, but, when one touches on the emotions of the human heart, it is another thing. You cannot abstract yourself from this contemplation; for man, that is yourself, and men, that is the reader. Whatever you do, your tale is a conversation between you and the reader. If you show him the evil coldly, without ever showing him the good, he is angry. He wonders if it is he that is bad, or if it is you. You work, however, to rouse him and to interest him; you will never succeed if you are not roused yourself, or if you hide it so well that he thinks you indifferent. He is right: supreme impartiality is an anti-human thing, and a novel ought to be human above everything. If it is not, the public is not pleased in its being well written, well composed and conscientious in every detail. The essential quality is not there: interest. The reader breaks away likewise from a book where all the characters are good without distinctions and without weaknesses; he sees clearly that that is not human either. I believe that art, this special art of narration, is only worth while through the opposition of characters; but, in their struggle, I prefer to see the right prevail. Let events overwhelm the honest men, I agree to that, but let him not be soiled or belittled by them, and let him go to the stake feeling that he is happier than his executioners.

GUSTAVE FLAUBERT

To George Sand

Wednesday, 9th March, 1876

You distress me a bit, dear master, by attributing esthetic opinions to me which are not mine. I believe that the rounding of the phrase is nothing. But that writing well is everything, because "writing well is at the same time perceiving well, thinking well and saying well" (Buffon). The last term is then dependent on the other two, since one has to feel strongly, so as to think, and to think, so as to express.

All the bourgeois can have a great deal of heart and delicacy, be full of the best sentiments and the greatest virtues, without becoming for all that, artists. In short, I believe that the form and the matter are two subtleties, two entities, neither of which can exist without the other.

This anxiety for external beauty which you reproach me with is for me a method. When I discover a bad assonance or a repetition in one of my phrases, I am sure that I am floundering in error; by dint of searching, I find the exact expression which was the only one and is, at the same time, the harmonious one. The word is never lacking when one possesses the idea.

GUSTAVE FLAUBERT

To George Sand

Monday evening, 3 April, 1876

I do not share in Tourgueneff's severity as regards *Jack,** nor in the immensity of his admiration for *Rougon.*† The one has charm, the other force. But neither one is concerned above all else with what is for me the end of art, namely, beauty. I remember having felt my heart beat violently, having felt a fierce pleasure in contemplating a wall of the Acropolis, a perfectly bare wall (the one on the left as you go up to the Propylaea). Well! I wonder if a book independently of what it says, cannot produce the same effect! In the exactness of its assembling, the rarity of its elements, the polish of its surface, the harmony of its ensemble, is there not an intrinsic virtue, a sort of divine force, something eternal as a principle? (I speak as a Platonist.) Thus, why is a relation necessary between the exact word and the musical word? Why does it happen that one always makes a

---

* [A novel by Alphonse Daudet.]
† [*Son Excellence Rougon,* a novel by Emile Zola. Both men were friends and, in a way, followers of Flaubert.]

verse when one restrains his thought too much? Does the law of numbers govern then the feelings and the images, and is what seems to be the exterior quite simply inside it? If I should continue a long time in this vein, I should blind myself entirely, for on the other side art has to be a good fellow; or rather art is what one can make it, we are not free. Each one follows his path, in spite of his own desire.

GUSTAVE FLAUBERT

To George Sand

Sunday evening . . . 1876

Well, dear master, and this is to answer your last letter, this is, I think what separates us essentially. You, on the first bound, in everything, mount to heaven, and from there you descend to the earth. You start from *a priori*, from the theory, from the ideal. Thence your pity for life, your serenity, and to speak truly, your greatness. —I, poor wretch, I am stuck on the earth as with soles of lead; everything disturbs me, tears me to pieces, ravages me, and I make efforts to rise. If I should take your manner of looking at the whole of life I should become laughable, that is all. For you preach to me in vain. I cannot have another temperament than my own; nor another esthetics than what is the consequence of it. You accuse me of not letting myself go, according to nature. Well, and that discipline? that virtue? what shall we do with it? I admire M. Buffon putting on cuffs when he wrote. This luxury is a symbol. In short I am trying simply to be as comprehensive as possible. What more can one exact?

As for letting my personal opinion be known about the people I put on the stage: no, no, a thousand times no! I do not recognize the right to that. If the reader does not draw from a book the moral that should be found there, the reader is an imbecile or the book is false from the point of view of accuracy. For, the moment that a thing is true, it is good. Obscene books likewise are immoral only because they lack truth. Things are not "like that" in life.

And observe that I curse what they agree to call realism, although they make me one of its high priests; reconcile all that.

SOME QUESTIONS

1. What is the major issue about fiction between George Sand and Gustave Flaubert?

2. How does that issue bear on what John Crowe Ransom says, in the exercise before this, about poetry?

3. In Flaubert's first letter, he quotes three sentences from Montesquieu with great admiration. Assume that the translation here has the virtues of the original. Do you like the passage quoted? Do you see any reason for Flaubert's admiration? Is the progress of Montesquieu's statement from the more particular to the more general? Is each successive sentence longer or shorter than the one before it? Does the cadence of each sentence suit what is said? Do the cadences of the whole passage aid the effect? Is the meaning clear? Are the words exact? Can you think of other considerations?

4. George Sand believes that Flaubert's unhappiness results somehow from his theory of fiction. Construct an argument to demonstrate that belief, based on what Sand says. Never mind whether you accept the argument; state it so she would accept it.

5. In the last paragraph of his first letter here, Flaubert says: "In short, I try to think well, in order to write well." In his second letter, he quotes Buffon, who identifies writing well with thinking well, perceiving well, and saying well.

From your experience with this book so far, do you agree or disagree with Buffon and Flaubert? What more can you say to defend what you believe about this matter?

6. Paraphrase Flaubert's defense of his theory and practice of fiction. Put it in the form of a single reasoned argument.

7. In his last letter, Flaubert says: "I admire M. Buffon putting on cuffs when he wrote." Why does he admire it? What has it to do with his theory of fiction? (John Keats sometimes dressed with great care and combed his hair before he wrote.)

8. In his last letter, Flaubert suggests that his aesthetic is a result of his temperament. Does that agree or disagree with Henry James's reflections in the exercise here? Justify your answer by comparison with James's own words.

EXERCISE

JACOB BURCKHARDT

From *Force and Freedom*

Real greatness is a mystery. The predicate is bestowed or with-
held far more by an obscure feeling than by real judgments based on
records, nor is it only the experts who bestow it, but a genuine con-
sensus of the opinion of many. Nor is fame in itself enough. The
general education of our time knows a vast army of more or less
famous men of all nations and times, yet with each single one of them
we must ask whether he is to be called great, and few stand the test.

Yet what is the standard? It is uncertain, fluctuating, illogical.
Sometimes the predicate is bestowed more on intellectual, sometimes
more on moral grounds, sometimes more by the conviction that comes
from written records, sometimes (and as we have said, oftener) by
mere feeling. Sometimes the personality counts more, sometimes the
persisting influence. Often judgment finds its place usurped by prejudice.

Finally it begins to dawn upon us that the whole of the personality which seems great to us is producing upon us, across the peoples
and the centuries, a *magical* after-effect, far beyond the limits of
mere tradition.

From this point, a further definition, though not an explanation,
of greatness is given by the words—unique, irreplaceable. The great
man is a man of that kind, a man without whom the world would
seem to us incomplete because certain great achievements only became possible through him in his time and place and are otherwise

unimaginable. He is an essential strand in the great web of causes and effects. "No man is irreplaceable," says the proverb. But the few that are, are great.

Of the discoverers of distant lands, Columbus alone was great, but he was very great because he staked his life and expended a vast power of will upon a hypothesis which gives him a rank among the greatest philosophers. The confirmation of the spherical shape of the earth was a premise of all subsequent thought, and all subsequent thought, in so far as it was liberated by that one premise, flashes back to Columbus.

And yet it might be possible to argue that the world could have done without Columbus. "America would soon have been discovered, even if Columbus had died in his cradle"—a thing that could not be said of Aeschylus, Pheidias and Plato. If Raphael had died in his cradle, the *Transfiguration* would assuredly never have been painted.

SOME QUESTIONS

1. Burckhardt says, in the first passage quoted above, that "greatness" includes the ideas "unique," "irreplaceable." These constitute a "further definition," in addition perhaps to the "*magical* after-effect" produced upon us. Now, from what Burckhardt says in the second passage about Columbus, is "irreplaceability" a necessary condition of "greatness"?

2. Do you agree that America would soon—or ever—have been discovered if Columbus had died in his cradle? Do you agree that if Raphael had died in his cradle, his pictures would never have been painted? If you assume both statements are true, do you see a difference between the *kinds* of achievement that are irreplaceable and those that are not? Try to list both kinds, and defend your choices. Where do you put invention, scientific discovery, philosophy, the arts? Are there some kinds of achievement that fit under both headings, depending on the man and his times? For example, is it true that the Monroe Doctrine, at least in all essentials, would have been proclaimed by almost any other President at about the same time? Is it true that another Greek would have conquered approximately the territories Alexander did, at about the same time, thus bringing

Greek civilization to the Near East? If you say "yes" to the first and "no" to the second, under which heading would you put political rule? 3. Burckhardt thinks that Columbus is the only discoverer "of distant lands" who was great, and he explains why. Does his explanation presuppose another element in the definition of "greatness"?

EXERCISE

G. M. TREVELYAN

From *History of England*

The heathen Danes and Norsemen destroyed for awhile the higher civilization of the island collected in its monasteries, and for awhile increased its disunion by establishing the Danelaw over against the areas ruled by Saxon and Celt. Yet before a hundred years were out, the Scandinavian invasions were seen to have greatly strengthened the forces of progress. For the Vikings were of a stock kindred to the Saxon, but even more full of energy, hardihood and independence of character, and with no less aptitude for poetry and learning. They brought back to the island those seafaring habits which the Saxons had lost in their sojourn on up-country farms, and it was due to them that a vigorous town life revived in England for the first time since the departure of the Romans. Had it not been for the Scandinavian blood infused into our race by the catastrophes of the Ninth Century, less would have been heard in days to come of British maritime and commercial enterprise.

SOME QUESTIONS

1. To explain anything one must use a general hypothesis. If you say "The green army defeated the blue army because the green army was larger," and add no more by way of explanation, you presuppose the general hypothesis that larger armies always defeat smaller armies. Often, when you learn what general hypothesis you have presupposed, you give up or change your explanation, because the general hypothesis is false, as it may be above. What general

hypothesis is presupposed by Trevelyan in his last sentence? Does it seem true?

2. What normative statements, or evaluations, are presupposed in the phrases "higher civilization" and "forces of progress"?

3. Is a contradiction involved in saying: (1) the Vikings were of a *stock* more full of energy, etc., than the Saxons; and (2) the Vikings brought back those seafaring *habits* the Saxons had lost by living on up-country farms?

4. If Trevelyan defended himself by arguing that since Scandinavian blood was infused into the English stock in the ninth century and only afterwards did England rule the seas, Scandinavian blood must have been the reason for English naval power, what fallacy could you accuse him of?

EXERCISE

JACOB BURCKHARDT

From *Judgments on History and Historians*

Only the civilized nations, not the primitive ones, are part of history in a higher sense. . . . Primitive peoples, however, interest us only when civilized nations come into conflict with them . . . Of the civilized peoples, our discipline does not embrace those whose culture did not flow into European civilization, for instance Japan and China. Of India, too, only the very oldest period concerns us—first, because of the Aryan tribal type shared with the Zend peoples, and then because of the contact with the Assyrians, Persians, Macedonians, and others. Our subject is that past which is clearly connected with the present and with the future. Our guiding idea is the course of civilization, the succession of levels of culture in various peoples and within individual peoples themselves. Actually, one ought to stress especially those historical realities from which threads run to our own period and culture.

SOME QUESTIONS

1. Can you tell, from this passage, what Burckhardt would regard as history in a lower sense?

2. Does the word "higher" make Burckhardt's first sentence *normative?* Or is he stating his opinion, throughout this passage, about what history really is, and so *defining* "history"? Or is he perhaps generalizing from all good historical writing to tell what its subject matter is, thus making an *empirical* assertion?

Perhaps you cannot answer these questions fully from this passage alone, but your arguments for and against these three possibilities should be rewarding. You may be helped by applying the principle of textual context, attending to the whole passage, and thinking especially of Burckhardt's use of "our": "our subject," "our guiding idea"? Is his use of the word just an example of the editorial plural—"we think," writes the editor—or does "our" refer to historians? Does the use of the word "one" in the last sentence help you decide?

3. "Our subject is that past which is clearly connected with the present and with the future." How do we know which things about the past are so connected? Or put it this way: if a present-day historian of ancient Rome is so exclusively devoted to his subject that he pays no attention to the present, or little attention—no one can *utterly* ignore the present, though many try—how would he, on Burckhardt's criterion, know what to write about? If he wouldn't, can we conclude that—at least according to Burckhardt—every historian must know about his own time? As for the future, can we think about it intelligibly except in terms of the present?

4. Is it possible, and even likely, that what we take to be the past events connected with the present are different from what the nineteenth century thought they were, and what the twenty-first century will think? Does our choice of such past events depend on what we think our present is like and on the theories of causation and historical influence we hold? If that is so, wouldn't the history of every age in the past have to be rewritten with every major change in the present?

EXERCISE

LORD MACAULAY

From "History"

Some capricious and discontented artists have affected to consider portrait-painting as unworthy of a man of genius. Some critics have spoken in the same contemptuous manner of history. Johnson puts the case thus: The historian tells either what is false or what is true: in the former case he is no historian; in the latter he has no opportunity for displaying his abilities: for truth is one; and all who tell the truth must tell it alike.

It is not difficult to elude both the horns of this dilemma. We will recur to the analogous art of portrait-painting. Any man with eyes and hands may be taught to take a likeness. The process, up to a certain point, is merely mechanical. If this were all, a man of talents might justly despise the occupation. But we could mention portraits which are resemblances—but not mere resemblances; faithful—but much more than faithful; portraits which condense into one point of time, and exhibit at a single glance the whole history of turbid and eventful lives—in which the eye seems to scrutinise us, and the mouth to command us—in which the brow menaces, and the lip almost quivers with scorn—in which every wrinkle is a comment on some important transaction. The account which Thucydides has given of the retreat from Syracuse is, among narratives, what Vandyck's Lord Strafford is among paintings.

Diversity, it is said, implies error: truth is one, and admits of no degrees. We answer that this principle holds good only in abstract reasonings. When we talk of the truth of imitation in the fine arts, we mean an imperfect and a graduated truth.

No picture is exactly like the original; nor is a picture good in proportion as it is like the original. When Sir Thomas Lawrence paints a handsome peeress, he does not contemplate her through a powerful microscope, and transfer to the canvas the pores of the skin, the blood-vessels of the eye, and all the other beauties which Gulliver discovered in the Brobdingnagian maids of honour. If he were to do this, the effect would not merely be unpleasant, but, unless the scale of the picture were proportionably enlarged, would be absolutely false. And, after all, a microscope of greater power than that which he had employed would convict him of innumerable omissions. The same may be said of history. Perfectly and absolutely true it cannot be; for, to be perfectly and absolutely true, it ought to record all the slightest particulars of the slightest transactions—all the things done and all the words uttered during the time of which it treats. The omission of any circumstance, however insignificant, would be a defect. If history were written thus, the Bodleian library would not contain the occurrences of a week. What is told in the fullest and most accurate annals bears an infinitely small proportion to what is suppressed. The difference between the copious work of Clarendon and the account of the civil wars in the abridgment of Goldsmith vanishes when compared with the immense mass of facts respecting which both are equally silent.

SOME QUESTIONS

1. Consider Johnson's argument, as Macaulay renders it. Surely Johnson does not mean that the Law of Gravitation cannot be stated in more than one way, that the words must be the same and in the same sequence. What then can he mean by "all who tell the truth must tell it alike"? Would you agree that his intention is, "whatever words we use to tell the truth, our meanings must be identical" or "whatever the sentences in which we write the truth, the propositions they express are the same"? If you do agree, does it follow that when two historians give the same information, but in quite different ways, neither has "opportunity for displaying his abilities"? Couldn't one write turgidly, and the other lucidly, one dully and the other excitingly? "Yes," you may say, but would Johnson be entitled to retort: "Those are their abilities as writers, not as historians; as historians their meanings are identical if they tell the same truth"?

2. Do you think that Macaulay's analogy of portrait painting is well chosen?

3. Do you agree with Macaulay that the principle, "truth is one, and admits of no degrees," holds good only in abstract reasoning? Let us dispense with the ticklish matter of degrees. Is Macaulay saying that truth is one and the same only in analytic propositions? But the Law of Gravitation is empirical and its meaning must be one and the same if it is to be stated correctly, whatever words you use. Perhaps Macaulay means "science" by his term "abstract reasoning." With what does he contrast it? With "imitation in the fine arts"? The contrast between science and art is a common one, so Macaulay may well mean "physical science" in a broad sense by the term "abstract reasoning," since he thinks of history as like portrait painting, rather than like science.

Now, what is it that Macaulay thinks portraits can render? The particular impression that the subject made on the painter? A special likeness to life? The essence or basic meaning of the subject's biography as revealed in his face? What can the historian render, so like what the portrait painted can, that Macaulay can compare the Greek historian Thucydides with the Flemish portraitist Van Dyck (or Vandyck, as he has it)?

4. Macaulay's last sentences above make a basic point about written history. The historian cannot tell all about any event. He must select. So if twenty historians discovered a mass of information about an event, and agreed on the truth of all of it, they would still have to select from that mass when they came to write the history of the event. And they might all select differently. So Johnson is refuted. But another difficulty arises. A serious historian doesn't toss a coin over each item, to decide whether he will include it in his history. If he selects, he must have a principle of selection. What could that principle be? Can you think of a principle that is implied by Macaulay's passage and our discussion of it?

EXERCISE

ARNOLD BENNETT

From Preface to *The Old Wives' Tale*

It has been asserted that unless I had actually been present at a public execution, I could not have written the chapter in which Sophia was at the Auxerre solemnity. I have not been present at a public execution, as the whole of my information about public executions was derived from a series of articles on them which I read in the Paris *Matin*. Mr. Frank Harris, discussing my book in "Vanity Fair," said it was clear that I had not seen an execution, (or words to that effect), and he proceeded to give his own description of an execution. It was a brief but terribly convincing bit of writing, quite characteristic and quite worthy of the author of "Montes the Matador" and of a man who has been almost everywhere and seen almost everything. I comprehended how far short I had fallen of the truth! I wrote to Mr. Frank Harris, regretting that his description had not been printed before I wrote mine, as I should assuredly have utilized it, and, of course, I admitted that I had never witnessed an execution.

He simply replied: "Neither have I." This detail is worth preserving, for it is a reproof to that large body of readers, who, when a novelist has really carried conviction to them, assert off hand: "O, that must be autobiography!"

SOME QUESTIONS

1. If Frank Harris had not seen an execution, but was prepared to describe one, was it fair of him to criticize Arnold Bennett's description by saying it was clear that Bennett had not seen an execution? Bennett seems to think Harris was justified. Why?

2. If a good description in a novel is said to be based necessarily on the novelist's experience, does it follow that he has actually witnessed a scene like the one described? If so, what about a good description of the way the condemned man *feels* on his way to the scaffold, and what he *thinks*? Is the only novelist capable of doing that, one who was condemned, and then reprieved at the last second, like Dostoievsky?

Surely, experience has something to do with writing good fiction. But what? To begin with, experience is only a necessary condition at most. It cannot be sufficient, or we would all be novelists, for we all have experience. Now, to what extent need the novelist's experience bear on his work? Does he have to have had a specific experience as the basis of every scene he writes? If he has never experienced fear in any form, it might be impossible for him to write of a condemned man's fears, or of anybody else's. But if he has experienced fear (and who hasn't?), can't his imagination and sympathy re-create the particulars of a condemned man's fears?

3. On the basis of the little argument in 2, can you distinguish meaningfully between the statement that convincing writing is based on the writer's experience and the statement that it is based on his autobiography?

EXERCISE

SAMUEL TAYLOR COLERIDGE

From *Biographia Literaria*

During the first year that Mr. Wordsworth and I were neighbours, our conversations turned frequently on the two cardinal points of poetry, the power of exciting the sympathy of the reader by a faithful adherence to the truth of nature, and the power of giving the interest of novelty by the modifying colours of imagination. The sudden charm, which accidents of light and shade, which moon-light or sunset diffused over a known and familiar landscape, appeared to represent the practicability of combining both. These are the poetry of nature. The thought suggested itself—(to which of us I do not recollect)—that a series of poems might be composed of two sorts. In the one, the incidents and agents were to be, in part at least, supernatural; and the excellence aimed at was to consist in the interesting of the affections by the dramatic truth of such emotions, as would naturally accompany such situations, supposing them real. And real in this sense they have been to every human being who, from whatever source of delusion, has at any time believed himself under supernatural agency. For the second class, subjects were to be chosen from ordinary life; the characters and incidents were to be such as will be found in every village and its vicinity, where there is a meditative and feeling mind to seek after them, or to notice them, when they present themselves.

In this idea originated the plan of the *Lyrical Ballads;* in which it was agreed, that my endeavours should be directed to persons and characters supernatural, or at least romantic; yet so as to transfer from our inward nature a human interest and a semblance of truth sufficient to procure for these shadows of imagination that willing suspension of disbelief for the moment, which constitutes poetic faith. Mr. Wordsworth, on the other hand, was to propose to himself as his object, to give the charm of novelty to things of every day, and to excite a feeling analogous to the supernatural, by awakening the mind's attention to the lethargy of custom, and directing it to the loveliness and the wonders of the world before us; an inexhaustible treasure, but for which, in consequence of the film of familiarity and selfish solicitude, we have eyes, yet see not, ears that hear not, and hearts that neither feel nor understand.

SOME QUESTIONS

1. What are the two kinds of poetry that Wordsworth and Coleridge planned to write for the *Lyrical Ballads?* List the characteristics of each kind as Coleridge describes it.

2. What does Coleridge mean when he says that "in consequence of the film of familiarity and selfish solicitude, we have eyes, yet see not, ears that hear not, and hearts that neither feel nor understand"? How can poetry, or any other art, remove the film, bring sight to our eyes, hearing to our ears, and feeling and understanding to our hearts?

3. Coleridge's phrase, "willing suspension of disbelief," has become famous. He uses it to define poetic faith. Is it a necessary condition for reading, so that poetry can have its proper effect? Why "willing"? Would an unwilling suspension of disbelief work as well?

PART II

Imaginative Writing

Fiction

ISAAK BABEL

In Odessa

I was the one to open the conversation.

"Reb Arye Leyb," I said to the old man, "let us talk about Benya Krik. Let us talk about his meteoric beginnings and his terrible end. Three black shadows block the paths of my imagination. Here is one-eyed Froim Grach. The rusty steel of his deeds—can you compare it to the dazzling strength of the King? And here is Kolka Pakovsky. This man's simple-minded ferocity had in it all that is needed for domination. And is it possible that Haim Drong couldn't recognize the brilliance of the new star? How is it, then, that Benya Krik alone reached the top of the rope ladder, while all the others were left hanging below on the limp rungs?"

Reb Arye Leyb, sitting on the cemetery wall, kept still. Before us stretched the green peace of the graves. A man who thirsts for knowledge must be patient. A man who possesses knowledge should be dignified. That is why Arye Leyb remained silent, perched on the cemetery wall. At last he said:

"Why he, why not they, you want to know. Well, forget for a while that you've got spectacles on your nose and autumn in your soul. Stop raising hell at your desk and stammering in public. Imagine for a moment that you're a fellow who raises hell in public squares and stammers on paper. You're a tiger, a lion, a wildcat. You can

197

spend the night with a Russian woman, and the Russian woman will be satisfied by you. You are twenty-five. If sky and earth had rings fastened to them, you would grab these rings and draw the sky down to the earth. And your papa is Mendel Krik, the teamster. What does such a father think about? He thinks about drinking a good glass of vodka, about socking someone on the jaw, about his horses—and about nothing else. You want to live, and he makes you die twenty times a day. What would you have done if you'd been in Benya Krik's boots? You'd have done nothing. But he did something. That's why he's King, while you fig with your fist in your pocket.

"Benya, he went to Froim Grach, who then already looked at the world with one eye and was what he is today. He said to Froim: 'Take me on, Froim. I want to be cast upon your shore. The shore I'm cast upon will gain by it.'

"Grach asked him: 'Who are you? Where are you coming from? And what do you live by?'

" 'Try me, Froim,' answered Benya, 'and let's stop chewing the rag.'

" 'Let's,' said Grach. 'I'll try you!'

"And the gangsters held a session to put their minds to the subject of Benya Krik. I wasn't at that session. But it is said that they did hold it. The late Lyovka Byk was elder then.

" 'What's going on under this Benchik's hat?' asked the late Lyovka Byk.

"One-eyed Grach gave his opinion: 'Benya doesn't talk much, but there's a flavor to his words. He says little, and you wish he'd say more.'

" 'If that's so,' exclaimed the late Lyovka, 'then let's try him on Tartakovsky.'

" 'Let's try him on Tartakovsky,' the council decided, and all those who housed a conscience blushed when they heard this decision. Why did they blush? You'll find out if you go where I'll lead you.

"Among us, Tartakovsky had the nicknames Yid-and-a-Half or Nine Holdups. He was called Yid-and-a-Half, because no one Jew could contain so much insolence and so much money as Tartakovsky. He was taller than the tallest policeman in Odessa and he weighed

more than the fattest Jewess. And he was nicknamed Nine Holdups
because the firm of Lyovka Byk and Company had held up his place
not ten or eight times, but exactly nine. It now fell to Benya's lot to
hold up Yid-and-a-Half for the tenth time. When Froim passed this
information on to him, Benya said 'Yes' and walked out, slamming
the door. Why did he slam the door? You'll find out if you go where
I'll lead you.

"Tartakovsky has the soul of a murderer, but he's one of ours.
He came from among us. He is our own flesh and blood, as if one
mother brought us into the world. Half Odessa was employed in his
stores. And it was his own Moldavanka people who made trouble for
him. Twice they kidnapped him for ransom, and once during a
pogrom they staged his funeral, with a choir too. That was when the
thugs from the Sloboda section were beating up the Jews on Bolshaya
Arnautskaya Street. Tartakovsky ran away from them and came
across a funeral procession with a choir.

" 'Who are they burying with a choir?' he asked.

"The passers-by told him it was Tartakovsky's funeral. The
procession reached the Sloboda cemetery. Then our people took a
machine-gun out of the coffin and made it hot for the Sloboda thugs.
But Yid-and-a-Half hadn't expected that. Yid-and-a-Half was scared
to death. And who in his position wouldn't have been scared?

"The tenth holdup of a man who had been buried once already
—that was really uncivil. Benya, who wasn't King then yet, understood it better than anyone else. But he had said 'Yes' to Grach, and
the same day he wrote Tartakovsky a letter like all letters of that
kind:

" 'Highly Esteemed Ruvin Ossipovich!

" 'Be so kind as to place under the rain-water barrel next Saturday . . .' and so on. 'Should you take it upon yourself to refuse, as
you have recently done on several occasions, a grave disappointment
in your family life awaits you.

Respectfully, one whom you know,
Benzion Krik.'

"Tartakovsky, no dawdler, wrote his answer without delay:

" 'Benya!

" 'If you were an idiot, I would have written to you as to an idiot. But I know that you are not, and God forbid that I should have to change my opinion. It looks as if you're making believe you're a child. Don't you know that there has been a bumper crop in Argentina and that we sit here and don't find one customer for our wheat? And upon my word, I'm tired of eating such bitter bread in my old age and having such a disagreeable time of it, after slaving all my life like the lowest teamster, and what do I have after a lifetime of hard labor? Ulcers, sores, aggravation, sleeplessness. Give up them fool ideas, Benya.

> Your friend, much more than you imagine,
> Ruvin Tartakovsky.'

"Yid-and-a-Half did his part. He wrote the letter. But the post-office didn't deliver it. When he got no answer, Benya got mad. The next day he showed up in Tartakovsky's office with four friends. Four masked young men carrying revolvers barged into the room.

" 'Stick 'em up!' they said and began brandishing their guns.

" 'Calm down, Solomon,' Benya remarked to one who shouted louder than the others, 'don't get into this habit of being nervous when you're on the job,' and turning to the clerk who was white as death and yellow as clay, he asked him: 'Is Yid-and-a-Half at the plant?'

" 'The proprietor is not at the plant,' answered the clerk, whose name was Josif Muginstein and who was the bachelor son of Aunt Pessya,—she sold chickens on Seredinsky Square.

" 'Who is in charge here, then?' they asked the unhappy Muginstein.

" 'I am in charge here,' answered the clerk, as green as green grass.

" 'Then with God's help, open the cashbox for us!' Benya ordered him, and so began an opera in three acts!

"Solomon, the nervous one, packed cash, securities, watches and jewelry into a suitcase; the late Josif stood facing him with lifted hands; in the meantime Benya was telling stories from the life of the Jewish people.

" 'If he makes believe he's a Rothschild,' Benya was saying, referring to Tartakovsky, 'then let him burn on a slow fire. Explain it to me, Muginstein, as to a friend: he gets a business letter from me; why couldn't he get into a trolley for five kopecks then, and ride up to my place and have a glass vodka with the family and a snack, taking potluck? What kept him from having a heart-to-heart talk with me? "Benya," he could have told me, "thus and thus, here is my bank balance, wait a couple of days, let me get my breath, give me a chance to turn around . . . ." What would I have answered? Hog don't meet hog, but man meets man. Muginstein, do you get me?'

" 'I do,' answered Muginstein and told a lie, because it wasn't at all clear to him why Yid-and-a-Half, a respectable, substantial man, one of the leading citizens, should take a trolley to have a bite with the family of Mendel Krik, the teamster.

"Meanwhile misfortune was prowling around the house like a beggar at dawn. Misfortune burst into the office with a bang. And although this time it took the shape of a Jew by the name of Savka Butzis, it was as drunk as a water carrier.

" 'Haw-haw-haw!' shouted the Jew Savka. 'Beg your pardon, Benchik, I'm late,' and he stamped his feet and waved his arms. Then he fired a shot, and the bullet struck Muginstein in the stomach.

"Are words needed here? There was a man, the man is no more. There lived an innocent bachelor, like a bird on a bough, and now he has perished, stupidly. Came a Jew who looked like a sailor and fired a shot, not at some bottle with a surprise in it, but at a living man. Are words needed here?

" 'Clear out!' shouted Benya, and was the last to go. But as he was running off, he took time to say to Butzis: 'I swear by my mother's grave, Savka, you'll lie beside him. . . .'

"Now tell me, young gentleman, you who cut coupons off other people's bonds, what would you have done if you'd been in Benya Krik's boots? You don't know how you would have acted. But he knew what to do. That's why he is King, while we two sit on the wall of the Second Jewish Cemetery and shade our faces from the sun with our palms.

"Aunt Pessya's unfortunate son did not die at once. An hour after he was brought to the hospital Benya appeared there. He summoned the doctor-in-charge and the nurse and, without taking his hands out of the pockets of his cream-colored pants, he said to them: 'I want to see the patient Josif Muginstein get well. Just in case, let me introduce myself: I'm Benzion Krik. Spare no expense. Camphor, air cushions, a private room—you must give him everything. If you don't, remember that no doctor, not even a doctor of philosophy, needs more than six feet of earth. . . .'

"Nevertheless Muginstein died the same night. And it was only then that Yid-and-a-Half let himself be heard all over Odessa.

" 'Where does the police begin,' he bellowed, 'and where does Benya end?'

" 'The police ends where Benya begins,' sensible people answered, but Tartakovsky wouldn't calm down and in the end this is what happened: a red automobile with a music box in it played the first march from the opera *Laugh, Pagliacci* in Seredinsky Square. In broad daylight the automobile raced up to the little house where Aunt Pessya lived.

"The automobile thundered, spat smoke, glittered brassily, spread a stench of gasoline, and played arias on its horn. A man leaped out of it and walked into the kitchen, where little Aunt Pessya was writhing on the earthen floor. Yid-and-a-Half sat on a chair, waving his arms.

" 'You gorilla!' he shouted when he caught sight of the visitor, 'you bandit, you, may the earth spit out your corpse! Nice fashion you've started, killing living men. . . .'

" 'Mosoo Tartakovsky,' Benya Krik said to him in a quiet voice, 'it's the second day now that I been mourning for the deceased as for my own brother. But I know that you don't give a damn for my young tears. And where, Mosoo Tartakovsky, in what strong box did you lock up shame? You had the gall to send the mother of our late Josif a miserable hundred bucks. My brain, let alone my hair, stood on end when I heard the news. . . .'

"Here Benya paused. He had on a chocolate jacket, cream-colored pants and raspberry boots.

" 'Ten grand, in a lump sum,' he roared, 'and a pension for the rest of her life, may she live a hundred and twenty years. If not, then let's leave this room, Mosoo Tartakovsky, and get into my car.'

"There was a row between the two. Yid-and-a-Half and Benya had words. I wasn't there when the argument took place. But those who were remember it. The two agreed on five thousand outright and a monthly payment of fifty roubles.

" 'Aunt Pessya,' Benya said then to the disheveled little woman who lay on the floor, 'if you need my life, you can have it, but everybody makes mistakes, even God. A terrible mistake has been made, Aunt Pessya. But wasn't it a mistake on God's part to settle the Jews in Russia, where they've had to suffer the tortures of hell? Would it be bad if the Jews lived in Switzerland, where they'd be surrounded by first-class lakes, mountain air and nothing but Frenchmen? Everybody makes mistakes, even God. Open your ears to what I'm saying, Aunt Pessya. You have five thousand in hand and fifty roubles a month till you die, may you live a hundred and twenty years. Josif will have a first-class funeral: six horses like six lions, two carriages for the wreaths, the choir from the Brody Synagogue, Minkovsky himself will sing at your late son's funeral.'

"The funeral took place the next morning. About this funeral ask the beggars who hang around the cemeteries. Ask the synagogue beadles about it, the kosher poultry mentor, the old women from the Second Poorhouse. Odessa never saw such a funeral, and the world will never see another like it. That day policemen put on cotton gloves. The synagogues were wide open, they were decorated with greenery and blazed with electric lights. Black plumes swayed above the heads of the white horses that drew the hearse. Sixty choir boys walked in front of the procession. Boys they were, but they sang with the voices of women. Elders of the synagogue of the kosher poultry dealers led Aunt Pessya, one at either elbow. Behind them marched members of the Society of Jewish Salesmen, then came attorneys-at-law, physicians and trained midwives. On one side of Aunt Pessya were poultrywomen from the Old Market, on the other the milkmaids from the Bugayovka district, wrapped in orange shawls. They stamped their feet like gendarmes on a holiday parade, and their wide hips gave off the odor of the sea and of milk. The employees of Ruvin Tartakovsky brought up the rear. There were a hundred of them, or two hundred, or two thousand. They wore black jackets with silk lapels and new boots that squeaked like suckling-pigs in a sack.

"And now I shall speak as the Lord did on Mount Sinai out of the burning bush. Fill your ears with my words. It was with my own eyes that I beheld all I beheld, sitting here on the wall of the Second Jewish Cemetery, alongside of lisping Moiseyka and Shimshon, from the cemetery office. It was I who saw it, I, Arye Leyb, the proud Jew who is neighbor to the dead.

"The hearse drove up to the cemetery chapel. The coffin was placed on the steps. Aunt Pessya trembled like a little bird. The cantor climbed out of his carriage and started the funeral service. Sixty choir boys echoed him. At that moment a red motor car shot out from behind a bend on the road. It played *Laugh, Pagliacci,* and came to a halt. The people were as quiet as the dead. The trees were silent, and the choir boys, and the beggars. Four men climbed out from under the red roof, and walking slowly, carried to the hearse a wreath of roses the like of which was never seen before. And when the service was over, four men placed their steel shoulders under the coffin and, with eyes blazing and chests thrust forward, marched in the ranks of the Society of Jewish Salesmen.

"In front walked Benya Krik, who had not yet been called King by anyone. He was the first to approach the grave. He stepped on the mound of earth and stretched out his arm.

"Kofman, of the burial brotherhood, ran up to him.

" 'What do you want to do, young man?' Kofman asked Benya.

" 'I want to make a speech,' answered Benya Krik.

"And he made a speech. It was heard by all who wanted to hear. It was heard by me, Arye Leyb, and by lisping Moiseyka, who was perched on the wall beside me.

" 'Gentlemen and ladies,' said Benya Krik, 'gentlemen and ladies,' he said, and the sun stood above his head like a sentry with a rifle. 'You have come here to pay your last respects to an honest toiler who perished for two cents. In my own name and in the name of all those who aren't present here, I thank you. Gentlemen and ladies, what did our dear Josif get out of life? A couple trifles. What was his occupation? He counted other people's money. What did he perish for? He perished for the whole working class. There are people already doomed to death, and there are people who haven't begun to live. And it just happened that a bullet that was flying at a doomed breast pierced that of Josif, who did not get anything out of life but a couple trifles. There are people who know how to drink vodka, and there are those who don't know how to drink vodka, and there are those who don't know how to drink it, but drink all the same. The result is that the first get pleasure from both joy and grief, while the second suffer for all those who drink vodka without knowing how. That is why, gentlemen and ladies, after we have said a prayer for our poor Josif, I will ask you to accompany to his grave Savely Butzis, unknown to you, but already deceased. . . .'

"After he made this speech, Benya Krik stepped down from the mound. The people, the trees, the cemetery beggars were all silent. Two grave-diggers carried an unpainted coffin to a near-by grave. The cantor, stammering, finished the prayers. Benya threw the first shovelful of earth into Josif's grave and walked over to Savka's. All the lawyers and the ladies with brooches followed him like sheep. He made the cantor chant the complete service over Savka, and the sixty choir boys joined in. Savka had never dreamed of such a service—believe the word of Arye Leyb, an old oldster.

"They say that on that day Yid-and-a-Half decided to retire from business. I wasn't there when he made that decision. But that neither the cantor nor the choir nor the burial brotherhood asked to be paid—that I saw with Arye Leyb's eyes. Arye Leyb is my name. And I could see nothing more, because the people, after walking slowly away from Savka's grave, began to run as from a house on fire. They rushed away in carriages, in carts and on foot. And only the four who had come in the red car drove off in it. The music box played its march; the car shook and was off.

" 'A King,' said lisping Moiseyka, looking after the automobile, the same Moiseyka who edges me off the best seat on the wall.

"Now you know everything. You know who was the first to utter the word, 'King!' It was Moiseyka. You know why he didn't apply that name either to one-eyed Grach or to ferocious Kolka. You know everything. But what good does it do you, if you still have spectacles on your nose and autumn in your soul? . . ."

COMMENTARY

Let us begin with some general considerations. This dazzling story, one of several by the Russian author Isaak Babel collectively entitled *Benya Krik, the Gangster,* is likely to bewilder an inexperienced reader at least as much as it pleases or amazes him. In some ways it sounds very off-hand. Benya's extortion note is not even given in full, for instance; the author just says "and so on," as if one received that sort of letter every day. On the other hand, the style [1] of the story is extremely elaborate, and its two principal events— the holdup and the funeral—seem to bear a formal relation to one another, as you think about them a little. The trouble (or complication [2]) involved in the holdup is brought to a close, or resolved,[2] by the funeral or funerals. But the stylized and formal character of the story may itself seem incongruous with its bloodthirsty material. The story, to tell the truth, has somewhat the air of a horse-opera: an exchange of fantastic letters, a crazy holdup, sudden killings, a powerlessness of the police, a funeral like something out of Chicago in the 1920's. Its theatrical quality is even insisted on by the author —"So began an opera in three acts!" he has the old man say of the holdup. Moreover, what sort of instruction is this for a rabbi, a learned man, to be giving a spectacled schoolboy? Why is a gangster held up to admiration? The story seems to give rise to all sorts of questions.

Should a story give rise to questions? This will depend on what we mean by the word "story." A story about a traveling salesman and a farmer's daughter gives rise to no questions; its purpose is achieved when you laugh. Let us use the word "anecdote" [3] for this rather than story. A second use of the word "story" applies it to the kind of narrative [4] you find in popular magazines. Formulas have been discovered for these stories, such as Boy-meets-Girl, Time-of-Troubles, Boy-gets-Girl; and the great majority of them conform closely to such formulas. Their purpose is nearly as simple as that of the anecdote; they wish to amuse, to entertain. The word "story" is a perfectly legitimate term for such narratives (a narrative is just something which is told). Plainly, however, when we call "In Odessa" a story we mean something different. A rack is a thing you put your hat on, and is also a thing that some of our ancestors stretched their sorry bodies on. By the grim comparison we suggest that the intention of a popular story writer is a casual and slight matter beside the complex intention of a serious story writer. A serious author is something like an inquisitor. He even asks questions. Indeed this is one of his major purposes, as it is also one of the purposes of poets and dramatists. He does not so much, however, ask questions of the reader as he forces the reader to put to himself the same questions about life that the author has had to put to himself.

The term "serious writer" cannot be defined briefly; but by the time we come to O. Henry's "The Gift of the Magi," you will feel the difference. "Popular writer" is not easy to define either; it has nothing to do with success or popularity, for many "popular stories" never get published at all, and many serious stories are world-famous.

Formulas are of little use to the serious writer. Each story is obliged to be an exploration. But just as the two kinds of rack have qualities in common (they are flat, you put things on them), so the popular story's desire to entertain persists in the serious or art-story. Even the character of the anecdote—a short happening narrated— persists in a large number of popular stories and some serious stories. The part of Benya Krik's career described in this story, for example, might easily have formed the subject of a simple anecdote. But, told in that way (how he got under way as a gangster, his first job, and its consequences), it would not have borne much relation to the story that we actually have; it would have raised no questions. And, for that matter, told as a popular story—but it could never have been told as a popular story, could it? This is not the stuff popular stories are made of. Leaving aside for the moment the serious writer's extra purposes, he aims at a different *kind* of entertainment. It is hardly an exaggeration to say that the popular writer wishes to make the reader forget himself and the serious writer wishes to make him *think* of himself. But with this remark we begin to face the difficult subject of identification,[5] which it will be better to postpone for a bit.

Having looked at the similarities among the three kinds of story, we come to their differences, which is what we are interested in. The identifying difference may be put very simply. Of an anecdote or a popular story we never dream of asking *what it is about,* whereas this is what deeply concerns us, as critical readers, with respect to serious stories. The anecdote or the popular story is not about anything, or it is just about itself; the question never comes up. We can see now that part of the strangeness of Babel's story must be a way of guaranteeing—by the author—that this question *will* come up.

What is the story about, then? Certainly we must not expect, by now, any very easy or rapid answer to this question.

There is a difficulty at once with the word "about." Suppose you have a conversation, a lengthy and tricky conversation, with someone on a subject of immense importance to you, and then you mention to a friend the fact that you have had a conversation, and he asks you, "What was it about?" Evidently there are several ways in which you can answer him, depending on the amount of time you have, the degree of your confidence in him, the quality of your desire to know his opinion, and so on. You can tell him very roughly the kind of things the talk was about, or you can go further and tell him what essentially mattered in it, or you can go further still and tell him *why* it was about this, and what, in your mind and feeling, the whole experience came to. These three ways of telling what a thing is about are roughly what we are going to mean here by subject,[6] substance,[7] and theme.[8] Subject is the stuff of the story, what is in it, and we will find this no simple matter. Let's take substance to stand for what is underlying and central in, or as of, the subject. Theme will be the reason for substance, its purpose—lying, that is to say, behind substance, as well as issuing from it. These three things are not perfectly distinct, of course, but it is convenient to distinguish them. We will be using all three ways of getting at what Babel's story is "about," because the time we have for a work of art is unlimited, if we aim at critical reading, and because we wish to deserve the *unlimited confidence* the author of this odd, wild story has reposed in us, and because probably we are curious to get at the feelings about life—not so much his opinions about it as the nature of the questions he asks about it, and his feelings—of one of the major story writers of our time.

A reservation or two, and a warning, before we begin. A reader's time, truly, is more or less unlimited. It depends on what he wants to read. A character in Wilkie Collins's fascinating novel *The Moonstone* read *Robinson Crusoe* all his life, citing it and consulting it as a Bible; many so read the Bible; the works of the chief poets of the world, Homer, Dante, and Shakespeare, have been used in this way for centuries. But a student's time is not (*as* a matriculated student) unlimited, nor is a teacher's. For this reason, and also for the reason that any work of art of fair scale is, strictly speaking, inexhaustible, our discussion will concentrate on what seems to matter *most,* especially as to subject. We will not even dream of attempting to touch on everything that matters with regard to "about." But then, and before then, there will be a new thing to consider. We have said scarcely anything about form [9] (plan, structure, style), which is the way that not only substance and theme but subject itself (apart from material [10]) come into being; this is literary art itself, and will need some consideration—not only for itself, but because no reasonably full account can be given of substance and theme until the form of a story is more or less clear. All this may seem to you rather abstract, but will immediately become less so. In any serious academic (or other) study—say, of descriptive or historical geology—we move between details and generalizations.

The material of Babel's story might be thought of like this. We have Benya Krik, twenty-five, reaching at the stars, but the son of a teamster (do not think of the flourishing Teamsters' Union; think of *dirt*, and remember that the locale of the story is a traditional society where a son follows his father's trade) and in addition a Jew, in Czarist Russia. Part of his life-story is recited by an old man (Reb Arye Leyb) sitting on the wall of the Second Jewish Cemetery, to a disciple, a schoolboy, "I," who has asked him why, of three magnificent gangsters, Benya is supreme. The old man answers the boy's question. Benya, tortured by longing, went into business; he offered his services, as a crook, to Froim Grach. It is to be noted—and will come up again under characterization [11] later—that he was not so rash, despite his energy and ambition, as to try to set up in business for himself. Evidently crime was highly organized. Grach, who runs a lawless outfit or gang under the patronage of an "elder" of the Jewish community, holds a conference and decides to take Benya on—to fix Tartakovsky. Madly rich, Jewish too, but wicked, Tartakovsky now is given a character sketch corresponding to the one we had of Benya. His insolence is beyond anything, he employs half Odessa in his stores, and he has been held up nine times.

Benya writes him an extortion note. Tartakovsky replies paternally, reproachfully. The letter goes astray, and Tartakovsky's place (apparently his main store) is held up by Benya with four masked assistants. While the loot is being packed, another gangster turns up late and drunk—one Savka Butzis—and for no reason shoots a clerk named Muginstein. As the gangsters run off, Benya threatens Butzis with the same fate.

Benya goes to the hospital and threatens the head doctor, ordering all special care for the clerk at his expense, but Muginstein dies. Then Benya goes, "in broad daylight," riding in a red automobile with a music box playing a march from *Laugh, Pagliacci,* to visit Muginstein's mother, Aunt Pessya. Finding Tartakovsky there, he argues him into promising her five thousand down and fifty rubles a month instead of the "miserable hundred bucks" Tartakovsky had sent her. He himself then apologizes to Aunt Pessya, who is lying on the floor, saying to her, "if you need my life, you can have it, but everybody makes mistakes, even God," and he tells her about the money settlement, and promises her son an absolutely exceptional funeral. (Nearly all peoples of the earth, except Americans, place great importance upon funerals; our general squeamishness about death doesn't let us.) This overwhelming funeral takes place. "Odessa never saw such a funeral, and the world will never see another like it. That day policemen put on cotton gloves." At the climactic moment, when the coffin is placed on the steps of the cemetery chapel and the cantor begins the service, Benya shoots up in his blaring car. In the sudden stillness, a vast wreath is carried to the hearse by four men from the car. The same four carry the coffin after the service. Benya steps on the grave-mound and makes a speech: ". . . Gentlemen and ladies, what did our dear Josif get out of life? A couple trifles. What was his occupation? He counted other people's money. . . . There are those who know how to drink vodka . . . and there are those who don't know how to drink it, but drink all the same. . . . That is why, gentlemen and ladies, after we have said a prayer for our poor Josif, I will ask you to accompany to his grave Savely Butzis, unknown to you, but already deceased. . . ." Another coffin is placed in a grave, and Benya has the cantor and sixty choir boys do the whole service over again—"Savka had never dreamed of such a service," as the old man says. A beggar sitting on the wall watching says: "A King."

Such, in three crude paragraphs which gravely and inevitably misrepresent the actual story, is what takes place—except that we have said very little of the framework.[12] Before we go on, notice that the three paragraphs correspond to the story's introduction, complication, and resolution. The conflict between Benya's character and his circumstances, producing his visit to Grach, and the community between Tartakovsky's circumstances (wealth) and character (insolence, making it certain that he will resist demands), make up the introduction. In one sense, the complication has begun already, since it is obvious that, Benya being what he is, some of Tartakovsky's money is going to pass into his possession, and complication flows from character and circumstances as much as or even more than it does from accident. Still, it seems fair to regard this as the introduction, setting the scene. About the complication—the letters and holdup— we will have something to say later. Here it will be sufficient to observe that Babel's employment of the haphazard helps strongly to produce, by contrast, the feeling of inevitability that accompanies a careful reading of the end of the story (the resolution). A letter is posted but not delivered. A gangster comes late (so that he does not know that all is going well) and drunk (so that he is given to convulsive physical actions). A clerk happens to be in front of the bullet. After these accidents, the four-stage resolution has the effect of a sequence of things *fated,* proceeding—in a degree even more complete than everything that has gone before—from Benya's character. He works to save Muginstein, he makes sure that the bereaved mother is really compensated (so far as compensation is possible in life), he arranges a magnificent funeral, and he avenges him. At the beginning of a story, nothing has happened; at the end of a good story, something—an action—has *completely* taken place.

But we have made too little of the fact that the whole thing is told by an old man to a boy as they sit on a cemetery wall. This frame-action is part of the story, of course. No view of what the story is about could satisfy us which did not take this into account. And now we are in a position to begin saying what the story is about, in terms of its subject, its substance, its theme. (Before you read on, try describing to yourself what you take its subject to be.)

The story answers the boy's question about the reason for the difference between Benya Krik, "the King," and two other superb criminals. What qualities above all *matter* in life, that is. Arye Leyb replies with a tale of Benya's beginning and how he came to be called "King." His energy was indispensable, of course; a high degree of energy marks one difference between achievement and failure or mediocrity. So was his daring; you note that all four parts of the resolution involve daring—his openly visiting the hospital, the mother, the funeral, and his not only murdering Butzis, but acknowledging the deed, as it were. But these qualities are not the real point.

His sense of *responsibility* is the real point. The world is not chaotic for Benya Krik; it makes sense. He makes it make sense. The major elements that require notice here are his imagination, his kindness, and his justice. Even a really good porter without imagination is hardly a working concept, much less a king; you require imagination in order to know what your people want, even before they tell you. Benya's imagination, if it needs illustration, is seen vividly enough in his car and in the funeral grandeur. Could a king be responsible—*be* a king—without imagination, the story asks, and answers: Certainly not. His kindness, voluntary, to Aunt Pessya, we remember. Benya strikes one as a sort of Robin Hood, extracting from the rich for the poor; and his references to classes of people in his speech on the grave-mound enforces this feeling, though we shall have more to say about this later. Now for his justice, which is what matters most. It is primitive, from our point of view perhaps —whatever "our" point of view is, at present. But it is the oldest of all Jewish justice: an eye for an eye, a death for a death. But as soon as we put it in the second way, we realize that our own law is the same as this (a slaying committed in the course of armed robbery is punished by death in those states which have capital punishment). Benya simply takes the law into his own hands, as he should do, being a King. Now it is proper that the old, who are wise, should instruct the young, who are ignorant: the old man and the boy sit on the wall. What is a fitting subject for such instruction? The center of life, which one of them has passed, the other not attained; and *in* the center of life, a man as a focus of power, whether for good or for evil, perhaps especially if for *both,* as most men are in some degree and a King in the highest degree. Yes, the qualities and responsibilities proper to a King, discoursed on by age for youth; and this is Babel's subject. It is not of course his whole subject, and we have not yet begun to take into account his irony,[13] which is basic and persistent. But now we are passing into the discussion of substance.

This story is tragic, yet funny, yet not funny. The world it describes, or rather creates and presents, is an atrocious one, lacking altogether, outside the figure of Benya Krik, in the compassion and justice that he brings into it. The context is Czarist Russia, with its special persecution for the *whole* Jewish community inside which the action [14] of the story takes place. "That was when the thugs from the Sloboda district were beating up the Jews on Bolshaya Arnaut-skaya Street." "That day policemen put on cotton gloves"—the special force of this brilliant sentence lies in one's sudden vision of the *usual* aspect of their hands: fists, clubs, whatever they used, as in Detroit in the 1930's. There is not much of this; not much is needed, and in general the Jews—that is, all the people of the story—are seen as too *low* to be of concern, even malignant concern, to the Russian society in which they live ("You can spend the night with a Russian woman, and the Russian woman will be satisfied by you" is an early, savage pointer to this broad assumption made by Babel). This fate of the Jews is crucial. "A terrible mistake has been made, Aunt Pessya. But wasn't it a mistake on God's part to settle the Jews in Russia, where they've had to suffer the tortures of hell?" The nerves of the story are singing with pain on this topic; *therefore,* Benya continues, like Danny Kaye: "Would it be bad if the Jews lived in Switzerland, where they'd be surrounded by first-class lakes, mountain air, and nothing but Frenchmen? Everybody makes mistakes, even God." The grotesquerie and comedy are defensive, one way of treating the intolerable; we will be studying a similar use of grotesquerie in "The Open Boat."

But on the whole we are, in the story, among Jews only. Their world is an atrocious place just in itself. "Tartakovsky has the soul of a murderer, but he's one of ours . . . it was his own Moldavanka people who made trouble for him. Twice they kidnapped him for ransom, and once during a pogrom they staged his funeral"—the phrase "during a pogrom" placed in this sentence shows how little Babel conceives the agony of the Jews to be due merely to persecution of them from above. They suffer because they are human beings. Businessmen with murderous souls confront gangsters who are in business ("the firm of Lyovka Byk and Company") under the aegis of an *elder* (a respected community leader). Benya himself is a gangster, and kills. That the entire narration takes place by a cemetery, and is told by one who has escaped from the war of life to one who has not entered upon it yet, testifies to the fundamental gloom of the story; at the beginning, we hear of the "green peace of the graves" directly after hearing of the three furious gangsters. Men are victims, not of Fate, but of other human beings. Life is wolfish; God is a blunderer. There is little religious faith in this story.

But there is a deep and vivid love, all the same, for this community (of which, of course, Babel had once been a part), with all its errors and crimes. This love is clearest in a paragraph cataloguing, as with tender pride, all those who attended the funeral—among them "the milkmaids from the Bugayovka district, wrapped in orange shawls" who "stamped their feet like gendarmes on a holiday parade, and their wide hips gave off the odor of the sea and of milk." His ridicule issues, not from contempt for them, but from his tragicomic [15] personal vision of their responsibility for their own misery or a large part of it. Here is the reason for the *Pagliacci* music—the clown who sings while his heart is breaking. Babel's pity, rich and hopeless, fills the story. His love and pity are unsparing, however, toward the reality of their life. The last words spoken by the helpless Muginstein before he is killed are a lie, and the author emphasizes this disconcerting fact. Even Arye Leyb mocks the boy for his weak sight, for the impossibility of his ever becoming Benya Krik. The story, which is *written* almost as a fantasy, is sharply realistic at this level.

The subject of a complex, ambitious story such as "In Odessa" is more readily identified, and can be more briefly described, than its substance. Its theme is more difficult still. But it will be possible to formulate the theme in just a few words as an introduction to some discussion of it. Why, let us ask, is a gangster held up to admiration? Our enquiry into the story's subject gave us one answer, or set of answers: exalted human qualities, even in a gangster, form a proper matter for transmitted wisdom. Our enquiry into substance suggested a more elaborate answer. Implicit already in the first answer was a certain humor—that it is to a *gangster,* in an oppressed race, that we have to be looking for these qualities. Of course this is ironic. If only the *boy* admired Benya Krik, we would learn nothing; boys do in fact make heroes of gangsters. But Reb Arye Leyb admires him too. We hardly feel either of them to be a fool, or vicious, and our second answer to the question began to show that it is not only ironic, but also *natural,* that they—and through them, we—should admire Benya, who is a superior product in an amusing but disgusting world. To say the least of it, he refuses to drown. Stifling, in danger of spiritual death, trapped between his circumstances and his desires, he goes to Froim Grach: "Take me on, Froim. I want to be cast upon your shore. The shore I'm cast on will gain by it." The image is that of shipwreck. All the others *are* shipwrecked, lost in their evils, stupidities, sufferings. *He* finds himself, both in the qualities that are proper for success in this savage world and in the qualities that would be proper (*are* proper, as is recognized by Arye Leyb) in another, higher world. He respects himself and feels for others and believes in justice. This second answer (substance) gives a much less optimistic account of things, it will be noticed, than the first did, but both are comparatively realistic. The third answer to the question, that given in terms of *theme,* is ideal, and imaginative, and is the true motor of the story's power. A reader does not at all have to be able to express, or even to "know" consciously, just what it is that he is responding to, any more than most of us do in music—hearing Mozart's Quartet K. 499 for example—or in architecture—seeing, entering, rounding the cathedral, say, at Seville, and looking down on its structure, as one is able to do (an expert does this from plans) from the even higher Moorish tower, the Giralda, beside it.

A short way to put the third answer might be this: Babel is seeking, and creating, *sources of authority.*

We live, in this story, in a world where authority has broken down. People are at each other's throats, and gouging. The American government's attempts in recent years, backed by the press and by a solid quantity of public opinion, to disinfect the leadership of the Teamsters' Union, which have ended so far in complete failure (Mr. Beck being succeeded by Mr. Hoffa, who is far stronger), are one of a thousand examples that could be cited of this twentieth-century

breakdown; the weakness of the Weimar Republic invited Hitler; *six*
more or less democratic regimes, brand new, in backward countries
in Asia and Africa, became military dictatorships in the single
year 1958. But already it is clear that the jungle atmosphere at the
bottom is produced by power vacuums at the top—into which jungle
elements move. Babel's story is complicated partly because it was
written *in* Soviet Russia *about* Czarist Russia, or the Jews under it in
one of the country's great southern cities, Odessa. We are going to
have to deal with several things. It would be better, and clearer,
if we could deal with them simultaneously, as the parts of the work can
go forward simultaneously in a musical composition for orchestra or
even for piano (the pianist has two hands), or in a Bach fugue. But
this is impossible for criticism, which is occasionally a minor branch
of literature: criticism is linear, a time-bound art, as music and
architecture are not (you hear various parts of a musical work's
thought at once, you "see" a temple or tomb in a second). Here there
is the jungle atmosphere, first, *as it results from a breakdown of*
authority. Then there are *false authorities* moving into the vacuum
at the top. And there is the imagination, partly ironic, of real Authority, new or surviving. We are obliged to follow these three strands of
one rope separately.

Jungle from breakdown. (This is not the same thing, of course,
as just jungle, studied under substance.) What authorities, in the
story, seem to be valued? A reader notices four: the "elder," the rabbi
—these are inside the community—the police (representatives of the
Czarist regime), God (the Jewish God). The elder, Lyovka Byk,
is head of a "crook"-firm. The rabbi, Arye Leyb, sits on a cemetery
wall, apparently waiting for death, without influence upon anything
except his small, bespectacled disciple. The police are powerless
against Benya (and of small assistance, apparently, to others—
witness Tartakovsky's having been held up nine times). God makes
mistakes.

Therefore: *false authorities.* (1) Benya Krik, with his simple-
minded, straight-forward illusion of the existence of democracy (his
conversation with Muginstein at the holdup). (2) Communism, which
is parodied by Benya in the funeral oration when he says of Muginstein, "He perished for the whole working class." These are the
authorities, one reigning when the story was written, one imagined
into the earlier time, an authoritarian crook, paralyzing the authorities, astonishing and delighting the community, doing his will, com-
pelling the imagination of old and young with utopian dreams. "Explain it to me, Muginstein," says Benya during the holdup, "as to a

friend: he gets a business letter from me; why couldn't he get into a trolley for five kopecks then, and ride up to my place and have a glass vodka with the family and a snack, taking potluck? What kept him from having a heart-to-heart talk with me? 'Benya,' he could have told me, 'thus and thus, here is my bank balance, wait a couple of days, let me get my breath, give me a chance to turn around . . .' What would I have answered? Hog don't meet hog, but man meets man. Muginstein, do you get me?" The democratic dream (try writing an extortion letter to the president of Macy's and then sit waiting at home for him to come visit you by subway, or bus—with the FBI) is seen in this touching passage—the loot is being packed— as central to the nature of man, post-animal. Men are equal. Benya believes this, in the teeth of all evidence, and Muginstein agrees (not truthfully) and is killed. The author's contempt, in this story, for both democratic and communist theory is plain. (Not surprisingly, his work proved unacceptable to the Soviet Union, and Babel himself disappeared twenty years ago.) What then does he believe in? It does not follow, from his dislike for two of the ruling political philosophies of our century, that he believes in anything. Increasingly, as the world progresses, people believe in nothing. Perhaps Babel is a nihilist?

Real authority, imagined. There are two sources of real authority imagined: one of action, Benya Krik, one of reflection, Arye Leyb. Benya is created as a folk-hero. He is made a practical man (he does not try to set up in "business" for himself, a tactic frowned on by organized crime) but essentially he operates in another sphere. He does not give charity like Robin Hood. We were wrong there. Money is not the point. He *does glory* (if we may put it this way)—Muginstein's funeral and Savka Butzis's—and he *does justice*—the atonement of Butzis's killing for Muginstein's. Note the rising order of the functions, first glory, then justice. These are what he gives them, and is King. The inability of the police to operate against him is magical; at this high creative level of the story, magic is allowable, and he even sways the police (in cotton gloves) to presence at the funeral— this because of the special Jewish demands made upon leaders, an absolutely fundamental topic to be taken up in a moment. He is a source of authority and of fixing-things-up, such as we need because God is hardly to be depended on. It is true that he only does a *bad* justice—such is clearly the author's thought—but this is because he has to work in a wicked, submerged world, where that is the only sort of justice (death for death) that is possible. He is only human; he makes mistakes. Or is he human? for God Himself makes mistakes. So much, with one very important reservation, for Benya. He is the King that history has denied the exiled, dispersed, persecuted, and suffering Jews. This is what, ironically, this marvelous story is really up to.

But he *becomes known* to us through the recital of his kingship by Arye Leyb to a boy. Not only must there *be* a king, but he must be recognized and named as such and his deed transmitted from generation to generation as a topic of traditional racial wisdom. Arye Leyb is the second great source of authority in the story. Note that he makes the boy *wait* for instruction; nothing could be more unlike the hurry-scurry empty give-and-take of American popular education than the tone of the framework of this story. "A man who thirsts for knowledge must be patient. A man who possesses knowledge should be dignified." Note that he himself qualifies his authority as a teller in a way suggesting that he alone can ("I wasn't at that session. But it is said that they did hold it."); for the boy his authority is absolute. Observe his saying at the end: "Now you know everything"—as if convinced that he has communicated an essential and all-encompassing secret of wisdom completely; in its own way, this story is a wisdom work [16] (a work telling one how life should be conducted) like the greatest of all Jewish wisdom works, the Poem of Job embodied (with later additions and corruptions) in the Old Testament *Book of Job*. Both poem and story are ironic and rebellious, but whereas one submits in the end to God's power (the sixth-century B.C. poem) the other imagines—only imagines—a different authority and power. Note the monumental strength of the narrator's assertion of authority: "Fill your ears with my words. It was with my own eyes that I beheld all I beheld, sitting here on the wall of the Second Jewish Cemetery. . . . It was I who saw it, I, Arye Leyb, the proud Jew who is neighbor to the dead." Pride is what the two sources of authority, the agent (Benya Krik) and the interpreter (Arye Leyb) have in common, the pride denied to the Jews now for two thousand years.

One point necessary to our account of the story's theme has been omitted with respect to each of the two characters. But we need a general consideration here. In reading any literary work of another time and place, it is necessary to think ourselves into the knowledge and frame of mind available to the contemporary reader of that work, so far as we can. We can never do this completely; but then no work of art is ever thoroughly understood anyway, even by the artist—as with all other things in life, we make out with approximations, a truth recognized in physics by one of its major twentieth-century laws, Heisenberg's Principle of Indeterminacy. We do it as well as we can, partly with learning, partly with imagination. The reader of *Macbeth* is better off if he knows that for Shakespeare and his audience the word "modern" did not mean up-to-date (with a shining connotation) but ordinary, trivial (with a pejorative connotation). This is a matter of learning, of detail. There is also a matter of learning whole national and racial attitudes, and imagination is needed for this. Japanese streets have no names, or had none until the American Army arrived and nearly went crazy; only an intersection had a name. Indians (in India) express approval by shaking their heads—a custom disconcerting to Western lecturers until they accustom themselves to it. These habits, particularly the first, are indicative of attitudes toward experience different from ours—a special vagueness (without discomfort about it) in the Japanese; and Indians visiting the West are astonished by the ordinary practices of politeness familiar to us. Now the Jews' particular respect for learning is fairly well known, even though living in American conditions many Jews have discarded it and adopted instead our American contempt for learning. But readers of this commentary who are not Jewish (and the writer of it cannot claim to be, any more than he is Russian, whether Czarist or Soviet) will have small idea of the *degree* of the Jewish feeling for learning and authority which is taken for granted in this story. The story that best conveys this feeling, perhaps, is a very funny one by the greatest of living Jewish philosophers, Martin Buber. The scene is a city in Central Europe where Buber was lecturing before World War I. After the lecture, "I went with some members of the association who had arranged the evening into a coffee house. I like to follow the speech before many, whose form allows no reply, with a conversation with a few in which person acts on person and my view is set forth directly through going into objection and question.

"We were just discussing a theme of moral philosophy when a well-built Jew of simple appearance and middle age came up to the table and greeted me. To my no doubt somewhat distant return greeting, he replied with words not lacking a slight reproof: 'Doctor! Do you not recognize me?' When I had to answer in the negative, he introduced himself as M., the brother of a former steward of my father's. I invited him to sit with us, inquired about his circumstances of life and then took up again the conversation with the young people. M. listened to the discussion, which had just taken a turn toward somewhat abstract formulations, with eager attentiveness. It was obvious that he did not understand a single word; the devotion with which he received every word resembled that of the believers who do not need to know the content of a litany since the arrangement of sounds and tones alone give them all that they need, and more than any content could.

"After a while, nonetheless, I asked him whether he had perhaps something to say to me; I should gladly go to one side with him and talk over his concern. He vigorously declined. The conversation began again and with M.'s listening. When another half hour had passed, I asked him again whether he did not perhaps have a wish that I might fulfill for him; he could count on me. No, no, he had no wish, he assured me. It had grown late; but, as happens to one in such hours of lively interchange, I did not feel weary; I felt fresher, in fact, than before, and decided to go for a walk with the young people. At this moment M. approached me with an unspeakably timid air. 'Doctor,' he said, 'I should like to ask you a question.' I bid the students wait and sat down with him at a table. He was silent. 'Just ask, Mr. M.,' I encouraged him; 'I shall gladly give you information as best I can.' 'Doctor,' he said, 'I have a daughter.' He paused; then he continued, 'And I also have a young man for my daughter.' Again a pause. 'He is a student of law. He passed the examinations with distinction.' He paused again, this time somewhat longer. I looked at him encouragingly; I supposed that he would entreat me to use my influence in some way on behalf of the presumptive son-in-law. 'Doctor,' he asked, 'is he a steady man?' I was surprised, but felt that I might not refuse him an answer. 'Now, Mr. M.,' I explained, 'after what you have said, it can certainly be taken for granted that he is industrious and able.' Still he questioned further. 'But Doctor,' he said, 'does he also have a good head?'—'That is even more difficult to answer,' I replied; 'but at any rate he has not succeeded with industry alone, he must also have something in his head.' Once again M. paused; then he asked, clearly as a final question, 'Doctor, should he now become a judge or a lawyer?'—'About that I can give you no information,' I answered. 'I do not know the young man, indeed, and even if I did know him, I should hardly be able to advise in this matter.' But then M. regarded me with a glance of almost melancholy renunciation, half-complaining, half-understanding, and spoke in an indescribable tone, composed in equal part of sorrow and humility: 'Doctor, you do not *want* to say—now, I thank you for what you have said to me.'

"This humorous and meaningful occurrence, which apparently has nothing to do with Hasidism, afforded me, nonetheless, a new and significant insight into it. As a child, I had received an image of the zaddik and through the sullied reality had glimpsed the pure idea, the idea of the genuine leader of a genuine community. Between youth and manhood this idea had arisen in me through knowledge of Hasidic teaching as that of the perfected man who realizes God in the world. But now in the light of this droll event, I caught sight in my inner experience of the zaddik's function as a leader. I, who am truly no zaddik, no one assured in God, rather a man endangered before God, a man wrestling ever anew for God's light, ever anew engulfed in God's abysses, nonetheless, when asked a trivial question and replying with a trivial answer, then experienced from within for the first time the true zaddik, questioned about revelations and replying in revelations. I experienced him in the fundamental relation of his soul to the world: in his responsibility."

To this *extreme* sense of the Jewish need for authority, and the Jewish people's sense of story telling, let us now connect the things omitted earlier about Benya Krik and Arye Leyb. One of the strangest remarks in Babel's story is one about Benya. One of the gangsters was packing the loot, Muginstein had his hands over his head, and "in the meantime Benya was telling stories from the life of the Jewish people." This remark means, probably, to identify the unusually laconic folk-hero, a doer, with the theme of traditional wisdom that belongs otherwise (but Benya's speech at the funeral, explaining his justice, is a second instance) to the frame of the story. The statement about, or rather by, Arye Leyb that we have not considered is the most exalted, perhaps, in the story: "And now I shall speak as the Lord did on Mount Sinai out of the burning bush . . ." Here we have actual divine authority claimed, in simile,[17] for the revelation (as we had better call it) of Benya Krik's arrival at the funeral(s)—the manifestation of his glory, his presence, and his justice. A Law is announced. What Law? A New Law, like Paul's in the New Testament? No, the same Law as Moses's—put *back* into force, as if the abrogation of the Old Law announced by Paul had failed (Czarist Russia was a strongly Christian society), and in order to have *any* Law it was necessary, with Benya Krik and his interpreter Arye Leyb (we will meet this notion of "interpreter" again in "The Open Boat"), to re-establish the old.

At this point we may see our account of the story's meaning as sufficiently full. How does this meaning reach the reader? Not reach him intellectually, for, as we saw, few readers will go so far as we have done here with formulation of the story's meaning; but reach him emotionally, so that he is moved, impressed, perhaps changed even, without being able to say exactly what it is that has worked on him. Identification is probably the chief means, and Buber's story gives us a fine example by way of contrast.

Buber's story, beautifully told as it is, is really an anecdote. The reader does not identify himself, in any *serious* sense, with either Buber or his anxious interlocutor. Buber's anecdote may have something in common, stylistically and thematically, with Babel's story; it has nothing in common with a popular magazine story, and this brings us to the realization of a paradoxical fact. The reader's identification with the characters, in a popular story, is far more complete than it can ever be in a serious story. The reason for this is just that the characters in a popular story are not made individuals, *so that they can be identified with unreservedly.* It is true that the identification— with the hero, the wife, the villain—is shallow and transient, and serves only the purpose of escape from the reader's self for a little while. None of the *learning* inevitably involved in a serious identification with another (imagined) human being takes place. Now this word "imagined" must contain our point. Buber's story is veracious, or *"true."* We do not, as readers or listeners, identify ourselves readily with actual other human beings; we are too conscious of our own reality. The kind of identification that takes place when we read biography probably ought to be regarded in two ways: first, as a mere intensifying of the very slight identification with the writer involved in *all* reading, even scientific reading, such as Darwin's *Origin of Species;* second, as a response to the fact that the subject of a biography is always to some extent *imagined* and *created* in the biography.

The identification that occurs in a serious work is often not very conscious. It takes place at deeper levels in the mind or spirit. The appeal made is very likely from deeper levels in the character to deeper levels in the reader. The identification is very incomplete— few people still sane have ever felt even for a moment that they *were* Hamlet or Don Quixote—but may be profound and lasting, because learning has accompanied it: the learning what it is like to be, or pretend to be, someone else, from which experience one resumes one's ordinary self in a new frame of mind. Not escape from one's self but discovery of one's self is the object.

In Babel's story, let us take up the hero, the villain, and the victims. The reader's primary identification of course is with Benya— otherwise the story would be nothing; but we do not reach Benya directly. The explanation of his royalty comes to us from the old man —throughout, we are sitting on the cemetery wall—and we hear it with the ears and excitement of the boy. We are really with the boy (it is impossible not to feel, by the way, that the author has put himself into the story, to some extent, in the figure of the boy). The double remove from the figure of the hero allows the story's mythical and magical qualities free play; we are less disposed to criticism, as we listen with the boy's open ears to the old man's authority. More will be said about this when we come to discuss point of view. Any very strong *personal* identification with Benya is forbidden; it would be undesirable, considering the stature the author wishes to secure for him; the reader is required to occupy a position of weakness and mere admiration. The circumstances of this primary identification govern our feelings with the other characters. We can identify with Tartakovsky only in his helplessness before Benya and his feelings upon attending his own "funeral"; on this note also, the villain as victim, his character disappears—he is said to have retired. When he is his usual self (playing, for example, *from above,* on Benya's sympathies, as in his letter) we attend to him with perfect objectivity. The actual victims, again, we reach indirectly. Muginstein, during the holdup, is "as green as green grass" as he says, pathetically, "I am in charge here," and just before he is shot he is more or less forced by Benya (who feels that everyone shares his own folk-democracy) to tell a lie. This is not very much to go on, though it shows us that identification is not a product only of characterization but also of mere function-in-the-story and of imagery.[18] With Savka there is no identification at all. But of Aunt Pessya we learn that at her son's great funeral she "trembled like a little bird"; here is unquestionably a moment of feeling with her. In this story of an oppressed people it is natural that identification should be through weakness. But perhaps it is true that in all serious literary works— *not* in popular ones, where the reverse is true—we are more inclined to identify with weakness and suffering than with strength and joy, perhaps because most people's lives are so much more fully characterized by the first two qualities than by the second two.

Several topics remain. It is as much by means of style and tone and imagery as by what is said, that an author's personal vision is communicated. Two of the most obvious elements of style in Babel's story are clearly the management of *pace* [19] and the richness of *imagery*. The tranquil setting of the narration—the man and boy at peace on the cemetery wall—contrasts sharply with the furious, jocular rapidity of the narrative itself with its violent content. This is emphasized, of course, by the ceremonious dialogue of man and boy in contrast with the unceremonious action described. But the contrast is not simple, because the element of ceremony enters also into the action, with the funeral, Benya Krik's apology to Aunt Pessya, and his funeral oration. The otherwise jerky action is also raised to a poetic level, and drawn out of its squalid urban setting to be seen against the general background of Nature, by the imagery—like a little bird, as green as green grass. This dimension of the story's style allows Babel to be much more offhand than he could otherwise be without losing stature and significance for his action.

Tone [20] is a term closely related to style, describing something which is a product of style but not quite the same thing and not lending itself readily to short definition. It corresponds rather to the tone of a man's voice in conversation—unmistakable, but not to be identified exactly with any combination of nameable elements. What adjectives shall we apply to Babel's tone here? Jaunty, and dubious. He needs both those qualities at once, because they affect each other; neither would be the same in isolation. The combination is one of the richest of all literary tones and one of the oldest. There is a passage in the Babylonian epic of *Gilgamesh,* some 4000 years old, which has a tone remarkably like Babel's in this story. The hero is approached by the Lady Ishtar and offered all sorts of things to become her lover. He remains unmoved. "Lady," he replies, "you speak of giving me riches, but you would demand far more in return. The food and clothing you would need would be such as befits a goddess; the house would have to be meet for a queen, and your robes of the finest weave. And why should I give you all this? You are but a draughty door, a palace tottering to its ruin, a turban which fails to cover the head, pitch that defiles the hand, a bottle that leaks, a shoe that pinches. Have you ever kept faith with a lover? Have you ever been true to your troth? When you were a girl there was Tammuz. But what happened to him? Year by year men mourn his fate!" and so on.* The blunt and poetic realism of the two works, their tone, the heroes' refusal to be surprised or overtaken, have much in common.

Finally, something must be said about point of view.[21] Most stories are told from the point of view of an omniscient narrator [22] (as he has been called), the author, who writes in the third person and knows everything. This is the direct opposite of the point of view of the dramatist, who never says a single word himself (except perhaps in stage directions, like Shaw); only the characters speak, and each of them is limited to his own knowledge. This is called the effaced narrator.[23] The advantages of the omniscient narrator technique are obvious; it is the method, for example, both of the epic of *Gilgamesh* and of *War and Peace.* But except in very powerful

---

* Theodor H. Gaster's admirable translation, in *The Oldest Stories in the World.*

hands it tends to lack immediacy, becoming something more resembling a report than a presentation. Babel's method is very different. It is first person narrative,[24] the second most usual way of telling a story. But to say this hardly describes it adequately. Because of the doubling of this technique in the story, it really resembles drama to some extent. The whole story is told by the boy. But since so much of what he tells us is exactly what the old man tells him, the story has the effect of a conversation—losing in scope what the *author* might have been able to tell us that the boy and the old man do not know, but gaining in directness, of course, not only because the old man speaks with the special authority of personal knowledge, but because we do not even hear him directly except with the pricked ears of ignorance and longing.

TERMS AND PRINCIPLES

1. *Style:* The mode of expressing thought in language, distinctive to a particular author or a particular work.

2. *Complication:* The name given in criticism to the entanglement of action, in most stories, which makes up the first part of the narrative (though frequently this is preceded by an *introduction*) and leads to the *resolution,* or second part, where the entanglement is straightened out or "resolved." This division of the parts of a story is artificial, of course; good stories seldom divide themselves so conveniently, the relations between their parts being organic. This term will be made clearer later; for the moment, it will be enough for you to ask yourself where your shoulder ends and your arm begins.

3. *Anecdote:* A short narrative of an incident of private life.

4. *Narrative:* A continued account of any series of occurrences; story.

5. *Identification:* The tendency of a reader to identify himself with a character or characters in an imaginative literary work, or even with the author of it.

6. *Subject:* The stuff of the story, what is in it. But this term is to be distinguished sharply from the notion of *action* or what happens in the story. In Babel's story the subject is identified as "the qualities and responsibilities proper to a King, discoursed on by age for youth."

7. *Substance:* What underlies the subject, what it bears on, and how. This might be considered as the broad, permanent

thought—or way of taking life—of the author, the "subject" being the particular instance embodied in the story in question. But the term shades forward into "theme" and the commentary should be studied for the distinctions.

8. *Theme:* A term which generalizes the activity, and outcome, of the substance; *why* the subject and substance are what they are. Theme comprehends the ideal, and the imaginative, more distinctly than the preceding terms.

9. *Form:* The systematic and structural pattern, and unity, in a literary work.

10. *Material:* What goes into a literary work, the separate elements as they (or some of them) may have existed in the author's mind before composition.

11. *Characterization:* The marking out by an author of his characters as distinct, by traits mentioned, description given, dialogue reported, etc.

12. *Framework, frame-action:* The action or dialogue which encloses, in some stories, the body of the story.

13. *Irony:* Briefly, conveyance of meaning by words, or events, whose intended meaning is different from their literal meaning, sometimes indeed the opposite. There is invariably some hidden force involved. This term too will need continued discussion.

14. *Action:* The movement of *events* in a story, novel, or drama. A very limited term, compared to most of those we have been using.

15. *Tragicomic:* A term in which emphasis is to be laid on the first of its two components. There are no tragic authors whose view of life is essentially comic; the term is reserved for apparently comic authors whose views are at least in part essentially tragic.

16. *Wisdom literature:* A term applied to certain books of the Old Testament—which is Christian as well as Hebrew—which aim at an explanation of how human life should be conducted.

17. *Simile:* An explicit likening of one thing to another.

18. *Imagery:* The term applied to whatever, in a literary work, makes its appeal to the reader's *senses,* as of sight, hearing, taste, touch, smell.

19. *Pace:* Rate of speed, as an element of style in a literary work or a part of it.

20. *Tone:* A term originally musical, now used for the prevail-

ing character or spirit in a literary work or anywhere in it, analogous to the tone of an individual human speaking or singing voice, not practically definable but to the acquainted ear unmistakable.

21. *Point of view:* Two rather different technical ways of looking at fiction are comprehended under this awkwardly elastic term. The first concerns the different kinds of narrators that are possible: the omniscient, the first person, and the effaced (see below for these). The second concerns something more like long shots and close-ups in a film. The long view gives us panoramas, summaries; the short view gives us *scenes,* incidents. Instead of just telling *about,* looking off at, it dramatizes. Of course these two ways of understanding point of view overlap.

22. *Omniscient narrator:* The author telling the story in the third person, knowing everything.

23. *Effaced narrator:* The author appearing in the story as little as possible, but without using a narrator inside the story. The method is usually scenic (see Point of view above)— short views predominate.

24. *First person narrator:* The author telling the story through one of its characters, or by putting himself into the story.

ERNEST HEMINGWAY

A Clean, Well-Lighted Place

It was late and every one had left the café except an old man who sat in the shadow the leaves of the tree made against the electric light. In the day time the street was dusty, but at night the dew settled the dust and the old man liked to sit late because he was deaf and now at night it was quiet and he felt the difference. The two waiters inside the café knew that the old man was a little drunk, and while he was a good client they knew that if he became too drunk he would leave without paying, so they kept watch on him.

"Last week he tried to commit suicide," one waiter said.

"Why?"

"He was in despair."

"What about?"

"Nothing."

"How do you know it was nothing?"

"He has plenty of money."

They sat together at a table that was close against the wall near the door of the café and looked at the terrace where the tables were all empty except where the old man sat in the shadow of the leaves of the tree that moved slightly in the wind. A girl and a soldier went by in the street. The street light shone on the brass number on his collar. The girl wore no head covering and hurried beside him.

"The guard will pick him up," one waiter said.

"What does it matter if he gets what he's after?"

"He had better get off the street now. The guard will get him. They went by five minutes ago."

The old man sitting in the shadow rapped on his saucer with his glass. The younger waiter went over to him.

"What do you want?"

The old man looked at him. "Another brandy," he said.

"You'll be drunk," the waiter said. The old man looked at him. The waiter went away.

"He'll stay all night," he said to his colleague. "I'm sleepy now. I never get into bed before three o'clock. He should have killed himself last week."

The waiter took the brandy bottle and another saucer from the counter inside the café and marched out to the old man's table. He put down the saucer and poured the glass full of brandy.

"You should have killed yourself last week," he said to the deaf man. The old man motioned with his finger. "A little more," he said. The waiter poured on into the glass so that the brandy slopped over and ran down the stem into the top saucer of the pile. "Thank you," the old man said. The waiter took the bottle back inside the café. He sat down at the table with his colleague again.

"He's drunk now," he said.

"He's drunk every night."

"What did he want to kill himself for?"

"How should I know."

"He hung himself with a rope."

"Who cut him down?"

"His niece."

"Why did they do it?"

"Fear for his soul."

"How much money has he got?"

"He's got plenty."

"He must be eighty years old."

"Anyway I should say he was eighty."

"I wish he would go home. I never get to bed before three o'clock. What kind of hour is that to go to bed?"

"He stays up because he likes it."

"He's lonely. I'm not lonely. I have a wife waiting in bed for me."

"He had a wife once too."

"A wife would be no good to him now."

"You can't tell. He might be better with a wife."

"His niece looks after him."

"I know. You said she cut him down."

"I wouldn't want to be that old. An old man is a nasty thing."

"Not always. This old man is clean. He drinks without spilling. Even now, drunk. Look at him."

"I don't want to look at him. I wish he would go home. He has no regard for those who must work."

The old man looked from his glass across the square, then over at the waiters.

"Another brandy," he said, pointing to his glass. The waiter who was in a hurry came over.

"Finished." he said, speaking with that omission of syntax stupid people employ when talking to drunken people or foreigners. "No more tonight. Close now."

"Another," said the old man.

"No. Finished." The waiter wiped the edge of the table with a towel and shook his head.

The old man stood up, slowly counted the saucers, took a leather coin purse from his pocket and paid for the drinks, leaving half a peseta tip.

The waiter watched him go down the street, a very old man walking unsteadily but with dignity.

"Why didn't you let him stay and drink?" the unhurried waiter asked. They were putting up the shutters. "It is not halfpast two."

"I want to go home to bed."

"What is an hour?"

"More to me than to him."

"An hour is the same."

"You talk like an old man yourself. He can buy a bottle and drink at home."

"It's not the same."

"No, it is not," agreed the waiter with a wife. He did not wish to be unjust. He was only in a hurry.

"And you? You have no fear of going home before your usual hour?"

"Are you trying to insult me?"

"No, hombre, only to make a joke."

"No," the waiter who was in a hurry said, rising from pulling down the metal shutters. "I have confidence. I am all confidence."

"You have youth, confidence, and a job," the older waiter said. "You have everything."

"And what do you lack?"

"Everything but work."

"You have everything I have."

"No. I have never had confidence and I am not young."

"Come on. Stop talking nonsense and lock up."

"I am of those who like to stay late at the café," the older waiter said. "With all those who do not want to go to bed. With all those who need a light for the night."

"I want to go home and into bed."

"We are of two different kinds," the older waiter said. He was now dressed to go home. "It is not only a question of youth and confidence although those things are very beautiful. Each night I am reluctant to close up because there may be some one who needs the café."

"Hombre, there are bodegas open all night long."

"You do not understand. This is a clean and pleasant café. It is well lighted. The light is very good and also, now, there are shadows of the leaves."

"Good night," said the younger waiter.

"Good night," the other said. Turning off the electric light he continued the conversation with himself. It is the light of course but it is necessary that the place be clean and pleasant. You do not want music. Certainly you do not want music. Nor can you stand before a bar with dignity although that is all that is provided for these hours. What did he fear? It was not fear or dread. It was a nothing that he knew too well. It was all a nothing and a man was nothing too. It was only that and light was all it needed and a certain cleanness and order. Some lived in it and never felt it but he knew it all was nada y pues nada y nada y pues nada. Our nada who art in nada, nada be thy name thy kingdom nada thy will be nada in nada as it is in nada. Give us this nada our daily nada and nada us our nada as we nada our nadas and nada us not into nada but deliver us from nada; pues nada. Hail nothing full of nothing, nothing is with thee. He smiled and stood before a bar with a shining steam pressure coffee machine.

"What's yours?" asked the barman.

"Nada."

"Otro loco mas," said the barman and turned away.

"A little cup," said the waiter.

The barman poured it for him.

"The light is very bright and pleasant but the bar is unpolished," the waiter said.

The barman looked at him but did not answer. It was too late at night for conversation.

"You want another copita?" the barman asked.

"No, thank you," said the waiter and went out. He disliked bars and bodegas. A clean, well-lighted café was a very different thing. Now, without thinking further, he would go home to his room. He would lie in the bed and finally, with daylight, he would go to sleep. After all, he said to himself, it is probably only insomnia. Many must have it.

This short, almost desperate, and beautiful story is an unusually fine example of a very special kind of story which is not anecdotal at all. If you were asked by somebody, "What happens in this story?" you would have to reply, "Nothing." Now *nothing* is exactly what the story is about: Nothing, and the steps we take against Nothing. The fact that there is no plot is part of the story's meaning: in a world characterized by "Nothing" what significant action could take place? Characterization is at a minimum also. The two waiters are only very gradually distinguished from one another; their voices in the beginning are choric,[1] just two men talking, any two men. Of the old man in the café we learn very little, and of the barman at the end, nothing. The older waiter is clearly the most important person in the story, but we do not really learn very much about him either. You could hardly say that the story is *about* him. The part usually played by plot and characterization, in conveying a story's meaning, is left in this story largely to setting [2] and atmosphere.[3]

Setting is not merely a geographical word, like "locale," saying where the action of a story is laid. Setting is a larger and more inclusive term, shading toward atmosphere, but referring rather to the physical than to the atmospheric or psychological presentation of the action—or, in the case of this story, non-action. Both setting and atmosphere are products of style.

Hemingway's style is famous for its simplicity—short, common words, short sentences—and is said to be realistic or naturalistic. Is it realistic? "I am of those who like to stay late at the café," the older waiter says. "With all those who do not want to go to bed. With all those who need a light for the night." Surely this is elaborately rhetorical, nobody actually talks this way, and one of the reasons (though only one) for the Spanish setting of the story is the author's desire to achieve from time to time this highly poetic and unnatural tone (as he can do by pretending to be translating from Spanish into English) without its seeming inconsistent with the curt talk, rapid description, and coarse and bitter material of the story. Hemingway's style is very complicated, that is to say. Even where it appears simple, it is not very simple. Let us look at the first two sentences.

"It was late and every one had left the café except an old man who sat in the shadow the leaves of the tree made against the electric light. In the day time the street was dusty, but at night the dew settled the dust and the old man liked to sit late because he was deaf and now at night it was quiet and he felt the difference." Now in just a moment we are going to learn that this old man tried to kill himself last week, even though he has plenty of money; in short, he is *in despair,* and the phrase is used by one of the waiters. That is why he is drinking himself drunk, as he does every night. Even in themselves Hemingway's opening sentences are rather stylized—the rhythms are insistent, alliteration [4] is employed (dew . . . dust . . . deaf . . . difference), even rhyme is (night: quiet), and "late" is repeated in a choric way. But as the opening of *this* story, which is to come to a climax in a violent parody of the Lord's Prayer, clearly these sentences have already begun the symbolism which is the reason for the story's being. It is *late,* not only on this evening, and in this man's life, but *in a tradition*—a religious tradition, specifically the Christian tradition (we are in a Catholic country, Spain); so late that the tradition cannot support or console, and suicide invites. There is thus a second reason, besides the physical debility that awaits all of us at the end of life, for the old man's being deaf: he is deaf to the Christian promises, he cannot hear them. He is *alone,* isolated, sitting in the "shadow" left by Nature in the modern artificial world. All the light desired in this story is artificial, as if Nature had abandoned man, and anything he may want he has to get for himself—precariously and briefly.

We are now in a position to hear better the first little conversation between the waiters:

"He was in despair."
"What about?"
"Nothing."
"How do you know it was nothing?"
"He has plenty of money."

This is not just a sour joke, though it is that too. We have to hear "Nothing" also as *something very positive,* the name given in this story to the modern condition of moral vacancy and meaninglessness which the old man feels, and so he tried to kill himself, and the older waiter feels, and so he suffers from insomnia: "It was a nothing that he knew too well. It was all a nothing and a man was nothing too. It was only that and light was all it needed and a certain cleanness and order. Some lived in it and never felt it but he knew it all was nada y pues nada y nada y pues nada" (nothing and then nothing and nothing and then nothing).

It is *feeling* this condition of nothingness, not the nothingness itself, which is Hemingway's real subject. His deep sympathy with the two sensitive men, the old man and the older waiter, is the story's strongest feeling. Neither is a passive victim. The old man has his "dignity"—a key word for Hemingway. When the younger waiter says "An old man is a nasty thing," the older waiter, without sentimentalizing or denying the general truth of this (very unpleasant) remark, defends the honor of this particular old man with precise observation: "Not always. This old man is clean. He drinks without spilling. Even now, drunk. Look at him." And when the impatience of the younger waiter has pushed him out, he walks away "unsteadily but with dignity." It is not much, human dignity, in the face of the human condition of nothingness, but it is what we can have.

The older waiter's symbol [5] for it is *light*—here a man-made device to hold off the darkness, not permanently, but as late as possible, and *in public,* as if man's essential loneliness were less intolerable where the forms of social life have to be observed, where one's dignity is called on. (The specific danger of being alone is, of course, suicide.) He formulates this, as it were, on behalf of the old man, and only gradually do we become aware that *his* plight is similar, he is an *older* waiter. In the beginning, as we saw, the two waiters are hardly differentiated. The view that money is all that matters in life, the little conversation about the soldier and the girl, cannot even be assigned to one or the other; it is just waiters' talk—waiters we think of as automatically cynical, like taxi drivers. (What is the purpose of the incident of the soldier and the girl? This shows us two people who *do* have a program, something to do that they want to do, as the younger waiter does and the two older do not; and it also established a context for this café in which nearly the whole story takes place—that context is war.) The older waiter begins to become distinct when he points out the cleanness of the old man. He is "unhurried," unlike the younger waiter, having no place to go. But his nerves do not strike one as being at all good: his coarse joke ("You have no fear of going home before your usual hour?") proceeds from some deep irritability, which is then partly explained by his "No. I have never had confidence and I am not young." More and more distinctly he has become the story's spokesman, the younger waiter being unfitted for this role by his insensitivity (in one of his very rare value-judgments, Hemingway implies that he is "stupid") and the old man by being too completely isolated. In the three-sentence speech quoted in the third paragraph of this analysis, he takes on himself the open role of spokesman, and he sees himself also as a custodian of certain values ("It is not only a question of youth and confidence although those things are very beautiful. Each night I am reluctant to close up because there may be some one who needs the café").

Light, cleanness, order, dignity: to hold the Nothing at bay. The reason these things are necessary is that everything else has failed. The parody of the Lord's Prayer has a deliberate effect of blasphemy, and thus explains why these symbols have been used—and why this story, for that matter, has come into existence. Notice how brilliantly the narrative is handled. Turning the light off in the café, he continues the conversation with himself. We are given no indication that he is moving, much less going somewhere else. The parody ends: "Hail nothing full of nothing, nothing is with thee. He smiled and stood before a bar with a shining steam pressure coffee machine." Without our knowledge he has been moving, while blaspheming, and the Lord's Prayer has brought him—where? Precisely where you cannot be with dignity, standing at a bar. Religion is a cheat. You might as well worship this sudden apparition, the shining steam pressure coffee machine, as the Christian God or *nada*.

When the barman asks what he wants, he answers "Nada," meaning "Nothing is all that is possible, so that is what I'll have." The barman does not understand, of course ("Otro loco mas" is One more lunatic, Another joker). The lack of understanding of the barman is the point of the end of the story. Insensitive, like the younger waiter, the barman leaves the older waiter isolated with his knowledge that all is *nada,* that this bar is unpolished, that a bar is not a dignified place, and that he himself will not sleep. The last two sentences of the story come like a lash, ranging him again, in his loneliness and desperate need for dignity, with the large class of human beings ("I am of those who . . .") who feel and suffer man's desertion by God —an invented God. (One of Hemingway's little poems takes a different tone with the same theme:

> The Lord is my shepherd.
> I shall not want
> Him for long.)

This essential human ordeal is for all men, but it is only recognized, the story suggests, in age; so that this is what our journey is toward. This, miserably, is what wisdom is of: Nada. Perhaps no story in English has ever been built so obsessively around one word (and the volume of stories in which it originally appeared was called by Hemingway *Winner Take Nothing*).

The angry desolation of the story has its roots in Hemingway's disillusion during the First World War, best expressed shortly in a famous passage of his novel *A Farewell to Arms*. An Italian and the hero are talking, and the Italian says, "We won't talk about losing. There is enough talk about losing. What has been done this summer cannot have been done in vain." "I did not say anything. I was always embarrassed by the words sacred, glorious, and sacrifice and the expression in vain. We had heard them, sometimes standing in the rain almost out of earshot, so that only the shouted words came through, and had read them, on proclamations that were slapped up by billposters over other proclamations, now for a long time, and I had seen nothing sacred, and the things that were glorious had no glory and the sacrifices were like the stockyards at Chicago if nothing was done with the meat except to bury it. There were many words that you could not stand to hear and finally only the names of places had dignity. Certain numbers were the same way and certain dates and these with the names of the places were all you could say and have them mean anything. Abstract words such as glory, honor, courage, or hallow were obscene beside the concrete names of villages, the numbers of roads, the names of rivers, the numbers of regiments and the dates." In the light of this passage, it is clearer why the older waiter has such difficulty in saying what it is that he hates—*nada*—and what it is that he sets against it—dignity—and why he has to use symbols to express his malignant dissatisfaction with the Christian universe.

TERMS AND PRINCIPLES

1. *Choric:* A chorus (from which "choral" and "choric") is a group talking or singing in unison. Greek tragedy developed from a religious chorus and always retained a chorus of some sort. The members are not distinguished from each other as individuals; they are just Theban elders or the townsmen of Corinth. They comment on the action or enter into it, but not as principals.
2. *Setting:* The place in which the action of a story, play, or poem goes on. But it also gives the physical characteristics of the action, and these provide some of the atmosphere.
3. *Atmosphere:* The psychological "feel" of a story or its characters, the psychic medium in which the events occur.
4. *Alliteration:* The recurrence of the same initial sound in words in close succession.
5. *Symbol:* The word "symbol" is used differently in philosophy and in literary criticism. In the former it means either anything that functions as a sign, i.e. refers to something else, or a conventional sign (words, flags, traffic lights) rather than a natural one (dark clouds, which mean rain). In literary

criticism, a "symbol" is usually a term whose meaning goes beyond the immediate story or event (as one says "home" in a context which reminds the reader of the idea that the soul's home is heaven).

EXERCISE

JAMES JOYCE

Araby

North Richmond Street, being blind, was a quiet street except at the hour when the Christian Brothers' School set the boys free. An uninhabited house of two storeys stood at the blind end, detached from its neighbours in a square ground. The other houses of the street, conscious of decent lives within them, gazed at one another with brown imperturbable faces.

The former tenant of our house, a priest, had died in the back drawing-room. Air, musty from having been long enclosed, hung in all the rooms, and the waste room behind the kitchen was littered with old useless papers. Among these I found a few paper-covered books, the pages of which were curled and damp: *The Abbot,* by Walter Scott, *The Devout Communicant* and *The Memoirs of Vidocq.* I liked the last best because its leaves were yellow. The wild garden behind the house contained a central apple-tree and a few straggling bushes under one of which I found the late tenant's rusty bicycle-pump. He had been a very charitable priest; in his will he had left all his money to institutions and the furniture of his house to his sister.

When the short days of winter came, dusk fell before we had well eaten our dinners. When we met in the street the houses had grown somber. The space of sky above us was the color of everchanging violet and towards it the lamps of the street lifted their feeble lanterns. The cold air stung us and we played till our bodies glowed. Our shouts echoed in the silent street. The career of our play brought us through the dark muddy lanes behind the houses where we ran the gauntlet of the rough tribes from the cottages, to the back doors of the dark dripping gardens where odors arose from the ashpits, to the dark odorous stables where a coachman smoothed and combed the horse or shook music from the buckled harness. When we returned to the street, light from the kitchen windows had filled the areas. If my uncle was seen turning the corner we hid in the shadow until we had seen him safely housed. Or if Mangan's sister came out on the doorstep to call her brother in to his tea we watched her from our shadow peer up and down the street. We waited to see whether she would remain or go in and, if she remained, we left our shadow and walked up to Mangan's steps resignedly. She was waiting for us, her figure defined by the light from the half-opened door. Her brother always teased her before he obeyed and I stood by the railings looking at her. Her dress swung as she moved her body and the soft rope of her hair tossed from side to side.

Every morning I lay on the floor in the front parlor watching her door. The blind was pulled down to within an inch of the sash so that I could not be seen. When she came out on the doorstep my heart leaped. I ran to the hall, seized my books and followed her. I kept her brown figure always in my eye and, when we came near the point at which our ways diverged, I quickened my pace and passed her. This happened morning after morning. I had never spoken to her, except for a few casual words, and yet her name was like a summons to all my foolish blood.

Her image accompanied me even in places the most hostile to romance. On Saturday evenings when my aunt when marketing I had to go to carry some of the parcels. We walked through the flaring streets, jostled by drunken men and bargaining women, amid the curses of laborers, the shrill litanies of shop-boys who stood on guard by the barrels of pigs' cheeks, the nasal chanting of street-singers, who sang a *come-all-you* about O'Donovan Rossa, or a ballad about the troubles in our native land. These noises converged in a single sensation of life for me: I imagined that I bore my chalice safely through a throng of foes. Her name sprang to my lips at moments in strange prayers and praises which I myself did not understand. My eyes were often full of tears (I could not tell why) and at times a flood from my heart seemed to pour itself out into my bosom. I thought little of the future. I did not know whether I would ever speak to her or not or, if I spoke to her, how I could tell her of my confused adoration. But my body was like a harp and her words and gestures were like fingers running upon the wires.

One evening I went into the back drawing-room in which the priest had died. It was a dark rainy evening and there was no sound in the house. Through one of the broken panes I heard the rain impinge upon the earth, the fine incessant needles of water playing in the sodden beds. Some distant lamp or lighted window gleamed below me. I was thankful that I could see so little. All my senses seemed to desire to veil themselves and, feeling that I was about to slip from them, I pressed the palms of my hands together until they trembled, murmuring: *"O love! O love!"* many times.

At last she spoke to me. When she addressed the first words to me I was so confused that I did not know what to answer. She asked me was I going to *Araby*. I forgot whether I answered yes or no. It would be a splendid bazaar, she said she would love to go.

"And why can't you?" I asked.

While she spoke she turned a silver bracelet round and round her wrist. She could not go, she said, because there would be a retreat that week in her convent. Her brother and two other boys were fighting for their caps and I was alone at the railings. She held one of the spikes, bowing her head towards me. The light from the lamp opposite our door caught the white curve of her neck, lit up her hair that rested there and, falling, lit up the hand upon the railing. It fell over one side of her dress and caught the white border of a petticoat, just visible as she stood at ease.

"It's well for you," she said.

"If I go," I said, "I will bring you something."

What innumerable follies laid waste my waking and sleeping thoughts after that evening! I wished to annihilate the tedious intervening days. I chafed against the work of school. At night in my bedroom and by day in the classroom her image came between me and the page I strove to read. The syllables of the word *Araby* were called to me through the silence in which my soul luxuriated and cast an Eastern enchantment over me. I asked for leave to go to the bazaar on Saturday night. My aunt was surprised and hoped it was not some Freemason affair. I answered few questions in class. I watched my master's face pass from amiability to sternness; he hoped I was not beginning to idle. I could not call my wandering thoughts together. I had hardly any patience with the serious work of life which, now that it stood between me and my desire, seemed to me child's play, ugly monotonous child's play.

On Saturday morning I reminded my uncle that I wished to go to the bazaar in the evening. He was fussing at the hall-stand, looking for the hat-brush, and answered me curtly:

"Yes, boy, I know."

As he was in the hall I could not go into the front parlor and lie at the window. I left the house in bad humor and walked slowly towards the school. The air was pitilessly raw and already my heart misgave me.

When I came home to dinner my uncle had not yet been home. Still it was early. I sat staring at the clock for some time and, when its ticking began to irritate me, I left the room. I mounted the staircase and gained the upper part of the house. The high, cold, empty gloomy rooms liberated me and I went from room to room singing. From the front window I saw my companions playing below in the street. Their cries reached me weakened and indistinct and, leaning my forehead against the cool glass, I looked over at the dark house where she lived. I may have stood there for an hour, seeing nothing but the brown-clad figure cast by my imagination, touched discreetly by the lamplight at the curved neck, at the hand upon the railings and at the border below the dress.

When I came downstairs again I found Mrs. Mercer sitting at the fire. She was an old garrulous woman, a pawnbroker's widow, who collected used stamps for some pious purpose. I had to endure the gossip of the tea-table. The meal was prolonged beyond an hour and still my uncle did not come. Mrs. Mercer stood up to go: she was sorry she couldn't wait any longer, but it was after eight o'clock and she did not like to be out late, as the night air was bad for her. When she had gone I began to walk up and down the room, clenching my fists. My aunt said:

"I'm afraid you may put off your bazaar for this night of Our Lord."

At nine o'clock I heard my uncle's latchkey in the hall-door. I heard him talking to himself and heard the hall-stand rocking when it had received the weight of his overcoat. I could interpret these signs. When he was midway through his dinner I asked him to give me the money to go to the bazaar. He had forgotten.

"The people are in bed and after their first sleep now," he said.

I did not smile. My aunt said to him energetically:

"Can't you give him the money and let him go? You've kept him late enough as it is."

My uncle said he was very sorry he had forgotten. He said he believed in the old saying: "All work and no play makes Jack a dull boy." He asked me where I was going and, when I had told him a second time he asked me did I know *The Arab's Farewell to his Steed.* When I left the kitchen he was about to recite the opening lines of the piece to my aunt.

I held a florin tightly in my hand as I strode down Buckingham Street towards the station. The sight of the streets thronged with buyers and glaring with gas recalled to me the purpose of my journey. I took my seat in a third-class carriage of a deserted train. After an intolerable delay the train moved out of the station slowly. It crept onward among ruinous houses and over the twinkling river. At Westland Row Station a crowd of people pressed to the carriage doors; but the porters moved them back, saying that it was a special train for the bazaar. I remained alone in the bare carriage. In a few minutes the train drew up beside an improvised wooden platform. I passed out on to the road and saw by the lighted dial of a clock that it was ten minutes to ten. In front of me was a large building which displayed the magical name.

I could not find any sixpenny entrance and, fearing that the bazaar would be closed, I passed in quickly through a turnstile, handing a shilling to a weary-looking man. I found myself in a big hall girdled at half its height by a gallery. Nearly all the stalls were closed and the greater part of the hall was in darkness. I recognised a silence like that which pervades a church after a service. I walked into the center of the bazaar timidly. A few people were gathered about the stalls which were still open. Before a curtain, over which the words *Café Chantant* were written in colored lamps, two men were counting money on a salver. I listened to the fall of the coins.

Remembering with difficulty why I had come I went over to one of the stalls and examined porcelain vases and flowered tea-sets. At the door of the stall a young lady was talking and laughing with two young gentlemen. I remarked their English accents and listened vaguely to their conversation.

"O, I never said such a thing!"

"O, but you did!"

"O, but I didn't!"

"Didn't she say that?"

"Yes. I heard her."

"O, there's a . . . fib!"

Observing me the young lady came over and asked me did I wish to buy anything. The tone of her voice was not encouraging; she seemed to have spoken to me out of a sense of duty. I looked humbly at the great jars that stood like eastern guards at either side of the dark entrance to the stall and murmured:

"No, thank you."

The young lady changed the position of one of the vases and went back to the two young men. They began to talk of the same subject. Once or twice the young lady glanced at me over her shoulder.

I lingered before her stall, though I knew my stay was useless, to make my interest in her wares seem the more real. Then I turned away slowly and walked down the middle of the bazaar. I allowed the two pennies to fall against the sixpence in my pocket. I heard a voice call from one end of the gallery that the light was out. The upper part of the hall was now completely dark.

Gazing up into the darkness I saw myself as a creature driven and derided by vanity; and my eyes burned with anguish and anger.

SOME QUESTIONS

1. What do you make of the first sentence of the story in relation to its theme? Perhaps an essential opposition might be seen at once

between the word "blind," as of the setting of the boy's drab life, and the word "free," as of his imagination of the bazaar. Notice that the freedom of the boys is set in contrast at once to the "brown imperturbable faces" of decent houses.

2. Is there an advantage in the first-person narrative here as against, say, third-person, in the displaying of the circumstances of the boy's life? Would an omniscient author have told us so *little* and so indirectly? The boy lives, not with his parents—they are presumably dead—but with his uncle and aunt, whom we hear about in terms of his hiding from his uncle and having to go with his aunt to do tasks. There is no complaint. The complaint is left to the reader, for this wretched orphan.

3. Until the blazing final sentence, the story is a superb illustration of the power of *understatement*.[1] Make a list of examples in the narrative. For instance, how do we learn that the boy is imaginative? There is nothing but a romantic book or so named, a color or so— yellow, "everchanging violet." How do we learn that he *was* a good student until his obsession with Mangan's sister?

4. Is the story written, in general, in terms of the long view— panorama, summary—or the short view—drama, scene? Are there any exceptions to the generalization?

5. What function is served by the boy's thought about the priest who used to live in his house? You will be helped here by noticing that what seems to matter to the boy about the priest is that he was charitable: he *gave* things; and that the boy uses the word "chalice" about his love; and that his fundamental desire is to *give* her something.

6. The boy's sacramental sense of her is enforced by one physical detail in particular—his lying prostrate as he watches her in the morning. Is there any physical detail, or are there any, suggesting strongly that this is not his only sense of her, and preparing for the staggering word "vanity" in the final sentence?

7. What do the ugly lists, in the sentences beginning "The career of our play brought us through . . ." and "We walked through . . ." in the third and fifth paragraphs, add to the extremely bare indications of his family life at the beginning of the story, by way of indicating how he feels about his life apart from his love?

8. How do we learn that his uncle drinks? Why did not the author simply tell us, through the boy, that the uncle drinks?

9. In this unusual story, complication and resolution are dealt with in an unusual way. There is a description of the situation, apart from Mangan's sister, then there is the girl, for whom he is a "harp"

on which she plays; here, she is a complication. But the situation-and-girl then form the new *given* situation, for which the complication is the bazaar as a promise. You will want to study for yourself the sequence of frustrations, beginning with the uncle's being in the hall on the morning of the great day. These compose, of course, for the new situation, the complication. But they continue until the final sentence of the story begins. Is this alone, then, the resolution? Not at all. All these frustrations are *part* of the resolution of which the final sentence is the climax. They are not accidental in the story's metaphysics, but inevitable—the bad weather, the tea-gossip, the late, irresponsible uncle, the slow train, the solitude, the poverty, the closed stalls, the banal conversation at a stall that is open. If they were accidental, the story would not lead to the word "vanity," as it does. Here is the question: the story looks, to a casual reader, as if it were going to lead to the notion of *self-pity*. But it does not. Why not?

10. You will be helped in answering the last question, which we do not pretend is an easy one, if you consider the possibility that the boy is taught, by his ultimate difficulties in the story, that he has sent himself off on a false quest—an almost purely romantic love (or indeed rather mixed), to which he has given a religious significance. Even the bazaar, which is only an avenue to the service of the beloved one, is equated with a church: "I recognized a silence like that which pervades a church after a service." Now what was the service here?—but a service of Mammon and women, gifts, flirting. What function is served by the "young lady" at the stall, and the idiocies she and her suitors utter?

11. The being "driven and derided by vanity" (and the consequent "anger and anguish") of the *climax* 2 of the story might be considered in several ways: first, his vanity, in the most ordinary sense, in the boy's hoping to recommend himself by a gift from him; then the vanity, vainness (from the point of view of the Church), in the love of creatures rather than of the Creator; and last, nihilism of the "Vanity of vanities, all is vanity" in *Ecclesiastes*. The order and importance of these possibilities is a question for your reflection and debate.

TERMS AND PRINCIPLES

1. *Understatement:* One understates when he says less than the literal truth. In imaginative literature, understatement can make the full, unrevealed truth stronger than if stated.
2. *Climax:* What a sequence comes to its end in; culmination.

EXERCISE

O. HENRY

The Gift of the Magi

One dollar and eighty-seven cents. That was all. And sixty cents of it was in pennies. Pennies saved one and two at a time by bulldozing the grocer and the vegetable man and the butcher until one's cheeks burned with the silent imputation of parsimony that such close dealing implied. Three times Della counted it. One dollar and eighty-seven cents. And the next day would be Christmas.

There was clearly nothing to do but flop down on the shabby little couch and howl. So Della did it. Which instigates the moral reflection that life is made up of sobs, sniffles, and smiles, with sniffles predominating.

While the mistress of the home is gradually subsiding from the first stage to the second, take a look at the home. A furnished flat at $8 per week. It did not exactly beggar description, but it certainly had that word on the lookout for the mendicancy squad.

In the vestibule below was a letter-box into which no letter would go, and an electric button from which no mortal finger could coax a ring. Also appertaining thereunto was a card bearing the name "Mr. James Dillingham Young."

The "Dillingham" had been flung to the breeze during a former period of prosperity when its possessor was being paid $30 per week. Now, when the income was shrunk to $20, the letters of "Dillingham" looked blurred, as though they were thinking seriously of contracting to a modest and unassuming D. But whenever Mr. James Dillingham Young came home and reached his flat above he was called "Jim" and greatly hugged by Mrs. James Dillingham Young, already introduced to you as Della. Which is all very good.

Della finished her cry and attended to her cheeks with the powder rag. She stood by the window and looked out dully at a gray cat walking a gray fence in a gray backyard. Tomorrow would be Christmas Day, and she had only $1.87 with which to buy Jim a present. She had been saving every penny she could for months, with this result. Twenty dollars a week doesn't go far. Expenses had been greater than she had calculated. They always are. Only $1.87 to buy a present for Jim. Her Jim. Many a happy hour she had spent planning for something nice for him. Something fine and rare and sterling—something just a little bit near to being worthy of the honor of being owned by Jim.

There was a pier-glass between the windows of the room. Perhaps you have seen a pier-glass in an $8 flat. A very thin and very agile person may, by observing his reflection in a rapid sequence of longitudinal strips, obtain a fairly accurate conception of his looks. Della, being slender, had mastered the art.

Suddenly she whirled from the window and stood before the glass. Her eyes were shining brilliantly, but her face had lost its color within twenty seconds. Rapidly she pulled down her hair and let it fall to its full length.

Now, there were two possessions of the James Dillingham Youngs in which they both took a mighty pride. One was Jim's gold watch that had been his father's and his grandfather's. The other was Della's hair. Had the Queen of Sheba lived in the flat across the air-shaft, Della would have let her hair hang out the window some day to dry just to depreciate Her Majesty's jewels and gifts. Had King Solomon been the janitor, with all his treasures piled up in the basement, Jim would have pulled out his watch every time he passed, just to see him pluck at his beard from envy.

So now Della's beautiful hair fell about her rippling and shining like a cascade of brown waters. It reached below her knee and made itself almost a garment for her. And then she did it up again nervously and quickly. Once she faltered for a minute and stood still while a tear or two splashed on the worn red carpet.

On went her old brown jacket; on went her old brown hat. With a whirl of skirts and with the brilliant sparkle still in her eyes, she fluttered out the door and down the stairs to the street.

Where she stopped the sign read: "Mme. Sofronie. Hair Goods of All Kinds." One flight up Della ran, and collected herself, panting. Madame, large, too white, chilly, hardly looked the "Sofronie."

"Will you buy my hair?" asked Della.

"I buy hair," said Madame. "Take yer hat off and let's have a sight at the looks of it."

Down rippled the brown cascade.

"Twenty dollars," said Madame, lifting the mass with a practised hand.

"Give it to me quick," said Della.

Oh, and the next two hours tripped by on rosy wings. Forget the hashed metaphor. She was ransacking the stores for Jim's present.

She found it at last. It surely had been made for Jim and no one else. There was no other like it in any of the stores, and she had turned all of them inside out. It was a platinum fob chain simple and chaste in design, properly proclaiming its value by substance alone and not by meretricious ornamentation—as all good things should do. It was even worthy of The Watch. As soon as she saw it she knew that it must be Jim's. It was like him. Quietness and value— the description applied to both. Twenty-one dollars they took from her for it, and she hurried home with the 87 cents. With that chain on his watch Jim might be properly anxious about the time in any company. Grand as the watch was, he sometimes looked at it on the sly on account of the old leather strap that he used in place of a chain.

When Della reached home her intoxication gave way a little to prudence and reason. She got out her curling irons and lighted the gas and went to work repairing the ravages made by generosity added to love. Which is always a tremendous task, dear friends—a mammoth task.

Within forty minutes her head was covered with tiny, close-lying curls that made her look wonderfully like a truant schoolboy. She looked at her reflection in the mirror long, carefully, and critically.

"If Jim doesn't kill me," she said to herself, "before he takes a second look at me, he'll say I look like a Coney Island chorus girl. But what could I do—oh! what could I do with a dollar and eighty-seven cents?"

At 7 o'clock the coffee was made and the frying-pan was on the back of the stove hot and ready to cook the chops.

Jim was never late. Della doubled the fob chain in her hand

and sat on the corner of the table near the door that he always entered. Then she heard his step on the stair way down on the first flight, and she turned white for just a moment. She had a habit of saying little silent prayers about the simplest everyday things, and now she whispered: "Please God, make him think I am still pretty."

The door opened and Jim stepped in and closed it. He looked thin and very serious. Poor fellow, he was only twenty-two—and to be burdened with a family! He needed a new overcoat and he was without gloves.

Jim stopped inside the door, as immovable as a setter at the scent of quail. His eyes were fixed upon Della, and there was an expression in them that she could not read, and it terrified her. It was not anger, nor surprise, nor disapproval, nor horror, nor any of the sentiments that she had been prepared for. He simply stared at her fixedly with that peculiar expression on his face.

Della wriggled off the table and went for him.

"Jim, darling," she cried, "don't look at me that way. I had my hair cut off and sold it because I couldn't have lived through Christmas without giving you a present. It'll grow out again—you won't mind, will you? I just had to do it. My hair grows awfully fast. Say 'Merry Christmas!' Jim, and let's be happy. You don't know what a nice—what a beautiful, nice gift I've got for you."

"You've cut off your hair?" asked Jim, laboriously, as if he had not arrived at that patent fact yet even after the hardest mental labor.

"Cut it off and sold it," said Della. "Don't you like me just as well, anyhow? I'm me without my hair, ain't I?"

Jim looked about the room curiously.

"You say your hair is gone?" he said, with an air almost of idiocy.

"You needn't look for it," said Della. "It's sold, I tell you—sold and gone, too. It's Christmas Eve, boy. Be good to me, for it went for you. Maybe the hairs of my head were numbered," she went on with a sudden serious sweetness, "but nobody could ever count my love for you. Shall I put the chops on, Jim?"

Out of his trance Jim seemed quickly to wake. He enfolded his Della. For ten seconds let us regard with discreet scrutiny some inconsequential object in the other direction. Eight dollars a week or a million a year—what is the difference? A mathematician or a wit would give you the wrong answer. The magi brought valuable gifts, but that was not among them. This dark assertion will be illuminated later on.

Jim drew a package from his overcoat pocket and threw it upon the table.

"Don't make any mistake, Dell," he said, "about me. I don't think there's anything in the way of a haircut or a shave or a shampoo that could make me like my girl any less. But if you'll unwrap that package you may see why you had me going a while at first."

White fingers and nimble tore at the string and paper. And then an ecstatic scream of joy; and then, alas! a quick feminine change to hysterical tears and wails, necessitating the immediate employment of all the comforting powers of the lord of the flat.

For there lay The Combs—the set of combs, side and back, that Della had worshipped for long in a Broadway window. Beautiful combs, pure tortoise shell, with jewelled rims—just the shade to wear in the beautiful vanished hair. They were expensive combs, she knew, and her heart had simply craved and yearned over them without the least hope of possession. And now, they were hers, but the tresses that should have adorned the coveted adornments were gone.

But she hugged them to her bosom, and at length she was able to look up with dim eyes and a smile and say: "My hair grows so fast, Jim!"

And then Della leaped up like a little singed cat and cried, "Oh, oh!"

Jim had not yet seen his beautiful present. She held it out to him eagerly upon her open palm. The dull precious metal seemed to flash with a reflection of her bright and ardent spirit.

"Isn't it a dandy, Jim? I hunted all over town to find it. You'll have to look at the time a hundred times a day now. Give me your watch. I want to see how it looks on it."

Instead of obeying, Jim tumbled down on the couch and put his hands under the back of his head and smiled.

"Dell," said he, "let's put our Christmas presents away and keep 'em a while. They're too nice to use just at present. I sold the watch to get the money to buy your combs. And now suppose you put the chops on."

The magi, as you know, were wise men—wonderfully wise men—who brought gifts to the Babe in the manger. They invented the art of giving Christmas presents. Being wise, their gifts were no doubt wise ones, possibly bearing the privilege of exchange in case of duplication. And here I have lamely related to you the uneventful chronicle of two foolish children in a flat who most unwisely sacrificed for each other the greatest treasures of their house. But in a last word to the wise of these days let it be said that of all who give gifts these two were the wisest. Of all who give and receive gifts, such as they are wisest. Everywhere they are wisest. They are the magi.

SOME QUESTIONS

1. This world-famous story contains a good instance of its author's favorite device,[1] the surprise (or "twist") ending. Can you describe its mechanism? Another good instance is that in his story called "After Twenty Years." Here two men meet. They had parted twenty years before, agreeing to meet at this time and place. One is now a wanted criminal, the other a policeman, who after meeting his old friend and recognizing him (but not being recognized—plausibility is not a chief point in this kind of story) sends a plain-clothes man around to arrest him. The plain-clothes man pretends to be the friend until he is noticed *not* to be: he arrests the criminal, showing him a note from the policeman, whose heart was too soft to allow him to make the arrest himself. Does this sort of story telling involve any cost in characterization? Does it seem to you to be legitimate,[2] or to be a trick played on the reader?

2. Sentimentality[3] is a quality not very easily defined but easily recognized, as we distinguish it from sentiment. Sentiment we think of as deep and steady, sentimentality as shallow and sporadic; one is difficult and true, the other easy and false. Does the story seem to you sentimental? Does it seem to aim at *an impression of life* or at tear-jerking?

3. We are told that "Had King Solomon been the janitor . . .

Jim would have pulled out his watch every time he passed, just to see him pluck at his beard from envy." Later we learn that "Grand as the watch was, he sometimes looked at it on the sly on account of the old leather strap that he used as a chain." Are these statements consistent with each other? Does the author care, or is he concerned only to make an effect by any means at any particular point in his narrative, without any sense of conscience about what he has been saying earlier or what he will be saying later?

4. Characterize Della and Jim. Do we learn anything about them that is not entirely to their credit, apart from a certain impulsive generosity, which after all is to their credit too, as the little moral at the end of the story is careful to point out? Do they seem believable people, composed of both good and bad qualities as the characters in serious stories are?

5. In various analyses and exercises we have studied the various kinds of narrator in fiction. We might call O. Henry's here the "cozy narrator." Point out examples of this quality. At one point he says "Forget the hashed metaphor," to which we might reply, "Why should we? Why didn't you fix it up?" The expression he has used is this: "The next two hours tripped by on rosy wings." Are the notions that time trips and flies trite? Are they made any less trite by being *confused?*

6. What do you imagine would be Ernest Hemingway's opinion of this story? Why?

7. Perhaps the real point, from which a writer might have taken off, in "After Twenty Years," would be the state of mind of the policeman as he meets his old friend turned criminal; but there is not a word about this in O. Henry's story. What do you think might be the real point, or points, in the present story, from which a writer might take off?

TERMS AND PRINCIPLES

1. *Device:* The way in which something is got done; contrivance.
2. *Legitimate:* A word of many meanings, most of them in the area of:—making its appeal to one's best judgment, or to standards of authenticity, or to the permanent. The opposite adjective always has a connotation of underhandedness, which is denied in "legitimate."
3. *Sentimentality:* Excess or affectation of feeling, or self-indulgence in it, generally with connotations of lack of genuineness and steadiness, qualities we associate with "senti-

ment." ("Connotation" we use here in the grammarian's sense, as we do throughout Part II; see Part I, pp. 94, 103.) We are referring to a word's secondary suggestions or associations, rather than to its intension.

EXERCISE

FRANZ KAFKA

A Fratricide

The evidence shows that this is how the murder was committed:

Schmar, the murderer, took up his post about nine o'clock one night in clear moonlight by the corner where Wese, his victim, had to turn from the street where his office was into the street he lived in.

The night air was shivering cold. Yet Schmar was wearing only a thin blue suit; the jacket was unbuttoned, too. He felt no cold; besides, he was moving about all the time. His weapon, half a bayonet and half a kitchen knife, he kept firmly in his grasp, quite naked. He looked at the knife against the light of the moon; the blade glittered; not enough for Schmar; he struck it against the bricks of the pavement till the sparks flew; regretted that, perhaps; and to repair the damage drew it like a violin bow across his boot sole while he bent forward, standing on one leg, and listened both to the whetting of the knife on his boot and for any sound out of the fateful side street.

Why did Pallas, the private citizen who was watching it all from his window near by in the second story, permit it to happen? Unriddle the mysteries of human nature! With his collar turned up, his dressing gown girt round his portly body, he stood looking down, shaking his head.

And five houses farther along, on the opposite side of the street, Mrs. Wese, with a fox-fur coat over her nightgown, peered out to look for her husband who was lingering unusually late tonight.

At last there rang out the sound of the doorbell before Wese's office, too loud for a doorbell, right over the town and up to heaven, and Wese, the industrious nightworker, issued from the building, still invisible in that street, only heralded by the sound of the bell; at once the pavement registered his quiet footsteps.

Pallas bent far forward; he dared not miss anything. Mrs. Wese, reassured by the bell, shut her window with a clatter. But Schmar knelt down; since he had no other parts of his body bare, he pressed only his face and his hands against the pavement; where everything else was freezing, Schmar was glowing hot.

At the very corner dividing the two streets Wese paused; only his walking stick came round into the other street to support him. A sudden whim. The night sky invited him, with its dark blue and its gold. Unknowing, he gazed up at it, unknowing he lifted his hat and stroked his hair; nothing up there drew together in a pattern to interpret the immediate future for him; everything stayed in its senseless, inscrutable place. In itself it was a highly reasonable action that Wese should walk on, but he walked on to Schmar's knife.

"Wese!" shrieked Schmar, standing on tiptoe, his arms outstretched, the knife sharply lowered, "Wese! You will never see Julia again!" And right into the throat and left into the throat and a third time deep into the belly stabbed Schmar's knife. Water rats, slit open, give out such a sound as came from Wese.

"Done," said Schmar, and pitched the knife, now superfluous bloodstained ballast, against the nearest house front, "The bliss of murder! The relief, the soaring ecstasy from the shedding another's blood! Wese, old nightbird, friend, alehouse crony, you are oozing away into the dark earth below the street. Why aren't you simply a bladder of blood so that I could stamp on you and make you vanish into nothingness? Not all we want comes true, not all the dreams that blossomed have borne fruit; your solid remains lie here, already indifferent to every kick. What's the good of the dumb question you are asking?"

Pallas, choking on the poison in his body, stood at the doubleleafed door of his house as it flew open. "Schmar! Schmar! I saw it all, I missed nothing." Pallas and Schmar scrutinized each other. The result of the scrutiny satisfied Pallas; Schmar came to no conclusion.

Mrs. Wese, with a crowd of people on either side, came rushing up, her face grown quite old with the shock. Her fur coat swung open, she collapsed on top of Wese; the nightgowned body belonged to Wese, the fur coat spreading over the couple like the smooth turf of a grave belonged to the crowd.

Schmar, fighting down with difficulty the last of his nausea, pressed his mouth against the shoulder of the policeman who, stepping lightly, led him away.

SOME QUESTIONS

1. There seems to be no narrator here at all. Who is the narrator? Distinguish the various points of view in the sketch (perhaps it is not fully enough developed for us to call it a story).

2. Is the method of the narrative realistic? Point out details that are (a) highly poetic, or (b) seem dreamlike. Normally an author *guarantees,* so to speak, what he tells us; he takes responsibility for the truth of what he tells. Does this author do so? Cite passages *both* pro and con.

3. Pallas is the spectator (his name suggests Pallas Athene, the Greek goddess of wisdom); he is overlooking, watching, a fundamental human action, as old as Cain and Abel. Why do you suppose the author says "he *dared* not miss anything"? When toward the end he and the murderer scrutinize each other, he—but only he—is said to be "satisfied"; what is meant by this?

4. "You will never see Julia again!" may be read as a triumphant revenging statement, or it may be read as a desperate cry of sympathy to his brother even as he kills him. Are we given the evidence (the author begins by talking about "evidence") that would enable us to make up our minds on this point?

5. Why is the expression "stepping lightly" used of the policeman at the end? Your answer might have two parts, one dealing with the policeman himself, his duty done, and the other dealing with what the detail tells us about how *Schmar* is walking.

6. How would you characterize Schmar's view of human life? One of his expressions ("Why aren't you simply a bladder of blood . . .") is strongly reminiscent of a general pronouncement on human life by one of the wisest and best of men, the emperor Marcus Aurelius, in his *Meditations:* "All this is foul smell and blood in a bag." Does the author sympathize with Schmar? Do his pressing on the pavement, and the final sentence, tell us anything about this?

STEPHEN CRANE

The Open Boat

A Tale Intended to be after the Fact: Being the Experience of Four Men from the Sunk Steamer Commodore

I

None of them knew the colour of the sky. Their eyes glanced level, and were fastened upon the waves that swept toward them. These waves were of the hue of slate, save for the tops, which were of foaming white, and all of the men knew the colours of the sea. The horizon narrowed and widened, and dipped and rose, and at all times its edge was jagged with waves that seemed thrust up in points like rocks.

Many a man ought to have a bathtub larger than the boat which here rode upon the sea. These waves were most wrongfully and barbarously abrupt and tall, and each froth-top was a problem in small-boat navigation.

The cook squatted in the bottom, and looked with both eyes at the six inches of gunwale which separated him from the ocean. His sleeves were rolled over his fat forearms, and the two flaps of his unbuttoned vest dangled as he bent to bail out the boat. Often he said, "Gawd! that was a narrow clip." As he remarked it he invariably gazed eastward over the broken sea.

The oiler, steering with one of the two oars in the boat, sometimes raised himself suddenly to keep clear of water that swirled in over the stern. It was a thin little oar, and it seemed often ready to snap.

The correspondent, pulling at the other oar, watched the waves and wondered why he was there.

The injured captain, lying in the bow, was at this time buried in that profound dejection and indifference which comes, temporarily at least, to even the bravest and most enduring when, willy-nilly, the firm fails, the army loses, the ship goes down. The mind of the master of a vessel is rooted deep in the timbers of her, though he command for a day or a decade; and this captain had on him the stern impression of a scene in the greys of dawn of seven turned faces, and later a stump of a topmast with a white ball on it, that slashed to and fro at the waves, went low and lower, and down. Thereafter there was something strange in his voice. Although steady, it was deep with mourning, and of a quality beyond oration or tears.

"Keep 'er a little more south, Billie," said he.

"A little more south, sir," said the oiler in the stern.

A seat in his boat was not unlike a seat upon a bucking broncho, and by the same token a broncho is not much smaller. The craft pranced and reared and plunged like an animal. As each wave came, and she rose for it, she seemed like a horse making at a fence outrageously high. The manner of her scramble over these walls of water is a mystic thing, and, moreover, at the top of them were ordinarily these problems in white water, the foam racing down from the summit of each wave requiring a new leap, and a leap from the air. Then, after scornfully bumping a crest, she would slide and race and splash down a long incline, and arrive bobbing and nodding in front of the next menace.

A singular disadvantage of the sea lies in the fact that after successfully surmounting one wave you discover that there is another behind it just as important and just as nervously anxious to do something effective in the way of swamping boats. In a ten-foot dinghy one can get an idea of the resources of the sea in the line of waves that is not probable to the average experience which is never at sea in a dinghy. As each slaty wall of water approached, it shut all else from the view of the men in the boat, and it was not difficult to imagine that this particular wave was the final outburst of the ocean, the last effort of the grim water. There was a terrible grace in the move of the waves, and they came in silence, save for the snarling of the crests.

In the wan light the faces of the men must have been grey. Their eyes must have glinted in strange ways as they gazed steadily astern. Viewed from a balcony, the whole thing would doubtless

have been weirdly picturesque. But the men in the boat had no time
to see it, and if they had had leisure, there were other things to occupy their minds. The sun swung steadily up the sky, and they knew
it was broad day because the colour of the sea changed from slate
to emerald green streaked with amber lights, and the foam was like
tumbling snow. The process of the breaking day was unknown to
them. They were aware only of this effect upon the colour of the
waves that rolled toward them.

In disjoined sentences the cook and the correspondent argued
as to the difference between a life-saving station and a house of
refuge. The cook had said: "There's a house of refuge just north of
the Mosquito Inlet Light, and as soon as they see us they'll come off
in their boat and pick us up."

"As soon as who see us?" said the correspondent.

"The crew," said the cook.

"Houses of refuge don't have crews," said the correspondent.
"As I understand them, they are only places where clothes and grub
are stored for the benefit of shipwrecked people. They don't carry
crews."

"Oh, yes, they do," said the cook.

"No, they don't," said the correspondent.

"Well, we're not there yet, anyhow," said the oiler, in the stern.

"Well," said the cook, "perhaps it's not a house of refuge that
I'm thinking of as being near Mosquito Inlet Light; perhaps it's a
life-saving station."

"We're not there yet," said the oiler in the stern.

II

As the boat bounced from the top of each wave the wind tore
through the hair of the hatless men, and as the craft plopped her
stern down again the spray slashed past them. The crest of each of
these waves was a hill, from the top of which the men surveyed for a
moment a broad tumultuous expanse, shining and wind-riven. It was
probably splendid, it was probably glorious, this play of the free sea,
wild with lights of emerald and white and amber.

"Bully good thing it's an on-shore wind," said the cook. "If not, where would we be? Wouldn't have a show."

"That's right," said the correspondent.

The busy oiler nodded his assent.

Then the captain, in the bow, chuckled in a way that expressed humour, contempt, tragedy, all in one. "Do you think we've got much of a show now, boys?" said he.

Whereupon the three were silent, save for a trifle of hemming and hawing. To express any particular optimism at this time they felt to be childish and stupid, but they all doubtless possessed this sense of the situation in their minds. A young man thinks doggedly at such times. On the other hand, the ethics of their condition was decidedly against any open suggestion of hopelessness. So they were silent.

"Oh, well," said the captain, soothing his children, "we'll get ashore all right."

But there was that in his tone which made them think; so the oiler quoth, "Yes! if this wind holds."

The cook was baling. "Yes! if we don't catch hell in the surf."

Canton-flannel gulls flew near and far. Sometimes they sat down on the sea, near patches of brown seaweed that rolled over the waves with a movement like carpets on a line in a gale. The birds sat comfortably in groups, and they were envied by some in the dinghy, for the wrath of the sea was no more to them than it was to a covey of prairie chickens a thousand miles inland. Often they came very close and stared at the men with black bead-like eyes. At these times they were uncanny and sinister in their unblinking scrutiny, and the men hooted angrily at them, telling them to be gone. One came, and evidently decided to alight on the top of the captain's head. The bird flew parallel to the boat and did not circle, but made short sidelong jumps in the air in chicken-fashion. His black eyes were wistfully fixed upon the captain's head. "Ugly brute," said the oiler to the bird. "You look as if you were made with a jackknife." The cook and the correspondent swore darkly at the creature. The captain naturally wished to knock it away with the end of the heavy painter, but he did not dare do it, because anything resembling an emphatic gesture would have capsized this freighted boat; and so, with his open hand, the captain gently and carefully waved the gull away. After it had been discouraged from the pursuit the captain breathed easier on account of his hair, and others breathed easier because the bird struck their minds at this time as being somehow gruesome and ominous.

In the meantime the oiler and the correspondent rowed. And also they rowed. They sat together in the same seat, and each rowed an oar. Then the oiler took both oars; then the correspondent took both oars; then the oiler; then the correspondent. They rowed and they rowed. The very ticklish part of the business was when the time came for the reclining one in the stern to take his turn at the oars. By the very last star of truth, it is easier to steal eggs from under a hen than it was to change seats in the dinghy. First the man in the stern slid his hand along the thwart and moved with care, as if he were of Sèvres. Then the man in the rowing-seat slid his hand along the other thwart. It was all done with the most extraordinary care. As the two sidled past each other, the whole party kept watchful eyes on the coming wave, and the captain cried: "Look out, now! Steady, there!"

The brown mats of seaweed that appeared from time to time were like islands, bits of earth. They were travelling, apparently, neither one way nor the other. They were, to all intents, stationary. They informed the men in the boat that it was making progress slowly toward the land.

The captain, rearing cautiously in the bow after the dinghy soared on a great swell, said that he had seen the lighthouse at Mosquito Inlet. Presently the cook remarked that he had seen it. The correspondent was at the oars then, and for some reason he too wished to look at the lighthouse; but his back was toward the far shore, and the waves were important, and for some time he could not seize an opportunity to turn his head. But at last there came a wave more gentle than the others, and when at the crest of it he swiftly scoured the western horizon.

"See it?" said the captain.

"No," said the correspondent, slowly; "I didn't see anything."

"Look again," said the captain. He pointed. "It's exactly in that direction."

At the top of another wave the correspondent did as he was bid, and this time his eyes chanced on a small, still thing on the edge of the swaying horizon. It was precisely like the point of a pin. It took an anxious eye to find a lighthouse so tiny.

"Think we'll make it, Captain?"

"If this wind holds and the boat don't swamp, we can't do much else," said the captain.

The little boat, lifted by each towering sea and splashed viciously by the crests, made progress that in the absence of seaweed was not apparent to those in her. She seemed just a wee thing wallowing, miraculously top up, at the mercy of five oceans. Occasionally a great spread of water, like white flames, swarmed into her.

"Bail her, cook," said the captain, serenely.

"All right, Captain," said the cheerful cook.

III

It would be difficult to describe the subtle brotherhood of men that was here established on the seas. No one said that it was so. No one mentioned it. But it dwelt in the boat, and each man felt it warm him. They were a captain, an oiler, a cook, and a correspondent, and they were friends—friends in a more curiously iron-bound degree than may be common. The hurt captain, lying against the water-jar in the bow, spoke always in a low voice and calmly; but he could never command a more ready and swiftly obedient crew than the motley three of the dinghy. It was more than a mere recognition of what was best for the common safety. There was surely in it a quality that was personal and heart-felt. And after this devotion to the commander of the boat, there was this comradeship, that the correspondent, for instance, who had been taught to be cynical of men, knew even at the time was the best experience of his life. But no one said that it was so. No one mentioned it.

"I wish we had a sail," remarked the captain. "We might try my overcoat on the end of an oar, and give you two boys a chance to rest." So the cook and the correspondent held the mast and spread wide the overcoat; the oiler steered; and the little boat made good way with her new rig. Sometimes the oiler had to scull sharply to keep a sea from breaking into the boat, but otherwise sailing was a success.

Meanwhile the lighthouse had been growing slowly larger. It had now almost assumed colour, and appeared like a little grey shadow on the sky. The man at the oars could not be prevented from turning his head rather often to try for a glimpse of this little grey shadow.

At last, from the top of each wave, the men in the tossing boat could see land. Even as the lighthouse was an upright shadow on the sky, this land seemed but a long black shadow on the sea. It certainly was thinner than paper. "We must be about opposite New Smyrna," said the cook, who had coasted this shore often in schooners. "Captain, by the way, I believe they abandoned that life-saving station there about a year ago."

"Did they?" said the captain.

The wind slowly died away. The cook and the correspondent were not now obliged to slave in order to hold high the oar. But the waves continued their old impetuous swooping at the dinghy, and the little craft, no longer under way, struggled woundily over them. The oiler or the correspondent took the oars again.

Shipwrecks are apropos of nothing. If men could only train for them and have them occur when the men had reached pink condition, there would be less drowning at sea. Of the four in the dinghy none had slept any time worth mentioning for two days and two nights previous to embarking in the dinghy, and in the excitement of clambering about the deck of a foundering ship they had also forgotten to eat heartily.

For these reasons, and for others, neither the oiler nor the correspondent was fond of rowing at this time. The correspondent wondered ingenuously how in the name of all that was sane could there be people who thought it amusing to row a boat. It was not an amusement; it was a diabolical punishment, and even a genius of mental aberrations could never conclude that it was anything but a horror to the muscles and a crime against the back. He mentioned to the boat in general how the amusement of rowing struck him, and the weary-faced oiler smiled in full sympathy. Previously to the foundering, by the way, the oiler had worked a double watch in the engine-room of the ship.

"Take her easy now, boys," said the captain. "Don't spend yourselves. If we have to run a surf you'll need all your strength, because we'll sure have to swim for it. Take your time."

Slowly the land arose from the sea. From a black line it became a line of black and a line of white—trees and sand. Finally the captain said that he could make out a house on the shore. "That's the house of refuge, sure," said the cook. "They'll see us before long, and come out after us."

The distant lighthouse reared high. "The keeper ought to be able to make us out now, if he's looking through a glass," said the captain. "He'll notify the life-saving people."

"None of those other boats could have got ashore to give word of this wreck," said the oiler, in a low voice, "else the life-boat would be out hunting us."

Slowly and beautifully the land loomed out of the sea. The wind came again. It had veered from the north-east to the south-east. Finally a new sound struck the ears of the men in the boat. It was the low thunder of the surf on the shore. "We'll never be able to make the lighthouse now," said the captain. "Swing her head a little more north, Billie."

"A little more north, sir," said the oiler.

Whereupon the little boat turned her nose once more down the wind, and all but the oarsman watched the shore grow. Under the influence of this expansion doubt and direful apprehension were leaving the minds of the men. The management of the boat was still most absorbing, but it could not prevent a quiet cheerfulness. In an hour, perhaps, they would be ashore.

Their backbones had become thoroughly used to balancing in the boat, and they now rode this wild colt of a dinghy like circus men. The correspondent thought that he had been drenched to the skin, but happening to feel in the top pocket of his coat, he found therein eight cigars. Four of them were soaked with sea-water; four were perfectly scatheless. After a search, somebdy produced three dry matches; and thereupon the four waifs rode impudently in their little boat and, with an assurance of an impending rescue shining in their eyes, puffed at the big cigars, and judged well and ill of all men. Everybody took a drink of water.

IV

"Cook," remarked the captain, "there don't seem to be any signs of life about your house of refuge."

"No," replied the cook. "Funny they don't see us!"

A broad stretch of lowly coast lay before the eyes of the men. It was of low dunes topped with dark vegetation. The roar of the surf was plain, and sometimes they could see the white lip of a wave as it spun up the beach. A tiny house was blocked out black upon the sky. Southward, the slim lighthouse lifted its little grey length.

Tide, wind, and waves were swinging the dinghy northward. "Funny they don't see us," said the men.

The surf's roar was here dulled, but its tone was nevertheless thunderous and mighty. As the boat swam over the great rollers the men sat listening to this roar. "We'll swamp sure," said everybody.

It is fair to say here that there was not a life-saving station within twenty miles in either direction; but the men did not know this fact, and in consequence they made dark and opprobrious remarks concerning the eyesight of the nation's life-savers. Four scowling men sat in the dinghy and surpassed records in the invention of epithets.

"Funny they don't see us."

The light-heartedness of a former time had completely faded. To their sharpened minds it was easy to conjure pictures of all kinds of incompetency and blindness and, indeed, cowardice. There was the shore of the populous land, and it was bitter and bitter to them that from it came no sign.

"Well," said the captain, ultimately, "I suppose we'll have to make a try for ourselves. If we stay out here too long, we'll none of us have strength left to swim after the boat swamps."

And so the oiler, who was at the oars, turned the boat straight for the shore. There was a sudden tightening of muscles. There was some thinking.

"If we don't all get ashore," said the captain—"if we don't all get ashore, I suppose you fellows know where to send news of my finish?"

They then briefly exchanged some addresses and admonitions. As for the reflections of the men, there was a great deal of rage in them. Perchance they might be formulated thus: "If I am going to be drowned—if I am going to be drowned—if I am going to be drowned, why, in the name of the seven mad gods who rule the sea, was I allowed to come thus far and contemplate sand and trees? Was I brought here merely to have my nose dragged away as I was about to nibble the sacred cheese of life? It is preposterous. If this old ninny-woman, Fate, cannot do better than this, she should be deprived of the management of men's fortunes. She is an old hen who knows not her intention. If she has decided to drown me, why did she not do it in the beginning and save me all this trouble? The whole affair is absurd.—But no; she cannot mean to drown me. She dare not drown me. She cannot drown me. Not after all this work." Afterward the man might have had an impulse to shake his fist at the clouds. "Just you drown me, now, and then hear what I call you!"

The billows that came at this time were more formidable. They seemed always just about to break and roll over the little boat in a turmoil of foam. There was a preparatory and long growl in the speech of them. No mind unused to the sea would have concluded that the dinghy could ascend these sheer heights in time. The shore was still afar. The oiler was a wily surfman. "Boys," he said swiftly, "she won't live three minutes more, and we're too far out to swim. Shall I take her to sea again, Captain?"

"Yes; go ahead!" said the captain.

This oiler, by a series of quick miracles and fast and steady oarsmanship, turned the boat in the middle of the surf and took her safely to sea again.

There was a considerable silence as the boat bumped over the furrowed sea to deeper water. Then somebody in gloom spoke: "Well, anyhow, they must have seen us from the shore by now."

The gulls went in slanting flight up the wind toward the grey, desolate east. A squall, marked by dingy clouds and clouds brick-red like smoke from a burning building, appeared from the south-east.

"What do you think of those life-saving people? Ain't they peaches?"

"Funny they haven't seen us."

"Maybe they think we're out here for sport! Maybe they think we're fishin'. Maybe they think we're damned fools."

It was a long afternoon. A changed tide tried to force them southward, but wind and wave said northward. Far ahead, where coast-line, sea, and sky formed their mighty angle, there were little dots which seemed to indicate a city on the shore.

"St. Augustine?"

The captain shook his head. "Too near Mosquito Inlet."

And the oiler rowed, and then the correspondent rowed; then the oiler rowed. It was a weary business. The human back can become the seat of more aches and pains than are registered in books for the composite anatomy of a regiment. It is a limited area, but it can become the theatre of innumerable muscular conflicts, tangles, wrenches, knots, and other comforts.

"Did you ever like to row, Billie?" asked the correspondent.

"No," said the oiler; "hang it!"

When one exchanged the rowing-seat for a place in the bottom of the boat, he suffered a bodily depression that caused him to be careless of everything save an obligation to wiggle one finger. There was cold sea-water swashing to and fro in the boat, and he lay in it. His head, pillowed on a thwart, was within an inch of the swirl of a wave-crest, and sometimes a particularly obstreperous sea came inboard and drenched him once more. But these matters did not annoy him. It is almost certain that if the boat had capsized he would have tumbled comfortably out upon the ocean as if he felt sure that it was a great soft mattress.

"Look! There's a man on the shore!"

"Where?"

"There! See 'im? See 'im?"

"Yes, sure! He's walking along."

"Now he's stopped. Look! He's facing us!"

"He's waving at us!"

"So he is! By thunder!"

"Ah, now we're all right! Now we're all right! There'll be a boat out here for us in half an hour."

"He's going on. He's running. He's going up to that house there."

The remote beach seemed lower than the sea, and it required a searching glance to discern the little black figure. The captain saw a floating stick, and they rowed to it. A bath towel was by some weird chance in the boat, and, tying this on the stick, the captain waved it. The oarsman did not dare turn his head, so he was obliged to ask questions.

"What's he doing now?"

"He's standing still again. He's looking, I think.—There he goes again—toward the house.—Now he's stopped again."

"Is he waving at us?"

"No, not now; he was, though."

"Look! There comes another man!"

"He's running."

"Look at him go, would you!"

"Why, he's on a bicycle. Now he's met the other man. They're both waving at us. Look!"

"There comes something up the beach."

"What the devil is that thing?"

"Why, it looks like a boat."

"Why, certainly, it's a boat."

"No; it's on wheels."

"Yes, so it is. Well, that must be the life-boat. They drag them along shore on a wagon."

"That's the life-boat, sure."

"No, by God, it's—it's an omnibus."

"I tell you it's a life-boat."

"It is not! It's an omnibus. I can see it plain. See? One of these big hotel omnibuses."

"By thunder, you're right. It's an omnibus, sure as fate. What do you suppose they are doing with an omnibus? Maybe they are going around collecting the life-crew, hey?"

"That's it, likely. Look! There's a fellow waving a little black flag. He's standing on the steps of the omnibus. There come those other two fellows. Now they're all talking together. Look at the fellow with the flag. Maybe he ain't waving it!"

"That ain't a flag, is it? That's his coat. Why, certainly, that's his coat."

"So it is; it's his coat. He's taken it off and is waving it around his head. But would you look at him swing it!"

"Oh, say, there isn't any life-saving station there. That's just a winter-resort hotel omnibus that has brought over some of the boarders to see us drown."

"What's that idiot with the coat mean? What's he signalling, anyhow?"

"It looks as if he were trying to tell us to go north. There must be a life-saving station up there."

"No; he thinks we're fishing. Just giving us a merry hand. See? Ah, there, Willie!"

"Well, I wish I could make something out of those signals. What do you suppose he means?"

"He don't mean anything; he's just playing."

"Well, if he'd just signal us to try the surf again, or to go to sea and wait, or go north, or go south, or go to hell, there would be some reason in it. But look at him! He just stands there and keeps his coat revolving like a wheel. The ass!"

"There come more people."

"Now there's quite a mob. Look! Isn't that a boat?"

"Where? Oh, I see where you mean. No, that's no boat."

"That fellow is still waving his coat."

"He must think we like to see him do that. Why don't he quit it? It don't mean anything."

"I don't know. I think he is trying to make us go north. It must be that there's a life-saving station there somewhere."

"Say, he ain't tired yet. Look at 'im wave!"

"Wonder how long he can keep that up. He's been revolving his coat ever since he caught sight of us. He's an idiot. Why aren't they getting men to bring a boat out? A fishing-boat—one of those big yawls—could come out here all right. Why don't he do something?"

"Oh, it's all right now."

"They'll have a boat out here for us in less than no time, now that they've seen us."

A faint yellow tone came into the sky over the low land. The shadows on the sea slowly deepened. The wind bore coldness with it, and the men began to shiver.

"Holy smoke!" said one, allowing his voice to express his impious mood, "if we keep on monkeying out here! If we've got to flounder out here all night!"

"Oh, we'll never have to stay here all night! Don't you worry. They've seen us now, and it won't be long before they'll come chasing out after us."

The shore grew dusky. The man waving a coat blended gradually into this gloom, and it swallowed in the same manner the omnibus and the group of people. The spray, when it dashed uproariously over the side, made the voyagers shrink and swear like men who were being branded.

"I'd like to catch the chump who waved the coat. I feel like socking him one, just for luck."

"Why? What did he do?"

"Oh, nothing, but then he seemed so damned cheerful."

In the meantime the oiler rowed, and then the correspondent rowed, and then the oiler rowed. Grey-faced and bowed forward, they mechanically, turn by turn, plied the leaden oars. The form of the lighthouse had vanished from the southern horizon, but finally a pale star appeared, just lifting from the sea. The streaked saffron in the west passed before the all-emerging darkness, and the sea to the east was black. The land had vanished, and was expressed only by the low and drear thunder of the surf.

"If I am going to be drowned—if I am going to be drowned— if I am going to be drowned, why, in the name of the seven mad gods who rule the sea, was I allowed to come thus far and contemplate sand and trees? Was I brought here merely to have my nose dragged away as I was about to nibble the sacred cheese of life?"

The patient captain, drooped over the water-jug, was sometimes obliged to speak to the oarsman.

"Keep her head up! Keep her head up!"

"Keep her head up, sir." The voices were weary and low.

This was surely a quiet evening. All save the oarsman lay heavily and listlessly in the boat's bottom. As for him, his eyes were just capable of noting the tall black waves that swept forward in a most sinister silence, save for an occasional subdued growl of a crest.

The cook's head was on a thwart, and he looked without interest at the water under his nose. He was deep in other scenes. Finally he spoke. "Billie," he murmured, dreamfully, "what kind of pie do you like best?"

V

"Pie!" said the oiler and the correspondent, agitatedly. "Don't talk about those things, blast you!"

"Well," said the cook, "I was just thinking about ham sandwiches and——"

A night on the sea in an open boat is a long night. As darkness settled finally, the shine of the light, lifting from the sea in the south, changed to full gold. On the northern horizon a new light appeared, a small bluish gleam on the edge of the waters. These two lights were the furniture of the world. Otherwise there was nothing but waves.

Two men huddled in the stern, and distances were so magnificent in the dinghy that the rower was enabled to keep his feet partly warm by thrusting them under his companions. Their legs indeed extended far under the rowing-seat until they touched the feet of the captain forward. Sometimes, despite the efforts of the tired oarsman, a wave came piling into the boat, an icy wave of the night, and the chilling water soaked them anew. They would twist their bodies for a moment and groan, and sleep the dead sleep once more, while the water in the boat gurgled about them as the craft rocked.

The plan of the oiler and the correspondent was for one to row until he lost the ability, and then arouse the other from his sea-water couch in the bottom of the boat.

The other plied the oars until his head drooped forward and the overpowering sleep blinded him; and he rowed yet afterward.

Then he touched a man in the bottom of the boat, and called his name. "Will you spell me for a little while?" he said, meekly.

"Sure, Billie," said the correspondent, awaking and dragging himself to a sitting position. They exchanged places carefully, and the oiler, cuddling down in the sea-water at the cook's side, seemed to go to sleep instantly.

The particular violence of the sea had ceased. The waves came without snarling. The obligation of the man at the oars was to keep the boat headed so that the tilt of the rollers would not capsize her, and to preserve her from filling when the crests rushed past. The black waves were silent and hard to be seen in the darkness. Often one was almost upon the boat before the oarsman was aware.

In a low voice the correspondent addressed the captain. He was not sure that the captain was awake, although this iron man seemed to be always awake. "Captain, shall I keep her making for that light north, sir?"

The same steady voice answered him. "Yes. Keep it about two points off the port bow."

The cook had tied a life-belt around himself in order to get even the warmth which this clumsy cork contrivance could donate, and he seemed almost stove-like when a rower, whose teeth invariably chattered wildly as soon as he ceased his labour, dropped down to sleep.

The correspondent, as he rowed, looked down at the two men sleeping underfoot. The cook's arm was around the oiler's shoulders, and, with their fragmentary clothing and haggard faces, they were the babes of the sea—a grotesque rendering of the old babes in the wood.

Later he must have grown stupid at his work, for suddenly there was a growling of water, and a crest came with a roar and a swash into the boat, and it was a wonder that it did not set the cook afloat in his life-belt. The cook continued to sleep, but the oiler sat up, blinking his eyes and shaking with the new cold.

"Oh, I'm awful sorry, Billie," said the correspondent, contritely.

"That's all right, old boy," said the oiler, and lay down again and was asleep.

Presently it seemed that even the captain dozed, and the correspondent thought that he was the one man afloat on all the oceans. The wind had a voice as it came over the waves, and it was sadder than the end.

There was a long, loud swishing astern of the boat, and a gleaming trail of phosphorescence, like blue flame, was furrowed on the black waters. It might have been made by a monstrous knife.

Then there came a stillness, while the correspondent breathed with open mouth and looked at the sea.

Suddenly there was another swish and another long flash of bluish light, and this time it was alongside the boat, and might almost have been reached with an oar. The correspondent saw an enormous fin speed like a shadow through the water, hurling the crystalline spray and leaving the long glowing trail.

The correspondent looked over his shoulder at the captain. His face was hidden, and he seemed to be asleep. He looked at the babes of the sea. They certainly were asleep. So, being bereft of sympathy, he leaned a little way to one side and swore softly into the sea.

But the thing did not then leave the vicinity of the boat. Ahead or astern, on one side or the other, at intervals long or short, fled the long sparkling streak, and there was to be heard the *whirroo* of the dark fin. The speed and power of the thing was greatly to be admired. It cut the water like a gigantic and keen projectile.

The presence of this biding thing did not affect the man with the same horror that it would if he had been a picnicker. He simply looked at the sea dully and swore in an undertone.

Nevertheless, it is true that he did not wish to be alone with the thing. He wished one of his companions to awake by chance and keep him company with it. But the captain hung motionless over the water-jar, and the oiler and the cook in the bottom of the boat were plunged in slumber.

VI

"If I am going to be drowned—if I am going to be drowned—if I am going to be drowned, why, in the name of the seven mad gods who rule the sea, was I allowed to come thus far and contemplate sand and trees?"

During this dismal night, it may be remarked that a man would conclude that it was really the intention of the seven mad gods to drown him, despite the abominable injustice of it. For it was certainly an abominable injustice to drown a man who had worked so hard, so hard. The man felt it would be a crime most unnatural. Other people had drowned at sea since galleys swarmed with painted sails, but still—

When it occurs to a man that nature does not regard him as important, and that she feels she would not maim the universe by disposing of him, he at first wishes to throw bricks at the temple, and he hates deeply the fact that there are no bricks and no temples. Any visible expression of nature would surely be pelleted with his jeers.

Then, if there be no tangible thing to hoot, he feels, perhaps, the desire to confront a personification and indulge in pleas, bowed to one knee, and with hands supplicant, saying, "Yes, but I love myself."

A high cold star on a winter's night is the word he feels that she says to him. Thereafter he knows the pathos of his situation.

The men in the dinghy had not discussed these matters, but each had, no doubt, reflected upon them in silence and according to his mind. There was seldom any expression upon their faces save the general one of complete weariness. Speech was devoted to the business of the boat.

To chime the notes of his emotion, a verse mysteriously entered the correspondent's head. He had even forgotten that he had forgotten this verse, but it suddenly was in his mind.

> *A soldier of the Legion lay dying in Algiers;*
> *There was lack of woman's nursing, there was dearth of*
> *woman's tears;*
> *But a comrade stood beside him, and he took that comrade's*
> *hand,*
> *And he said, "I never more shall see my own, my native land."*

In his childhood the correspondent had been made acquainted with the fact that a soldier of the Legion lay dying in Algiers, but he had never regarded the fact as important. Myriads of his school-fellows had informed him of the soldier's plight, but the dinning had naturally ended by making him perfectly indifferent. He had never considered it his affair that a soldier of the Legion lay dying in Algiers, nor had it appeared to him as a matter for sorrow. It was less to him than the breaking of a pencil's point.

Now, however, it quaintly came to him as a human, living thing. It was no longer merely a picture of a few throes in the breast of a poet, meanwhile drinking tea and warming his feet at the grate; it was an actuality—stern, mournful, and fine.

The correspondent plainly saw the soldier. He lay on the sand with his feet out straight and still. While his pale left hand was upon his chest in an attempt to thwart the going of his life, the blood came between his fingers. In the far Algerian distance, a city of low square forms was set against a sky that was faint with the last sunset hues. The correspondent, plying the oars and dreaming of the slow and slower movements of the lips of the soldier, was moved by a profound and perfectly impersonal comprehension. He was sorry for the soldier of the Legion who lay dying in Algiers.

The thing which had followed the boat and waited had evidently grown bored at the delay. There was no longer to be heard the slash of the cutwater, and there was no longer the flame of the long trail. The light in the north still glimmered, but it was apparently no nearer to the boat. Sometimes the boom of the surf rang in the correspond-ent's ears, and he turned the craft seaward then and rowed harder. Southward, some one had evidently built a watch-fire on the beach. It was too low and too far to be seen, but it made a shimmering, roseate reflection upon the bluff in back of it, and this could be dis-cerned from the boat. The wind came stronger, and sometimes a wave suddenly raged out like a mountain cat, and there was to be seen the sheen and sparkle of a broken crest.

The captain, in the bow, moved on his water-jar and sat erect. "Pretty long night," he observed to the correspondent. He looked at the shore. "Those life-saving people take their time."

"Did you see that shark playing around?"

"Yes, I saw him. He was a big fellow, all right."

"Wish I had known you were awake."

Later the correspondent spoke into the bottom of the boat. "Billie!" There was a slow and gradual disentanglement. "Billie, will you spell me?"

"Sure," said the oiler.

As soon as the correspondent touched the cold, comfortable sea-water in the bottom of the boat and had huddled close to the cook's life-belt he was deep in sleep, despite the fact that his teeth played all the popular airs. This sleep was so good to him that it was but a moment before he heard a voice call his name in a tone that demonstrated the last stages of exhaustion. "Will you spell me?"

"Sure, Billie."

The light in the north had mysteriously vanished, but the correspondent took his course from the wide-awake captain.

Later in the night they took the boat farther out to sea, and the captain directed the cook to take one oar at the stern and keep the boat facing the seas. He was to call out if he should hear the thunder of the surf. This plan enabled the oiler and the correspondent to get respite together. "We'll give those boys a chance to get into shape again," said the captain. They curled down and, after a few preliminary chatterings and trembles, slept once more the dead sleep. Neither knew they had bequeathed to the cook the company of another shark, or perhaps the same shark.

As the boat caroused on the waves, spray occasionally bumped over the side and gave them a fresh soaking, but this had no power to break their repose. The ominous slash of the wind and the water affected them as it would have affected mummies.

"Boys," said the cook, with the notes of every reluctance in his voice, "she's drifted in pretty close. I guess one of you had better take her to sea again." The correspondent, aroused, heard the crash of the toppled crests.

As he was rowing, the captain gave him some whisky-and-water, and this steadied the chills out of him. "If I ever get ashore and anybody shows me even a photograph of an oar——"

At last there was a short conversation.

"Billie!—Billie, will you spell me?"

"Sure," said the oiler.

VII

When the correspondent again opened his eyes, the sea and the sky were each of the grey hue of the dawning. Later, carmine and gold was painted upon the waters. The morning appeared finally, in its splendour, with a sky of pure blue, and the sunlight flamed on the tips of the waves.

On the distant dunes were set many little black cottages, and a tall white windmill reared above them. No man, nor dog, nor bicycle appeared on the beach. The cottages might have formed a deserted village.

The voyagers scanned the shore. A conference was held in the boat. "Well," said the captain, "if no help is coming, we might better try a run through the surf right away. If we stay out here much longer we will be too weak to do anything for ourselves at all." The others silently acquiesced in this reasoning. The boat was headed for the beach. The correspondent wondered if none ever ascended the tall wind-tower, and if then they never looked seaward. This tower was a giant, standing with its back to the plight of the ants. It represented in a degree, to the correspondent, the serenity of nature amid the struggles of the individual—nature in the wind, and nature in the vision of men. She did not seem cruel to him then, nor beneficent, nor treacherous, nor wise. But she was indifferent, flatly indifferent. It is, perhaps, plausible that a man in this situation, impressed with the unconcern of the universe, should see the innumerable flaws of his life, and have them taste wickedly in his mind, and wish for another chance. A distinction between right and wrong seems absurdly clear to him, then, in this new ignorance of the grave-edge, and he understands that if he were given another opportunity he would mend his conduct and his words, and be better and brighter during an introduction or at a tea.

"Now, boys," said the captain, "she is going to swamp sure. All we can do is to work her in as far as possible, and then when she swamps, pile out and scramble for the beach. Keep cool now, and don't jump until she swamps sure."

The oiler took the oars. Over his shoulders he scanned the surf. "Captain," he said, "I think I'd better bring her about and keep her head-on to the seas and back her in."

"All right, Billie," said the captain. "Back her in." The oiler swung the boat then, and, seated in the stern, the cook and the correspondent were obliged to look over their shoulders to contemplate the lonely and indifferent shore.

The monstrous inshore rollers heaved the boat high until the men were again enabled to see the white sheets of water scudding up the slanted beach. "We won't get in very close," said the captain. Each time a man could wrest his attention from the rollers, he turned his glance toward the shore, and in the expression of the eyes during this contemplation there was a singular quality. The correspondent, observing the others, knew that they were not afraid, but the full meaning of their glances was shrouded.

As for himself, he was too tired to grapple fundamentally with the fact. He tried to coerce his mind into thinking of it, but the mind was dominated at this time by the muscles, and the muscles said they did not care. It merely occurred to him that if he should drown it would be a shame.

There were no hurried words, no pallor, no plain agitation. The men simply looked at the shore. "Now, remember to get well clear of the boat when you jump," said the captain.

Seaward the crest of a roller suddenly fell with a thunderous crash, and the long white comber came roaring down upon the boat.

"Steady now," said the captain. The men were silent. They turned their eyes from the shore to the comber and waited. The boat slid up the incline, leaped at the furious top, bounced over it, and swung down the long back of the wave. Some water had been shipped, and the cook bailed it out.

But the next crest crashed also. The tumbling, boiling flood of white water caught the boat and whirled it almost perpendicular. Water swarmed in from all sides. The correspondent had his hands on the gunwale at this time, and when the water entered at that place he swiftly withdrew his fingers, as if he objected to wetting them.

The little boat, drunken with this weight of water, reeled and snuggled deeper into the sea.

"Bail her out, cook! Bail her out!" said the captain.

"All right, Captain," said the cook.

"Now, boys, the next one will do for us sure," said the oiler. "Mind to jump clear of the boat."

The third wave moved forward, huge, furious, implacable. It fairly swallowed the dinghy, and almost simultaneously the men tumbled into the sea. A piece of life-belt had lain in the bottom of the boat, and as the correspondent went overboard he held this to his chest with his left hand.

The January water was icy, and he reflected immediately that it was colder than he had expected to find it off the coast of Florida. This appeared to his dazed mind as a fact important enough to be noted at that time. The coldness of the water was sad; it was tragic. This fact was somehow mixed and confused with his opinion of his own situation, so that it seemed almost a proper reason for tears. The water was cold.

When he came to the surface he was conscious of little but the noisy water. Afterward he saw his companions in the sea. The oiler was ahead in the race. He was swimming strongly and rapidly. Off to the correspondent's left, the cook's great white and corked back bulged out of the water; and in the rear the captain was hanging with his one good hand to the keel of the overturned dinghy.

There is a certain immovable quality to a shore, and the correspondent wondered at it amid the confusion of the sea.

It seemed also very attractive; but the correspondent knew that it was a long journey, and he paddled leisurely. The piece of life-preserver lay under him, and sometimes he whirled down the incline of a wave as if he were on a hand-sled.

But finally he arrived at a place in the sea where travel was beset with difficulty. He did not pause swimming to inquire what manner of current had caught him, but there his progress ceased. The shore was set before him like a bit of scenery on a stage, and he looked at it and understood with his eyes each detail of it.

As the cook passed, much farther to the left, the captain was calling to him, "Turn over on your back, cook! Turn over on your back and use the oar."

"All right, sir." The cook turned on his back, and, paddling with an oar, went ahead as if he were a canoe.

Presently the boat also passed to the left of the correspondent, with the captain clinging with one hand to the keel. He would have appeared like a man raising himself to look over a board fence if it were not for the extraordinary gymnastics of the boat. The correspondent marvelled that the captain could still hold to it.

They passed on nearer to shore—the oiler, the cook, the captain —and following them went the water-jar, bouncing gaily over the seas.

The correspondent remained in the grip of this strange new enemy—a current. The shore, with its white slope of sand and its green bluff topped with little silent cottages, was spread like a picture before him. It was very near to him then, but he was impressed as one who, in a gallery, looks at a scene from Brittany or Algiers.

He thought: "I am going to drown? Can it be possible? Can it be possible? Can it be possible?" Perhaps an individual must consider his own death to be the final phenomenon of nature.

But later a wave perhaps whirled him out of this small deadly current, for he found suddenly that he could again make progress toward the shore. Later still he was aware that the captain, clinging with one hand to the keel of the dinghy, had his face turned away from the shore and toward him, and was calling his name. "Come to the boat! Come to the boat!"

In his struggle to reach the captain and the boat, he reflected that when one gets properly wearied drowning must really be a comfortable arrangement—a cessation of hostilities accompanied by a large degree of relief; and he was glad of it, for the main thing in his mind for some moments had been horror of the temporary agony. He did not wish to be hurt.

Presently he saw a man running along the shore. He was undressing with most remarkable speed. Coat, trousers, shirt, everything flew magically off him.

"Come to the boat!" called the captain.

"All right, Captain." As the correspondent paddled, he saw the captain let himself down to bottom and leave the boat. Then the correspondent performed his one little marvel of the voyage. A large wave caught him and flung him with ease and supreme speed completely over the boat and far beyond it. It struck him even then as an event in gymnastics and a true miracle of the sea. An overturned boat in the surf is not a plaything to a swimming man.

The correspondent arrived in water that reached only to his waist, but his condition did not enable him to stand for more than a moment. Each wave knocked him into a heap, and the undertow pulled at him.

Then he saw the man who had been running and undressing, and undressing and running, come bounding into the water. He dragged ashore the cook, and then waded toward the captain; but the captain waved him away and sent him to the correspondent. He was naked—naked as a tree in winter; but a halo was about his head, and he shone like a saint. He gave a strong pull, and a long drag, and a bully heave at the correspondent's hand. The correspondent, schooled in the minor formulæ, said, "Thanks, old man." But suddenly the man cried, "What's that?" He pointed a swift finger. The correspondent said, "Go."

In the shallows, face downward, lay the oiler. His forehead touched sand that was periodically, between each wave, clear of the sea.

The correspondent did not know all that transpired afterward. When he achieved safe ground he fell, striking the sand with each particular part of his body. It was as if he had dropped from a roof, but the thud was grateful to him.

It seemed that instantly the beach was populated with men with blankets, clothes, and flasks, and women with coffee-pots and all the remedies sacred to their minds. The welcome of the land to the men from the sea was warm and generous; but a still and dripping shape was carried slowly up the beach, and the land's welcome for it could only be the different and sinister hospitality of the grave.

When it came night, the white waves paced to and fro in the

moonlight, and the wind brought the sound of the great sea's voice to the men on the shore, and they felt that they could then be interpreters.

COMMENTARY

I

The other stories we have studied have been definitely stories, invented things. Babel's epic [1] figure Benya Kirk is said to have had an original, or model, in some actual Odessa gangster, but how fully the author's imagination is at work in that story we have seen. A story like Hemingway's "A Clean Well-Lighted Place" comes to us as almost pure invention. Even if Hemingway once happened to witness such an occurrence as he describes and based his story on it—but the word "occurrence" is obviously not a possible word here, is it? There is a café at night, an old man, two waiters talk, close up, one goes away and thinks. The absence of explicit resort to the author's detailed experience of reality is complete.

Stephen Crane's story presents itself to us—or he presents it to us—as a very different matter. The shipwreck, of which the men's experience in the boat is the aftermath, actually occurred, on a definite date early in 1897, and when Crane got ashore safely with the captain and the cook he wrote a long dispatch to his New York paper (he was a reporter) about the shipwreck, which it published. His dispatch does not describe the experience in the boat. Now the story is said by him, in the subtitle, to be "after" (in accordance with) the *fact, "being* the *experience* of" and so on. Shall we expect then to hear the true story of the ordeal? It would certainly seem so, and a very interesting article by Mr. Cyrus Day of the University of Delaware has lately appeared,* studying the story from this point of view: as a full and veracious account of what took place between the foundering and the landing. Mr. Day inquires into the ethics of the captain's having left his ship at all, into the specifications of the dinghy, the speed of the wind at the time of the wreck and afterward (using U.S. Weather Bureau records), the distance from land, Crane's seamanship as an author, the oiler's and the captain's actual seamanship (apparently), and other such matters. He emerges with a rather dim view of most of these topics and appears to feel that he has discredited the story.

* "Stephen Crane and the Ten-foot Dinghy," *Boston University Studies in English* (1958) iii, 193–213.

But all this has nothing really to do with the story at all, impor-- tant though it certainly may be from a *biographical* point of view. It is a little as if we called in a fashion expert, expert in color, to determine whether the sides of the face of the mistress of the Elizabethan poet Thomas Campion, whom he calls "Rose-cheekt Laura," have been accurately described or not; supposing, for this purpose of research, that we are able to resurrect the lady in something resembling her original condition. The author's *intentions*—as to which we were quoting Crane—do not matter very much; it is what he does that counts. Besides, we quoted him very imperfectly. He only says *"intended* to be after the Fact"—a word that recognizes, of course, the impossibility of exact correspondence between any event in nature and any literary account (whether work of art or not). He also says "A *Tale,"* using a word of which the connotations are (as the dictionary says) "a false story," "a mere story"; a word rather like the American word "yarn," meaning a tall tale told by a sailor, partly incredible. Crane used language with great precision. In short, whether we ignore his intentions or take them into account, we may disregard the question whether much of the story is *true.* Many even experienced readers, like Mr. Day, never learn to do this. Imaginative art *takes off from* reality (including the reality of the unconscious); but it takes off, becoming something else. As readers we are interested in what, and how.

II

In investigating these things, our best tacks with "The Open Boat" will be: the first page of the story, particularly its style, and then the story's form-and-outline as a whole. It is misleading, of course, to separate the topics thus into two sections, but it is also not only unavoidable but helpful to the kind of clarity we aim at in this book.

What is the opening sentence of the first page up to? "None of them knew the colour of the sky." Why are we told first a fact so flat and odd? A *negative* fact? Perhaps we are being told this *instead* of something else that we expected to hear. But the story begins with this sentence! you may say. No, it began with its title, and sub-title, and it is in the light of both these that we read the first sentence. Then an expectation *has* been disappointed; for when one hears of an open boat, and four men in it from a sunk steamer, the first thing one thinks of is the excellent view which they unfortunately have of the sky and their deep interest in the weather that it will be foreshadowing. "Completely wrong," Crane is saying: "You know nothing about the matter." Instead, the men are watching the sea, with anxiety about the waves presumably (we do not *know* yet—the sea may even be calm), and watching the horizon, with an equal anxiety to see it (we do not know yet how far out they are). The line, thus, is far more *businesslike* than anything one expected. It has the effect, shall we say, of bringing the reader's gaze—as if taking him by the back of the neck—*down* from the skyey expectations of the title and sub-title to what is *level* (this word then occurs immediately) and a matter of human efficiency. (The general method of disappointment-of-expectation, which characterizes this story, is an intermittent feature of most literary art; it will be dealt with again when we come to A Note on Prosody, p. 314, and "The Love Song of J. Alfred Prufrock," p. 337.) Crane's opening sentence is *anti-heroic*, that is to say, standing as it does like a blunt sentry, in the forefront of what looked to be an epic of the sea. Anti-heroic and ironic, in view of the "big" opening (high-keyed, exalted) that the reader presumably expected.

But it is a curious fact that this very prosaic though active sentence makes a line of formal verse. It is an iambic pentameter, what is called a heroic verse, with trochaic substitution in the opening foot (see p. 316 for these terms, or you can look them up in the Glossary). No doubt the line is not so intense or highly colored as the first line of a *poem* on this subject might be. But the character of the rhythm, being formal, is antithetical to the sentence's anti-heroic muscular meaning and tone. As you can see by now, this author desires to take possession of the reader, on several fronts simultaneously, *at once*. In a longer analysis, one could do very much with this first sentence. Here, just three additional points. One is slight, that the word "sea" excludes directly any possibility of a lake-disaster, say, and states the true scale of the experience to come. A second is more substantial, namely, that the quality of the thought of the sentence already, here at the outset, forces the reader to begin to think *with* the men. What looks like an impersonal declarative sentence is really in its effect personal, questioning, psychological. At the end of just a page or so, this process of obliging the reader to enter the boat (and share the men's experience) has gone so far that Crane can say "the faces of the men must have been grey" and we are inside—though *not* yet with the correspondent, only with all four.

Our third point is formal. We have spoken of complication and resolution, as large sections of a whole literary work. The terms may be applied also, and help our understanding of form, to details in a work. Clearly, Crane's opening sentence, by *not* being about the sky but about—what? well, something else—introduces a complication: what is the other thing (*why* were we disappointed?) and what about it? After this short sentence, the longer second and third are not only explanatory but *resolving,* and the resolution comes in almost the rhythm of the complication: "and all of the men knew the colours of the sea."

A wave has passed. Almost at once a second wave begins. "Many a man" is mock-heroic [2] in tone (burlesquing heroic style) and the bathtub carries on the low-comedy sense. But the effect of the sentence is not comic. This dry, gay, senseless remark—as one critic has said—enables Crane to contrast, as in a flash of lightning, the most comfortable and sheltered situation conceivable (a bath in one's own bathtub) with on the other hand the sinister wilderness of wave and wind, where a man *owns* ("ought to have") nothing except, precariously, his life. But there is something more. A bathtub exists to fill with water—and with this sinister glimpse of the dinghy shipping water (we have not even been openly told yet that she is), the second complication is over. The wave is about to break, and in the famous sentence that follows it does break: "These waves were most wrongfully and barbarously abrupt and tall . . ." The sentence itself appears to swell and tower like a wave in the ear and mind, after the light, odd, little sentence preceding: its long, mournful middle-sounds ("most wrongfully and barbarously") are succeeded so rapidly by the extremely surprising, fast word "abrupt" and the even shorter, also sinister "tall," that it is a little as if a comber had loomed and broken over oneself. But the key word is "barbarously." The men are here in a world that has nothing to do with bathtubs. Civilization has been obliterated, for them, and their ordeal is going to be primitive, barbarous. Notice, finally, that the tone has risen so very high in the part of the sentence we have been studying, that Crane, in order to be able to get on with his narrative, drops his tone sharply in its second half, to make a technical remark; which has also the effect of saying that the barbarous is being confronted, at any rate, with skill.

So much for the opening paragraph, which is certainly one of the fastest, subtlest, toughest operations in American prose. Then each of the four men in the boat has a little paragraph to himself. These need our separate attention, but the first thing to be observed about the four of them, with respect to what we were saying a moment ago, is negative: we spoke of "skill," and it immediately follows that *not one* of the four men is a proper sailor. Instead we have men (in poor condition, as it will turn out) from the galley, the engine room, the passenger cabins, and the bridge—and the man from the bridge is injured. It follows that they will not be able to summon much except courage and endurance to save themselves. The author is clearly an author strongly given to irony.

Crane's treatment of the first man, the cook, is the reverse of heroic. There does not seem to be anything wrong with him and yet he is not doing anything; his costume is undignified, so is his speech, so is his fatness, so is the evident fear with which he regards the two inches of gunwale. This general impression is somewhat neutralized, however, by the last thing we hear, that he "invariably gazed eastward over the broken sea." This tone is more elevated than that of the rest of the paragraph, his intensity is communicated, and, after all, he does seem to be exercising a role: he is lookout.

We might expect, from this paragraph, that the cook would not play a *very* special role in the story, but rather that of the ordinary guy caught up in a predicament very exceptional. (We would be quite right in entertaining this expectation, as it happens.) You will have noted already that the mock-heroic tone partly characteristic of the opening paragraph makes the semi-clownish cook the perfect character, of the four, to introduce first. However, we may well expect to hear *more,* and especially more that is emotional or psychological, about the others.

What is our surprise, then, to hear far *less* about the oiler— almost nothing except that he is steering with a thin little oar and raises his body sometimes to avoid water. Is he going to prove even more insignificant in the story than the cook? Or is the author holding his fire, as with the cook there seems no reason to think he may be doing? All we can note at the moment is surprise.

Of the correspondent we hear, if possible, less still. He is rowing, watching, wondering "why he was there." But is this less? Surely with "wondering" we enter briefly the mind of the correspondent, as we never did the cook's mind, much less the oiler's. The notion of an *explanation* for the ordeal begins, with this verb, to reverberate in the story. It is suggested to us, in addition, technically, that at least one of our main points of view—notwithstanding the general tact of Crane's third person narrative—is going to be that of the correspondent.

Now for the captain, and it is obvious, instantly, that one of the things Crane has been doing with the others is holding his fire in order to do a proper job on the captain. Injured, shipless, he is lying down (the others squat or sit), and the quality of his reflection and memory (of his foundering ship) is conveyed by Crane in language which has none of the irony that has characterized the opening page down to this point. The others are anxious, working. He is withdrawn. One realizes at once that his situation is not going fully to be that of the others: in a sense, his defeat has already taken place, Fate can do nothing worse to him. He still gives orders—his "profound dejection and indifference" do not extend to an abandonment of his duty to the others; but he gives them in a voice "deep with mourning, and of a quality beyond oration or tears," and one does not receive an impression that the captain's fate is going to be the major concern of this story.

Whom, then, does it seem the story is going to be about?—at the end of this first page, that is; for a good reader is sensitive to as many as possible of an author's announcements and foreshadowings (*and omissions,* which is often the way announcements are made and suggestions conveyed).

The cook? Hardly. Of course the author may have surprises in store for us; but a good author does not work in terms of surprises so much as of expectation, discussed later. It is unlikely that Crane will have misled us to that extent. The cook—just as we know him so far (and do we ever learn more?)—does not seem fitted to be either the hero or the victim of a tale one of whose keynotes is set by the august paragraph about the captain. We have to say hero *or* victim, naturally, because we do not know how the story will turn out. But is it likely, do you think, to turn out either a simple tragedy or a simple escape-story?—considering the complexities of tone we have been examining on its first page?

The oiler? Conceivably; for we know nothing about him yet; the author may be making us wait, and it is a little striking that the first thing we learn, after the four characterizing paragraphs, is the oiler's name. Those paragraphs have already made it apparent that we are in the hands of an author who does not lightly reveal his characters' names: he is concerned rather with their roles, perhaps with their fates.

The correspondent? Conceivably; but, if so, in a very different way from the way the story will be about the oiler if it proves to be. The correspondent, as one would expect, reflects and inquires.

Or all four?

A study of the story's form will take us further, now, but you see how intense and elaborate is the initial impression made just by one paragraph and a little cast of characters.

III

The ordeal dramatized in the story has three parts, each growing out of, and superseding, the part preceding (this is true even of the first part, as will be clear in a moment), and each having a theme different from what one expected. The seven sections into which Crane has divided his story, that is, we may see as three waves. Each gathers, swells, breaks, and is followed by another, until the final word of the story brings the movements to a conclusion. But then this word itself shows that the three movements were one movement only. Far more than is the case even with most really good stories, "The Open Boat" reserves its true meaning to its actual final word.

What would the title, and the initial line of explanation ("A Tale" etc.), lead us to expect the story to be about? Hardship, certainly; fear; the relation between man and Nature. But the first wave of the story (sections I–III) is not about these things, essentially. It is about comradeship—the relation between man and man —and its basic tone is optimistic. At first no land is visible at all, then II ends with a "pin" appearing on the horizon, and the words "serenely" and "cheerful" are applied to the men. Section III strengthens this feeling at its close with the exquisite iteration [3] "Slowly the land arose from the sea. . . . Slowly and beautifully the land loomed out of the sea," and the men light cigars. The climax of this wave comes at the beginning of III, with "the subtle brotherhood of men that was here established on the seas." A man, that is to say, in his ordeal, is not alone; he may trust other men, and must, and does, and finds that they will help him. This is a *preliminary* conclusion, in the light of the rest of the story, but two things are to be noted about it at once. In the first place, it is, for this author, an unusually *hopeful* way of seeing man's situation. In Crane's earlier works, *Maggie* and *The Red Badge of Courage,* and in his later stories, such as "The Blue Hotel," men are seen as either completely alone or as *collaborating into disaster.* In the second place, this brotherhood is not arrived at easily or at once. As against the cliché that men in adversity stick together, Crane is careful to show these men quarreling toward the end of section I; so that the establishment of brotherhood comes as an achievement.

The second wave (sections IV–VI) is concerned powerfully to question both this brotherhood and the nature of the ordeal itself. Its tone is very dark; all three of its sections end in gloom.

Already in part one, it was clear that the brotherhood was established against an enemy, the Sea, which is envisaged as animal: "There was a terrible grace in the move of the waves, and they came in silence, save for the *snarling* of the crests" and "There was a preparatory and long *growl* in the speech of them." The nature of this enemy is now to be explored. But the brotherhood itself—to deal with this first—is seen as both partial and incompletely operative. It does not include the men on the shore, who can only stand and wave, not help. So, are men able to help their fellow-man in crisis, after all? Moreover, the brotherhood does not spare the correspondent his agony in the night—though we have to qualify this statement with a reminder that the captain *is* awake and with him, without his knowing it until later. Men must undergo their crises of rage and fear essentially alone.

To move now toward the nature of the enemy: man's fear is of death, but his rage is directed rather toward what is going to cause his death—that is to say, nature. But is nature man's enemy? To the extent that it is going to cause his death, one would think so. But in that it *cannot receive rage,* it is not after all an enemy: "he at first wishes to throw bricks at the temple, and he hates deeply the fact that there are no bricks and no temples." The final formulation of the truth about nature is reserved to the third part of the story: here it is enough to know that *nature is not an enemy,* so far as man's *expression of emotion* is concerned. Therefore, in one of Crane's subtlest passages (in section VI), the rage and fear are transformed into *self-love* and *self-pity.* Nature does not hate man but does not love him either, and does not pity him; and so if he needs these emotions, he must supply them himself. There is irony, of course, even in this view, but it is a tenderer irony than most of Crane's, and the paragraphs about the soldier of the Legion dying in Algiers form one of his most beautiful achievements. (Technically, they get their effect by holding back and holding back in order to accumulate enormous pressure on the simple word "sorry" in the final sentence, making it ring in the mind.)

The dramatization of nature, in the correspondent's mind, as the shark, then, was false or misleading, and in the third part of the story we hear what nature *is:* she is "indifferent, flatly indifferent." Emotion directed toward her—anger or entreaty—is wasted. What is wanted is something very different: *understanding* of her. With this conception, however, we are approaching the word with which the story ends, and before entering on that final subject it is necessary to understand the death of the oiler.

The oiler's death is the price paid by the men for the salvation of the other three. He dies as a sacrifice.[4] Nature is indifferent, but the arrangements of nature—so to put it—exact tribute. From the narrative point of view, it has to be the oiler who dies because of the disqualifications of the other three. The cook is lacking in dignity, the correspondent is the perceiving mind, and the captain is already injured (a sacrifice must be in perfect condition). But somebody must die; man (the four men in the boat) does not escape scot-free from ordeal; and so the oiler perishes.

And now for the word "interpreters," toward which the entire story has been moving.

This unexpected and dramatic word lifts the story explicitly to a plane that has earlier only been implied. The experience, and *only* the experience, of nature's most dangerous and demanding ordeals, fits man to do what it is most his duty and power to do: to *explain*—explain what nature is, what man is, what matters. The whole story, then, has in some sense been a *metaphor,* and the ordeal of the boat only an *instance* of what can happen to man and what it means, what qualities the experience of nature requires. The best imaginable comment on Crane's word "interpreters" is the splendid passage with which William Faulkner closed his Nobel Prize address in 1950. "I decline to accept the end of man. It is easy enough to say that man is immortal simply because he will endure: that when the last ding-dong of doom has clanged and faded from the last worthless rock hanging tideless in the last red and dying evening, that even then there will still be one more sound: that of his puny inexhaustible voice, still talking. I refuse to accept this. I believe that man will not merely endure: he will prevail. He is immortal, not because he alone among creatures has an inexhaustible voice, but because he has a soul, a spirit capable of compassion and sacrifice and endurance. The poet's, the writer's, duty is to write about these things. It is his privilege to help man endure by lifting his heart, by reminding him of the courage and honor and hope and pride and compassion and pity and sacrifice which have been the glory of his past. The poet's voice need not merely be the record of man, it can be one of the props, the pillars to help him endure and prevail."

TERMS AND PRINCIPLES

1. *Epic:* Here, larger than life size, heroic.
2. *Mock-heroic:* Burlesquing the heroic style.
3. *Iteration:* Repetition.

4. *Sacrifice:* This is almost a technical word, so important is it in modern literature, perhaps in all literature. It comes, the notion of sacrifice, from primitive religion: an offering to a feared deity: something important has to be given up, voluntarily, in order that some fate may be escaped. From Homer to Henry James the idea has obsessed the creative mind, and it is one of the keys to "The Open Boat," as to Tolstoy's story "Master and Man" and other masterpieces.

EXERCISE

FRANZ KAFKA

Three Parables

AN IMPERIAL MESSAGE

The Emperor, so it runs, has sent a message to you, the humble subject, the insignificant shadow cowering in the remotest distance before the imperial sun; the Emperor from his deathbed has sent a message to you alone. He has commanded the messenger to kneel down by the bed, and has whispered the message to him; so much store did he lay on it that he ordered the messenger to whisper it back into his ear again. Then by a nod of the head he has confirmed that it is right. Yes, before the assembled spectators of his death—all the obstructing walls have been broken down, and on the spacious and loftily-mounting open staircases stand in a ring the great princes of the Empire—before all these he has delivered his message. The messenger immediately sets out on his journey; a powerful, an indefatigable man; now pushing with his right arm now with his left, he cleaves a way for himself through the throng; if he encounters resistance he points to his breast, where the symbol of the sun glitters; the way, too, is made easier for him than it would be for any other man. But the multitudes are so vast; their numbers have no end. If he could reach the open fields how fast he would fly, and soon doubtless you would hear the welcome hammering of his fists on your door. But instead how vainly does he wear out his strength; still he is only mak-

ing his way through the chambers of the innermost palace; never will
he get to the end of them; and if he succeeded in that nothing would be
gained; he must fight his way next down the stairs; and if he succeeded
in that nothing would be gained; the courts would still have to be
crossed; and after the courts the second outer palace; and once more
stairs and courts; and once more another palace; and so on for thousands of years; and if at last he should burst through the outermost
gate—but never, never can that happen—the imperial capital would
lie before him, the center of the world, crammed to bursting with its
own refuse. Nobody could fight his way through here, least of all one
with a message from a dead man.—But you sit at your window when
evening falls and dream it to yourself.

BEFORE THE LAW

"Before the Law stands a doorkeeper on guard. To this doorkeeper there comes a man from the country who begs for admittance
to the Law. But the doorkeeper says that he cannot admit the man at
the moment. The man, on reflection, asks if he will be allowed, then,
to enter later. 'It is possible,' answers the doorkeeper, 'but not at this
moment.' Since the door leading into the Law stands open as usual
and the doorkeeper steps to one side, the man bends down to peer
through the entrance. When the doorkeeper sees that, he laughs and
says: 'If you are so strongly tempted, try to get in without my permission. But note that I am powerful. And I am only the lowest doorkeeper. From hall to hall keepers stand at every door, one more
powerful than the other. Even the third of these has an aspect that
even I cannot bear to look at.' These are difficulties which the man
from the country has not expected to meet; the Law, he thinks, should
be accessible to every man and at all times, but when he looks more
closely at the doorkeeper in his furred robe, with his huge pointed
nose and long, thin, Tartar beard, he decides that he had better wait
until he gets permission to enter. The doorkeeper gives him a stool
and lets him sit down at the side of the door. There he sits waiting
for days and years. He makes many attempts to be allowed in and
wearies the doorkeeper with his importunity. The doorkeeper often

engages him in brief conversation, asking him about his home and about other matters, but the questions are put quite impersonally, as great men put questions, and always conclude with the statement that the man cannot be allowed to enter yet. The man, who has equipped himself with many things for his journey, parts with all he has, however valuable, in the hope of bribing the doorkeeper. The doorkeeper accepts it all, saying, however, as he takes each gift: 'I take this only to keep you from feeling that you have left something undone.' During all these long years the man watches the doorkeeper almost incessantly. He forgets about the other doorkeepers, and this one seems to him the only barrier between himself and the Law. In the first years he curses his evil fate aloud; later, as he grows old, he only mutters to himself. He grows childish, even the fleas in the doorkeeper's fur collar, he begs the very fleas to help him and to persuade the doorkeeper to change his mind. Finally his eyes grow dim and he does not know whether his eyes are only deceiving him. But in the darkness he can now perceive a radiance that streams immortally from the door of the Law. Now his life is drawing to a close. Before he dies, all that he has experienced during the whole time of his sojourn condenses in his mind into one question, which he has never yet put to the doorkeeper. He beckons the doorkeeper, since he can no longer raise his stiffening body. The doorkeeper has to bend far down to hear him, for the difference in size between them has increased very much to the man's disadvantage. 'What do you want to know now?' asks the doorkeeper, 'you are insatiable.' 'Everyone strives to attain the Law,' answers the man, 'how does it come about, then, that in all these years no one has come seeking admittance but me?' The doorkeeper perceives that the man is at the end of his strength and that his hearing is failing, so he bellows in his ear: 'No one but you could gain admittance through this door, since this door was intended only for you. I am now going to shut it.' "

"So the doorkeeper deluded the man," said K. immediately, strongly attracted by the story.

"Don't be too hasty," said the priest, "don't take over an opinion without testing it. I have told you the story in the very words of the scriptures. There's no mention of delusion in it."

"But it's clear enough," said K., "and your first interpretation of it was quite right. The doorkeeper gave the message of salvation to the man only when it could no longer help him."

"He was not asked the question any earlier," said the priest, "and you must consider, too, that he was only a doorkeeper, and as such he fulfilled his duty."

"What makes you think he fulfilled his duty?" asked K. "He didn't fulfill it. His duty might have been to keep all strangers away, but his man, for whom the door was intended, should have been let in."

"You have not enough respect for the written word and you are altering the story," said the priest. "The story contains two important statements made by the doorkeeper about admission to the Law, one at the beginning, the other at the end. The first statement is: that he cannot admit the man at the moment, and the other is: that this door was intended only for the man. If there were a contradiction between the two, you would be right and the doorkeeper would have deluded the man. But there is no contradiction. The first statement, on the contrary, even implies the second. One could almost say that in suggesting to the man the possibility of future admittance the doorkeeper is exceeding his duty. At that moment his apparent duty is only to refuse admittance, and indeed many commentators are surprised that the suggestion should be made at all, since the doorkeeper appears to be a precisian with a stern regard for duty. He does not once leave his post during these many years, and he does not shut the door until the very last minute; he is conscious of the importance of his office, for he says: 'I am powerful'; he is respectful to his superiors, for he says: 'I am only the lowest doorkeeper'; he is not garrulous, for during all these years he puts only what are called 'impersonal questions'; he is not to be bribed, for he says in accepting a gift: 'I take this only to keep you from feeling that you have left something undone'; where his duty is concerned he is to be moved neither by pity nor rage, for we are told that the man 'wearied the doorkeeper with his importunity'; and finally even his external appearance hints at a pedantic character, the large, pointed nose and the long, thin, black Tartar beard. Could one imagine a more faithful doorkeeper?

Yet the doorkeeper has other elements in his character which are likely to advantage anyone seeking admittance and which make it comprehensible enough that he should somewhat exceed his duty in suggesting the possibility of future admittance. For it cannot be denied that he is a little simple-minded and consequently a little conceited. Take the statements he makes about his power and the power of the other doorkeepers and their dreadful aspect which even he cannot bear to see—I hold that these statements may be true enough, but that the way in which he brings them out shows that his perceptions are confused by simpleness of mind and conceit. The commentators note in this connection: 'The right perception of any matter and a misunderstanding of the same matter do not wholly exclude each other.' One must at any rate assume that such simpleness and conceit, however sparingly indicated, are likely to weaken his defense of the door; they are breaches in the character of the doorkeeper. To this must be added the fact that the doorkeeper seems to be a friendly creature by nature, he is by no means always on his official dignity. In the very first moments he allows himself the jest of inviting the man to enter in spite of the strictly maintained veto against entry; then he does not, for instance, send the man away, but gives him, as we are told, a stool and lets him sit down beside the door. The patience with which he endures the man's appeals during so many years, the brief conversations, the acceptance of the gifts, the politeness with which he allows the man to curse loudly in his presence the fate for which he himself is responsible—all this lets us deduce certain motions of sympathy. Not every doorkeeper would have acted thus. And finally, in answer to a gesture of the man's he stoops low down to give him the chance of putting a last question. Nothing but mild impatience—the doorkeeper knows that this is the end of it all—is discernible in the words: 'You are insatiable.' Some push this mode of interpretation even further and hold that these words express a kind of friendly admiration, though not without a hint of condescension. At any rate the figure of the doorkeeper can be said to come out very differently from what you fancied."

"You have studied the story more exactly and for a longer time than I have," said K. They were both silent for a little while. Then K. said: "So you think the man was not deluded?"

"Don't misunderstand me," said the priest, "I am only showing you the various opinions concerning that point. You must not pay too much attention to them. The scriptures are unalterable and the comments often enough merely express the commentator's bewilderment. In this case there even exists an interpretation which claims that the deluded person is really the doorkeeper."

"That's a far-fetched interpretation," said K. "On what is it based?"

"It is based," answered the priest, "on the simple-mindedness of the doorkeeper. The argument is that he does not know the Law from inside, but he knows only the way that leads to it, where he patrols up and down. His ideas of the interior are assumed to be childish, and it is supposed that he himself is afraid of the other guardians whom he holds up as bogies before the man. Indeed, he fears them more than the man does, since the man is determined to enter after hearing about the dreadful guardians of the interior, while the doorkeeper has no desire to enter, at least not so far as we are told. Others again say that he must have been in the interior already, since he is after all engaged in the service of the Law and can only have been appointed from inside. This is countered by arguing that he may have been appointed by a voice calling from the interior, and that the third doorkeeper is more than he can endure. Moreover, no indication is given that during all these years he ever made the one remark about the doorkeepers. He may have been forbidden to do so, but there is no mention of that either. On these grounds the conclusion is reached that he knows that he is in a state of delusion. But he is deceived also about his relation to the man from the country. For he is subject to the man and does not know it. He treats the man instead as his own subordinate, as can be recognized from many details that must still be fresh in your mind. But, according to this view of the story, it is just as clearly indicated that he is really subordinated to the man. In the first place, a bondsman is always subject to a free man. Now the man from the country is really free, he can go where he likes, it is only the Law that is closed to him, and access to the Law is forbidden him only by one individual, the doorkeeper. When he sits down on the stool by the side of the door and stays there for the rest of his life, he does it of his own free will; in the story there is no mention of any compulsion. But the doorkeeper is bound to his post by his very office, he does not dare strike out into the country, nor apparently may he go into the interior of the Law, even should he wish to. Besides, although he is in the service of the Law, his service is confined to this one entrance; that is to say, he serves only this man for whom alone the entrance is intended. On that ground too he is subject to the man. One must assume that for many years, for as long as it takes a man to grow up to the prime of life, his service was in a sense empty formality, since he had to wait for a man to come, that is to say, someone in the prime of life, and so had to wait a long time before the purpose of his service could be fulfilled, and, more-over, had to wait on the man's pleasure, for the man came of his own free will. But the termination of his service also depends on the man's term of life, so that to the very end he is subject to the man. And it is emphasized throughout that the doorkeeper apparently real-izes nothing of all this. That is not in itself remarkable, since accord-ing to this interpretation the doorkeeper is deceived in a much more important issue, affecting his very office. At the end, for example, he says regarding the entrance to the Law: 'I am now going to shut it,' but at the beginning of the story we are told that the door leading into the Law stands always open, and if it stands open always, that is to say, at all times, without reference to the life or death of the man, then the doorkeeper is incapable of closing it. There is some difference of opinions about the motive behind the doorkeeper's statement, whether he said he was going to close the door merely for the sake of giving an answer, or to emphasize his devotion to duty, or to bring the man into a state of grief and regret in his last moments. But there is no lack of agreement that the doorkeeper will not be able to shut the door. Many indeed profess to find that he is subordinate to the man even in wisdom, towards the end, at least, for the man sees the radi-ance that issues from the door of the Law while the doorkeeper in his official position must stand with his back to the door, nor does he say anything to show that he has perceived the change."

"That is well argued," said K., after repeating to himself in a low voice several passages from the priest's exposition. "It is well argued, and I am inclined to agree that the doorkeeper is deluded. But that has not made me abandon my former opinion, since both conclusions are to some extent compatible. Whether the doorkeeper is clear-sighted or deluded does not dispose of the matter. I said the man is deluded. If the doorkeeper is clear-sighted, one might have doubts about that, but if the doorkeeper himself is deluded, then his delusion must of necessity be communicated to the man. That makes the doorkeeper not, indeed, a swindler, but a creature so simple-minded that he ought to be dismissed at once from his office. You mustn't forget that the doorkeeper's delusions do himself no harm but do infinite harm to the man."

"There are objections to that," said the priest. "Many aver that the story confers no right on anyone to pass judgment on the doorkeeper. Whatever he may seem to us, he is yet a servant of the Law; that is, he belongs to the Law and as such is set beyond human judgment. In that case one dare not believe that the doorkeeper is subordinate to the man. Bound as he is by his service, even at the door of the Law, he is incomparably freer than anyone at large in the world. The man is only seeking the Law, the doorkeeper is already attached to it. It is the Law that has placed him at his post; to doubt his integrity is to doubt the Law itself."

"I don't agree with that point of view," said K. shaking his head, "for if one accepts it, one must accept as true everything the doorkeeper says. But you yourself have sufficiently proved how impossible it is to do that."

"No," said the priest, "it is not necessary to accept everything as true, one must only accept it as necessary."

"A melancholy conclusion," said K. "It turns lying into a universal principle."

COURIERS

They were offered the choice between becoming kings or the couriers of kings. The way children would, they all wanted to be couriers. Therefore there are only couriers who hurry about the world, shouting to each other—since there are no kings—messages that have become meaningless. They would like to put an end to this miserable life of theirs but they dare not because of their oaths of service.

SOME QUESTIONS

1. A parable [1] is a short tale designed to inculcate a moral truth. There are two points to be noticed about the term. Unlike an allegory,[2] which corresponds point-to-point with some pre-existent moral scheme, a parable is partly just narrative; its correspondence is general, suggestive, not exact. The second point is related to this; there is an element of mystery, usually, about a parable. Christ insists, especially in the Gospel According to St. Mark, on the difficulty of his own parables; and the word parable is closely related to riddle. What can you say about the appropriateness of the *form*, then, to the meaning of the first of these parables?

2. Of what nature do you imagine the imperial message to be?

3. Discriminate the elements optimistic and pessimistic, for the "humble subject" waiting, in the author's presentation.

4. The second parable forms part of a chapter called "In the Cathedral" late in Kafka's novel *The Trial,* and is so complicated that we can only take up certain points here. You note that there are at least two fundamental difficulties, *immediately,* with the priest's story. The doorkeeper *says* that other doorkeepers stand one after another inside, even the third of whom is so extraordinary that he cannot bear to look at him; then how does he know about the others? He also says at the end that he is going to close the door, whereas we have already learned that it always stands open. It follows that we cannot trust anything the doorkeeper says, and every word that he utters has to be subjected by us to the most rigorous skepticism. Test his statements now for yourself. Is it true that he cannot admit the man at the moment? Is it true that he is powerful, or have we only his word for it? Perhaps the man was wrong not to enter immediately, without paying any attention to the doorkeeper. When the doorkeeper says, "try to get in without my permission," perhaps there is a second meaning in addition to the threat and exactly opposite to it—namely, an entreaty, an instruction, if only the man understood it correctly. You will want to study the rest of the parable for yourself, following this line, that perhaps the man's power and freedom were greater than he imagined.

5. Of course, he fails, however. What does the Law symbolize, with its "radiance that streams immortally" from its door? In attempting to answer this question, you will want to know that the author was a Jew (the Torah, or the Law, is the first five books of the He-

brew, and for that matter, the Christian, Bible) writing in a Christian culture (the scene of the parable is a cathedral).

6. The commentary is rabbinical in method. Is it intended only to elucidate, or also to mislead? If you think the latter is true, why?

7. What do you understand by the word "necessary" at the end of the second parable?

8. What is meant by the "oaths of service" in the third parable? Do you imagine that a sense of duty is fundamental to Kafka's thought? Duty to what? Is the *nature* of the duty defined, beyond being said to be—in this parable—the carrying of messages? Messages about what? (Compare the first parable.) What is meant by "there are no kings"?

9. Is suicide regarded here as a human right or not? (The Stoics saw it as one; Epictetus gives as his reason for *not* committing suicide only the light sentence, "It is fitting for me to join in the game while it lasts." What would Kafka have thought of this?)

TERMS AND PRINCIPLES

1. *Parable:* A short fictitious story from which a moral is to be drawn.

2. *Allegory:* A story in which the actions represent other actions and the characters other characters, or types. So there are at least two meanings, each sometimes even in a different series, for every incident.

Section Two

Poetry

ANDREW MARVELL

To His Coy Mistress

Had we but world enough, and time,
This coyness, lady, were no crime.
We would sit down and think which way
To walk, and pass our long love's day;
Thou by the Indian Ganges' side
Shouldst rubies find; I by the tide
Of Humber would complain. I would
Love you ten years before the Flood,
And you should, if you please, refuse
Till the conversion of the Jews.
My vegetable love should grow
Vaster than empires, and more slow.
An hundred years should go to praise
Thine eyes, and on thy forehead gaze;
Two hundred to adore each breast,
But thirty thousand to the rest;
An age at least to every part,
And the last age should show your heart.
For, lady, you deserve this state,
Nor would I love at lower rate.
    But at my back I always hear

Time's wingéd chariot hurrying near,
And yonder all before us lie
Deserts of vast eternity.
Thy beauty shall no more be found,
Nor in thy marble vault shall sound
My echoing song; then worms shall try
That long-preserved virginity:
And your quaint honor turn to dust,
And into ashes all my lust.
The grave's a fine and private place,
But none, I think, do there embrace.
    Now therefore while the youthful hue
Sits on thy skin like morning dew,
And while thy willing soul transpires
At every pore with instant fires,
Now let us sport us while we may;
And now, like amorous birds of prey,
Rather at once our time devour,
Than languish in his slow-chapped power.
Let us roll all our strength, and all
Our sweetness, up into one ball;
And tear our pleasures with rough strife
Thorough the iron gates of life.
Thus, though we cannot make our sun
Stand still, yet we will make him run.

COMMENTARY

If we give this poem only a casual reading, we shall come away believing that the poet is saying something like this: that his lady should stop all this coy nonsense and yield to him at once. But is he saying just this? Or is he saying something else? If we study the poem a little, we shall discover that the poet is saying several things at the same time, which from the logical point of view are contradictory. But poetry is not formal logic. In this poem, some of the deepest conflicts and contradictions in human experience are given lucidity and order through the masterly use of two ancient *conventions*.[1] We have selected this poem for discussion not only because it is a masterpiece, but because it is a perfect example of the use of convention in poetry.

Without some understanding of poetic conventions, one will conclude that the poet's argument is, at best, pagan, and, at worst, downright immoral. Why does the lady seem to be holding out indefinitely? Is she waiting for a proposal of marriage? Why doesn't the poet propose marriage and write an entirely different poem, celebrating the betrothal? If she is already married, why doesn't he let her alone? The convention of the engagement followed by marriage is ancient and powerful, and common to all societies and religions; it has inspired many great poems, and will inspire more, because all men acknowledge it. Marvell's convention looks arbitrary and eccentric.

But we are not entitled to these speculations because they are not entertained as possibilities within the conventions of the poem. Every poem has its own leading convention: it is a signal from the poet to the reader that the incident or the idea will be presented from a certain point of view, which may be shared or only partly shared, or merely understood, or asking for understanding, by the reader. Thus, a poetic convention eliminates, for the occasion, many emotions and situations which common sense tells us are constant in human relations. Our feelings are, in fact, of infinite variety; but the one thing that a poet cannot deal with in a given poem is unlimited possibility. The poet must concentrate, if he is going to be coherent. The leading convention of "To His Coy Mistress" makes for a certain concentration of complex human attitudes. It seems to say that the poet must plead forever, and the lady forever refuse.

Much has happened in the western world in the three hundred years since this poem was written. Its special convention will possibly seem now to be either trivial or irrelevant, or both. Common sense tells us that if the relation between the sexes is to be conducted from what seems to be Marvell's point of view, human life cannot go on. Would common sense not discredit the convention as fantasy or even nonsense? What are we to think about the poet's perpetual devotion and the lady's perpetual chastity? We know that men and women in Marvell's age were perhaps no better than they are now; memoirs of the period, particularly of aristocratic and court society, suggest that they may have been even worse. What, then, is the poet talking about? Was not this strained relation between the poet and the lady artificial, or at least atypical, even when Marvell wrote the poem?

The answer is that it was artificial even then. We shall look at the convention more closely in a moment; but meanwhile, if what we have said about it is true, how could Marvell take it seriously enough to accept its limitations? Or is the poet after all completely serious? In the first paragraph the poet offers the lady certain exaggerated devotions, but on a certain *condition. If,* he says, there were no such thing as time, courtship could go on indefinitely, and consummation indefinitely postponed: but, says the poet, since time is limited, she should give it at once. This first paragraph ends with the couplet:

> For, Lady, you deserve this state,
> Nor would I love at lower rate.

If we have already suspected that his courtly devotion (which we shall describe presently) is too good to be true, this couplet seems to say that he has used the courtly convention for a purpose not yet clear to us, but for a purpose which at any rate contradicts its literal meaning, which is: perpetual courtship vs. perpetual chastity. The phrase "at lower rate" is not in the vocabulary of romantic sentiment and seduction: it undercuts ironically the courtly language, and suddenly puts the poet's courtship into a perspective of intellectual detachment. "Lower rate" shifts the context of the poet's plea, and we see his love as a kind of mechanism which has a *rate of speed.* This speed, in an infinitude of time, would be too exhausting to maintain, since human beings are finite creatures, subject to age, decay and death; not machines.

Is the poet actually saying this? So it seems. But what are we to make of the famous lines which introduce the second paragraph of the poem?

> But at my back I always hear
> Time's wingéd chariot hurrying near,
> And younder all before us lie
> Deserts of vast eternity.

The wit of the first paragraph has disappeared, and we have a straightforward statement of man's temporal limitations. Up to now the poet has been saying, wittily and ironically, that the lady should bestow her favors at once because time is short. He now says the same thing, in a different tone, from which the irony is missing. For the moment Marvell seems to have forgotten that he is a Christian and a Platonist; he gives us the classical vision of time carrying us relentlessly to "endless night." His image for this is a "desert," where all that we were on earth disappears; this eternity is not the fulfillment of our natures in the Christian heaven.

The lines come out of a different tradition from that of

courtly love, but their theme is brilliantly assimilated to the courtly convention. This theme, as we shall see, dominates and qualifies the poet's use of the convention. What is this theme? *Carpe diem* (seize the day); eat, drink, and be merry, for tomorrow we die. But Marvell seems to be saying only part of this: *tomorrow we die.* For in this second paragraph his attitude is somber and melancholy, and we are not urged to make merry. Nevertheless, Marvell is giving us the philosophy of classical hedonism which he had got from Horace and Catullus. He and his contemporaries—Marvell was Milton's assistant as Latin Secretary to Cromwell—knew Latin as well as they knew English; they looked upon the ancient poets as their superiors, as models to imitate. The Latin poets were not merely literary models: they had become, since the Renaissance, a part of the culture of every educated European; the substance, not merely the style, of Latin poetry was deeply embedded in the thought and feeling of Marvell and his contemporaries, existing alongside the Christian tradition, complicating and even modifying it.

Before we go further into the poem, we must pause to look more closely at the literary convention of courtly love. It seems to have originated and flourished in Provence, in southern France, in the twelfth century; was taken over by certain Italian poets (including Dante) in the thirteenth; and in the fourteenth century was given its familiar elements by the Italian poet Petrarch (1304–1374), whose famous sonnet sequence to an idealized woman named Laura became a model for generations of poets all over Europe. Two hundred and fifty years after Petrarch the courtly convention was powerful in England. The Tudor and Elizabethan poets developed and modified it; Shakespeare's sonnets, perhaps the greatest in English, would be very different, or might not have been written at all, had Petrarch not written his.

A literary convention that feeds the imagination of poets for hundreds of years cannot be taken lightly. If what we have said about courtly love makes it seem trivial, we had better take second thought. We have asked the question: If the lady is already married, why doesn't the poet let her alone? In the courtly convention, the lady almost had to be married. The poetical homage to the lady idealized her as the type of purity, beauty, and elegance, and it was a rule of the "game" that she should not yield to the "courtship" of the poet. Our verb "to court" survives from this social and literary convention. It meant the payment of homage to a person of distinction, a member of the *court,* before it came to mean the formal attentions of a gentleman to a lady before marriage, or without the possibility of marriage. (The lady represented ideal womanhood, and the cult of her worship was called *domnei,* from the late Latin *domina,* lady, and cognate with the French *dame* and the Italian *donna*). That this rarefied convention became at times the cloak of gross sensual indulgence is beside the point; what must be borne in mind is the fact that the cult came into existence at all. It accounts for some of the subtlest and most highly civilized poetry ever written; its masters were Arnaut Daniel, Guiraut de Bornelh, and Bernart de Ventadorn, all of whom flourished around the year 1200. Dante refined the convention still further when he wrote of "ladies who have *intelligence* of love." The worship of mortal women was related to the cult of the Virgin Mary, whose influence reached its climax in the cathedrals of Chartres and Notre Dame.

The power of the cult becomes the more remarkable when we remember that an English poet, Andrew Marvell, writing four hundred and fifty years after Arnaut Daniel, could write a poem which is, in effect, a courtly address to a lady beyond the poet's reach. Is the convention, then, intrinsically ridiculous? No; for it represented to many generations of Europeans the pattern of what the relation between the sexes should be; and it contains as much "common sense" as the modern cult of woman who is at once the "comrade" of man and the romantic mistress; who, as wife, can be discarded (divorced) if the husband "falls in love" with another woman; or the "comrade-mistress" may do likewise. The continuance of sexual desire as the basis of marriage would seem to be no more realistic than the formal devotion to women who are beyond our reach. Such considerations are by no means beside the point when we read "To His Coy Mistress." And if we have sketched in what may appear to be too large a background for one short poem, we can only say that the more we know the better; we probably still don't know enough to read this poem.

The situations of poems come out of life; the words exist and are used before they get into poems; and we have got to have some historical sense of the situation and some knowledge of what the words meant when the poet used them. But given some of this knowledge, or as much as we can acquire, our next task is to look at the poem as a self-contained discourse, as a kind of organic whole. We say "a *kind* of organic whole"; it would be more precise to say something *like* an organic whole; for poems are not living organisms like ourselves. When they have the maximum of coherence and order, when every word seems to go with every other, we say that *by analogy* the poem has organic form, or aesthetic unity.[2]

We have indicated that Marvell, in the first section, seems not to take the convention of perpetual worship quite seriously. He subjects the implicit idea ("My devotion is eternal") to realistic analysis through hyperbole.[3] He says in effect that if the devotion is humorless and eternal, here are the consequences: You, lady, may spend years by the Ganges in India searching for rubies. Notice the ironic characterization of the lady: though her chastity is unyielding, she will spend this false, impossible eternity not in ascetic meditation, but in adorning her person with precious stones. I, the lover, thousands of miles away, by an English river, the Humber, miles that are not real because both time and space no longer exist, will eternally "complain." Notice the sudden ironic understatement in the verb; it conveys the sense of moderate unhappiness, not of powerful and continuous passion. Time being unreal, the lovers may reverse "time," and begin the courtship before Noah's Ark; or they may look ahead to the end of the world, for it was an old Christian belief that the Jews would be converted to Christianity on the Day of Judgment. Perhaps the wittiest exaggeration of all is in the phrase "my vegetable love." This is frequently cited as the supreme example of "metaphysical wit."[4] It is difficult to explain the exact meaning of this kind of wit. For convenience we may describe it as the simultaneous perception of a human emotion and of its opposite. If we reject our sense of reality, says the poet, and pretend that we are not subject to decay and death after a short term of life, we are rejecting the rational intelligence. What organisms lack the rational intelligence? In the descending scale from man, animals; but Marvell glances at the extreme case: vegetable organisms. If we accept the courtly convention of eternal devotion in a world without space and time, we are behaving no more intelligently than a vegetable, which has no intelligence. Thus, vegetables cannot *know:* they can only *grow.* So the poet's love, in an implied simile, becomes a monstrous plant gradually spreading out into the entire world. The metaphysical wit here, then, consists in carrying out to its extreme implications, with literal logic, the absurdity of courtly love if it is accepted as a mode of practical conduct between men and women.

In the first paragraph, then, the poet discerns the assumptions underlying his lady's refusal—assumptions which she does not perceive. In the second paragraph ("But at my back I always hear"), he tells her what will actually happen to them, since they are mortal beings, if she continues obdurate. The "tone," as we have remarked, becomes somber; but the attitude of the poet is still by no means simple; we shall not be able to discover univocally what he "really believes." "To His Coy Mistress" is not a direct expression of personal emotion; it is, as we have already said, an enormously complex discourse in which contradictory ideas and conflicting attitudes are given ordered expression through the controlled use of metaphorical language.

The limitations of man, the actualities of the human condition, will after the normal span of life bring both lover and mistress to the grave. If the lady will not yield to him, her virginity nevertheless will eventually be violated:

> . . . then worms shall try
> That long-preserved virginity:
> And your quaint honor turn to dust
> And into ashes all my lust.

The irony in the verb "try," which here means to test, to attempt, suggests the classical, pagan belief that the soul dies with the body. Her virginity, which was of the body in life, remains of the body in death; the worm will ironically accomplish what the lover was not permitted to do. The irony consists in the sudden revelation to the lady of a possibility which she had not considered: irony being in its most general definition a *speaking two ways,* or a seeing two ways. To conclude the second paragraph, the poet offers the lady the extreme consequences of her ironical position:

> The grave's a fine and private place,
> But none, I think, do there embrace.

Here the irony is complete. To get fully its impact we must look at the words "fine" and "private." "Fine," from the Latin *finire,* means "to end"; the past participle, *finitus,* means finished, in the sense of "ended," but also "brought to perfection." Death is ironically the perfection of the lady's virginity, the actuality for which she has "preserved" it. "Private," from the past participle of *privari,* means bereaved, or otherwise set apart from the public. Well, the poet seems to say, you want privacy, and *now you'll get it to perfection* throughout the real eternity, which is death, not the false eternity of perpetual courtship.

The third paragraph, beginning

> Now therefore while the youthful hue
> Sits on thy skin like morning dew

is the conclusion of the "argument"; it is like the conclusion of an Aristotelian syllogism, the first and second paragraph of the poem resembling the major and minor premises. This poem, like many others of its time, has a quasi-logical development which *looks like logical thinking*. But the "thought" of the poem is not true logic; it is rather a *rhetorical* enthymeme,[5] in syllogistic form, which the poet uses to give his appeal the air of a certain reasonableness, poise, and courtesy. The poet is not beating his breast in anguish; he is speaking well within one of the universal aspects of the courtly convention—that is, the polite address of a gentleman to a lady. Even the ironic wit, which undercuts the convention, from another point of view confirms it, since the wit indicates emotional control and a poised courtesy toward the lady.

This third and last paragraph is the most brilliant, and was probably the most difficult to write. Note the impact of the simple conjunctive adverb *therefore*—scarcely a "poetic" word, but a word which here subtly imposes upon the lady (and the reader) the illusion that what the poet is about to say follows logically from what has been said. Let us summarize again the "argument":

1. *Major premise.* The courtly convention, examined realistically, is nonsense, because time and space are real, and do not offer lovers an infinity in which to practice perpetual devotion and perpetual chastity. Logically, this first section can be seen as a hypothetical proposition in universal form; that is, *if* earthly time and space were infinite, then such and such would follow; but they are not infinite.

2. *Minor premise.* This exhibits the *particular* example of the plight of human beings under the limitations of finite existence. They die, and there is no fulfillment in the grave of what was left undone in life.

3. *Conclusion.* "Now therefore," says the poet, since we must die, let us live to the fullest.

But does he actually say this in the third paragraph? He does and he does not.

The explicit meaning of the third paragraph develops from the classical theme of the second. Since our most cherished virtues, like female chastity, end in the grave, let us make the most of life. This is the explicit meaning brought out in detail in a series of brilliant images. While the lady is young and has the "youthful hue," let her yield. But notice, from here on, the violence of the imagery in which the poet imagines the act of love. The lady's *soul* "transpires"— which means here to sweat through the "pores" of her skin. (This is an Aristotelian sense of the *soul* as the *form* of the body). Her soul must sweat with the "instant fires" of passion. "Instant" is the Latin *instare,* meaning to stand forth, to be huge; thus it is something at once gross and grotesque. "And now like amorous birds of prey / Rather at once our time devour": this is animal lust, not human passion fused with that sense of the whole person which is love. But rather this than "languish in his [time's] slow-chapped power," through the false eternity of courtly devotion and chastity. "Slow-chapped power": the slow, relentless *jaws* of time, which is here implicitly imagined as an animal. (Persons have jaws; animals, chaps). To "tear our pleasures with rough strife" extends the imagery of animal lust. "Thorough the iron gates of life" has given the critics a good deal of trouble because the "iron gates" cannot be located in any known traditional or conventional symbolism. We must take the risk of a rather bold interpretation. The gate through which we enter life is the female sexual organ, and life enters the womb through the act of love. Does not the adjective "iron" suggest the resistance encountered by the child in entering the world, and the violence of the act by which the child is conceived?

In these observations on the imagery of paragraph three, we have deliberately postponed looking at the "ball" as the image for the union of the lovers. We know that in Greek philosophy the sphere was considered the perfect geometrical figure: it combines the idea of infinity (one may travel forever upon its surface without coming to an end) with the idea of a limit (the volume of a given sphere is a finite number). For this reason the sphere, or ball, became a symbol of perfect unity; the configuration of its surface has no "parts"— unlike the surface of a hexagonal solid, for example. If the "ball" means what we are guessing that it may mean, how can we reconcile its implications with the gross presentation of physical love that has preceded it? The answer is as simple as the question is difficult. We cannot reconcile *logically* the union of lovers in lust with a symbol of unity in the mind or spirit. All that we are entitled to say of this logical, but not poetic, contradiction, is that through the symbol of the ball the poet *glances* at the possibility of a mystery: spiritual union through the body.

At last we come up against the kind of conclusion that the poet, considering, through two major conventions, the complexities of love, is able to give us. The schematic, logical conclusion that seemed to follow from the two first sections, does not follow without ambiguity. There is, in fact, no logical conclusion at all. We are given a dilemma, which may be stated as follows: On the one hand, there is the absurdity of perpetual devotion to perpetual chastity; on the other, there is the extreme of animal lust. There is nothing in the middle. Is the poet rejecting the possibility of the middle ground where human love as we know it exists? So it seems; but we cannot be sure. For there is always the ball, in which the lovers concentrate their "strength" and their "sweetness"—qualities that are very human and that imply a serenity and a balance of desire which the violence of lust would eliminate. The perfect lucidity and order with which the poet has set forth this conflict is of the poetic order, not of the logical or philosophical. Any attempt to paraphrase "To His Coy Mistress" from the point of view of one side of the conflict would omit half of the poem.

TERMS AND PRINCIPLES

1. *Convention:* A usage, in literature or painting, say, or for that matter in behavior (as hand-shaking) or thought, which is *agreed upon,* not experimental or idiosyncratic. The Commentary will make the term clearer than any short notation can.

2. *Aesthetic unity:* As the text explains, it is only by analogy that we speak of a work of art's having organic form, for it is not alive. But if we contrast the notion of the *mechanical* in bad art with the notion of the *organic* in good art, we can see that there is a sense in which it is useful to say that a poem or statue *is* alive: all of its parts grow from and supplement each other in an aesthetic unity which is entirely different from the mere piecemeal perfection of a machine.

3. *Hyperbole:* Extravagant exaggeration.

4. *Metaphysical wit:* A term quite impossible to define; see the text. The term comes from a celebrated passage in Samuel Johnson's *Life of Cowley* where the addiction of Donne and Cowley and other poets of the seventeenth century to far-fetched conceits (for this word see the following Commentary, on Donne) was noticed and criticized.

5. *Rhetorical enthymeme:* An argument of probability only, which is given the air, however, of logic, of demonstration, of certainty. An enthymeme is a syllogism with one of its three parts unstated, but assumed. Thus the syllogism, "All men are mortal, Socrates is a man, therefore Socrates is mortal," becomes an enthymeme when stated as, "All men are mortal, so Socrates is mortal," or "All men are mortal and Socrates is a man," or "Socrates is a man, so Socrates is mortal."

   A *rhetorical* enthymeme is intended to persuade rather than to demonstrate. Leaving out one step in the implied syllogism makes it easier to overlook any reference to proof.

JOHN DONNE

A Valediction Forbidding Mourning

As virtuous men pass mildly away,
　　And whisper to their souls to go,
Whilst some of their sad friends do say,
　　"The breath goes now," and some say, "No":

So let us melt, and make no noise,
　　No tear-floods, nor sigh-tempests move,
'Twere profanation of our joys
　　To tell the laity our love.

Moving of the earth brings harms and fears;
　　Men reckon what it did and meant;
But trepidation of the spheres,
　　Though greater far, is innocent.

Dull sublunary lovers' love
　　(Whose soul is sense) cannot admit
Absence, because it doth remove
　　Those things which elemented it.

But we, by a love so much refined
　　That ourselves know not what it is,
Inter-assured of the mind,
　　Care less eyes, lips, and hands to miss.

Our two souls, therefore, which are one,
　　Though I must go, endure not yet
A breach, but an expansion,
　　Like gold to airy thinness beat.

If they be two, they are two so
　　As stiff twin compasses are two;

Thy soul, the fixed foot, makes no show
  To move, but doth if the other do.

And though it in the center sit,
  Yet, when the other far doth roam,
It leans, and hearkens after it,
  And grows erect as that comes home.

Such wilt thou be to me, who must
  Like the other foot, obliquely run:
Thy firmness draws my circle just,
  And makes me end where I begun.

COMMENTARY

I

From the end of the seventeenth century until about forty years ago, it was difficult to read the Metaphysical poets with sympathy and understanding. Largely through the influence of T. S. Eliot, the twentieth century began to read Donne with an open mind. The poem that we are about to discuss is one of the great achievements of this Metaphysical school, and to read it properly we must disabuse our minds of certain prejudices about the use of intellect in poetry, along with a popular superstition that intellectual poetry is inevitably cold and passionless.

It was Samuel Johnson who was largely responsible for the opinion that the Metaphysicals were coldly intellectual. In a famous passage in his *Life of Cowley,* Johnson denounced the Metaphysical poets because they dealt with "heterogeneous ideas yoked by violence together." It is beyond our purpose to discuss the basis of this opinion. It is enough to say that Johnson along with his contemporaries thought that the language of poetry should not depart too far from everyday usage. He thought that Donne and the other Metaphysical poets were merely trying to astonish the reader with rare fragments of learning, and that the "conceits," [1] or extended metaphors, of the Metaphysical poets were beyond the reach of ordinary intelligent men and made their poetry cold and remote. Actually, as we shall see, Donne's "A Valediction" is one of the most passionate poems in the English language.

Approaching the poem for the first time, we may have difficulty in identifying the action [2] of the poem; several readings may be necessary in order to determine "what is happening." What is happening is actually very simple and is something that could happen to any mature man and woman who are in love.

Let us look at the title first. A "valediction" is simply a farewell, and this valediction is the farewell of a husband to his wife, asking her not to grieve over his absence as he departs for a trip. The poem presents a brilliantly complex argument to justify the husband's injunction to his wife. A brief paraphrase of the argument is as follows: Do not mourn my absence because I am really not going to be away; no, surprisingly enough, in a sense we will be closer together now than when we were not physically separated. The paradox [3] of this argument is at once apparent, and as we know from reading other poetry of the early seventeenth century, the rhetoric [4] of paradox is a constant feature of Metaphysical poetry.

Let us now examine the argument in detail.

The first two stanzas contain an elaborate simile [5] which only after repeated reading reveals its relation to the parting of two lovers. The exact moment of death for "virtuous men" is compared to the spiritual union of the lovers, who, by the sacrament of uniting, leave their former selves behind and pass into another life, just as the dying men pass from physical existence into the life of the spirit. It is a Christian commonplace that in order to achieve grace we must die to our former selves. Thus, the poet is saying, "As men quietly die into the afterlife, so let us, the lovers, 'melt and make no noise'— let us achieve this wholly private experience of union without any outward show of emotion." The outward show would render the union profane; the secret of this union is known only to the lovers, who thus achieve a priestly knowledge that cannot be explained to the laity, that is, to the people in the world who have not had this experience. This preliminary part of the argument is indispensable to the success of the paradox around which the poem is constructed, for Donne is telling us that the spiritual union of lovers is indestructible, not conditioned by time and place. These first two stanzas are also very important in setting the tone [6] of the poem: a secular love is treated with the awe appropriate to religious feeling, and the lovers are compared to the priests, the elect.

The next two stanzas place the action in a cosmic setting. Donne here makes use of a doctrine sometimes called "The Great Chain of Being," which was central to the world-view of the seventeenth century. According to this theory, Man, as microcosm, contains in his nature all the elements of the cosmos at large. He is of the earth in the very nature of his body, and of the highest spiritual realms by virtue of his rational soul. That part of man which is of the earth is subject to the agitations and shocks alluded to in the lines

> Moving of earth brings harms and fears;
> Men reckon what it did and meant;

His spiritual half is related through the Chain of Being to the "trepidation of the spheres." This trepidation, Donne says, is greater than the violence of any earthly phenomena, but because it is progressively farther from the earth as we proceed outward to the empyrean which encloses the cosmos, it is "innocent," it brings no harm; simple, because it is in essence spiritual.

Having set the cosmic stage, Donne now locates upon it the kind of lovers who are united only through the senses. This "dull, sublunary lovers' love," being below the sphere of the moon is hence of the earth and merely physical. Such lovers cannot tolerate physical separation, since absence removes those things which "elemented" (constituted) their love (as elements constitute a compound).

Donne next proceeds not by strict logic but by means of a rhetorical enthymeme, a device or argument in which one of the propositions, usually a premise, is understood but not stated. The suppressed "proposition" can be stated thus: *"We* are *supra-*lunar lovers and are above sense-experience."* He uses this device to distinguish his lovers from the merely sublunary ones. Their love has so refined the lovers that the intellect, he says, is no longer capable of describing it; but the two lovers are "inter-assured," through intuitive recognition, and they therefore care less than the physical lovers do about physical contact. Note that Donne's lovers do not say they don't care *at all*—they simply care *less.* For in this magnificent flight of analogy which affirms the reality of spiritual love, Donne does not reject its physical basis; in fact, the higher love becomes known *through* the physical.

We now approach the great similes of the malleable gold and the draftsman's compasses.

Donne begins by playing a sly rhetorical trick upon us. He says, "Our two souls therefore, which are one," almost as if he had proved by strict argument the absolute union of the souls, when he has merely asserted it imaginatively, by masterful analogy.[7] He then declares that the lovers' souls, instead of suffering a breach through absence, achieve an expansion: having become a unitary soul, they actually become larger. As presented here, the "expansion" is a spatial correlative [8] for the nonspatial idea of increased spirituality. Brilliant as the argument is, so paraphrased, it would not be beyond the range of any intelligent poet of Donne's generation. The great stroke of genius is the fourth line of this stanza, the simile "Like gold to airy thinness beat." With a sleight of hand that defies critical analysis, Donne climaxes the abstract argument by converting it into a concrete image which is visual and at the same time symbolic of the spiritual situation of the lovers. Gold is itself an ancient artificial symbol derived from the light of the sun, which represents both spiritual light and the source of all life. A sheet of gold may theoretically be beaten to such thinness that its surface will progressively occupy greater two-dimensional space into infinity. Thus we see the souls of the lovers not divided but infinitely extended. And to this idea of extension Donne joins, with the word "airy," that of progressive refinement.

The next and final phase of the argument seems at first to employ a simile that is new, but actually is subtly related to that of the malleable gold. Donne begins with a concession to our common sense. He knows quite well, even after the formidable "argument" for the spiritual union of the lovers, that he must come back to two human beings—a man and a woman—in the world which all men inhabit. So he says, "If they be two," they are two in a sense that does not really destroy their oneness, as we can see by an analogy between the lovers and the draftsman's compass. This compass has two legs, but they are joined at the top. Notice the brilliant appositeness of the compass as a vehicle [9] for expressing the apparently contradictory ideas of physical separation and spiritual union. As the compass describes a circle, one leg—here the woman—remains in the center, while the other leg—the man—draws a circle at any conceivable distance from the center. But the motion of the masculine leg is controlled by "the fixed foot" of the woman. And though the points of the legs are separated in space, they remain joined at the "top," that is, through the soul. Notice, moreover, that the figure described by the masculine leg of the compass is a circle—the perfect geometrical figure, which even in pre-Christian times was the symbol both of absolute symmetry and of the human soul.

This is very nearly the end of the argument, except for a few minor but very brilliant extensions of the simile. To the feminine leg of the compass the poet attributes the power of listening: it "leans and hearkens" after the masculine leg; but notice that Donne does not overdo it to the point where a listening compass would become an absurdity.

At the end, when the wandering masculine leg of the compass begins to return to the center, the fixed feminine leg grows erect, and finally the two legs form one straight perpendicular line, representing physical reunion as the final symbol of their spiritual unity. The woman makes the circle "just," that is, perfect, and "makes me end where I begun." In other words, the husband began his trip by leaving his wife, and he is now back with her. He began his life in the womb and, as the lover, he is now in a sense returning to the womb in the physical embrace with his beloved. There is perhaps no poem in the English language which sets forth with so great intellectual and imaginative resources the profound relation between physical and spiritual love.

TERMS AND PRINCIPLES

1. *Conceit:* Extended metaphor; a witty thought or analogy carried out far more elaborately than the usual simile or metaphor.
2. *Action:* In a poem or story or play, what happens in a narrative sense.
3. *Paradox:* A seemingly self-contradictory statement or situation; that which seems absurd but is or may be true. (See Part I, pp. 13, 15.)
4. *Rhetoric:* The theory and practice of eloquence: the use of all the arts of language to persuade or delight.
5. *Simile:* A likening of one thing to another, made explicitly.
6. *Tone:* The prevailing *voice* (tint, shade, temper, mood) of a literary work, comparable to the individual speaking voice of a man or woman.
7. *Analogy:* A resemblance in certain respects between things otherwise different.
8. *Correlative:* A person or thing correspondingly related to another (person or thing).
9. *Vehicle:* A means of conveyance, a medium.

📖 *A Note on Prosody*

You may sometimes have wondered why poems are written in verse. But verse is in fact the older medium, older than prose. Originally, everything, from magical spells to recipes to agricultural works, was written in verse; and its effectiveness as a medium is still acknowledged by advertisements and commercials that set your teeth on edge. The deep reasons for its effectiveness—having to do, probably, with the rhythms of the blood, of the seasons, of night and day, with children's desire (and men's) to have things done over again in the way they were done at first—lie outside our present scope. But it is clear that a verse-pattern (the metrical convention being used by a poet in a given poem) aims at creating *expectation,* which can then be (1) satisfied, or (2) disappointed, causing surprise, both satisfaction and surprise bringing pleasure. Very few lines in most poems are *perfectly* regular; and it is in the counterpoint [1] between the pattern demanded by the verse-form (let us call this: song [2]) and what actually occurs in the meter (let us call this: speech [3])—it is in this continually altering relation or counterpoint that the poet makes his individual verse heard and develops his subject.

These remarks will be clearer with some illustration from Donne's versification [4] in this poem and Carew's prosody in "A Song," the poem we consider next.

The basic English foot [5] (and to a lesser extent the basic American foot) is the iamb,[6] an unaccented syllable followed by an accented syllable. The standard English line, in which most of the poetry of Shakespeare and Milton is written, for instance, consists of five of these feet, and is called an iambic pentameter.[7] Donne's meter in "A Valediction" is iambic tetrameter: [8] four of these feet to a line, gathered into quatrains [9] rhyming *abab.* His first stanza [10] may be scanned [11] as follows:

$$\text{Ăs vír|tŭoŭs mén | páss míld|lў ăwaý}$$

—but the first line is in fact so unlike what we have been saying that we must pause.

In *three* of the four feet Donne has violated his norm.[12] Small wonder that Ben Jonson, the Elizabethan literary critic (and lovely poet) declared that Donne deserved hanging for his practices in versification. But how do we know what his norm is? Surely this first line establishes it? No, it is established by lines 2 and 3, and then the rest of the poem. Most poets establish it at once, and it might not be easy to find another example of a violation so extreme so early. What Donne is doing here is substituting, in order to have speech working strongly at once against song, other kinds of foot for iambs: anapests [13] in the second and fourth feet, a spondee [14] in the third. (You now know three of the five usual English feet; the fourth is a trochee,[15] reversing the iamb, the fifth is a dactyl,[16] which is a reversal of the anapest.) The result is a line—not cacophonous,[17] as many of Donne's lines are—but one of the most beautiful in English, a line like a sigh. The pronounced middle pause, and the substitutions, together with vowels and consonants and the meaning of the words and the genius of the poet, have produced this memorable line.

Carew in his "Song" is using the same meter. He uses it more conventionally, of course. The poem is smooth, as Donne with his more energetic temperament, stronger brain, passions, and interest in realism, would never have dreamed of making a poem. Not that Carew's "Song" does not deserve its fame, these last three hundred years. But notice that Carew also is not perfectly regular: his first foot is a trochee, though his poem gives you no such sense of metrical experiment and ambition as Donne's.

TERMS AND PRINCIPLES

1. *Counterpoint:* The art of combining melodies, proceeding simultaneously.
2. *Song:* The melody to which something is sung.
3. *Speech:* That which is spoken.
4. *Versification:* The making of verse, or the analyzing of it.
5. *Foot:* A division of a line of poetry.
6. *Iamb:* A foot of two syllables, an unstressed followed by a stressed.
7. *Pentameter:* A verse (line) of five feet—in the case of iambic pentameter, all iambs of course, *in theory,* though as is pointed out in the text very few lines of poetry are perfectly regular. The *norm* will be iambic, however.
8. *Tetrameter:* A verse-line of four feet.
9. *Quatrain:* A stanza of four lines. See next term.
10. *Stanza:* A group of lines of verse forming a definite pattern.
11. *Scan:* Analyze metrically (metrics is the science of versification).
12. *Norm:* Pattern, rule.
13. *Anapest:* A foot consisting of three syllables, two unstressed syllables followed by a stressed one.
14. *Spondee:* A foot consisting of two syllables, both stressed.
15. *Trochee:* A foot of two syllables, the first stressed, the second not.
16. *Dactyl:* A foot of three syllables, a stressed followed by two unstressed. Can you supply examples, for yourself, of these four main kinds of English verse-feet?
17. *Cacophonous:* Disagreeable, discordant, in sound.

THOMAS CAREW

A Song

Ask me no more where Jove bestows,
When June is past, the fading rose;
For in your beauty's orient deep
These flowers, as in their causes, sleep.

Ask me no more whither do stray
The golden atoms of the day;
For in pure love heaven did prepare
Those powders to enrich your hair.

Ask me no more whither doth haste
The nightingale, when May is past;
For in your sweet dividing throat
She winters, and keeps warm her note.

Ask me no more where those stars light
That downwards fall in dead of night;
For in your eyes they sit, and there
Fixéd become, as in their sphere.

Ask me no more if east or west
The phoenix builds her spicy nest;
For unto you at last she flies,
And in your fragrant bosom dies.

COMMENTARY

We have included "A Song" by Thomas Carew not because it is
a great poem but because it exhibits another phase of the courtly convention which we have seen in the greater poems by Marvell and
Donne. Carew uses only one aspect of this courtly convention, and he
brilliantly joins to it an ancient *rhetorical* convention, which does not

pertain to any particular poetic subject matter but is strictly speaking a rhetorical device. Sometimes called the *ubi sunt* formula, it asks the question, Where are the vanished glories and joys of human life? * The classical statement of this idea in the affirmative rather than the interrogative is, *Sic transit gloria mundi* (Thus passes away the glory of the world).

Back of what seems to be the very simple question—Where are? —lies the shadow of an ancient philosophical problem, that of the One and the Many, or the Permanent and the Changing. The evanescence of our sense perceptions—sight, smell, hearing, taste, and touch —the instability of human love and loyalty, all these have perplexed poets and philosophers since men first developed the arts of reflection.

Carew's "A Song" is obviously an address by the poet either to a real or imaginary woman. In any case, she is the idealized woman of courtly poetry, and this both explains and justifies the hyperbole of the language. Several features of the courtly convention are missing, chiefly the plea to the invincibly chaste lady to yield her favors. Here the poet asks the lady for nothing; he is content to praise her. The praise takes the form of the philosophical problem that we have already mentioned: She represents the One, the principle of Permanence, which gathers up and preserves for all time those natural and human phenomena that disappear in the ceaseless flux.

At a first reading, it seems that the poet is asking a different question in each of the five stanzas. Actually, the questions are one question:—Where is vanished beauty? And the five answers are likewise one answer:—Beauty has not vanished; it is preserved in the lady. The considerable interest of the poem consists in the poet's powers of invention. He asks this one question in five strikingly different ways. The language is uniformly arresting and precise. The seventeenth-century diction of Carew is markedly different from the diction of modern poetry represented by T. S. Eliot's "The Love Song of J. Alfred Prufrock," not only because of changes in sensibility and in the English language, but also because of differences in poetic intention. Carew and the best of his contemporaries were concerned with the precise rendition of objective images, whereas the modern poet does not care as much about the precision of the image as such as about the exact representation of subtle psychological states and changes.

* The most famous example of the use of this device is contained in François Villon's *Ballade des Dames du Temps Jadis,* with the line that concludes each stanza (in the English translation by D. G. Rossetti): "But where are the snows of yester-year?"

In the first stanza, the first word which arrests our attention is the verb "bestows." To bestow something is to commit a formal act of a certain magnitude. Jove as god takes the withered rose and preserves it in the beauty of the lady. The next arresting phrase is "orient deep," which can be interpreted to mean deep orient, where "orient" is the East and the rising sun. The phrase "as in their causes" glances at the scholastic or Thomistic idea of cause as "potency"—matter awaiting its fulfillment as form; here, more specifically, it refers to the seeds or buds of the roses. The lady's beauty thus contains within it, dormant, the rose which will come to new life. When the rose withers, instead of being wholly destroyed it achieves a new being in the formal beauty of the lady. (By "formal" we mean *achieved, complete.*)

The second stanza requires very little comment. "The golden atoms of the day," the one phrase of interest, refers to the belief held by the ancient philosophers that the small motes sometimes visible in a sunbeam were actual components of life, rather than the mere dust particles we know them to be.

In stanza three, the word "dividing" is a technical musical term for the "execution of a rapid passage, originally conceived as the dividing of each of a succession of long notes into several short ones" (New English Dictionary). The nightingale is the traditional symbol of poetry and beauty surviving the onslaughts of change, as in the myth of Philomela.* She lives eternally in the lady's voice, which is only another variant of the symbol of permanence.

In stanza four the "meteors" are conceived as fixed stars of the Ptolemaic cosmos, in which they occupy the eighth concentric sphere. These fixed stars, like all physical things, are subject to change, and some of them fall and lose their place in the order of nature. But, says the poet, even if they lose their natural position, they find its equivalent in the lady's eyes, which are their "new sphere," where they enjoy a new order of existence.

The last stanza brilliantly gathers up the implications of the preceding "conceits," in the image of the phoenix. The phoenix is the fabulous bird who every hundred years, according to legend, is consumed by fire and is born anew from the ashes. It is the ancient stock symbol of Permanence in Change. Here the phoenix flies to the

* There are many stories of Philomela, but Ovid's was most influential. She was ravished by Tereus, the husband of her sister, Procne. Although Tereus kept her prisoner and cut out her tongue so she would be silent, she wove her story into tapestry, which Procne saw. The sisters killed Procne's children and served them to Tereus. The gods made Procne a swallow and Philomela a nightingale. Nightly, Philomela pours out her grief in song.

lady's bosom and "dies." The poet does not tell us explicitly that she arises again, but we know by implication that her new embodiment is the lady herself, who is constantly reborn and thus, as the perpetual re-creation of vanished beauty, cannot die.

Again a rhetorical "trick" has been employed. In strict logic, the lady is mortal and must, of course, eventually die. But the poet, by his use of analogy, persuades us—for a time at least—to suspend ordinary logic and enter sympathetically into the "logic of feeling" by which the poem develops.

The five questions Carew asks are, we saw, one question. The five answers he gives are also one answer. The single underlying question was, Where does beauty go when it disappears? And the underlying answer is, It reappears in another form. Beauty never dies. It is permanent through change, moving in the ceaseless flux of nature from one form to another.

EXERCISE

ALUN LEWIS

Song

(On seeing dead bodies floating off the Cape)

> The first month of his absence
> I was numb and sick
> And where he'd left his promise
> Life did not turn or kick.
> The seed, the seed of love was sick.
>
> The second month my eyes were sunk
> In the darkness of despair,
> And my bed was like a grave
> And my ghost was lying there
> And my heart was sick with care.
>
> The third month of his going
> I thought I heard him say
> "Our course deflected slightly
> On the thirty-second day—"
> The tempest blew his words away.

And he was lost among the waves,
His ship rolled helpless in the sea,
The fourth month of his voyage
He shouted grievously
"Beloved, do not think of me."

The flying fish like kingfishers
Skim the sea's bewildered crests,
The whales blow steaming fountains,
The seagulls have no nests
Where my lover sways and rests.

We never thought to buy and sell
This life that blooms or withers in the leaf,
And I'll not stir, so he sleeps well,
Though cell by cell the coral reef
Builds an eternity of grief.

But oh, the drag and dullness of my Self;
The turning seasons wither in my head;
All this slowness, all this hardness,
The nearness that is waiting in my bed,
The gradual self-effacement of the dead.

SOME QUESTIONS

This poem by the remarkable young Welsh poet Alun Lewis, who was killed in India during World War II, seems to have been inspired by the sight of men dead at sea during his voyage East; presumably he thought of the wife he had left in England, and he puts his poem in the mouth of a woman so bereaved.

1. Does the title of the poem prepare the reader for the anxious realism [1] of the first stanza? What is the subject of this first stanza? The tone is one of intense *regret,* so the man and woman cannot have been merely lovers; they are husband and wife. Do you think they have been married long or not? Why?

2. In view of the later action of the poem, has the last line of the first stanza a secondary meaning? If so, what is it? How would you describe the technical device [2]—as a simile, a metaphor, or a symbol?

3. The subject of the first stanza is a beginning of life (or a failure of it); the symbolism of the second stanza (grave, ghost) is the ending of life. In what way does the word "bed" bind the two stanzas together? Does "sick"?

4. If we take the first stanza to be unexpectedly realistic, and the second to be (therefore) unexpectedly imaginative, do both of these modes [3] continue into stanza three? In what lines, if so, and in what order?

5. What is the tone of the quotations from the man in stanzas three and four? Does she actually hear a voice? What is the *meaning* of her imagining his technical statement in stanza three? Is her mind following and continually envisaging his problems? What is the meaning of the quotation from him in stanza four?

6. In stanza five, what is the function of the word "bewildered" —that is, is it really the crests that are bewildered? Is this a transferred function? What is the function of "nests"?

7. Is it significant that she thinks of creatures that are *above* the sea's surface and *under* it? In what way?

8. What is the function of the word "lover"?

9. How do you think of the action of her mind (in the poet's intention) as of the phrase "sways and rests"?

10. The subject of the first two lines of the sixth stanza is suicide. She rejects it in line 3; why? Suicide is an escape. Do the last two lines of the stanza suggest that she imagines any *other* escape from her mourning?

11. Is immortality a topic in this poem?

12. The intense realism of the first stanza is taken up again—not that it has been exactly abandoned in between—in the last stanza. What is the subject here? Is, after all, an escape for her envisaged? Is there a relation between this last stanza and the final line of stanza four? What is it?

13. Why did not the poet put what he had to say in this poem in words of one syllable, in declarative sentences, and publish it on the editorial page of the London *Times?* Is a poet's job to tell people what to think, or to say what *he* thinks, or what *he feels,* or to force readers (good readers) to have *experiences?* Or is it some combination of these? Does life itself, for human beings, consist of words of one syllable, in declarative sentences?

14. What is meant, in the final line, by *"self-*effacement"? Is this notion romantic [4] or realistic?

1. *Realism:* A word with many meanings and ambiguous banners; here the meaning is "the taking a practical view in human problems."
2. *Device:* The means by which something gets done; conveyance.
3. *Mode:* Manner of existing; mood.
4. *Romantic:* Another mysterious word; here the meaning is extravagant, fictitious (both are common dictionary meanings).

EXERCISE

WILLIAM WORDSWORTH

Sonnet

> Surprised by joy—impatient as the Wind
> I turned to share my transport—Oh! with whom
> But Thee, deep buried in the silent tomb,
> That spot which no vicissitude can find?
> Love faithful love, recalled thee to my mind—
> But how could I forget thee? Through what power,
> Even for the least division of an hour,
> Have I been so beguiled as to be blind
> To my most grievous loss?—That thought's return
> Was the worst pang that sorrow ever bore,
> Save one, one only, when I stood forlorn,
> Knowing my heart's best treasure was no more;
> That neither present time, nor years unborn
> Could to my sight that heavenly face restore.

SOME QUESTIONS

A sonnet is a poem of fourteen lines (usually) in iambic pentameter (usually). The two main types in English and American poetry are: (1) the Petrarchan, which divides into eight lines (octave) and six lines (sestet), rhyming *abba, abba,* nearly always in the octave, but with various arrangements of three rhymes in the last six lines; (2) the Shakespearian, a much easier and looser form, consisting of three quatrains, *abab, cdcd, efef,* with a couplet, *gg.* The Shakespearian sonnet generally goes in for variations on a theme, with a two-line conclusion which even Shakespeare was seldom able to make interesting. The Petrarchan sonnet—of which type is Wordsworth's?—is more complex, in the interaction of the octave and the sestet, particularly where there is a run-over of one into the other.

1. The sonnet is addressed to the poet's dead daughter. Is there a secondary meaning,[1] then, for the word "heavenly" in the last line? What is it?

2. What is the real meaning here of the verb *bore* in line 10? You will notice "unborn" later. How is this theme relevant to the action of the poem?

3. The fact that even human sorrow dies with time is the subject of the last stanza [2] of Alun Lewis's "Song." Is the same subject [3] present here? In what lines or passages?

4. Essentially the poem moves from joy to a grief which reminds the poet of a deeper grief, the worst in fact of his life. What is gained by approaching a grief through a joy, and then a deeper grief through a lesser one?

5. Another way of putting the movement of the poet's thought, or feeling, is that we move from the transient (the joy) to the permanent (loss). Is a general truth about human life implied, then, in the emotional and intellectual structure [4] of the sonnet? How would you formulate it?

6. What is the meaning of "vicissitude"? In that it means a change of fortune *either* from good to bad or from bad to good, how is it a key word in the poem? You notice that it is the most elaborate word in the poem, and comes after a large number of short, simple words. Does this give it emphasis?

TERMS AND PRINCIPLES

1. *Secondary meaning:* Many expressions used in imaginative literature—poetry, fiction, drama—must be regarded as having two or more meanings, of which it is convenient to regard one as primary, the literal, and the others, depending as they do more on suggestion than statement, as secondary, tertiary, and so on.

2. *Stanza:* A group of lines of verse forming a definite pattern.

3. *Subject:* What a piece of writing is *about*. See Babel Commentary, page 206.
4. *Structure:* Arrangement of parts; manner of organization.

EXERCISE

ANONYMOUS

A Handsome Young Airman

A handsome young airman lay dying,
And as on the aerodrome he lay,
To the mechanics who round him came sighing
These last dying words he did say:

"Take the cylinders out of my kidney,
The connecting-rod out of my brain,
Take the cam-shaft from out of my backbone,
And assemble the engine again."

SOME QUESTIONS

This is not a professional poem—not, that is, the work of a professional poet. It was made by some unknown Englishman during World War I, and has been passed along verbally.
1. The first stanza is extremely romantic. Point out the details that show this to be true.
2. Is the second stanza romantic?
3. In the light of the second stanza, does the romanticism of the first stanza require a second look? How further would you characterize it now?
4. A man becomes fond not only of his horse but of his car or his plane. Is this the only point of the second stanza, or is some connection being made with one form of immortality? What are some other forms of immortality that have been imagined by man?
5. We contrast the limp and elegiac first stanza with the energetic, even violent second. Could we see these in terms of the complication and resolution that we were studying in the structure of short stories?

EXERCISE

ANONYMOUS

The Twa Corbies

I

As I was walking all alane,
I heard twa corbies making a mane:
The tane unto the tither did say,
"Whar sall we gang and dine the day?"

II

"—In behint yon auld fail dyke
I wot there lies a new-slain knight;
And naebody kens that he lies there
But his hawk, his hound, and his lady fair.

III

"His hound is to the hunting gane,
His hawk to fetch the wild-fowl hame,
His lady's ta'en anither mate,
Sae we may mak' our dinner sweet.

IV

"Ye'll sit on his white hause-bane,
And I'll pike out his bonny blue e'en;
Wi'ae lock o' his gowden hair
We'll theek our nest when it grows bare.

V

"Mony's the one for him maks mane,
But nane sall ken whar he is gane;
O'er his white banes when they are bare,
The wind sall blaw for evermair."

SOME QUESTIONS

Because of the Scottish vowel-changes and diction, you will want some practice in reading this poem aloud, until it feels easy to you. The most usual change is from English "o" to Scottish "a," as in Twa, alane, mane, naebody, gane, hame, Sae, -bane, nane, banes, blaw. Some words are changed slightly in other ways: "tane" and "tither" are "one" and "other," "behint" is "behind," "e'en" is "eyes," "gowden" is "golden," "sall" is "shall." A few words need glossing [1]: "corbies" are ravens, "gang" is go, "fail dyke" is a turf-wall, "wot" is know, and so is "ken," "hause-bane" is collar-bone, "pike" is pick or pierce, "ae" is one, "theek" is thatch.

1. This bleak and exquisitely beautiful old poem is what is called a folk-poem, by which we mean that we do not know who wrote it, *not* that it was written by a folk, for poetry is made only by poets. It is not quite a ballad,[2] which is a simple straightforward narrative poem [3] in short stanzas. This is neither simple nor straightforward, and it *implies* a story rather than tells it. Can you tell who killed the knight, for instance?

2. An approach to that question might concern the narrative element of the consideration of *time* in the poem, as in a detective story, say. It is important to fix the time of the crime, so that we may know who has an alibi, and so on. This poem is a little like a detective story, in fact. Well, the knight is "new-slain," and yet his lady has had time to marry again. We infer that she remarried very rapidly. And yet his body has not even been found, for burial, so there is no general certainty of his death. Still, she not only knows that he is dead (else how could she remarry?) but she knows where his body is, as lines 7 and 8 tell us. Yet she does nothing to bury him, but remarries. Clearly she is either the killer or an accomplice of the killer. Perhaps the latter of the two possibilities is more likely, the murder being done by her lover, whom she has now married. In short, the knight was surrounded by treachery, without knowing it. How do we know that he was unsuspecting? Is it easy to kill a suspicious and armed man?

3. Is the theme of faithlessness reinforced in the poem? That is, do we have to reckon with any betrayals except the wife's (and the lover's, if he knew the husband, as presumably he did)?

4. Are these other betrayals important in themselves, or only as they help to create an *atmosphere* of faithlessness, in the animal as well as the human world, and so lead on to the *natural* cruelty of the ravens themselves?

5. Suppose we heard that his lady had remarried, and *then*

learned that his hound and his hawk were, under new masters, about their business: would this be sentimental?

6. How old was the knight? Does the color of his hair tell us anything about that? Is the pathos of his desolate treacherous death increased by what we learn about his age?

7. Can we consider the color of his hair, "gowden," a symbol? What do you think it symbolizes? (Remember what you know about the Golden Age, or as Shakespeare puts it in *As You Like It,* the Golden World—"an imaginary past time of innocence and happiness," as the dictionary says.) Is to be unsuspicious a virtue? From what point of view?

8. What is the analogical meaning of the last two lines of stanza four? One connotation of "nest" is: a safe home. Is a connection being made, by the anonymous poet, between the home of the knight, which *all* of his beautiful hair could not make other than treacherous, and the home of the ravens, which one lock of it will make comfortable? What is implied here about the moral demands made by man (and his hopes, and their chances for satisfaction), and the demands made by the natural world?

9. With the question just asked, at the end of 8, we are reaching toward a sort of metaphysics in the poem. This is an almost ruthless poem. Can you point to any line which asserts an *alternative* to the pattern of faithlessness?

10. As of the same question at the end of 8, can we contrast the moan made by the ravens—for dinner—with the implied demand made in life by the knight for faithfulness? On what non-natural bases would he make this demand?

11. As of question 9, is there any suggestion of hypocrisy in the line involved (line 17)? Is this suggestion strong or slight? (Note that her remarriage would have freed her from any considerable pretense of mourning.)

12. "Knight," in this poem, is of course a Christian term—"one of gentle birth and bred to arms," says the dictionary, "admitted in feudal times to a certain honorable military rank." Does this fact have anything to say to the meaning of line 18? What is the *literal* meaning of the line? (Note that he must have been killed on a pleasure expedition, since his hawk and his hound know where his body lies; note also, as of question 11, that "nane" refers very closely back to "Mony's the one," so that the suggestion of hypocrisy there is very slight indeed, since the widow knows very well where he has gone.) What is the secondary, Christian meaning of the line? How does this second meaning help prevent any possible sentimentality in the treat-

ment, by the poet, of the figure whom we may regard as the hero (and victim) of the poem? Is it of interest, in relation to the general feelings of the poet about human life, that the hero of the poem should also be its victim?

13. Is the adjective "fair," used about the lady, ambiguous? If so, how?

14. Do the last two lines of the poem help emphasize the Christian ambiguity of the line (18) just before them? How?

15. The body of the poem is a speech by a raven. Is the reader invited to believe that ravens talk? What is meant by the poet in putting this into a raven's mouth?

16. Who is the narrator in this poem? What are we told about him? What is the reason, or what are the reasons, for the deep emphasis, only heard truly as you read the poem for the second or tenth time, upon "all alane"? Is the fact that there are *two* ravens relevant to the meaning that we attach to "all alane" and to the guilt and remarriage of the lady? What do you imagine to have been the deep *motive* of this magnificent poem?

17. The first line of the poem is purely human and isolated, the final line is natural and general. Can we infer anything from this fact about the *unconscious* opinions of the poet? (It is necessary to say "unconscious" because he may not either have planned or noticed this relation.)

TERMS AND PRINCIPLES

1. *Glossing:* Explaining a word or expression.
2. *Ballad:* A simple straightforward narrative poem in short stanzas.
3. *Narrative poem:* A poem that tells a story.

JOHN CROWE RANSOM

The Equilibrists

> Full of her long white arms and milky skin
> He had a thousand times remembered sin.
> Alone in the press of people traveled he,
> Minding her jacinth, and myrrh, and ivory.

Mouth he remembered: the quaint orifice
From which came heat that flamed upon the kiss,
Till cold words came down spiral from the head,
Grey doves from the officious tower illsped.

Body: it was a white field ready for love,
On her body's field, with the gaunt tower above,
The lilies grew, beseeching him to take,
If he would pluck and wear them, bruise and break.

Eyes talking: Never mind the cruel words,
Embrace my flowers, but not embrace the swords.
But what they said, the doves came straightway flying
And unsaid: Honor, Honor, they came crying.

Importunate her doves. Too pure, too wise,
Clambering on his shoulder, saying, Arise,
Leave me now, and never let us meet,
Eternal distance now command thy feet.

Predicament indeed, which thus discovers
Honor among thieves, Honor between lovers.
O such a little word is Honor, they feel!
But the grey word is between them cold as steel.

At length I saw these lovers fully were come
Into their torture of equilibrium;
Dreadfully had forsworn each other, and yet
They were bound each to each, and they did not forget.

And rigid as two painful stars, and twirled
About the clustered night their prison world,
They burned with fierce love always to come near,
But Honor beat them back and kept them clear.

Ah, the strict lovers, they are ruined now!
I cried in anger. But with puddled brow
Devising for those gibbeted and brave
Came I descanting: Man, what would you have?

For spin your period out, and draw your breath,
A kinder saeculum begins with Death.
Would you ascend to Heaven and bodiless dwell?
Or take your bodies honorless to Hell?

In Heaven you have heard no marriage is,
No white flesh tinder to your lecheries,
Your male and female tissue sweetly shaped
Sublimed away, and furious blood escaped.

Great lovers lie in Hell, the stubborn ones
Infatuate of the flesh upon the bones;
Stuprate, they rend each other when they kiss,
The pieces kiss again, no end to this.

But still I watched them spinning, orbited nice.
Their flames were not more radiant than their ice.
I dug in the quiet earth and wrought the tomb
And made these lines to memorize their doom:—

Epitaph

Equilibrists lie here; stranger, tread light;
Close, but untouching in each other's sight;
Mouldered the lips and ashy the tall skull,
Let them lie perilous and beautiful.

COMMENTARY

This poem was written in the early 1920's, and it is, as we shall
see, a modern poem; that is, it probably could not have been written
before the twentieth century. But a good deal of the diction [1] is archaic
and formal, and the occasional colloquial tone [2] would be difficult to
locate in any period. Moreover, the main convention of the poem—
the courtly convention—is a very old one.

This convention of courtly love, as we have seen in the analysis
of Marvell's "To His Coy Mistress," is probably the most powerful
single tradition in the history of European poetry. It has been employed, with modifications, in a great deal of twentieth-century verse.
Whether or not John Crowe Ransom was consciously using this con-

vention in writing "The Equilibrists," we can discern its main outlines here, though the poet gives the convention with a particular twist. Thus, in the poetry of courtly love, it was indispensable that the love should not be consummated, but that the lover should continue to praise and beseech the lady, who always keeps him off. The lovers in Mr. Ransom's poem do not consummate their passion either; as in the poetry of the troubadours, the chastity of the beloved is assumed. But Mr. Ransom introduces a variant upon the classic situation: Here the lover participates in the rejection or renunciation no less than the beloved does. (For a more extensive discussion of this convention, see the commentary on Marvell's "To His Coy Mistress," p. 299.)

Let us look at the language of the poem.

The first four stanzas contain a series of images [3] of the lady's body—her arms and skin, her mouth, her eyes, and the entire beautiful body, which the lover remembers as a "white field ready for love." The description is never purely sensuous but is conveyed through complicated metaphors [4] and allusions. And the images are not used for their own sake, as a reverie upon the beloved's physical charms; instead they are presented at once from the point of view of a conflict which engages the lover:

> Full of her long white arms and milky skin
> He had a thousand times remembered sin.

The nature of this conflict in the lover's mind is foreshadowed in the very first stanza.

In the stanza that follows, the poet complicates the romantic imagery by referring it to the physical, naturalistic basis of love. The mouth is an "orifice"—an anatomical term—and the "heat" is not romantic fervor but simply the heat of the body. Then, through the development of another kind of metaphor, the woman's body becomes a medieval fortress, gaunt and forbidding. The tower is the head, from which appear the doves of conscience. These doves have a traditional setting: their first connotation is the white doves of Venus, which are depicted in art as preceding the Goddess of Love in her chariot. Their other connotation is Christian—the white dove of the Holy Ghost. But the poet brilliantly alters the doves' conventional symbolism for his particular purpose. The doves of this poem are gray doves. They are thus the symbols neither of sensual indulgence nor of the Holy Spirit as comforter. Mr. Ransom recalls the tradition only to reject it. These are the gray doves of conscience, forbidding and grim. But here again we must qualify this description; for what the doves say to the lover is not entirely puritanical and repressive. Their message, in fact, comes from a different perspective

—that of honor. The concept of honor was, of course, not originally Christian, but had its beginnings in pagan morality and was later a part of the standard code of behavior or "etiquette" of the medieval courtier. In other words, the doves enjoin the lover to renounce the beloved not merely for reasons of right and wrong but for considerations of honor, since he is a gentleman, the idea of the gentleman being neutral with respect to Christian morality.

After the doves have spoken, the reader begins to wonder what this renunciation is all about. He may well ask, Why has the renunciation been necessary? What has happened? Is there some external impediment to the consummation of this love, or is it some obscure private difficulty? A good reader will ask these questions, but he will not necessarily expect them to be answered. Our understanding of the drama of the poem would not in any sense be increased if the poet told us that the lady was married to another man, or that a cruel father had forbidden her to see her lover again. An inferior poet might have given us these details, a practice that Henry James defined as "the fallacy of weak specifications," [5] the introduction of irrelevant or unnecessary details which only detract from the power and mystery of the bare, unexplained central drama. The purpose of the poet is to set forth the dramatic conflict, whatever its origins and causes may have been.

The parting injunction of the doves to the lover is to leave— "Eternal distance now command thy feet." At the end of this stanza, the fifth, the poet appears in person and meditates upon the situation. His first remark is:

> Predicament indeed, which thus discovers
> Honor among thieves, Honor between lovers.

Observe the wit which equates thieves and lovers. It establishes a certain detachment, a formal control on the part of the narrator, which, as we shall see, tends to universalize the particular situation of these two lovers and to make it unnecessary for him to invade the privacy of the lovers' motivations and emotions.

The poet begins in the seventh stanza to develop the central metaphor form which the title of the poem is derived, that is, the metaphor of equilibrium. The lovers have achieved a certain relation to each other which may be described as a perfect balance of attraction and renunciation. At a certain fixed distance from each other, they cannot come together in the lovers' embrace; they can renounce, but they cannot reject one another.

In the next stanza we have one of the most brilliant extended metaphors in modern poetry. In order to convey dynamically to the reader this peculiar equilibrium of the lovers, the poet hit upon the kind of analogy or "conceit" which the seventeenth-century Metaphysical poets brought into English verse. This particular metaphor, however, could not have been invented in the seventeenth century. It is derived from modern astronomy, which has revealed to us the existence of huge twin stars revolving round each other; their centrifugal force keeps them apart, but at the same time the pull of gravitation draws them together. As a result they are orbited in equilibrium.

The poet shifts ground again in the ninth stanza as he begins to meditate on the nature of honor and of the renunciation that it demands. The line "Ah, the strict lovers, they are ruins now," expresses the ordinary human and compassionate attitude that most people would feel for the predicament of these lovers. But what the poet is going to say eventually is that through the tragic irony [6] of the renunciation these lovers achieve a moral victory which would not otherwise have been possible for them.

In stanzas ten and eleven, we get that curious fusion of Christian and classical feeling which was characteristic of Andrew Marvell and his contemporaries:

For spin your period out and draw your breath,
A kinder saeculum begins with Death.

We notice that "Death" is a semi-personification; [7] it has overtones of Hades or Orcus or some region of the classical underworld. And this implication is reinforced by the word "saeculum," the Latin word for age or epoch.

The naturalistic implications of the description of the woman's body in the four first stanzas are extended in the eleventh stanza with the words "lecheries," and "male and female tissue." The phrase "sublimed away" is derived from alchemy: in the alembic the spiritual essences are presumably distilled from the baser materials, and the "furious blood" no longer exists with the spirit.

In the twelfth stanza we have a powerful scene in which damned lovers are presented with a kind of Dantesque realism and, we may add, with Dantesque ambiguity. The lovers are condemned to an eternal physical embrace in which they rend each other with destructive passion. But the scene is one of considerable magnificence—horror and awe are both present here. The poet thus approaches the end of the poem with a far from simple or univocal view of the renunciation of his lovers. He concludes by retaining on the whole his original tragic interpretation of their plight: they are ceaselessly "spinning," but they are at the same time "orbited nice." The renunciation of these equilibrists has precision, dignity, and order.

The final stanza, the Epitaph, reminds us of the epitaph of Gray's "Elegy Written in a Country Churchyard," but its purpose is quite different. We see the lovers buried in the same grave, "Close, but untouching in each other's sight." The "tall skull," the tower of stanza three, now "ashy," reminds us of Marvell's "And your quaint honor turn to dust, And into ashes all my lust." In death as in life, the situation of the lovers is "perilous and beautiful." The adjective "beautiful," refers, we may assume, to their tragic victory.

TERMS AND PRINCIPLES

1. *Diction:* Choice of words or language (as whether to use, depending on the context, "car" or "automobile"). In this sense, the word has nothing whatever to do with speaking or accent.
2. *Colloquial tone:* Tone of ordinary speech.
3. *Image:* Anything in a literary work which makes its appeal primarily to the senses, as of hearing, seeing, taste, touch.
4. *Metaphor:* A figure of speech by which something is spoken of as *being* what it only *resembles*.
5. *Weak specification:* The introduction of irrelevant or unnecessary details.
6. We have described *irony* as a "speaking two ways." Here the poet says the lovers are "ruined," but yet they achieve a secret moral victory. The irony is *tragic* because the victory is won at the price of their destruction.
7. *Semi-personification:* An incomplete attribution of human traits to an abstract quality.

EXERCISE

WALTER DE LA MARE

The Song of the Mad Prince

Who said, "Peacock Pie"?
The old King to the sparrow:
Who said, "Crops are ripe"?

Rust to the harrow:
Who said, "Where sleeps she now?
Where rests she now her head,
Bathed in eve's loveliness"?—
That's what I said.

Who said, "Ay, mum's the word"?
Sexton to willow:
Who said, "Green dusk for dreams,
Moss for a pillow"?
Who said, "All Time's delight
Hath she for narrow bed;
Life's troubled bubble broken"?—
That's what I said.

SOME QUESTIONS

1. The poem is called "The Song of the *Mad* Prince," so we will not expect ordinary coherence. Indeed it is like a nursery rhyme, enigmatic and short. But does the second stanza make clear at any rate that it is an elegy? For whom?

2. At the same time, is it perfectly certain, by the end of stanza 1, that "she" is dead? Perhaps she has merely gone away (lines 5–6)?

3. Do the mysterious conversations at the beginning of the poem help us to answer question 2? A pie made of peacock flesh would be exotic, and *rare;* nothing is so *common* as an English sparrow, to whom the remark is addressed, by a King. Is this suggested ambiguity helpful to the theme of the poem? Do the connotations of the word "Peacock" bring the concept of Beauty into the poem at once? And then a "pie" made of peacock, *killed:* is this helpful to the theme?

4. We have seen that the suggestions of the first distich * are startling: a peacock is made into a pie, a King addresses a sparrow about it. We might call the suggestions of the distich anomalous. Does the second distich contrast with them in its generality and ordinariness? Things come to their completion, ready for harvest. Does the rusting of the harrow indicate a normal passage of time? But does it also suggest tarnishing—something bright dimming? Is this useful to the theme?

5. Try to paraphrase line 7 as it might be put in ordinary prose.

* Two lines or verses that make a complete sense.

Is its meaning likely to occur in ordinary prose? The line is dreamlike, leading on from the first part of the question toward the second stanza.

6. A sexton is a church officer who digs graves. Does the poem suddenly turn sinister with this word?

7. Is an injunction to silence appropriately put into the mouth of a sexton? Why?

8. You notice, comparing line 1 with line 9, that "Ay" is extra-metrical, unexpected. Is this technical fact related to the emphasis the poet desires for the word? What would be the difference in tone here if he had written "Yes" instead of "Ay"?

9. What are connotations of "dusk"?

10. Does the penultimate line suggest that her life was happy?

11. The intense constricting that occurs in line 14 (all time), after the expansion of line 13 (narrow bed) suggests something about the passage from life to death. What can you say about this?

12. The fact that it is a Prince who is mourning her tells us that she was young and, almost certainly of high birth herself: do these circumstances increase the pathos of her death?

13. How would you formulate, now, the theme of the poem? Is it possible, or even likely, that the Prince is mad with grief for her?

14. Analyze the sound of "troubled bubble broken."

T. S. ELIOT

The Love Song of J. Alfred Prufrock

> S'io credesse che mia risposta fosse
> A persona che mai tornasse al mondo,
> Questa fiamma staria senza piu scosse.
> Ma perciocche giammai di questo fondo
> Non torno vivo alcun, s'i'odo il vero,
> Senza tema d'infamia ti rispondo.

Let us go then, you and I,
When the evening is spread out against the sky
Like a patient etherised upon a table;
Let us go, through certain half-deserted streets,
The muttering retreats
Of restless nights in one-night cheap hotels

And sawdust restaurants with oyster-shells:
Streets that follow like a tedious argument
Of insidious intent
To lead you to an overwhelming question. . .
Oh, do not ask, "What is it?"
Let us go and make our visit.

In the room the women come and go
Talking of Michelangelo.

The yellow fog that rubs its back upon the window-panes,
The yellow smoke that rubs its muzzle on the window-panes
Licked its tongue into the corners of the evening,
Lingered upon the pools that stand in drains,
Let fall upon its back the soot that falls from chimneys,
Slipped by the terrace, made a sudden leap,
And seeing that it was a soft October night,
Curled once about the house, and fell asleep.
And indeed there will be time
For the yellow smoke that slides along the street,
Rubbing its back upon the window-panes;
There will be time, there will be time
To prepare a face to meet the faces that you meet;
There will be time to murder and create,
And time for all the works and days of hands
That lift and drop a question on your plate;
Time for you and time for me,
And time yet for a hundred indecisions,
And for a hundred visions and revisions,
Before the taking of a toast and tea.

In the room the women come and go
Talking of Michelangelo.
And indeed there will be time
To wonder, "Do I dare" and, "Do I dare?"
Time to turn back and descent the stair,
With a bald spot in the middle of my hair—

[They will say: "How his hair is growing thin!"]
My morning coat, my collar mounting firmly to the chin,
My necktie rich and modest, but asserted by a simple pin—
[They will say: "But how his arms and legs are thin!"]
Do I dare
Disturb the universe?
In a minute there is time
For decisions and revisions which a minute will reverse.

For I have known them all already, known them all—
Have known the evenings, mornings, afternoons,
I have measured out my life with coffee spoons;
I know the voices dying with a dying fall
Beneath the music from a farther room.
   So how should I presume?

And I have known the eyes already, known them all—
The eyes that fix you in a formulated phrase,
And when I am formulated, sprawling on a pin,
When I am pinned and wriggling on the wall,
Then how should I begin
To spit out all the butt-ends of my days and ways?
   And how should I presume?

And I have known the arms already, known them all—
Arms that are braceleted and white and bare
[But in the lamplight, downed with light brown hair!]
Is it perfume from a dress
That makes me so digress?
Arms that lie along a table, or wrap about a shawl.
   And should I then presume?
   And how should I begin?

       *   *   *   *   *   *

Shall I say, I have gone at dusk through narrow streets
And watched the smoke that rises from the pipes
Of lonely men in shirt-sleeves, leaning out of windows? . . .

I should have been a pair of ragged claws
Scuttling across the floors of silent seas.

      *   *   *   *   *   *

And the afternoon, the evening, sleeps so peacefully!
Smoothed by long fingers,
Asleep . . . tired . . . or it malingers,
Stretched on the floor, here beside you and me.
Should I, after tea and cakes and ices,
Have the strength to force the moment to its crisis?
But though I have wept and fasted, wept and prayed,
Though I have seen my head [grown slightly bald] brought in upon a
   platter,
I am no prophet—and here's no great matter;
I have seen the moment of my greatness flicker,
And I have seen the eternal Footman hold my coat, and snicker,
And in short, I was afraid.

And would it have been worth it, after all,
After the cups, the marmalade, the tea,
Among the porcelain, among some talk of you and me,
Would it have been worth while,
To have bitten off the matter with a smile,
To have squeezed the universe into a ball
To roll it toward some overwhelming question,
To say: "I am Lazarus, come from the dead,
Come back to tell you all, I shall tell you all"—
If one, settling a pillow by her head,
  Should say: "That is not what I meant at all.
  That is not it, at all."

And would it have been worth it, after all,
Would it have been worth while,
After the sunsets and the dooryards and the sprinkled streets,
After the novels, after the teacups, after the skirts that trail along the
   floor—
And this, and so much more?—
It is impossible to say just what I mean!

But as if a magic lantern threw the nerves in patterns on a screen:
Would it have been worth while
If one, settling a pillow or throwing off a shawl,
And turning toward the window, should say:
  "That is not it at all,
  That is not what I meant, at all."

*   *   *   *   *   *

No! I am not Prince Hamlet, nor was meant to be;
Am an attendant lord, one that will do
To swell a progress, start a scene or two,
Advise the prince; no doubt, an easy tool,
Deferential, glad to be of use,
Politic, cautious, and meticulous;
Full of high sentence, but a bit obtuse;
At times, indeed, almost ridiculous—
Almost, at times, the Fool.

I grow old . . . I grow old . . .
I shall wear the bottoms of my trousers rolled.

Shall I part my hair behind? Do I dare to eat a peach?
I shall wear white flannel trousers, and walk upon the beach.
I have heard the mermaids singing, each to each.

I do not think that they will sing to me.

I have seen them riding seaward on the waves
Combing the white hair of the waves blown back
When the wind blows the water white and black.

We have lingered in the chambers of the sea
By sea-girls wreathed with seaweed red and brown
Till human voices wake us, and we drown.

COMMENTARY

Suppose we begin with Eliot's title, "The Love Song of J. Alfred Prufrock." Is the second half of the title quite what the first part led us to expect? A man named J. Alfred Prufrock could hardly be expected to sing a love song; he sounds too well dressed. His name

takes something away from the notion of a love song; the form of
the title, that is to say, is reductive.[1] How does he begin singing?

> Let us go then, you and I,
> When the evening is spread out against the sky . . .

That sounds very pretty—lyrical [2]—he does seem, after all, in spite
of his name, to be inviting her for an evening; there is a nice rhyme
—it sounds like other dim romantic verse. Then comes the third line:

> Like a patient etherised upon a table.

With this line, modern poetry begins.

In the first place, the third line proves that the author of the first
two lines did not mean them. They were a come-on, designed merely
to get the reader off guard, so that he could be knocked down. The
form, again, is reductive; an expectation has been created only to be
diminished or destroyed. (Presently, by the way, it will prove that
"you" is not the woman at all, since "you" is invited to make a visit
with "I" *to* her; we can hardly say yet who "you" is; an assumption
has been destroyed.) And the word "then"—"Let us go *then*"—is
really very unpromising; if he had only said "Let us go" it would
have sounded much more as if they were going to go; "Let us go
then" sounds as if he had been giving it thought, and thought suggests
hesitation. Of course he never goes at all: the visit, involving the
"overwhelming question," the proposal of marriage, is never made.
Here again we come on a reduction.

Also, the simile is not visual: it only pretends to be. No reader
could possibly be assisted in seeing the evening spread out against the
sky by having his attention suddenly and violently called to a patient
laid out on an operating table. The device of simile is being put to a
novel use, violating the ordinary logic of verse, just as the abrupt
vision of a hospital violates the lyrical notion of an evening stroll.

What does the line mean? We are obliged to resort to suggestion,
not to logic. The situation of a patient under ether is unenviable,
risky: he is about to be cut into, soon he may be dead. This fear is
basic to the poem; Prufrock finally says in fact, "I was afraid." On
the other hand, the situation of the patient can be regarded as desirable, in that he *has* made a decision, and now the result is out of his
hands, he has no further responsibility, it is up to the surgeon to save
him or not. This desire—to *have made* the proposal, and to have his
fate left up to the woman—is also basic to the poem. We may think
of that as quite a lot of work to get done in one line. Of course, the
suggestion that Prufrock sees himself as *ill* is important also, and we
will return to this.

Now, between the title, with its slight effect of double-take, and these opening lines, with their full effect of double-take, the poet has inserted an epigraph [5] in Italian, six lines of it. Does the poet imagine the reader knows Italian? Hardly, or a knowledge of Italian is of very little help. All the lines say is, "If I thought what I am going to tell you would ever get back to the world, you would hear nothing from me. But as it is," and so on. One has to know *who* is speaking, and what he then goes on, in Dante's *Divine Comedy,* to say. This is a lost soul, in Hell, damned in particular because he tried to purchase absolution *before* committing a crime. We are obliged to consider, that is, as of Prufrock with his dilemma of whether or not to propose marriage, whether the fundamental reason he does not do so—his sin—is his refusal to take the ordinary inevitable human risks: he wants to know beforehand whether he will be accepted or not—in fact he does *think* he knows already what will happen—but this belongs later for us.

Our point just now is that everything we have been saying paints a picture as different as possible from any that you may have of a writer sitting down to entertain, beguile, charm, and lull a reader or readers. Obstacles and surprise, of no pleasant kind, are this poet's stock-in-trade. The reader's expectation that *one* thing will happen is the first to be attacked. Several things are going to be happening simultaneously. One feels, even, a certain hostility toward the reader on the part of the poet—as if he were saying: You are a stupid reader, do not think you are going to have an easy time here, come along if you want to, but I couldn't care less, I am very busy with my intricate and difficult subject, naturally you will hear some interesting things if you do come along. The modern poet, characteristically, has *lost confidence in his* readers (this is not altogether surprising, considering the quality of most contemporary education); but so far from causing him to reduce his demands therefore, this loss of confidence has led to an *increase* in his demands. Good poetry has never been easy to read with any advanced understanding, but it has seldom been made so deliberately difficult.

Shall we connect this deliberate difficulty with the reductive devices studied earlier and suggest that the poet's impatience with the reader is based on the fact that the reader's mind is full of vague and grandiose assumptions which seem to the poet contemptible? The poet sees himself as a warning voice, like a Hebrew prophet calling on the people to repent, to understand better themselves and the world. Of course this *is* a reduced world. In one celebrated view, we have undergone three crucial scientific revolutions. The first was the astronomical, in the sixteenth century—Copernicus and Galileo are the major names—which taught man that so far from occupying a splendid position at the heart of the universe, he lived in a suburb, and one of no importance. He digested this unwelcome information very slowly. Then he was informed, by Darwin and others, a hundred years ago, that in addition to his ignominious physical location, he was not unique, but continuous with the animals whom he had always patronized. Our periods of time are getting much shorter. He had barely fifty years in which to learn to accept this biological insult, when the psychological revolution associated with the name of Freud informed man that in addition to his displaced and reduced astronomical and biological status, he was not even king inside, but stood at the mercy of gigantic unconscious forces within himself. All this ought to have rendered him distinctly uneasy, let us say, and has done so, depending on his degree of self-awareness; but hardly to a degree acceptable to the exceptional self-awareness of the poet. Eliot had pretty certainly not read Freud when he wrote this poem. In some ways however their thought is parallel, for the "you" whom Prufrock invites to go with him for the visit must be another part of his own personality, whom he vainly invites to join him in the great task before them—the instinctual part of man (as against the façade that knows itself, the I, the ego) for which Freud was to borrow the word "id" from Groddeck.

But the "you" is perhaps also the reader, the actual reader, addressed thus surprisingly in this dramatic monologue; and this device is French, part of the general air of elaborate sophistication adopted by Eliot in this poem. This tone is not original; it is borrowed from the French symbolist poet Jules Laforgue (1860–1887), under whose influence Eliot first found his own voice. Some of the characteristic properties in "Prufrock" are Laforgue's, allusions to Hamlet, and the sirens. But there is influence also from Elizabethan drama, in the speech-rhythms (the poem is written in what is called "free verse,"[3] which only means that the laws it obeys are different from those of traditional stanza or blank verse);[4] and there is influence from prose words, especially the expatriate American novelist Henry James's. In any event, Laforgue could never have conceived or written the poem. He only supplied the *manner,* and anyway his music—very beautiful sometimes—is hardly Eliot's.

Eliot's mind is very deep. The manner is highly sophisticated. But perhaps we ought not to call the poem sophisticated. Let us call it primitive.

The poem pretends to be a love song. It is something much more practical. It is a study—a debate by Prufrock with himself—over the *business* of proposing marriage, agreeing to lay your fate in someone else's hands, undertaking to spend your life with her, to beget and rear children, and so on. He never makes it. The first half of the poem looks forward to the proposal, the second half looks back on how it *would* have gone if it had gone at all. The poem is intensely anti-romantic, and its extremely serious subject, in a so-called Love Song, is another rebuke to the (probably romantic) reader. Primitive societies take a dim view of not marrying. Hawaiian mythology, for instance, describes a god called Nanggananaag, whose job it is to stand with an immense club on the Road to Paradise and smash off it, into nothingness, any unmarried male who, having died, tries to get by. This way of thinking is precisely Eliot's. Late in the poem Prufrock looks forward with dismay (and a certain jaunty pathos) to his endless bachelorhood—the sameness and triviality that are the lot of one who never succeeded in adopting his human responsibilities at all. It is clear that the poet sympathizes with Prufrock. It is also clear that the poet damns Prufrock. Some of the basic emotions of the poem are primitive also—fear, malice—but lust is absent, and the prevailing surface tone is one of civilized, overcivilized anxiety. Prufrock's feelings are rather abstract; he never makes the woman real at all, except in one terrible respect, which let us reserve a little. He is concerned with himself. He is mentally ill, neurotic, incapable of love. But the problem that he faces is a primitive problem.

Modern poetry—which has so awkward a fame for sophistication—strikes one as remarkably primitive, at its best—dealing, that is, with what is central, fundamental, ancient, permanent (so far as we can see) in human concerns. The profound, and not accidental, affinity between primitive graphic and plastic art, and the work of men like Picasso and Matisse, needs no illustration. The primitivism of "Prufrock" has some affinities, perhaps, with the poetry of Whitman, but is otherwise unlike anything American, Victorian, Romantic, Eighteenth Century, Seventeenth Century, and Elizabethan, not to speak of Chaucer. Who ever wrote a poem before on *getting a mate?* —joining the tribe? Once we put it so crudely as this, we can see that the poet is greatly disturbed by what seems to everyone else a very simple matter. Or: does it? The terrifying ordeal of deciding to propose marriage is a real enough thing, for men and women alike. But this is a civilized matter as well as primitive. Let us consider rather things *we* take for granted, which the poet refuses to take for granted. Americans are loyal, for example, and desire to live. Do they? We all know this, but the Army does not. More than one third of all captured American personnel in Korea engaged in treasonable activities—*not* because they were brainwashed (they were not), not because they were communists, but because they didn't really believe in anything, including their country; and more than one third of all captured American personnel in Korea *died*—of the callousness of their comrades, of their own ignorance, indiscipline, and lack of respect for learning (as of what was safe to eat, and so on). Of 200 captured Turks, not *one* died.* The modern poet is in the peculiar position of reminding his reader of what the reader's great-grandfather knew but what he, the reader, has strangely forgotten. He is on the side of the Turks— primitive qualities, loyalty, survival, simple things. We are in a better position now to understand both his shock-tactics and the deep interest in *history* which often conceals from the casual reader his real, crude, primitive, subject.

Eliot brings to bear on Prufrock's dilemma four figures out of the spiritual history of man: Michelangelo, John the Baptist, Lazarus, and Hamlet. Prufrock identifies himself, in his imagination, with Lazarus; he says that he is *not* the Baptist or Hamlet. About the first all he says is:

> In the room the women come and go
> Talking of Michelangelo.

What are we to make of this? There is a twittering of women's voices. Their subject? A type of volcanic masculine energy—sculptor, architect, as well as painter—at the height of one of the supreme periods of human energy, the Italian Renaissance. Chit-chat. *Reduction,* we may say. Michelangelo, everything that mattered about him forgotten or not understood, has become a topic for women's voices—destructive, without even realizing it. Then Prufrock says

> Though I have seen may head [grown slightly bald]
>   brought in upon a platter,
> I am no prophet . . .

The situation is a visit, or the imagination of a visit, to the woman; it was *women* who got the Baptist beheaded. We might phrase the meaning as: I announce no significant time to come, I am the forerunner of (not children, not a Saviour) nothing. Then Prufrock is speculating about how it *would* have been, IF he had

> squeezed the universe into a ball
> To roll it toward some overwhelming question,
> To say: "I am Lazarus, come from the dead,
> Come back to tell you all, I shall tell you all"—

---

* These facts are from the Army's study of the dreadful subject as reported by Eugene Kinkead in *The New Yorker,* October 26, 1957.

We have seen Prufrock already imagined as dead, the suggestion of the epigraph,[5] and at the end of the poem he drowns. Here he thinks of himself as *come back*. Lazarus, perhaps, is the person whom one would most like to interview—another character from sacred history, not Christ's forerunner but the subject of the supreme miracles (reported, unfortunately, only in the Fourth Gospel)—the one man who would tell us . . . what it is like. Prufrock has a message, for the women, that is or ought to be of similar importance: here I am, out of my loneliness, at your feet; I am this man full of love, trust, hope; decide my fate.

Now—postponing Hamlet for a second—what Prufrock imagines the woman as saying in return for his Lazarus—communication explains his despair:

> If one, settling a pillow by her head,
> Should say: "That is not what I mean, at all.
> That is not it, at all."

Here the reason for his inability to propose becomes clear. He is convinced that she will (or would) respond with the most insulting and unmanning of all attitudes: Let's be *friends;* I never thought of you as a lover or husband, only a friend. What the women's voices did to Michelangelo her voice is here imagined as doing to him, demanning him; the sirens' voices at the end of the poem are yet to come. This is the central image of Prufrock's fear; what he cannot face. We see better now why the image of an *operation* turned up so early in the poem, and the paranoid * passages swing into focus:

> when I am formulated, sprawling on a pin,
> When I am pinned and wriggling on the wall . . .

and:

> as if a magic lantern threw the nerves in patterns
> on a screen . . .

A reasonable study of these fears of exposure would take us not only into our well-known Anglo-Saxon fear of ridicule but into folklore and psychoanalysis.

As for Hamlet, Prufrock says he is "not Prince Hamlet." He is not even the hero, that is to say, of his own tragedy; let us have in mind again the scientific revolutions and also the hero of one of Franz Kafka's novels, *The Trial,* who suddenly says, when recounting his arrest afterward, "Oh, I've forgotten the most important person of all, myself." Prufrock is merely, he says, an extra courtier, an

---

* A term of mental illness characterized by delusions of persecution.

adviser (to himself a very bad adviser—the name "Alfred" means ironically good counselor, and the character in Dante who supplies the epigraph was an evil counselor). But of course he *is* Hamlet—in one view of Shakespeare's character: a man rather of reflection than of action, on whom has been laid an intolerable burden (of revenge, by the way), and who suffers from sexual nausea (owing to his mother's incest) and deserts the woman he loves.

The resort to these four analogues from artistic and sacred history suggests a man—desperate, in his ordeal—ransacking the past for help in the present, and *not finding it*—finding only ironic parallels, or real examples, of his predicament. The available tradition, the poet seems to be saying, is of no use to us. It supplies only analogies and metaphors for our pain. Needless to say, the author of this poem was not a Christian; he became one years later.

Prufrock cannot act. He can, however, reflect and feel and imagine. Here we might think of W. B. Yeats's lines in a celebrated poem called "The Second Coming":

> The best lack all conviction, while the worst
> Are full of passionate intensity.

Prufrock would be among Yeats's "best" only for sensitivity and intelligence, it is true, his human failure being otherwise complete. Let us explore a little however, his *positive* courses of imagination; and Hamlet's desertion of Ophelia, and his "intolerable burden," as we called it, point our way.

Prufrock's not proposing to the lady (there is no suggestion that anyone else will) might be thought of as aggressive: at whatever cost to himself, he deprives her of a mate, a normal married life. For such fear and humiliation as he suffers, we should expect some sort of revenge taken. But Prufrock suffers from the inhibitions that we might imagine as accompanying a man of such crucial indecision. He has difficulty in expressing himself, for instance, and this difficulty is brought prominently into the poem—as Henry James, especially in a novel called *The Sacred Fount,* brought into his book all the process of the development of the subject which is ordinarily relegated to an author's working notes. Notice particularly the lines

> And how should I begin?
> It is impossible to say just what I mean!

His incoherence is a token of his struggle, and it is hardly surprising that his resentment against the woman in the poem emerges only in malicious detail ("catty" we would call this) as—of her arms

> in the lamplight, downed with light brown hair!

What does come forward openly is his imagination of escape from the dilemma altogether.

Hamlet's burden was the responsibility, urged by his father's ghost, to take revenge on his uncle the King for his father's murder —except that the ghost, of course, may be a demon sent to tempt him. He is found considering suicide as an avenue of escape from this equivocal (equi-vocal, two-voiced) responsibility. Prufrock's burden is that of proposing marriage when he does not know whether he may not be ridiculed. His desire, from the outset, to have the whole thing over with, no matter how, we have seen already in the line about the "patient etheriscd upon a table." At the very end of the poem, in an excited and brilliant passage which might be characterized as one of negative exaltation, he imagines— like Hamlet—his death, as an escape at any rate from the dread anxiety of his ordeal. These are mermaids, sirens, the women of the poem come into the open as killers:

> I have seen them riding seaward on the waves
> Combing the white hair of the waves blown back
> When the wind blows the water white and black.
>
> We have lingered in the chambers of the sea
> By sea-girls wreathed with seaweed red and brown
> Till human voices wake us, and we drown.

This death is *desired*—like the hospital situation—as well as feared. But the basic image of escape occurs in the dead center of the poem, in a couplet, without much relation to anything apparently, *lacking* which this would be a much less impressive poem than it is. These are the lines:

> I should have been a pair of ragged claws
> Scuttling across the floors of silent seas.

You notice, first, that this is not much of a couplet,[6] though it *is* a heroic couplet;[7] the off-rhyme speaks of incongruity. As abruptly, second, as we were transferred from the prospect of a romantic evening to a hospital, are we here plunged, away from modern social life ("I have measured out my life with coffee spoons"), into—into what? Man's biological past, continuous with him, but unimaginably remote, long before he emerged into the tidal areas: Prufrock sees himself, in his desire, as his own ancestor, *before this ordeal came up,* when he was sufficient unto himself, a "pair," not needing a mate. Now the whole crustacean is not imagined—only the fighting part, which is taken for the whole—the claws. But these do not seem to be in very good condition ("ragged") and unquestionably we must take them also to be full of fear ("scuttling"), like Prufrock now. But the seas are *silent:* no woman speaks. Therefore the situation is desirable, protected. We really need to resort to the later formulations of Freud to understand this. When a human being encounters a problem beyond his capacity to meet, Freud thought, *regression* occurs: the whole organization of the emotional and instinctual person escapes from the intolerable reality by reverting to an earlier, or ancient, stage of his individual development—paying the price of symptoms, but securing partial oblivion. The antagonism toward civilization in Eliot's couplet is unmistakable. It contains, indeed, a sort of list of the penalties that civilization has exacted from man's instinctual life—having cost him: open expression of hatred, fear, remorse, intolerable responsibilities.

"I am no prophet," Prufrock says. It must be obvious, however, that this extraordinarily ambitious poem, including as it does acrid sketches not only of man's spiritual but his biological history, is not designed as entertainment, whatever the author may say to us (Eliot has defined poetry as "a superior amusement"), and whatever his mask *inside* the poem: the sophisticate, the disillusioned, the dandy with his particular social problem in Boston, as Baudelaire had had his in Paris and Belgium and Laforgue his in Berlin. The poet has adopted the guise of light verse, but he writes as a prophet, without any trace of conciliation toward any possible audience. He does not write *directly*. He uses the mask of Prufrock—whose fate is like that of what are called the Vigliacchi in Dante. These sinners did neither good nor evil, and so they cannot be admitted even to Hell, lest the damned feel a certain superiority to them; they suffer eternally in what is called the vestibule of Hell. It is better, as Eliot says in one of his critical essays, to do evil than to do nothing. At least one exists in a relation to the moral world. Under this mask he sets up a ruinous antithesis to Victorian hope—in particular, to what must have seemed to him the vacuous optimism of the most recent master of dramatic monologue in English before him, Browning. Civilization is not condemned. Who would condemn the bomb tests?—which make more doubtful every year the composition of all the bones of all the human children yet to be born, besides those growing? The *results* of civilization are dramatized, that is all; above all, the destruction of the ability to love, and—in the well-meaning man—to be decisive. The poet speaks, in this poem, of a society sterile and suicidal.

TERMS AND PRINCIPLES

1. *Reductive:* Beginning with something from which one then takes away.
2. *Lyrical:* Songlike (used here ironically, of course).
3. *Free verse:* Verse in which the laws obeyed are different from, and have not been so acceptably formulated as, those obeyed by traditional verse; both as of foot-structure, and rhyme.
4. *Blank verse:* Unrhymed iambic pentameter.
5. *Epigraph:* A motto or citation at the beginning of a literary work.
6. *Couplet:* Two successive lines of verse that rhyme with each other.
7. *Heroic couplet:* A couplet of which the meter is iambic pentameter.

EXERCISE

WILLIAM BUTLER YEATS

Sailing to Byzantium

I

That is no country for old men. The young
In one another's arms, birds in the trees
—Those dying generations—at their song,
The salmon-falls, the mackerel-crowded seas,
Fish, flesh, or fowl, commend all summer long
Whatever is begotten, born, and dies.
Caught in that sensual music all neglect
Monuments of unageing intellect.

II

An aged man is but a paltry thing,
A tattered coat upon a stick, unless
Soul clap its hands and sing, and louder sing
For every tatter in its mortal dress,

Nor is there singing school but studying
Monuments of its own magnificence;
And therefore I have sailed the seas and come
To the holy city of Byzantium.

III

O sages standing in God's holy fire
As in the gold mosaic of a wall,
Come from the holy fire, perne in a gyre,
And be the singing-masters of my soul.
Consume my heart away; sick with desire
And fastened to a dying animal
It knows not what it is; and gather me
Into the artifice of eternity.

IV

Once out of nature I shall never take
My bodily form from any natural thing,
But such a form as Grecian goldsmiths make
Of hammered gold and gold enamelling
To keep a drowsy Emperor awake;
Or set upon a golden bough to sing
To lords and ladies of Byzantium
Of what is past, or passing, or to come.

There are no questions in this exercise. We just want you to read it, and our note, after Eliot's poem.

❦ *A Note*

Yeats, an Irishman, was born a whole generation earlier than Eliot, so that he was thirty-five by 1900 and internationally famous, although his work did not become really good for another fifteen years; he is a very unusual case of a striking late development. Our poem was written when he was about fifty, at the height of his powers, and it is a poem of age, very energetic age, as "Prufrock," artificially fatigued and dandy-ish, is a poem of youth. Both poems are rather *learned,* having nothing about them of the unpremeditated or improvisatorial, or occasional. Both are intensely ambitious. Both are concerned with history, and both engage the theme of the poet-as-prophet. But in these last two respects the two poems, and poets, are also so different that we may as well stop comparing them, except to note that the *impulse toward rejection,* common to both, is oddly enough even stronger in Yeats than in Eliot, so that his poem actually begins with a complete rejection of both the modern *and* the natural world.

Yeats's poem is romantic, and represents from this point of view a continuation of a tradition (a native English tradition) rather than a break with it, as Eliot's poem does. His stanza—developed from a study of the eight-line stanza in Spenser and Keats, and in certain remarkable minor poets such as Abraham Cowley—is both so traditional and so characteristic of Yeats that one hardly sees influence in it at all.

There is a theory of history in this poem also, and, as in Eliot's poem, the past is used as a touchstone for the present. Here, however, the poet is concerned not only with spiritual history but with actual history—about which he is willing to indulge in fancies that the author of "Prufrock" would scarcely countenance. "I think," Yeats once wrote, "if I could be given a month of antiquity and leave to spend it where I chose, I would spend it in Byzantium a little before Justinian opened St. Sophia and closed the Academy of Plato. [This would be at the beginning of the sixth century A.D.] I think I could find in some little wineshop some philosophical worker in mosaic who could answer all my questions. . . . I think that in early Byzantium, maybe never before or since in recorded history, religious, aesthetic and practical life were one . . . The painter, the mosaic worker, the worker in gold and silver, the illuminator of sacred books, were almost impersonal, almost perhaps without the consciousness of individual design, absorbed in their subject-matter and that the vision of a whole people."

The fractioning of consciousness we noted in "Prufrock" is here also a topic of dislike. What is desired is unitary, romantic, abolishing change, and almost abolishing personality—"were almost impersonal" he says—a strange requirement for a romantic writer, as if consciousness were for this poet, as for "Prufrock," a *burden,* desired to be got rid of. We are certainly, here, full in the modern period. But the function of the poet as prophet is celebrated without a trace of the irony to be found in "Prufrock"; except that, again, it is not the poet directly, but the poet masked—in Yeats's poem, the immortal construct of a golden bird who will sing forever

> To lords and ladies of Byzantium
> Of what is past, or passing, or to come.

Not, we observe, to the modern reader, toward whom Yeats is as impatient as Eliot, although he is less openly scornful. Yeats's unwillingness to adopt the values of the modern period was so sharp, in fact, that instead of merely criticizing them in terms of the values of the past, as Eliot has done, Yeats invented a whole theory—rather crazy—of history and human temperament, described in a book called *A Vision*—the gyres in this poem, revolving inside each other in opposite directions, come from his theory; but we have put this elaborate poem here neither for our analysis nor for specific exercises set to you, but as a subject of meditation. Expert readers find, sometimes or often, that it is only twenty years after they have known and loved a poem that it opens its true nature to them.

EXERCISE

DYLAN THOMAS

A Refusal to Mourn the Death, by Fire, of a Child in London

> Never until the mankind making
> Bird beast and flower
> Fathering and all humbling darkness
> Tells with silence the last light breaking
> And the still hour
> Is come of the sea tumbling in harness
>
> And I must enter again the round
> Zion of the water bead
> And the synagogue of the ear of corn
> Shall I let pray the shadow of a sound
> Or sow my salt seed
> In the least valley of sackcloth to mourn

The majesty and burning of the child's death.
I shall not murder
The mankind of her going with a grave truth
Nor blaspheme down the stations of the breath
With any further
Elegy of innocence and youth.

Deep with the first dead lies London's daughter,
Robed in the long friends,
The grains beyond age, the dark veins of her mother,
Secret by the unmourning water
Of the riding Thames.
After the first death, there is no other.

SOME QUESTIONS

This is a poem by the great Welsh poet, now dead, Dylan
Thomas, about the death, in World War II, of a girl. It is a majestic
and somehow rather simple poem in which very complicated imagery
from both the Old Testament and the New Testament is employed
in order to reject *both,* and all, the religious consolations. Then this
rejection is itself used as a consolation, such as we can have. Even
a modern poem so passionate as this, perhaps, is inclined to be
critical, the passage attacked here being the one in the Book of
Revelation about "the second death"—the death by sin, to Hell.

1. The poem begins with one tremendous sentence containing
both the first two stanzas and running over into the third. This sentence is periodic; [1] its syntax, that is, is such as to forbid a period's
being put anywhere into it before it comes to its end. Does this
magisterial control on the part of the poet suggest to you anything
about the syntactical confusion in the opening lines?

2. If this confusion, then, is deliberate, can you half-explain
its details?

3. "Fathering" is Judaeo-Christian: the Earth is seen as the
(pagan) Mother in the last stanza. What is the status of the *riding*
Thames (London's great river) in this progression?

4. What expected word does "pray" replace in line 10? What is
the relation between the two words?

5. What is meant by "the sea tumbling in harness"? Can the
Continental mountain chains be in question?

6. In "the stations of the breath" a Christian symbol is employed. To what end?

7. The last two lines of the third stanza are among the most heartbreaking in English poetry. Can you help account for this— but only help—by noticing that there *has been* no elegy, except line 13? What are the other elements involved?

8. Why "grains"? Why "veins"?

TERMS AND PRINCIPLES

1. *Periodic sentence:* A sentence whose structure is opposed to that of a "loose" sentence, which will allow the insertion of a period, bringing it to an end as a grammatical whole, at some point *before* its end.

EXERCISE

WILLIAM SHAKESPEARE

From *Pericles*

A terrible childbed hast thou had, my dear;
No light, no fire: the unfriendly elements
Forgot thee utterly; nor have I time
To give thee hallow'd to thy grave, but straight
Must cast thee, scarcely coffin'd, in the ooze;
Where, for a monument upon thy bones
And aye-remaining lamps, the belching whale
And humming water must o'er-whelm thy corse,
Lying with simple shells. . . .

SOME QUESTIONS

This is a speech from Act III of Shakespeare's play *Pericles*. A king is speaking, on shipboard during a tempest, a sort of funeral service over the body of his wife, who died in childbirth and whose body has to be put overboard at once, owing to the sailors' superstition about having a dead body on board during a storm. "Corse" is the Elizabethan word for corpse, with a pun (of course) on "course," a very broad word here equivalent to Fate.

1. The speech has three parts: the lament over the unnatural circumstances of the Queen's giving birth, the King's personal lament about the present necessity of the unnatural burial, and his imagination of the future of her body. There is a crescendo of pain. But is it also true that the speech rises to a sort of resolution that is *not* painful, in that the unnaturalness of the first two parts gives way, at any rate, to a sort of *naturalness* in the third part? What is the function of the word "simple," in some ways the most unexpected word in this whole amazing speech? Is a dead body in any way "simple" compared to a living one, so that there is a decorum after all in the final relation indicated here?

2. The words "terrible" and "my dear" in the first line form a harrowing contrast. Is the anomaly of the contrast of any use to the rest of the speech, as a foreshadowing?

3. Does the word "unfriendly" deliberately understate? What are the "elements"?

4. Can we see the understatement of "unfriendly" as related to the violence of the word "utterly" (which we must hear almost as a cry)?

5. What does the word "hallow'd" mean? Is the suggestion continued anywhere in the speech?

6. What is the meaning of "belching," as of a whale? What is the connotation, however?

7. The syntax makes the "aye-remaining lamps" and the "humming water" correlative. Does this structural relation tell us anything about the meaning here of the astonishing word "humming"? Is the chanting that would accompany the formal burial of a Queen somehow, ironically, implied? Is the word "humming" low-keyed here or high-keyed?

8. What is the connotation of the word "shell" that brings the agitation of the speech to a dignified and appropriate close?

✿ Section Three

Drama

✿

WILLIAM SHAKESPEARE

The Tragedy of Macbeth

DRAMATIS PERSONAE

DUNCAN, *King of Scotland*

MALCOLM,
DONALBAIN, } *his sons*

MACBETH,
BANQUO, } *Generals of the Scottish Army*

MACDUFF,
LENNOX,
ROSS,
MENTEITH,
ANGUS,
CAITHNESS, } *Noblemen of Scotland*

FLEANCE, *son to* BANQUO

SIWARD, *Earl of Northumberland, General of the English forces*

YOUNG SIWARD, *his son*

SEYTON, *an Officer attending on* MACBETH

BOY, *son to* MACDUFF

A Captain

An English Doctor

A Scottish Doctor

A Porter

358

An Old Man
Murderers
LADY MACBETH
LADY MACDUFF
A Gentlewoman, attending on LADY MACBETH
HECATE
Three Witches
The Ghost of BANQUO
Apparitions
Lords, Gentlemen, Officers, Soldiers, Messengers, Attendants
       SCENE: *Scotland and England*

Act I

SCENE I: *Scotland. An open place*

[*Thunder and lightning. Enter three* WITCHES]
FIRST WITCH.   When shall we three meet again
In thunder, lightning, or in rain?
SECOND WITCH.   When the hurlyburly's done,
When the battle's lost and won.
THIRD WITCH.   That will be ere the set of sun.
FIRST WITCH.   Where the place?
SECOND WITCH.   Upon the heath.
THIRD WITCH.   There to meet with Macbeth.
FIRST WITCH.   I come, Graymalkin!
SECOND WITCH.   Paddock calls.
THIRD WITCH.   Anon!   10
ALL.   Fair is foul, and foul is fair.
Hover through the fog and filthy air. [*Exeunt.*]

SCENE II: *A camp near Forres*

[*Alarum within. Enter* KING DUNCAN, MALCOLM, DONALBAIN,
LENNOX, *with attendants, meeting a bleeding* CAPTAIN.]
       KING.   What bloody man is that? He can report,
As seemeth by his plight, of the revolt
The newest state.

MALCOLM. This is the sergeant
Who like a good and hardy soldier fought
'Gainst my captivity. Hail, brave friend!
Say to the King the knowledge of the broil
As thou didst leave it.

    CAPTAIN.   Doubtful it stood,
As two spent swimmers that do cling together
And choke their art. The merciless Macdonwald
(Worthy to be a rebel, for to that   10
The multiplying villainies of nature
Do swarm upon him) from the Western Isles
Of kerns and gallowglasses is supplied;
And Fortune, on his damned quarrel smiling,
Showed like a rebel's whore. But all's too weak;
For brave Macbeth (well he deserves that name),
Disdaining Fortune, with his brandished steel,
Which smoked with bloody execution
(Like valor's minion), carved out his passage
Till he faced the slave;   20
Which ne'er shook hands nor bade farewell to him
Till he unseamed him from the nave to the chops
And fixed his head upon our battlements.

    KING.   O valiant cousin! worthy gentleman!

    CAPTAIN.   As whence the sun 'gins his reflection
Shipwracking storms and direful thunders break,
So from that spring whence comfort seemed to come
Discomfort swells. Mark, King of Scotland, mark.
No sooner justice had, with valor armed,
Compelled these skipping kerns to trust their heels   30
But the Norweyan lord, surveying vantage,
With furbished arms and new supplies of men,
Began a fresh assault.

    KING.   Dismayed not this
Our captains, Macbeth and Banquo?

    CAPTAIN.   Yes,
As sparrows eagles, or the hare the lion.

If I say sooth, I must report they were
As cannons overcharged with double cracks, so they
Doubly redoubled strokes upon the foe.
Except they meant to bathe in reeking wounds,
Or memorize another Golgotha,   40
I cannot tell—
But I am faint; my gashes cry for help.

    KING.   So well thy words become thee as thy wounds;
They smack of honor both. Go get him surgeons.

    [*Exit* CAPTAIN, *attended.*]
    [*Enter* ROSS *and* ANGUS.]

Who comes here?

    MALCOLM.   The worthy Thane of Ross.

    LENNOX.   What a haste looks through his eyes! So should he
    look
That seems to speak things strange.

    ROSS.   God save the King!

    KING.   Whence cam'st thou, worthy thane?

    ROSS.   From Fife, great King,
Where the Norweyan banners flout the sky
And fan our people cold. Norway himself,   50
With terrible numbers,
Assisted by that most disloyal traitor
The Thane of Cawdor, began a dismal conflict,
Till that Bellona's bridegroom, lapped in proof,
Confronted him with self-comparisons,
Point against point, rebellious arm 'gainst arm,
Curbing his lavish spirit; and to conclude,
The victory fell on us.

    KING.   Great happiness!

    ROSS.   That now
Sweno, the Norways' king, craves composition;
Nor would we deign him burial of his men   60
Till he disbursed, at Saint Colme's Inch,
Ten thousand dollars to our general use.

    KING.   No more that Thane of Cawdor shall deceive

Our bosom interest. Go pronounce his present death
And with his former title greet Macbeth.

ROSS.   I'll see it done.

DUNCAN.   What he hath lost noble Macbeth hath won. [*Exeunt.*]

SCENE III: *A blasted heath*

[*Thunder. Enter the three* WITCHES.]

FIRST WITCH.   Where hast thou been, sister?

SECOND WITCH.   Killing swine.

THIRD WITCH.   Sister, where thou?

FIRST WITCH.   A sailor's wife had chestnuts in her lap
And mounched and mounched and mounched. "Give me," quoth
  I.
"Aroint thee, witch!" the rump-fed ronyon cries.
Her husband's to Aleppo gone, master o' the "Tiger";
But in a sieve I'll thither sail
And, like a rat without a tail,
I'll do, I'll do, and I'll do.   10

SECOND WITCH.   I'll give thee a wind.

FIRST WITCH.   Th' art kind.

THIRD WITCH.   And I another.

FIRST WITCH.   I myself have all the other,
And the very ports they blow,
All the quarters that they know
I' the shipman's card.
I'll drain him dry as hay.
Sleep shall neither night nor day
Hang upon his penthouse lid.   20
He shall live a man forbid.
Weary sev'nights, nine times nine,
Shall he dwindle, peak, and pine.
Though his bark cannot be lost,
Yet it shall be tempest-tost.
Look what I have.

SECOND WITCH.   Show me! show me!

FIRST WITCH.   Here I have a pilot's thumb,

Wracked as homeward he did come.

[*Drum within.*]

THIRD WITCH.   A drum, a drum!   30
Macbeth doth come.

ALL.   The Weird Sisters, hand in hand,
Posters of the sea and land,
Thus do go about, about,
Thrice to thine, and thrice to mine,
And thrice again, to make up nine.
Peace! The charm's wound up.

[*Enter* MACBETH *and* BANQUO.]

MACBETH.   So foul and fair a day I have not seen.

BANQUO.   How far is't called to Forres? What are these,
So withered, and so wild in their attire,   40
That look not like the inhabitants o' the earth,
And yet are on't? Live you? or are you aught
That man may question? You seem to understand me,
By each at once her choppy finger laying
Upon her skinny lips. You should be women,
And yet your beards forbid me to interpret
That you are so.

MACBETH.   Speak, if you can. What are you?

FIRST WITCH.   All hail, Macbeth! Hail to thee, Thane of Glamis!

SECOND WITCH.   All hail, Macbeth! Hail to thee, Thane of
   Cawdor!

THIRD WITCH.   All hail, Macbeth, that shalt be King hereafter!   50

BANQUO.   Good sir, why do you start and seem to fear
Things that do sound so fair? I' the name of truth,
Are ye fantastical, or that indeed
Which outwardly ye show? My noble partner
You greet with present grace and great prediction
Of noble having and of royal hope,
That he seems rapt withal. To me you speak not.
If you can look into the seeds of time
And say which grain will grow and which will not,

Speak then to me, who neither beg nor fear   60
Your favors nor your hate.

FIRST WITCH.   Hail!

SECOND WITCH.   Hail!

THIRD WITCH.   Hail!

FIRST WITCH.   Lesser than Macbeth, and greater.

SECOND WITCH.   Not so happy, yet much happier.

THIRD WITCH.   Thou shalt get kings, though thou be none.

So all hail, Macbeth and Banquo!

FIRST WITCH.   Banquo and Macbeth, all hail!

MACBETH.   Stay, you imperfect speakers, tell me more!   70
By Sinel's death I know I am Thane of Glamis,
But how of Cawdor? The Thane of Cawdor lives,
A prosperous gentleman; and to be King
Stands not within the prospect of belief,
No more than to be Cawdor. Say from whence
You owe this strange intelligence, or why
Upon this blasted heath you stop our way
With such prophetic greeting. Speak, I charge you.

[*Witches vanish.*]

BANQUO.   The earth hath bubbles, as the water has,
And these are of them. Whither are they vanished?   80

MACBETH.   Into the air, and what seemed corporal melted
As breath into the wind. Would they had stayed!

BANQUO.   Were such things here as we do speak about?
Or have we eaten on the insane root
That takes the reason prisoner?

MACBETH.   Your children shall be kings.

BANQUO.   You shall be King.

MACBETH.   And Thane of Cawdor too. Went it not so?

BANQUO.   To the selfsame tune and words. Who's here?

[*Enter* ROSS *and* ANGUS.]

ROSS.   The King hath happily received, Macbeth,
The news of thy success; and when he reads   90
Thy personal venture in the rebels' fight,
His wonders and his praises do contend

pay.
loyalty I owe,
' part
ies
en and servants,
doing everything

Welcome hither.
will labor
Noble Banquo,
nor must be known   30
me infold thee

There if I grow,

My plenteous joys,
ek to hide themselves
ons, kinsmen, thanes,
es are the nearest, know
ur estate upon
lm, whom we name hereafter
mberland; which honor must
nied invest him only,
bleness, like stars, shall shine   40
rs. From hence to Inverness,
further to you.
ETH.   The rest is labor, which is not used for you.
elf the harbinger, and make joyful
ng of my wife with your approach;
bly take my leave.
NG.   My worthy Cawdor!
CBETH [*Aside*].   The Prince of Cumberland! That is a step
I must fall down, or else o'erleap,
way it lies. Stars, hide your fires!   50
ht see my black and deep desires.
nk at the hand; yet let that be,

Which should be thine or his. Silenced with that,
In viewing o'er the rest o' the selfsame day,
He finds thee in the stout Norweyan ranks,
Nothing afeared of what thyself didst make,
Strange images of death. As thick as hail
Came post with post, and every one did bear
Thy praises in his kingdom's great defense
And poured them down before him.

ANGUS.   We are sent   100
To give thee from our royal master thanks;
Only to herald thee into his sight,
Not pay thee.

ROSS.   And for an earnest of a greater honor,
He bade me, from him, call thee Thane of Cawdor;
In which addition, hail, most worthy Thane!
For it is thine.

BANQUO.   What, can the devil speak true?

MACBETH.   The Thane of Cawdor lives. Why do you dress me
In borrowed robes?

ANGUS.   Who was the Thane lives yet,
But under heavy judgment bears that life   110
Which he deserves to lose. Whether he was combined
With those of Norway, or did line the rebel
With hidden help and vantage, or that with both
He labored in his country's wrack, I know not;
But treasons capital, confessed and proved,
Have overthrown him.

MACBETH [*Aside*].   Glamis, and Thane of Cawdor!
The greatest is behind.—[*To* ROSS *and* ANGUS.] Thanks for your
pains.
[*Aside to* BANQUO.] Do you not hope your children shall be kings,
When those that gave the Thane of Cawdor to me
Promised no less to them?

BANQUO [*Aside to Macbeth*].   That, trusted home,   120
Might yet enkindle you unto the crown,
Besides the Thane of Cawdor. But 'tis strange!

And oftentimes, to win us to our harm,
The instruments of darkness tell us truths,
Win us with honest trifles, to betray's
In deepest consequence.—
Cousins, a word, I pray you.
  MACBETH [*Aside*]. Two truths are told,
As happy prologues to the swelling act
Of the imperial theme.—I thank you, gentlemen.—
[*Aside.*] This supernatural soliciting
Cannot be ill; cannot be good. If ill,
Why hath it given me earnest of success,
Commencing in a truth? I am Thane of Cawdor.
If good, why do I yield to that suggestion
Whose horrid image doth unfix my hair
And make my seated heart knock at my ribs
Against the use of nature? Present fears
Are less than horrible imaginings.
My thought, whose murder yet is but fantastical,
Shakes so my single state of man that function 140
Is smothered in surmise and nothing is
But what is not.
  BANQUO. Look how our partner's rapt.
  MACBETH [*Aside*]. If chance will have me King, why, chance
    may crown me,
Without my stir.
  BANQUO. New honors come upon him,
Like our strange garments, cleave not to their mold
But with the aid of use.
  MACBETH [*Aside*]. Come what come may,
Time and the hour runs through the roughest day.
  BANQUO. Worthy Macbeth, we stay upon your leisure.
  MACBETH. Give me your favor. My dull brain was wrought
With things forgotten. Kind gentlemen, your pains 150
Are registered where every day I turn
The leaf to read them. Let us toward the King.

  MACBETH. The service and the
More is thy due than more than all can
In doing it pays itself. Your Highnes
Is to receive our duties; and our du
Are to your throne and state child
Which do but what they should b
Safe toward your love and hono
  KING.
I have begun to plant thee an
To make thee full of growing.
That hast no less deserved,
No less to have done so, let
And hold thee to my hear
  BANQUO.
The harvest is your ow
  KING.
Wanton in fullness, se
In drops of sorrow. S
And you whose plac
We will establish o
Our eldest, Malco
The Prince of C
Not unaccomp
But signs of n
On all deserv
And bind us
  MACB
I'll be mys
The hear
So, hum

They a
With one
That very f
Implored you
A deep repentan
Became him like th
As one that had been
To throw away the dea
As 'twere a careless trifle.
  KING. T
To find the mind's construction
He was a gentleman on whom I b
An absolute trust.
  [*Enter* MACBETH, BANQUO, ROS
    O worthiest cousin,
The sin of my ingratitude even now
Was heavy on me! Thou art so far before
That swiftest wing of recompense is slow
To overtake thee. Would thou hadst less deserved,
That the proportion both of thanks and payment
Might have been mine! Only I have left to say,

Which the eye fears, when it is done, to see. [*Exit.*]

KING.   True, worthy Banquo: he is full so valiant,
And in his commendations I am fed;
It is a banquet to me. Let's after him,
Whose care is gone before to bid us welcome.
It is a peerless kinsman.

[*Flourish. Exeunt.*]

SCENE V: *Inverness. Macbeth's castle*

[*Enter* MACBETH'S WIFE, *alone, with a letter.*]

LADY [*Reads*].   "They met me in the day of success; and I
have learned by the perfect'st report they have more in them than
mortal knowledge. When I burned in desire to question them further,
they made themselves air, into which they vanished. Whiles I stood
rapt in the wonder of it, came missives from the King, who all-hailed
me Thane of Cawdor, by which title, before, these Weird Sisters
saluted me, and referred me to the coming on of time with 'Hail,
King that shalt be!' This have I thought good to deliver thee, my
dearest partner of greatness, that thou mightst not lose the dues of
rejoicing by being ignorant of what greatness is promised thee. Lay
it to thy heart, and farewell."

Glamis thou art, and Cawdor, and shalt be
What thou art promised. Yet do I fear thy nature.
It is too full o' the milk of human kindness
To catch the nearest way. Thou wouldst be great;
Art not without ambition, but without   20
The illness should attend it. What thou wouldst highly,
That wouldst thou holily; wouldst not play false,
And yet wouldst wrongly win. Thou'ldst have, great Glamis,
That which cries "Thus thou must do," if thou have it;
And that which rather thou dost fear to do
Than wishest should be undone. Hie thee hither,
That I may pour my spirits in thine ear
And chastise with the valor of my tongue
All that impedes thee from the golden round

Which fate and metaphysical aid doth seem   30
To have thee crowned withal.
> [*Enter* MESSENGER.]
>   What is your tidings?
MESSENGER.   The King comes here tonight.
LADY.   Thou'rt mad to say it!
Is not thy master with him? who, were't so,
Would have informed for preparation.
> MESSENGER.   So please you, it is true. Our Thane is coming.
One of my fellows had the speed of him,
Who, almost dead for breath, had scarcely more
Than would make up his message.
LADY.   Give him tending;
He brings great news.
> [*Exit* MESSENGER.]
>   The raven himself is hoarse
That croaks the fatal entrance of Duncan   40
Under my battlements. Come, you spirits
That tend on mortal thoughts, unsex me here,
And fill me, from the crown to the toe, top-full
Of direst cruelty! Make thick my blood;
Stop up the access and passage to remorse,
That no compunctious visitings of nature
Shake my fell purpose nor keep peace between
The effect and it! Come to my woman's breasts
And take my milk for gall, you murd'ring ministers,
Wherever in your sightless substances   50
You wait on nature's mischief! Come, thick night,
And pall thee in the dunnest smoke of hell,
That my keen knife see not the wound it makes,
Nor heaven peep through the blanket of the dark
To cry "Hold, hold!"
> [*Enter* MACBETH.]
>   Great Glamis! worthy Cawdor!
Greater than both, by the all-hail hereafter!
Thy letters have transported me beyond

This ignorant present, and I feel now
The future in the instant.

MACBETH.   My dearest love,
Duncan comes here tonight.

LADY.   And when goes hence?   60

MACBETH.   Tomorrow, as he purposes.

LADY.   O, never
Shall sun that morrow see!
Your face, my Thane, is as a book where men
May read strange matters. To beguile the time,
Look like the time; bear welcome in your eye,
Your hand, your tongue; look like the innocent flower,
But be the serpent under't. He that's coming
Must be provided for; and you shall put
This night's great business into my dispatch,
Which shall to all our nights and days to come   70
Give solely sovereign sway and masterdom.

MACBETH.   We will speak further.

LADY.   Only look up clear.
To alter favor ever is to fear.
Leave all the rest to me. [*Exeunt.*]

SCENE VI: *The same. Before* MACBETH'S *castle*

[*Hautboys and torches. Enter* KING DUNCAN, MALCOLM, DONAL-
BAIN, BANQUO, LENNOX, MACDUFF, ROSS, ANGUS, *and attendants.*]

KING.   This castle hath a pleasant seat. The air
Nimbly and sweetly recommends itself
Unto our gentle senses.

BANQUO.   This guest of summer,
The temple-haunting martlet, does approve
By his loved mansionry that the heaven's breath
Smells wooingly here. No jutty, frieze,
Buttress, nor coign of vantage, but this bird
Hath made his pendent bed and procreant cradle.
Where they most breed and haunt, I have observed
The air is delicate.

[*Enter* LADY MACBETH.]

KING.   See, see, our honored hostess!   10
The love that follows us sometime is our trouble,
Which still we thank as love. Herein I teach you
How you shall bid God 'ield us for your pains
And thank us for your trouble.

LADY.   All our service
In every point twice done, and then done double,
Were poor and single business to contend
Against those honors deep and broad wherewith
Your Majesty loads our house. For those of old,
And the late dignities heaped up to them,
We rest your hermits.

KING.   Where's the Thane of Cawdor?   20
We coursed him at the heels and had a purpose
To be his purveyor; but he rides well,
And his great love, sharp as his spur, hath holp him
To his home before us. Fair and noble hostess,
We are your guest tonight.

LADY.   Your servants ever
Have theirs, themselves, and what is theirs, in compt,
To make their audit at your Highness' pleasure,
Still to return your own.

KING.   Give me your hand;
Conduct me to mine host. We love him highly
And shall continue our graces towards him.   30
By your leave, hostess. [*Exeunt.*]

SCENE VII: *The same. Macbeth's castle*

[*Hautboys. Torches. Enter a sewer, and divers servants with
dishes and service over the stage. Then enter* MACBETH.]

MACBETH.   If it were done when 'tis done, then 'twere well
It were done quickly. If the assassination
Could trammel up the consequence, and catch,
With his surcease, success, that but this blow
Might be the be-all and the end-all here,

But here, upon this bank and shoal of time,
We'ld jump the life to come. But in these cases
We still have judgment here, that we but teach
Bloody instructions, which, being taught return
To plague the inventor. This even-handed justice 10
Commends the ingredience of our poisoned chalice
To our own lips. He's here in double trust:
First, as I am his kinsman and his subject,
Strong both against the deed; then, as his host,
Who should against his murderer shut the door,
Not bear the knife myself. Besides, this Duncan
Hath borne his faculties so meek, hath been
So clear in his great office, that his virtues
Will plead like angels, trumpet-tongued, against
The deep damnation of his taking-off; 20
And pity, like a naked new-born babe,
Striding the blast, or heaven's cherubin, horsed
Upon the sightless couriers of the air,
Shall blow the horrid deed in every eye,
That tears shall drown the wind. I have no spur
To prick the sides of my intent, but only
Vaulting ambition, which o'erleaps itself
And falls on th' other.
     [*Enter* LADY MACBETH.]
               How now? What news?
LADY.   He has almost supped. Why have you left the chamber?
MACBETH.   Hath he asked for me?
LADY.   Know you not he has? 30
MACBETH.   We will proceed no further in this business.
He hath honored me of late, and I have bought
Golden opinions from all sorts of people,
Which would be worn now in their newest gloss,
Not cast aside so soon.
LADY.   Was the hope drunk
Wherein you dressed yourself? Hath it slept since?
And wakes it now to look so green and pale

At what it did so freely? From this time
Such I account thy love. Art thou afeard
To be the same in thine own act and valor   40
As thou art in desire? Wouldst thou have that
Which thou esteem'st the ornament of life,
And live a coward in thine own esteem,
Letting "I dare not" wait upon "I would,"
Like the poor cat i' the adage?

    MACBETH.   Prithee peace!
I dare do all that may become a man.
Who dares do more is none.

    LADY.   What beast was't then
That made you break this enterprise to me?
When you durst do it, then you were a man;
And to be more than what you were, you would   50
Be so much more the man. Nor time nor place
Did then adhere, and yet you would make both.
They have made themselves, and that their fitness now
Does unmake you. I have given suck, and know
How tender 'tis to love the babe that milks me.
I would, while it was smiling in my face,
Have plucked my nipple from his boneless gums
And dashed the brains out, had I so sworn as you
Have done to this.

    MACBETH.   If we should fail?

    LADY.   We fail.
But screw your courage to the sticking place,   60
And we'll not fail. When Duncan is asleep
(Whereto the rather shall his day's hard journey
Soundly invite him), his two chamberlains
Will I with wine and wassail so convince
That memory, the warder of the brain,
Shall be a fume, and the receipt of reason
A limbeck only. When in swinish sleep
Their drenched natures lie as in a death,
What cannot you and I perform upon

The unguarded Duncan? what not put upon   70
His spongy officers, who shall bear the guilt
Of our great quell?

MACBETH.   Bring forth men-children only,
For thy undaunted mettle should compose
Nothing but males. Will it not be received,
When we have marked with blood those sleepy two
Of his own chamber and used their very daggers,
That they have done't?

LADY.   Who dares receive it other,
As we shall make our griefs and clamor roar
Upon his death?

MACBETH.   I am settled and bend up
Each corporal agent to this terrible feat.   80
Away, and mock the time with fairest show;
False face must hide what the false heart doth know. [*Exeunt.*]

Act II

SCENE I: *The same. Court of* MACBETH'S *castle*

[*Enter* BANQUO, *and* FLEANCE *with a torch before him.*]

BANQUO.   How goes the night, boy?

FLEANCE.   The moon is down; I have not heard the clock.

BANQUO.   And she goes down at twelve.

FLEANCE.   I take't, 'tis later, sir.

BANQUO.   Hold, take my sword. There's husbandry in heaven;
Their candles are all out. Take thee that too.
A heavy summons lies like lead upon me,
And yet I would not sleep. Merciful powers,
Restrain in me the cursed thoughts that nature
Gives way to in repose!

[*Enter* MACBETH, *and a servant with a torch.*]
                Give me my sword.

Who's there?   10

MACBETH.   A friend.

BANQUO.   What, sir, not yet at rest? The King's abed.

He hath been in unusual pleasure and
Sent forth great largess to your offices.
This diamond he greets your wife withal
By the name of most kind hostess, and shut up
In measureless content.

    MACBETH.   Being unprepared,
Our will became the servant to defect,
Which else should free have wrought.

    BANQUO.   All's well.
I dreamt last night of the three Weird Sisters.   20
To you they have showed some truth.

    MACBETH.   I think not of them.
Yet when we can entreat an hour to serve,
We would spend it in some words upon that business,
If you would grant the time.

    BANQUO.   At your kind'st leisure.

    MACBETH.   If you shall cleave to my consent, when 'tis,
It shall make honor for you.

    BANQUO.   So I lose none
In seeking to augment it but still keep
My bosom franchised and allegiance clear,
I shall be counseled.

    MACBETH.   Good repose the while!

    BANQUO.   Thanks, sir. The like to you!   30

    [*Exeunt* BANQUO *and* FLEANCE.]

    MACBETH.   Go bid thy mistress, when my drink is ready,
She strike upon the bell. Get thee to bed.

    [*Exit Servant.*]
Is this a dagger which I see before me,
The handle toward my hand? Come, let me clutch thee!
I have thee not, and yet I see thee still.
Art thou not, fatal vision, sensible
To feeling as to sight? or art thou but
A dagger of the mind, a false creation,
Proceeding from the heat-oppressed brain?
I see thee yet, in form as palpable   40

As this which now I draw.
Thou marshal'st me the way that I was going,
And such an instrument I was to use.
Mine eyes are made the fools o' the other senses,
Or else worth all the rest. I see thee still;
And on thy blade and dudgeon gouts of blood,
Which was not so before. There's no such thing.
It is the bloody business which informs
Thus to mine eyes. Now o'er the one half-world
Nature seems dead, and wicked dreams abuse   50
The curtained sleep. Witchcraft celebrates
Pale Hecate's offerings; and withered murder,
Alarumed by his sentinel, the wolf,
Whose howl's his watch, thus with his stealthy pace,
With Tarquin's ravishing strides, towards his design
Moves like a ghost. Thou sure and firm-set earth,
Hear not my steps which way they walk, for fear
Thy very stones prate of my whereabout
And take the present horror from the time,
Which now suits with it. Whiles I threat, he lives;   60
Words to the heat of deeds too cold breath gives.
                        [*A bell rings.*]
I go, and it is done. The bell invites me.
Hear it not, Duncan, for it is a knell
That summons thee to heaven, or to hell. [*Exit.*]

SCENE II: *The same*

[*Enter* LADY MACBETH.]

LADY.   That which hath made them drunk hath made me bold;
What hath quenched them hath given me fire.
Hark! Peace!
It was the owl that shrieked, the fatal bellman
Which gives the stern'st good-night. He is about it.
The doors are open, and the surfeited grooms
Do mock their charge with snores. I have drugged their possets,
That death and nature do contend about them

Whether they live or die.

MACBETH [*Within.*]   Who's there? What, ho?

LADY.   Alack, I am afraid they have awaked,   10
And 'tis not done! The attempt, and not the deed,
Confounds us. Hark! I laid their daggers ready;
He could not miss 'em. Had he not resembled
My father as he slept, I had done't.

    [*Enter* MACBETH.]

                                    My husband!

MACBETH.   I have done the deed. Didst thou not hear a noise?

LADY.   I heard the owl scream and the crickets cry.
Did not you speak?

MACBETH.   When?

LADY.   Now.

MACBETH.   As I descended?

LADY.   Ay.

MACBETH.   Hark!
Who lies i' the second chamber?

LADY.   Donalbain.   20

MACBETH.   This is a sorry sight.

LADY.   A foolish thought, to say a sorry sight.

MACBETH.   There's one did laugh in's sleep, and one cried
    "Murder!"
That they did wake each other. I stood and heard them.
But they did say their prayers and addressed them
Again to sleep.

LADY.   There are two lodged together.

MACBETH.   One cried "God bless us!" and "Amen!" the other,
As they had seen me with these hangman's hands,
List'ning their fear. I could not say "Amen!"
When they did say "God bless us!"

LADY.   Consider it not so deeply.   30

MACBETH.   But wherefore could I not pronounce "Amen"?
I had most need of blessing, and "Amen"
Stuck in my throat.

LADY.   These deeds must not be thought

After these ways. So, it will make us mad.

MACBETH.   Methought I heard a voice cry "Sleep no more!
Macbeth does murder sleep"—the innocent sleep,
Sleep that knits up the raveled sleave of care,
The death of each day's life, sore labor's bath,
Balm of hurt minds, great nature's second course,
Chief nourisher in life's feast—

LADY.   What do you mean?   40

MACBETH.   Still it cried "Sleep no more!" to all the house;
"Glamis hath murdered sleep, and therefore Cawdor
Shall sleep no more! Macbeth shall sleep no more!"

LADY.   Who was it that thus cried? Why, worthy Thane,
You do unbend your noble strength to think
So brainsickly of things. Go get some water
And wash this filthy witness from your hand.
Why did you bring these daggers from the place?
They must lie there. Go carry them and smear
The sleepy grooms with blood.

MACBETH.   I'll go no more.   50
I am afraid to think what I have done;
Look on't again I dare not.

LADY.   Infirm of purpose!
Give me the daggers. The sleeping and the dead
Are but as pictures. 'Tis the eye of childhood
That fears a painted devil. If he do bleed,
I'll gild the faces of the grooms withal,
For it must seem their guilt. [*Exit. Knocking within.*]

MACBETH.   Whence is that knocking?
How is't with me when every noise appals me?
What hands are here? Ha! they pluck out mine eyes!
With all great Neptune's ocean wash this blood   60
Clean from my hand? No. This my hand will rather
The multitudinous seas incarnadine,
Making the green one red.

[*Enter* LADY MACBETH.]

LADY.   My hands are of your color, but I shame

To wear a heart so white. [*Knock.*] I hear a knocking
At the south entry. Retire we to our chamber.
A little water clears us of this deed.
How easy is it then! Your constancy
Hath left you unattended. [*Knock.*] Hark! more knocking.
Get on your nightgown, lest occasion call us   70
And show us to be watchers. Be not lost
So poorly in your thoughts.

    MACBETH.   To know my deed, 'twere best not know myself.
[*Knock.*]
Wake Duncan with thy knocking! I would thou couldst!
[*Exeunt.*]

          SCENE III: *The same*

[*Enter a* PORTER. *Knocking within.*]

    PORTER.   Here's a knocking indeed! If a man were porter of
hell gate, he should have old turning the key. [*Knock.*] Knock,
knock, knock! Who's there, i' the name of Belzebub? Here's a farmer
that hanged himself on the expectation of plenty. Come in time!
Have napkins enow about you; here you'll sweat for't. [*Knock.*]
Knock, knock! Who's there, in the other devil's name? Faith, here's
an equivocator, that could swear in both the scales against either
scale; who committed treason enough for God's sake, yet could not
equivocate to heaven. O, come in, equivocator! [*Knock.*] Knock,
knock, knock! Who's there? Faith, here's an English tailor come
hither for stealing out of a French hose. Come in, tailor. Here you
may roast your goose. [*Knock.*] Knock, knock! Never at quiet! What
are you? But this place is too cold for hell. I'll devil-porter it no further. I had thought to have let in some of all professions that go
the primrose way to the everlasting bonfire. [*Knock.*] Anon, anon!
[*Opens the gate.*] I pray you remember the porter.

[*Enter* MACDUFF *and* LENNOX.]

    MACDUFF.   Was it so late, friend, ere you went to bed,
That you do lie so late?

    PORTER.   Faith, sir, we were carousing till the second cock;
and drink, sir, is a great provoker of three things.

MACDUFF.   What three things does drink especially provoke?   30

PORTER.   Marry, sir, nose-painting, sleep, and urine. Lechery, sir, it provokes, and unprovokes: it provokes the desire, but it takes away the performance. Therefore much drink may be said to be an equivocator with lechery: it makes him, and it mars him; it sets him on, and it takes him off; it persuades him, and disheartens him; makes him stand to, and not stand to; in conclusion, equivocates him in a sleep, and, giving him the lie, leaves him.   40

MACDUFF.   I believe drink gave thee the lie last night.

PORTER.   That it did, sir, i' the very throat on me; but I requited him for his lie; and, I think, being too strong for him, though he took up my legs sometime, yet I made a shift to cast him.

MACDUFF.   Is thy master stirring?

[*Enter* MACBETH.]

Our knocking has awaked him; here he comes.

LENNOX.   Good morrow, noble sir.

MACBETH.   Good morrow, both.

MACDUFF.   Is the King stirring, worthy Thane?

MACBETH.   Not yet.   50

MACDUFF.   He did command me to call timely on him;
I have almost slipped the hour.

MACBETH.   I'll bring you to him.

MACDUFF.   I know this is a joyful trouble to you;
But yet 'tis one.

MACBETH.   The labor we delight in physics pain.
This is the door.

MACDUFF.   I'll make so bold to call,
For 'tis my limited service. [*Exit.*]

LENNOX.   Goes the King hence today?

MACBETH.   He does; he did appoint so.

LENNOX.   The night has been unruly. Where we lay,
Our chimneys were blown down; and, as they say,   60
Lamentings heard i' the air, strange screams of death,
And prophesying, with accents terrible,
Of dire combustion and confused events

New hatched to the woeful time. The obscure bird
Clamored the livelong night. Some say the earth
Was feverous and did shake.

MACBETH.   'Twas a rough night.

LENNOX.   My young remembrance cannot parallel
A fellow to it.

[*Enter* MACDUFF.]

MACDUFF.   O horror, horror, horror! Tongue nor heart
Cannot conceive nor name thee!

MACBETH *and* LENNOX.   What's the matter?   70

MACDUFF.   Confusion now hath made his masterpiece!
Most sacrilegious murder hath broke ope
The Lord's anointed temple and stole thence
The life o' the building!

MACBETH.   What is't you say? the life?

LENNOX.   Mean you his Majesty?

MACDUFF.   Approach the chamber, and destroy your sight
With a new Gorgon. Do not bid me speak.
See, and then speak yourselves.

[*Exeunt* MACBETH *and* LENNOX.]
                         Awake, awake!

Ring the alarum bell. Murder and treason!
Banquo and Donalbain! Malcolm! awake!   80
Shake off this downy sleep, death's counterfeit,
And look on death itself! Up, up, and see
The great doom's image! Malcolm! Banquo!
As from your graves rise up and walk like sprites
To countenance this horror! Ring the bell!

[*Bell rings.*]

[*Enter* LADY MACBETH.]

LADY.   What's the business,
That such a hideous trumpet calls to parley
The sleepers of the house? Speak, speak!

MACDUFF.   O gentle lady,
'Tis not for you to hear what I can speak!
The repetition in a woman's ear   90

Would murder as it fell.

    [*Enter* BANQUO.]

                            O Banquo, Banquo,

Our royal master's murdered!

    LADY.   Woe, alas!

What, in our house?

    BANQUO.   Too cruel anywhere.

Dear Duff, I prithee contradict thyself

And say it is not so.

    [*Enter* MACBETH, LENNOX, *and* ROSS.]

    MACBETH.   Had I but died an hour before this chance,

I had lived a blessed time; for from this instant

There's nothing serious in mortality;

All is but toys; renown and grace is dead;

The wine of life is drawn, and the mere lees   100

Is left this vault to brag of.

    [*Enter* MALCOLM *and* DONALBAIN.]

    DONALBAIN.   What is amiss?

    MACBETH.   You are, and do not know't.

The spring, the head, the fountain of your blood

Is stopped, the very source of it is stopped.

    MACDUFF.   Your royal father's murdered.

    MALCOLM.   O, by whom?

    LENNOX.   Those of his chamber, as it seemed, had done't.

Their hands and faces were all badged with blood;

So were their daggers, which unwiped we found

Upon their pillows.

They stared and were distracted. No man's life   110

Was to be trusted with them.

    MACBETH.   O, yet I do repent me of my fury

That I did kill them.

    MACDUFF.   Wherefore did you so?

    MACBETH.   Who can be wise, amazed, temp'rate, and furious,

Loyal and neutral, in a moment? No man.

The expedition of my violent love

Outrun the pauser, reason. Here lay Duncan,

His silver skin laced with his golden blood,
And his gashed stabs looked like a breach in nature
For ruin's wasteful entrance; there, the murderers,   120
Steeped in the colors of their trade, their daggers
Unmannerly breeched with gore. Who could refrain
That had a heart to love and in that heart
Courage to make's love known?

LADY.   Help me hence, ho!

MACDUFF.   Look to the lady.

MALCOLM [*Aside to Donalbin*].   Why do we hold our tongues,
That most may claim this argument for ours?

DONALBAIN [*Aside to Malcolm*].   What should be spoken here,
Where our fate, hid in an auger hole,
May rush and seize us? Let's away,
Our tears are not yet brewed.

MALCOLM [*Aside to Donalbain*].   Not our strong sorrow   130
Upon the foot of motion.

BANQUO.   Look to the lady.

[LADY MACBETH *is carried out*.]

And when we have our naked frailties hid,
That suffer in exposure, let us meet
And question this most bloody piece of work,
To know it further. Fears and scruples shake us.
In the great hand of God I stand, and thence
Against the undivulged pretense I fight
Of treasonous malice.

MACDUFF.   And so do I.

ALL.   So all.

MACBETH.   Let's briefly put on manly readiness.
And meet i' the hall together.

ALL.   Well contented.   140

[*Exeunt all but* MALCOLM *and* DONALBAIN.]

MALCOLM.   What will you do? Let's not consort with them.
To show an unfelt sorrow is an office
Which the false man does easy. I'll to England.

DONALBAIN.   To Ireland I. Our separated fortune

Shall keep us both the safer. Where we are,
There's daggers in men's smiles; the near in blood,
The nearer bloody.

MALCOLM.   This murderous shaft that's shot
Hath yet not lighted, and our safest way
Is to avoid the aim. Therefore to horse!
And let us not be dainty of leave-taking   150
But shift away. There's warrant in that theft
Which steals itself when there's no mercy left. [*Exeunt.*]

SCENE IV: *The same. Outside Macbeth's castle*

[*Enter* ROSS *with an* OLD MAN.]

OLD MAN.   Threescore and ten I can remember well;
Within the volume of which time I have seen
Hours dreadful and things strange; but this sore night
Hath trifled former knowings.

ROSS.   Ah, good father,
Thou seest the heavens, as troubled with man's act,
Threaten his bloody stage. By the clock 'tis day,
And yet dark night strangles the traveling lamp.
Is't night's predominance, or the day's shame,
That darkness does the face of earth entomb
When living light should kiss it?

OLD MAN.   'Tis unnatural,   10
Even like the deed that's done. On Tuesday last
A falcon, tow'ring in her pride of place,
Was by a mousing owl hawked at and killed.

ROSS.   And Duncan's horses (a thing most strange and certain),
Beauteous and swift, the minions of their race,
Turned wild in nature, broke their stalls, flung out,
Contending 'gainst obedience, as they would make
War with mankind.

OLD MAN.   'Tis said they eat each other.

ROSS.   They did so, to the amazement of mine eyes
That looked upon't.

[*Enter* MACDUFF.]

Here comes the good Macduff.   20

How goes the world, sir, now?

MACDUFF.   Why, see you not?

ROSS.   Is't known who did this more than bloody deed?

MACDUFF.   Those that Macbeth hath slain.

ROSS.   Alas, the day!

What good could they pretend?

MACDUFF.   They were suborned.

Malcolm and Donalbain, the King's two sons,

Are stol'n away and fled, which puts upon them

Suspicion of the deed.

ROSS.   'Gainst nature still!

Thriftless ambition, that will raven up

Thine own live's means! Then 'tis most like

The sovereignty will fall upon Macbeth.   30

MACDUFF.   He is already named, and gone to Scone

To be invested.

ROSS.   Where is Duncan's body?

MACDUFF.   Carried to Colmekill,

The sacred storehouse of his predecessors

And guardian of their bones.

ROSS.   Will you to Scone?

MACDUFF.   No, cousin, I'll to Fife.

ROSS.   Well, I will thither.

MACDUFF.   Well, may you see things well done there. Adieu,

Lest our old robes sit easier than our new!

ROSS.   Farewell, father.

OLD MAN.   God's bension go with you, and with those   40

That would make good of bad, and friends of foes!

[*Exeunt omnes.*]

Act III

SCENE I: *Forres. The palace*

[*Enter* BANQUO.]

BANQUO.   Thou hast it now—King, Cawdor, Glamis, all,

As the Weird Women promised; and I fear
Thou play'dst most foully for't. Yet it was said
It should not stand in thy posterity,
But that myself should be the root and father
Of many kings. If there come truth from them
(As upon thee, Macbeth, their speeches shine),
Why, by the verities on thee made good,
May they not be my oracles as well
And set me up in hope? But, hush, no more!   10

[*Senet sounded. Enter* MACBETH, *as King;* LADY MACBETH, *as
Queen;* LENNOX, ROSS, *lords, and attendants.*]

MACBETH. Here's our chief guest.

LADY.   If he had been forgotten,
It had been as a gap in our great feast,
And all-thing unbecoming.

MACBETH.   Tonight we hold a solemn supper, sir,
And I'll request your presence.

BANQUO.   Let your Highness
Command upon me, to the which my duties
Are with a most indissoluble tie
For ever knit.

MACBETH.   Ride you this afternoon?

BANQUO. Ay, my good lord.   20

MACBETH. We should have else desired your good advice
(Which still hath been both grave and prosperous)
In this day's council; but we'll take tomorrow.
Is't far you ride?

BANQUO.   As far, my lord, as will fill up the time
'Twixt this and supper. Go not my horse the better,
I must become a borrower of the night
For a dark hour or twain.

MACBETH.   Fail not our feast.

BANQUO. My lord, I will not.

MACBETH.   We hear our bloody cousins are bestowed   30
In England and in Ireland, not confessing
Their cruel parricide, filling their hearers

With strange invention. But of that tomorrow,
When therewithal we shall have cause of state
Craving us jointly. Hie you to horse. Adieu,
Till you return at night. Goes Fleance with you?

BANQUO.   Ay, my good lord. Our times does call upon's.

MACBETH.   I wish your horses swift and sure of foot,
And so I do commend you to their backs.
Farewell.   40

[*Exit* BANQUO.]

Let every man be master of his time
Till seven at night. To make society
The sweeter welcome, we will keep ourself
Till supper time alone. While then, God be with you!

[*Exeunt Lords and others. Manent* MACBETH *and a servant.*]

Sirrah, a word with you. Attend those men
Our pleasure?

SERVANT.   They are, my lord, without the palace gate.

MACBETH.   Bring them before us.

[*Exit Servant.*]

                                        To be thus is nothing,
But to be safely thus. Our fears in Banquo
Stick deep, and in his royalty of nature   50
Reigns that which would be feared. 'Tis much he dares,
And to that dauntless temper of his mind
He hath a wisdom that doth guide his valor
To act in safety. There is none but he
Whose being I do fear; and under him
My genius is rebuked, as it is said
Mark Antony's was by Cæsar. He chid the Sisters
When first they put the name of King upon me,
And bade them speak to him. Then, prophet-like,
They hailed him father to a line of kings.   60
Upon my head they placed a fruitless crown
And put a barren scepter in my gripe,
Thence to be wrenched with an unlineal hand,
No son of mine succeeding. If't be so,

For Banquo's issue have I filled my mind;
For them the gracious Duncan have I murdered;
Put rancors in the vessel of my peace
Only for them, and mine eternal jewel
Given to the common enemy of man
To make them kings, the seed of Banquo kings!   70
Rather than so, come, Fate, into the list,
And champion me to the utterance! Who's there?

[*Enter* SERVANT *and two* MURDERERS.]

Now go to the door and stay there till we call.

[*Exit* SERVANT.]

Was it not yesterday we spoke together?

    MURDERERS.   It was, so please your Highness.

    MACBETH.   Well then, now
Have you considered of my speeches? Know
That it was he, in the times past, which held you
So under fortune, which you thought had been
Our innocent self. This I made good to you
In our last conference, passed in probation with you   80
How you were borne in hand, how crossed; the instruments;
Who wrought with them; and all things else that might
To half a soul and to a notion crazed
Say "Thus did Banquo."

    FIRST MURDERER.   You made it known to us.

    MACBETH.   I did so; and went further, which is now
Our point of second meeting. Do you find
Your patience so predominant in your nature
That you can let this go? Are you so gospeled
To pray for this good man and for his issue,
Whose heavy hand hath bowed you to the grave   90
And beggared yours for ever?

    FIRST MURDERER.   We are men, my liege.

    MACBETH.   Ay, in the catalogue ye go for men,
As hounds and greyhounds, mongrels, spaniels, curs,
Shoughs, water-rugs, and demi-wolves are clept
All by the name of dogs. The valued file

Distinguishes the swift, the slow, the subtle,
The housekeeper, the hunter, every one
According to the gift which bounteous nature
Hath in him closed; whereby he does receive
Particular addition, from the bill   100
That writes them all alike; and so of men.
Now, if you have a station in the file,
Not i' the worst rank of manhood, say't;
And I will put that business in your bosoms
Whose execution takes your enemy off,
Grapples you to the heart and love of us,
Who wear our health but sickly in his life,
Which in his death were perfect.

    SECOND MURDERER.   I am one, my liege,
Whom the vile blows and buffets of the world
Have so incensed that I am reckless what   110
I do to spite the world.

    FIRST MURDERER.   And I another,
So weary with disasters, tugged with fortune,
That I would set my life on any chance,
To mend it or be rid on't.

    MACBETH.   Both of you
Know Banquo was your enemy.

    MURDERERS.   True, my lord.

    MACBETH.   So is he mine, and in such bloody distance
That every minute of his being thrusts
Against my near'st of life; and though I could
With barefaced power sweep him from my sight
And bid my will avouch it, yet I must not,   120
For certain friends that are both his and mine,
Whose loves I may not drop, but wail his fall
Who I myself struck down. And thence it is
That I to your assistance do make love,
Masking the business from the common eye
For sundry weighty reasons.

    SECOND MURDERER.   We shall, my lord,

Perform what you command us.

FIRST MURDERER.   Though our lives—

MACBETH.   Your spirits shine through you. Within this hour
     at most
I will advise you where to plant yourselves,
Acquaint you with the perfect spy o' the time,   130
The moment on't; for't must be done tonight,
And something from the palace (always thought
That I require a clearness), and with him,
To leave no rubs nor blotches in the work,
Fleance his son, that keeps him company,
Whose absence is no less material to me
Than is his father's, must embrace the fate
Of that dark hour. Resolve yourselves apart;
I'll come to you anon.

MURDERERS.   We are resolved, my lord.

MACBETH.   I'll call upon you straight. Abide within.   140

[*Exeunt* MURDERERS.]

It is concluded. Banquo, thy soul's flight,
If it find heaven, must find it out tonight. [*Exit.*]

SCENE II: *The same*

[*Enter* MACBETH'S LADY *and a* SERVANT.]

LADY.   Is Banquo gone from court?

SERVANT.   Ay, madam, but returns again tonight.

LADY.   Say to the King I would attend his leisure
For a few words.

SERVANT.   Madam, I will. [*Exit.*]

LADY.   Naught's had, all's spent,
Where our desire is got without content.
'Tis safer to be that which we destroy
Than by destruction dwell in doubtful joy.

[*Enter* MACBETH.]

How now, my lord? Why do you keep alone,
Of sorriest fancies your companions making,
Using those thoughts which should indeed have died   10

With them they think on? Things without all remedy
Should be without regard. What's done is done.
    MACBETH.   We have scorch'd the snake, not killed it.
She'll close and be herself, whilst our poor malice
Remains in danger of her former tooth.
But let the frame of things disjoint, both the worlds suffer,
Ere we will eat our meal in fear and sleep
In the affliction of these terrible dreams
That shake us nightly. Better be with the dead,
Whom we, to gain our peace, have sent to peace,   20
Than on the torture of the mind to lie
In restless ecstasy. Duncan is in his grave;
After life's fitful fever he sleeps well.
Treason has done his worst: nor steel nor poison,
Malice domestic, foreign levy, nothing,
Can touch him further.
    LADY.   Come on.
Gentle my lord, sleek o'er your rugged looks;
Be bright and jovial among your guests tonight.
    MACBETH.   So shall I, love; and so, I pray, be you.
Let your remembrance apply to Banquo;   30
Present him eminence both with eye and tongue:
Unsafe the while, that we
Must lave our honors in these flattering streams
And make our faces vizards to our hearts,
Disguising what they are.
    LADY.   You must leave this.
    MACBETH.   O, full of scorpions is my mind, dear wife!
Thou know'st that Banquo, and his Fleance, lives.
    LADY.   But in them Nature's copy's not eterne.
    MACBETH.   There's comfort yet; they are assailable.
Then be thou jocund. Ere the bat hath flown   40
His cloistered flight, ere to black Hecate's summons
The shard-borne beetle with his drowsy hums
Hath rung night's yawning peal, there shall be done
A deed of dreadful note.

LADY.   What's to be done?

MACBETH.   Be innocent of the knowledge, dearest chuck,
Till thou applaud the deed. Come, seeling night,
Scarf up the tender eye of pitiful day,
And with thy bloody and invisible hand
Cancel and tear to pieces that great bond
Which keeps me pale! Light thickens, and the crow   50
Makes wing to the rooky wood.
Good things of day begin to droop and drowse,
Whiles night's black agents to their preys do rouse.
Thou marvell'st at my words; but hold thee still:
Things bad begun make strong themselves by ill.
So prithee go with me.

        [*Exeunt.*]

        SCENE III: *The same. A park near the palace*

[*Enter three* MURDERERS.]

FIRST MURDERER.   But who did bid thee join with us?

THIRD MURDERER.   Macbeth.

SECOND MURDERER.   He needs not our mistrust, since he
    delivers
Our offices, and what we have to do,
To the direction just.

FIRST MURDERER.   Then stand with us.
The west yet glimmers with some streaks of day.
Now spurs the lated traveler apace
To gain the timely inn, and near approaches
The subject of our watch.

THIRD MURDERER.   Hark! I hear horses.

BANQUO [*Within*].   Give us a light there, ho!

SECOND MURDERER.   Then 'tis he! The rest
That are within the note of expectation   10
Already are i' the court.

FIRST MURDERER.   His horses go about.

THIRD MURDERER.   Almost a mile; but he does usually,
So all men do, from hence to the palace gate

Make it their walk.

[*Enter* BANQUO, *and* FLEANCE *with a torch.*]

SECOND MURDERER.   A light, a light!

THIRD MURDERER.   'Tis he.

FIRST MURDERER.   Stand to't.

BANQUO.   It will be rain tonight.

FIRST MURDERER.   Let it come down!

[*They set upon* BANQUO.]

BANQUO.   O, treachery! Fly, good Fleance, fly, fly, fly!

Thou mayst revenge. O slave!

[*Dies.* FLEANCE *escapes.*]

THIRD MURDERER.   Who did strike out the light?

FIRST MURDERER.   Was't not the way?

THIRD MURDERER.   There's but one down; the son is fled.

SECOND MURDERER.   We have lost

Best half of our affair.   21

FIRST MURDERER.   Well, let's away, and say how much is done.

[*Exeunt.*]

SCENE IV: *The same. Hall in the palace*

[*Banquet prepared. Enter* MACBETH, LADY MACBETH, ROSS, LEN-
NOX, *lords, and attendants.*]

MACBETH.   You know your own degrees, sit down. At first

And last the hearty welcome.

LORDS.   Thanks to your Majesty.

MACBETH.   Ourself will mingle with society

And play the humble host.

Our hostess keeps her state, but in best time

We will require her welcome.

LADY.   Pronounce it for me, sir, to all our friends,

For my heart speaks they are welcome.

[*Enter* FIRST MURDERER, *to the door.*]

MACBETH.   See, they encounter thee with their hearts' thanks.

Both sides are even: here I'll sit i' the midst.   10

Be large in mirth; anon we'll drink a measure

The table round. [*Moves toward* MURDERER.] There's blood upon thy
    face.
    MURDERER.   'Tis Banquo's then.
    MACBETH.   'Tis better thee without than he within.
Is he dispatched?
    MURDERER.   My lord, his throat is cut. That I did for him.
    MACBETH.   Thou art the best o' the cutthroats! Yet he's good
That did the like for Fleance. If thou didst it,
Thou art the nonpareil.
    MURDERER.   Most royal sir,
Fleance is scaped.   20
    MACBETH [*Aside*].   Then comes my fit again. I had else been
    perfect;
Whole as the marble, founded as the rock,
As broad and general as the casing air.
But now I am cabined, cribbed, confined, bound in
To saucy doubts and fears.—But Banquo's safe?
    MURDERER.   Ay, my good lord. Safe in a ditch he bides,
With twenty trenched gashes on his head,
The least a death to nature.
    MACBETH.   Thanks for that!
There the grown serpent lies; the worm that's fled
Hath nature that in time will venom breed,   30
No teeth for the present. Get thee gone. Tomorrow
We'll hear ourselves again.
    [*Exit* MURDERER.]
    LADY.   My royal lord,
You do not give the cheer. The feast is sold
That is not often vouched, while 'tis a-making,
'Tis given with welcome. To feed were best at home.
From thence, the sauce to meat is ceremony;
Meeting were bare without it.
    [*Enter the* GHOST OF BANQUO, *and sits in* MACBETH'S place.]
    MACBETH.   Sweet remembrancer!
Now good digestion wait on appetite,

And health on both! [Moves toward MURDERER.] Thy
face.

LENNOX.   May't please your Highness sit.

MACBETH.   Here had we now our country's honor, roofed,   40
Were the graced person of our Banquo present;
Who may I rather challenge for unkindness
Than pity for mischance!

ROSS.   His absence, sir,
Lays blame upon his promise. Please't your Highness
To grace us with your royal company?

MACBETH.   The table's full.

LENNOX.   Here is a place reserved, sir.

MACBETH.   Where?

LENNOX.   Here, my good lord. What is't that moves your Highness?

MACBETH.   Which of you have done this?

LORDS.   What, my good lord?

MACBETH.   Thou canst not say I did it. Never shake   50
Thy gory locks at me.

ROSS.   Gentlemen, rise. His Highness is not well.

LADY.   Sit, worthy friends. My lord is often thus,
And hath been from his youth. Pray you keep seat.
The fit is momentary; upon a thought
He will again be well. If much you note him,
You shall offend him and extend his passion.
Feed, and regard him not.—Are you a man?

MACBETH.   Ay, and a bold one, that dare look on that
Which might appal the devil.

LADY.   O proper stuff!   60
This is the very painting of your fear.
This is the air-drawn dagger which you said
Led you to Duncan. O, these flaws and starts
(Impostors to true fear) would well become
A woman's story at a winter's fire,
Authorized by her grandam. Shame itself!
Why do you make such faces? When all's done,
You look but on a stool.

MACBETH.   Prithee see there! behold! look! lo! How say you?
Why, what care I? If thou canst nod, speak too.   70
If charnel houses and our graves must send
Those that we bury back, our monuments
Shall be the maws of kites.
    [*Exit* GHOST.]
    LADY.   What, quite unmanned in folly?
    MACBETH.   If I stand here, I saw him.
    LADY.   Fie, for shame!
    MACBETH.   Blood hath been shed ere now, i' the olden time,
Ere humane statute purged the gentle weal;
Ay, and since too, murders have been performed
Too terrible for the ear. The time has been
That, when the brains were out, the man would die,
And there an end! But now they rise again,   80
With twenty mortal murders on their crowns,
And push us from our stools. This is more strange
Than such a murder is.
    LADY.   My worthy lord,
Your noble friends do lack you.
    MACBETH.   I do forget.
Do not muse at me, my most worthy friends.
I have a strange infirmity, which is nothing
To those that know me. Come, love and health to all!
Then I'll sit down. Give me some wine, fill full.
    [*Enter* GHOST.]
I drink to the general joy o' the whole table,
And to our dear friend Banquo, whom we miss.   90
Would he were here! To all, and him, we thirst,
And all to all.
    LORDS.   Our duties, and the pledge.
    MACBETH.   Avaunt, and quit my sight! Let the earth hide thee!
Thy bones are marrowless, thy blood is cold;
Thou hast no speculation in those eyes
Which thou dost glare with!
    LADY.   Think of this, good peers,

But as a thing of custom. 'Tis no other.
Only it spoils the pleasure of the time.
      MACBETH.   What man dare, I dare.
Approach thou like the rugged Russian bear,   100
The armed rhinoceros, or the Hyrcan tiger;
Take any shape but that, and my firm nerves
Shall never tremble. Or be alive again
And dare me to the desert with thy sword.
If trembling I inhabit then, protest me
The baby of a girl. Hence, horrible shaddow!
Unreal mock'ry, hence!
      [*Exit* GHOST.]
                              Why, so! Being gone,
I am a man again. Pray you sit still.
      LADY.   You have displaced the mirth, broke the good meeting
With most admired disorder.
      MACBETH.   Can such things be,   110
And overcome us like a summer's cloud
Without our special wonder? You make me strange
Even to the disposition that I owe,
When now I think you can behold such sights
And keep the natural ruby of your cheeks
When mine is blanched with fear.
      ROSS.   What sights, my lord?
      LADY.   I pray you speak not. He grows worse and worse;
Question enrages him. At once, good night.
Stand not upon the order of your going,
But go at once.
      LENNOX.   Good night, and better health   120
Attend his Majesty!
      LADY.   A kind good night to all!
      [*Exeunt lords and attendants.*]
      MACBETH.   It will have blood, they say: blood will have blood.
Stones have been known to move and trees to speak;
Augures and understood relations have
By maggot-pies and choughs and rooks brought forth

The secret'st man of blood. What is the night?

LADY.   Almost at odds with morning, which is which.

MACBETH.   How say'st thou that Macduff denies his person
At our great bidding?

LADY.   Did you send to him, sir?

MACBETH.   I hear it by the way; but I will send.   130
There's not a one of them but in his house
I keep a servant fee'd. I will tomorrow
(And betimes I will) to the Weird Sisters.
More shall they speak; for now I am bent to know
By the worst means the worst. For mine own good
All causes shall give way. I am in blood
Stepped in so far that, should I wade no more,
Returning were as tedious as go o'er.
Strange things I have in head, that will to hand,
Which must be acted ere they may be scanned.   140

LADY.   You lack the season of all natures, sleep.

MACBETH.   Come, we'll to sleep. My strange and self-abuse
Is the initiate fear that wants hard use.
We are yet but young in deed. [*Exeunt.*]

SCENE V: *A heath*

[*Thunder. Enter the three* WITCHES, *meeting* HECATE.]

FIRST WITCH.   Why, how now, Hecate? You look angerly.

HECATE.   Have I not reason, beldams as you are,
Saucy and overbold? How did you dare
To trade and traffic with Macbeth
In riddles and affairs of death;
And I, the mistress of your charms,
The close contriver of all harms,
Was never called to bear my part
Or show the glory of our art?
And, which is worse, all you have done   10
Hath been but for a wayward son,
Spiteful and wrathful, who, as others do,
Loves for his own ends, not for you.

But make amends now. Get you gone
And at the pit of Acheron
Meet me i' the morning. Thither he
Will come to know his destiny.
Your vessels and your spells provide,
Your charms and everything beside.
I am for the air. This night I'll spend   20
Unto a dismal and a fatal end.
Great business must be wrought ere noon.
Upon the corner of the moon
There hangs a vap'rous drop profound.
I'll catch it ere it come to ground;
And that, distilled by magic sleights,
Shall raise such artificial sprites
As by the strength of their illusion
Shall draw him on to his confusion.
He shall spurn fate, scorn death, and bear   30
His hopes 'bove wisdom, grace, and fear;
And you all know security
Is mortals' chiefest enemy.
        [*Music and a song within. "Come away, come away," etc.*]
Hark! I am called. My little spirit, see,
Sits in a foggy cloud and stays for me. [*Exit.*]
        FIRST WITCH.   Come, let's make haste. She'll soon be back
    again. [*Exeunt.*]

SCENE VI: *Forres. The Palace*

[*Enter* LENNOX *and another* LORD.]
        LENNOX.   My former speeches have but hit your thoughts,
Which can interpret farther. Only I say
Things have been strangely borne. The gracious Duncan
Was pitied of Macbeth. Marry, he was dead!
And the right valiant Banquo walked too late;
Whom, you may say (if't please you) Fleance killed,
For Fleance fled. Men must not walk too late.
Who cannot want the thought how monstrous

It was for Malcolm and for Donalbain
To kill their gracious father? Damned fact!   10
How it did grieve Macbeth! Did he not straight,
In pious rage, the two delinquents tear,
That were the slaves of drink and thralls of sleep?
Was not that nobly done? Ay, and wisely too!
For 'twould have angered any heart alive
To hear the men deny't. So that I say
He has borne all things well; and I do think
That, had he Duncan's sons under his key
(As, an't please heaven, he shall not), they should find
What 'twere to kill a father. So should Fleance.   20
But peace! for from broad words, and 'cause he failed
His presence at the tyrant's feast, I hear
Macduff lives in disgrace. Sir, can you tell
Where he bestows himself?
    LORD.   The son of Duncan,
From whom this tyrant holds the due of birth,
Lives in the English court, and is received
Of the most pious Edward with such grace
That the malevolence of fortune nothing
Takes from his high respect. Thither Macduff
Is gone to pray the holy King upon his aid   30
To wake Northumberland and warlike Siward;
That by the help of these (with Him above
To ratify the work) we may again
Give to our tables meat, sleep to our nights,
Free from our feasts and banquets bloody knives,
Do faithful homage and receive free honors—
All which we pine for now. And this report
Hath so exasperate the King that he
Prepares for some attempt of war.
    LENNOX.   Sent he to Macduff?
    LORD.   He did; and with an absolute "Sir, not I!"   40
The cloudy messenger turns me his back
And hums, as who should say, "You'll rue the time

That clogs me with this answer."

LENNOX.   And that well might
Advise him to a caution t' hold what distance
His wisdom can provide. Some holy angel
Fly to the court of England and unfold
His message ere he come, that a swift blessing
May soon return to this our suffering country
Under a hand accursed!

LORD.   I'll send my prayers with him.

[*Exeunt.*]

Act IV

SCENE I: *A cavern. In the middle, a boiling cauldron*

[*Thunder. Enter the three* WITCHES.]

FIRST WITCH.   Thrice the brinded cat hath mewed.

SECOND WITCH.   Thrice, and once the hedge-pig whined.

THIRD WITCH.   Harpier cries; 'tis time, 'tis time.

FIRST WITCH.   Round about the cauldron go;
In the poisoned entrails throw.
Toad, that under cold stone
Days and nights has thirty-one
Swelt'red venom sleeping got,
Boil thou first i' the charmed pot.

ALL.   Double, double, toil and trouble;   10
Fire burn, and cauldron bubble.

SECOND WITCH.   Fillet of a fenny snake,
In the cauldron boil and bake;
Eye of newt, and toe of frog,
Wool of bat, and tongue of dog,
Adder's fork, and blindworm's sting,
Lizard's leg, and howlet's wing;
For a charm of pow'rful trouble
Like a hell-broth boil and bubble.

ALL.   Double, double, toil and trouble;   20
Fire burn, and cauldron bubble.

THIRD WITCH.   Scale of dragon, tooth of wolf,
Witch's mummy, maw and gulf
Of the ravined salt-sea shark,
Root of hemlock, digged i' the dark;
Liver of blaspheming Jew,
Gall of goat, and slips of yew
Slivered in the moon's eclipse;
Nose of Turk and Tartar's lips;
Finger of birth-strangled babe   30
Ditch-delivered by a drab:
Make the gruel thick and slab.
Add thereto a tiger's chaudron
For the ingredience of our cauldron.
          ALL.   Double, double, toil and trouble;
Fire burn, and cauldron bubble.
          SECOND WITCH.   Cool it with a baboon's blood,
Then the charm is firm and good.
          [*Enter* HECATE *and the other three* WITCHES.]
          HECATE.   O, well done! I commend your pains,
And every one shall share i' the gains.   40
And now about the cauldron sing
Like elves and fairies in a ring,
Enchanting all that you put in.
          [*Music and a song, "Black spirit," etc.*]
          SECOND WITCH.   By the pricking of my thumbs,
Something wicked this way comes.
                              Open locks,
                              Whoever knocks!
          [*Enter* MACBETH.]
          MACBETH.   How now, you secret, black, and midnight hags?
What is't you do?
          ALL.   A deed without a name.
          MACBETH.   I conjure you by that which you profess   50
(Howe'er you come to know it), answer me.
Though you untie the winds and let them fight
Against the churches; though the yesty waves

Confound and swallow navigation up;
Though bladed corn be lodged and trees blown down;
Though castles topple on their warders' heads;
Though palaces and pyramids do slope
Their heads to their foundations; though the treasure
Of nature's germens tumble all together,
Even till destruction sicken—answer me   60
To what I ask you.

    FIRST WITCH.   Speak.

    SECOND WITCH.   Demand.

    THIRD WITCH.   We'll answer.

    FIRST WITCH.   Say, if th' hadst rather hear it from our mouths
Or from our masters.

    MACBETH.   Call 'em! Let me see 'em.

    FIRST WITCH.   Pour in sow's blood, that hath eaten
Her nine farrow; grease that's sweaten
From the murderer's gibbet throw
Into the flame.

    ALL.   Come, high or low;
Thyself and office deftly show!

    [*Thunder. First Apparition, an Armed Head.*]

    MACBETH.   Tell me, thou unknown power—

    FIRST WITCH.   He knows thy thought.   70
Hear his speech, but say thou naught.

    FIRST APPARITION.   Macbeth! Macbeth! Macbeth! Beware Mac-
      duff;
Beware the Thane of Fife. Dismiss me. Enough. [*He descends.*]

    MACBETH.   Whate'er thou art, for thy good caution thanks!
Thou hast harped my fear aright. But one word more—

    FIRST WITCH.   He will not be commanded. Here's another,
More potent than the first.

    [*Thunder. Second Apparition, a Bloody Child.*]

    SECOND APPARITION.   Macbeth! Macbeth! Macbeth!

    MACBETH.   Had I three ears, I'ld hear thee.

    SECOND APPARITION.   Be bloody, bold, and resolute; laugh to
      scorn

The pow'r of man, for none of woman born   80
Shall harm Macbeth. [*Descends.*]

    MACBETH.   Then live, Macduff. What need I fear of thee?
But yet I'll make assurance double sure
And take a bond of fate. Thou shall not live!
That I may tell pale-hearted fear it lies
And sleep in spite of thunder.

    [*Thunder. Third Apparition, a Child Crowned, with a tree in his hand.*]

                            What is this
That rises like the issue of a king
And wears upon his baby-brow the round
And top of sovereignty?

    ALL.   Listen, but speak not to't.

    THIRD APPARITION.   Be lion-mettled, proud, and take no care   90
Who chafes, who frets, or where conspirers are.
Macbeth shall never vanquished be until
Great Birnam Wood to high Dunsinane Hill
Shall come against him. [*Descends.*]

    MACBETH.   That will never be.
Who can impress the forest, bid the tree
Unfix his earth-bound root? Sweet bodements, good!
Rebellious dead rise never till the Wood
Of Birnam rise, and our high-placed Macbeth
Shall live the lease of nature, pay his breath
To time and mortal custom. Yet my heart   100
Throbs to know one thing. Tell me, if your art
Can tell so much—shall Banquo's issue ever
Reign in this kingdom?

    ALL.   Seek to know no more.

    MACBETH.   I will be satisfied. Deny me this,
And an eternal curse fall on you! Let me know.
Why sinks that cauldron? and what noise is this?

    [*Hautboys.*]

    FIRST WITCH.   Show!
    SECOND WITCH.   Show!

THIRD WITCH.   Show!

ALL.   Show his eyes, and grieve his heart!   110
Come like shadows, so depart!

[*A show of eight Kings, the eighth with a glass in his hand, and*
BANQUO *last.*]

MACBETH.   Thou art too like the spirit of Banquo. Down!
Thy crown does sear mine eyeballs. And thy hair,
Thou other gold-bound brow, is like the first.
A third is like the former. Filthy hags!
Why do you show me this? A fourth? Start, eyes!
What, will the line stretch out to the crack of doom?
Another yet? A seventh? I'll see no more.
And yet the eighth appears, who bears a glass
Which shows me many more; and some I see   120
That twofold balls and treble scepters carry.
Horrible sight! Now I see 'tis true;
For the blood-boltered Banquo smiles upon me
And points at them for his. [*Apparitions descend.*] What? Is this so?

FIRST WITCH.   Ay, sir, all this is so. But why
Stands Macbeth thus amazedly?
Come, sisters, cheer we up his sprites
And show the best of our delights.
I'll charm the air to give a sound
While you perform your antic round,   130
That this great king may kindly say
Our duties did his welcome pay.

[*Music. The* WITCHES *dance, and vanish.*]

MACBETH.   Where are they? Gone? Let this pernicious hour
Stand aye accursed in the calendar!
Come in, without there!

[*Enter* LENNOX.]

LENNOX.   What's your Grace's will?

MACBETH.   Saw you the Weird Sisters?

LENNOX.   No, my lord.

MACBETH.   Came they not by you?

LENNOX.   No indeed, my lord.

MACBETH.   Infected be the air whereon they ride,
And damned all those that trust them! I did hear
The galloping of horse. Who was't came by?   140
   LENNOX.   'Tis two or three, my lord, that bring you word
Macduff is fled to England.
   MACBETH.   Fled to England?
   LENNOX.   Ay, my good lord.
   MACBETH [*Aside*].   Time, thou anticipat'st my dread exploits.
The flighty purpose never is o'ertook
Unless the deed go with it. From this moment
The very firstlings of my heart shall be
The firstlings of my hand. And even now,
To crown my thoughts with acts, be it thought and done!
The castle of Macduff I will surprise,   150
Seize upon Fife, give to the edge o' the sword
His wife, his babes, and all unfortunate souls
That trace him in his line. No boasting like a fool!
This deed I'll do before this purpose cool.
But no more sights!—Where are these gentlemen?
Come, bring me where they are. [*Exeunt.*]

SCENE II: *Fife.* MACDUFF'S *castle*

[*Enter* MACDUFF'S WIFE, *her* SON, *and* ROSS.]
   WIFE.   What had he done to make him fly the land?
   ROSS.   You must have patience, madam.
   WIFE.   He had none.
His flight was madness. When our actions do not,
Our fears do make us traitors.
   ROSS.   You know not
Whether it was his wisdom or his fear.
   WIFE.   Wisdom? To leave his wife, to leave his babes,
His mansion, and his titles, in a place
From whence himself does fly? He loves us not,
He wants the natural touch. For the poor wren,
(The most diminutive of birds) will fight,   10
Her young ones in her nest, against the owl.

All is the fear, and nothing is the love,
As little is the wisdom, where the flight
So runs against all reason.
    ROSS.   My dearest coz,
I pray you school yourself. But for your husband,
He is noble, wise, judicious, and best knows
The fits o' the season. I dare not speak much further;
But cruel are the times, when we are traitors
And do not know ourselves; when we hold rumor
From what we fear, yet know not what we fear,   20
But float upon a wild and violent sea
Each way, and none.—I take my leave of you.
Shall not be long but I'll be here again.
Things at the worst will cease, or else climb upward
To what they were before.—My pretty cousin,
Blessing upon you!
    WIFE.   Fathered he is, and yet he's fatherless.
    ROSS.   I am so much a fool, should I stay longer,
It would be my disgrace and your discomfort.
I take my leave at once. [*Exit.*]
    WIFE.   Sirrah, your father's dead;   30
And what will you do now? How will you live?
    SON.   As birds do, mother.
    WIFE.   What, with worms and flies?
    SON.   With what I get, I mean; and so do they.
    WIFE.   Poor bird! thou'dst never fear the net nor lime,
The pitfall nor the gin.
    SON.   Why should I, mother? Poor birds they are not set for.
My father is not dead, for all your saying.
    WIFE.   Yes, he is dead. How wilt thou do for a father?
    SON.   Nay, how will you do for a husband?
    WIFE.   Why, I can buy me twenty at any market.   40
    SON.   Then you'll buy 'em to sell again.
    WIFE.   Thou speak'st with all thy wit; and yet, i' faith,
With wit enough for thee.
    SON.   Was my father a traitor, mother?

WIFE. Ay, that he was!

SON. What is a traitor?

WIFE. Why, one that swears, and lies.

SON. And be all traitors that do so?

WIFE. Every one that does so is a traitor and must be hanged.

SON. And must they all be hanged that swear and lie? 51

WIFE. Every one.

SON. Who must hang them?

WIFE. Why, the honest men.

SON. Then the liars and swearers are fools; for there are liars
and swearers enow to beat the honest men and hang up
them.

WIFE. Now God help thee, poor monkey!
But how wilt thou do for a father? 60

SON. If he were dead, you'ld weep for him. If you would not,
it were a good sign that I should quickly have a new father.

WIFE. Poor prattler, how thou talk'st!

[*Enter a* MESSENGER.]

MESSENGER. Bless you, fair dame! I am not to you known,
Though in your state of honor I am perfect.
I doubt some danger does approach you nearly.
If you will take a homely man's advice,
Be not found here. Hence with your little ones!
To fright you thus methinks I am too savage; 70
To do worse to you were fell cruelty,
Which is too nigh your person. Heaven preserve you!
I dare abide no longer. [*Exit.*]

WIFE. Whither should I fly?
I have done no harm. But I remember now
I am in this earthly world, where to do harm
Is often laudable, to do good sometime
Accounted dangerous folly. Why then, alas,
Do I put up that womanly defense
To say I have done no harm?—What are these faces?

[*Enter* MURDERERS.]

MURDERER. Where is your husband? 80

WIFE.   I hope, in no place so unsanctified
Where such as thou mayst find him.
MURDERER.   He's a traitor.
SON.   Thou liest, thou shag-eared villain!
MURDERER.   What, you egg!
[*Stabbing him.*]
Young fry of treachery!
SON.   He has killed me, mother.
Run away, I pray you! [*Dies.*]
[*Exit* LADY MACDUFF, *crying* "Murder!" *followed by* MUR-
DERERS.]

SCENE III: *England. Before the King's palace*

[*Enter* MALCOLM *and* MACDUFF.]
MALCOLM.   Let us seek out some desolate shade, and there
Weep our sad bosoms empty.
MACDUFF.   Let us rather
Hold fast the mortal sword and, like good men,
Bestride our downfall'n birthdom. Each new morn
New widows howl, new orphans cry, new sorrows
Strike heaven on the face, that it resounds
As if it felt with Scotland and yelled out
Like syllable of dolor.
MALCOLM.   What I believe, I'll wail;
What know, believe; and what I can redress,
As I shall find the time to friend, I will.
What you have spoke, it may be so perchance.
This tyrant, whose sole name blisters our tongues,
Was once thought honest; you have loved him well;
He hath not touched you yet. I am young; but something
You may discern of him through me, and wisdom
To offer up a weak, poor, innocent lamb
T' appease an angry god.
MACDUFF.   I am not treacherous.
MALCOLM.   But Macbeth is.
A good and virtuous nature may recoil

In an imperial charge. But I shall crave your pardon. 20
That which you are, my thoughts cannot transpose.
Angels are bright still, though the brightest fell.
Though all things foul would wear the brows of grace,
Yet grace must still look so.

MACDUFF.   I have lost my hopes.

MALCOLM.   Perchance even there where I did find my doubts.
Why in that rawness left you wife and child,
Those precious motives, those strong knots of love,
Without leave-taking? I pray you,
Let not my jealousies be your dishonors,
But mine own safeties. You may be rightly just, 30
Whatever I shall think.

MACDUFF.   Bleed, bleed, poor country!
Great tyranny, lay thou thy basis sure,
For goodness dare not check thee! Wear thou thy wrongs;
The title is affeered! Fare thee well, lord.
I would not be the villain that thou think'st
For the whole space that's in the tryant's grasp
And the rich East to boot.

MALCOLM.   Be not offended.
I speak not as in absolute fear of you.
I think our country sinks beneath the yoke;
It weeps, it bleeds, and each new day a gash 40
Is added to her wounds. I think withal
There would be hands uplifted in my right;
And here from gracious England have I offer
Of goodly thousands. But, for all this,
When I shall tread upon the tyrant's head
Or wear it on my sword, yet my poor country
Shall have more vices than it had before,
More suffer and more sundry ways than ever,
By him that shall succeed.

MACDUFF.   What should he be?

MALCOLM.   It is myself I mean; in whom I know 50
All the particulars of vice so grafted

That, when they shall be opened, black Macbeth
Will seem as pure as snow, and the poor state
Esteem him as a lamb, being compared
With my confineless harms.

MACDUFF.   Not in the legions
Of horrid hell can come a devil more damned
In evils to top Macbeth.

MALCOLM.   I grant him bloody,
Luxurious, avaricious, false, deceitful,
Sudden, malicious, smacking of every sin
That has a name. But there's no bottom, none,   60
In my voluptuousness. Your wives, your daughters,
Your matrons, and your maids could not fill up
The cistern of my lust; and my desire
All continent impediments would o'erbear
That did oppose my will. Better Macbeth
Than such an one to reign.

MACDUFF.   Boundless intemperance
In nature is a tyranny. It hath been
The untimely emptying of the happy throne
And fall of many kings. But fear not yet
To take upon you what is yours. You may   70
Convey your pleasures in a spacious plenty,
And yet seem cold—the time you may so hoodwink.
We have willing dames enough. There cannot be
That vulture in you to devour so many
As will to greatness dedicate themselves,
Finding it so inclined.

MALCOLM.   With this there grows
In my most ill-composed affection such
A stanchless avarice that, were I King,
I should cut off the nobles for their lands,
Desire his jewels, and this other's house,   80
And my more-having would be as a sauce
To make me hunger more, that I should forge
Quarrels unjust against the good and loyal,

Destroying them for wealth.

MACDUFF.   This avarice
Sticks deeper, grows with more pernicious root
Than summer-seeming lust; and it hath been
The sword of our slain kings. Yet do not fear.
Scotland hath foisons to fill up your will
Of your mere own. All these are portable,
With other graces weighed.   90

MALCOLM.   But I have none. The king-becoming graces,
As justice, verity, temp'rance, stableness,
Bounty, perseverance, mercy, lowliness,
Devotion, patience, courage, fortitude,
I have no relish of them, but abound
In the division of each several crime,
Acting it many ways. Nay, had I pow'r, I should
Pour the sweet milk of concord into hell,
Uproar the universal peace, confound
All unity on earth.

MACDUFF.   O Scotland, Scotland!   100

MALCOLM.   If such a one be fit to govern, speak.
I am as I have spoken.

MACDUFF.   Fit to govern?
No, not to live. O nation miserable,
With an untitled tyrant bloody-scept'red,
When shalt thou see thy wholesome days again,
Since that the truest issue of thy throne
By his own interdiction stands accursed
And does blaspheme his breed? Thy royal father
Was a most sainted king; the queen that bore thee,
Oft'ner upon her knees than on her feet,   110
Died every day she lived. Fare thee well!
These evils thou repeat'st upon thyself
Have banished me from Scotland. O my breast,
Thy hope ends here!

MALCOLM.   Macduff, this noble passion,
Child of integrity, hath from my soul

Wiped the black scruples, reconciled my thoughts
To thy good truth and honor. Devilish Macbeth
By many of these trains hath sought to win me
Into his power; and modest wisdom plucks me
From over-credulous haste; but God above   120
Deal between thee and me! for even now
I put myself to thy direction and
Unspeak mine own detraction, here abjure
The taints and blames I laid upon myself
For strangers to my nature. I am yet
Unknown to woman, never was forsworn,
Scarcely have coveted what was mine own,
At no time broke my faith, would not betray
The devil to his fellow, and delight
No less in truth than life. My first false speaking   130
Was this upon myself. What I am truly,
Is thine and my poor country's to command;
Whither indeed, before thy here-approach,
Old Siward with ten thousand warlike men
Already at a point was setting forth.
Now we'll together; and the chance of goodness
Be like our warranted quarrel! Why are you silent?

    MACDUFF.   Such welcome and unwelcome things at once
'Tis hard to reconcile.

    [Enter a DOCTOR.]

    MALCOLM.   Well, more anon. Comes the King forth, I pray
you?   140

    DOCTOR.   Ay, sir. There are a crew of wretched souls
That stay his cure. Their malady convinces
The great assay of art; but at his touch,
Such sanctity hath heaven given his hand,
They presently amend.

    MALCOLM.   I thank you, doctor.

    [Exit DOCTOR.]

    MACDUFF.   What's the disease he means?

    MALCOLM.   'Tis called the evil:

A most miraculous work in this good king,
Which often since my here-remain in England
I have seen him do. How he solicits heaven
Himself best knows; but strangely-visited people,   150
All swol'n and ulcerous, pitiful to the eye,
The mere despair of surgery, he cures,
Hanging a golden stamp about their necks,
Put on with holy prayers; and 'tis spoken,
To the succeeding royalty he leaves
The healing benediction. With this strange virtue,
He hath a heavenly gift of prophecy,
And sundry blessings hang about his throne
That speak him full of grace.
     [*Enter* ROSS.]
    MACDUFF.   See who comes here.
    MALCOLM.   My countryman; but yet I know him not.   160
    MACDUFF.   My ever gentle cousin, welcome hither.
    MALCOLM.   I know him now. Good God betimes remove
The means that makes us strangers!
    ROSS.   Sir, amen.
    MACDUFF.   Stands Scotland where it did?
    ROSS.   Alas, poor country,
Almost afraid to know itself! It cannot
Be called our mother, but our grave; where nothing,
But who knows nothing, is once seen to smile;
Where sighs and groans, and shrieks that rent the air,
Are made, not marked; where violent sorrow seems
A modern ecstasy. The dead man's knell   170
Is there scarce asked for who; and good men's lives
Expire before the flowers in their caps,
Dying or ere they sicken.
    MACDUFF.   O, relation
Too nice, and yet too true!
    MALCOLM.   What's the newest grief?
    ROSS.   That of an hour's age doth hiss the speaker;
Each minute teems a new one.

MACDUFF.   How does my wife?

ROSS.   Why, well.

MACDUFF.   And all my children?

ROSS.   Well too.

MACDUFF.   The tyrant has not battered at their peace?

ROSS.   No, they were well at peace when I did leave 'em.

MACDUFF.   Be not a niggard of your speech. How goes't?   180

ROSS.   When I came hither to transport the tidings
Which I have heavily borne, there ran a rumor
Of many worthy fellows that were out;
Which was to my belief witnessed the rather
For that I saw the tyrant's power afoot.
Now is the time of help. Your eye in Scotland
Would create soldiers, make our women fight
To doff their dire distresses.

MALCOLM.   Be't their comfort
We are coming thither. Gracious England hath
Lent us good Siward and ten thousand men.   190
An older and a better soldier none
That Christendom gives out.

ROSS.   Would I could answer
This comfort with the like! But I have words
That would be howled out in the desert air,
Where hearing should not latch them.

MACDUFF.   What concern they?
The general cause? or is it a fee-grief
Due to some single breast?

ROSS.   No mind that's honest
But in it shares some woe, though the main part
Pertains to you alone.

MACDUFF.   If it be mine,
Keep it not from me, quickly let me have it.   200

ROSS.   Let not your ears despise my tongue for ever,
Which shall possess them with the heaviest sound
That ever yet they heard.

MACDUFF.   Humh! I guess at it.

ROSS.   Your castle is surprised; your wife and babes
Savagely slaughtered. To relate the manner
Were, on the quarry of these murdered deer,
To add the death of you.
    MALCOLM.   Merciful heaven!
What, man! Ne'er pull your hat upon your brows.
Give sorrow words. The grief that does not speak
Whispers the o'erfraught heart and bids it break.   210
    MACDUFF.   My children too?
    ROSS.   Wife, children, servants, all
That could be found.
    MACDUFF.   And I must be from thence?
My wife killed too?
    ROSS.   I have said.
    MALCOLM.   Be comforted.
Let's make us med'cines of our great revenge
To cure this deadly grief.
    MACDUFF.   He has no children. All my pretty ones?
Did you say all? O hell-kite! All?
What, all my pretty chickens and their dam
At one fell swoop?
    MALCOLM.   Dispute it like a man.
    MACDUFF.   I shall do so;   220
But I must also feel it as a man.
I cannot but remember such things were
That were most precious to me. Did heaven look on
And would not take their part? Sinful Macduff,
They were all struck for thee! Naught that I am,
Not for their own demerits, but for mine,
Fell slaughter on their souls. Heaven rest them now!
    MALCOLM.   Be this the whetstone of your sword. Let grief
Convert to anger; blunt not the heart, enrage it.
    MACDUFF.   O, I could play the woman with mine eyes   230
And braggart with my tongue! But, gentle heavens,
Cut short all intermission. Front to front
Bring thou this fiend of Scotland and myself.

Within my sword's length set him. If he scape,
Heaven forgive him too!

MALCOLM.   This tune goes manly.
Come, go we to the King. Our power is ready;
Our lack is nothing but our leave. Macbeth
Is ripe for shaking, and the pow'rs above
Put on their instruments. Receive what cheer you may.
The night is long that never finds the day. [*Exeunt.*]   240

Act V

SCENE I: *Dunsinane. Macbeth's castle*

[*Enter a* DOCTOR OF PHYSIC *and a* WAITING GENTLEWOMAN.]
DOCTOR.   I have two nights watched with you, but can perceive no truth in your report. When was it she last walked?
GENTLEWOMAN.   Since his Majesty went into the field I have seen her rise from her bed, throw her nightgown upon her, unlock her closet, take forth paper, fold it, write upon't, read it, afterwards seal it, and again return to bed; yet all this while in a most fast sleep.
DOCTOR.   A great perturbation in nature, to receive at once the benefit of sleep and do the effects of watching! In this slumb'ry agitation, besides her walking and other actual performances, what (at any time) have you heard her say?
GENTLEWOMAN.   That, sir, which I will not report after her.
DOCTOR.   You may to me, and 'tis most meet you should.
GENTLEWOMAN.   Neither to you nor any one, having no witness to confirm my speech.   20
[*Enter* LADY MACBETH, *with a taper.*]
Lo you, here she comes! This is her very guise, and, upon my life, fast asleep! Observe her; stand close.
DOCTOR.   How came she by that light?
GENTLEWOMAN.   Why, it stood by her. She has light by her continually. 'Tis her command.
DOCTOR.   You see her eyes are open.
GENTLEWOMAN.   Ay, but their sense is shut.

DOCTOR. What is it she does now? Look how she rubs her hands. 30

GENTLEWOMAN. It is an accustomed action with her, to seem thus washing her hands. I have known her continue in this a quarter of an hour.

LADY. Yet here's a spot.

DOCTOR. Hark, she speaks! I will set down what comes from her, to satisfy my remembrance the more strongly.

LADY. Out, damned spot! out, I say! One; two. Why then 'tis time to do't. Hell is murky. Fie, my lord, fie! a soldier, and afeard? What need we fear who knows it, when none can call our pow'r to accompt? Yet who would have thought the old man to have had so much blood in him?

DOCTOR. Do you mark that?

LADY. The Thane of Fife had a wife. Where is she now? What, will these hands ne'er be clean? No more o' that, my lord, no more o' that! You mar all with this starting. 50

DOCTOR. Go to, go to! You have known what you should not.

GENTLEWOMAN. She has spoke what she should not, I am sure of that. Heaven knows what she has known.

LADY. Here's the smell of the blood still. All the perfumes of Arabia will not sweeten this little hand. Oh, oh, oh!

DOCTOR. What a sigh is there! The heart is sorely charged. 60

GENTLEWOMAN. I would not have such a heart in my bosom for the dignity of the whole body.

DOCTOR. Well, well, well.

GENTLEWOMAN. Pray God it be, sir.

DOCTOR. This disease is beyond my practice. Yet I have known those which have walked in their sleep who have died holily in their beds.

LADY. Wash your hands, put on your nightgown, look not so pale! I tell you yet again, Banquo's buried. He cannot come out on's grave. 70

DOCTOR. Even so?

LADY. To bed, to bed! There's knocking at the gate. Come,

come, come, come, give me your hand! What's done cannot be undone. To bed, to bed, to bed! [*Exit.*]

DOCTOR.   Will she go now to bed?

GENTLEWOMAN.   Directly.

DOCTOR.   Foul whisp'rings are abroad. Unnatural deeds
Do breed unnatural troubles. Infected minds   80
To their deaf pillows will discharge their secrets.
More needs she the divine than the physician.
God, God forgive us all! Look after her;
Remove from her the means of all annoyance,
And still keep eyes upon her. So good night.
My mind she has mated, and amazed my sight.
I think, but dare not speak.

GENTLEWOMAN.   Good night, good doctor. [*Exeunt.*]

SCENE II: *The country near Dunsinane*

[*Drum and colors. Enter* MENTEITH, CAITHNESS, ANGUS, LEN-
NOX, *soldiers.*]

MENTEITH.   The English pow'r is near, led on by Malcolm,
His uncle Siward, and the good Macduff.
Revenges burn in them; for their dear causes
Would to the bleeding and the grim alarm
Excite the mortified man.

ANGUS.   Near Birnam Wood
Shall we well meet them; that way are they coming.

CAITHNESS.   Who knows if Donalbain be with his brother?

LENNOX.   For certain, sir, he is not. I have a file
Of all the gentry. There is Siward's son
And many unrough youths that even now   10
Protest their first of manhood.

MENTEITH.   What does the tyrant?

CAITHNESS.   Great Dunsinane he strongly fortifies.
Some say he's mad; others, that lesser hate him,
Do call it valiant fury; but for certain
He cannot buckle his distempered cause
Within the belt of rule.

ANGUS.   Now does he feel
His secret murders sticking on his hands.
Now minutely revolts upbraid his faith-breach.
Those he commands move only in command,
Nothing in love. Now does he feel his title   20
Hang loose about him, like a giant's robe
Upon a dwarfish thief.

    MENTEITH.   Who then shall blame
His pestered senses to recoil and start,
When all that is within him does condemn
Itself for being there?

    CAITHNESS.   Well, march we on
To give obedience where 'tis truly owed.
Meet we the med'cine of the sickly weal;
And with him pour we in our country's purge
Each drop of us.

    LENNOX.   Or so much as it needs
To dew the sovereign flower and drown the weeds.   30
Make we our march towards Birnam. [*Exeunt, marching.*]

SCENE III: *Dunsinane. A room in the castle*

[*Enter* MACBETH, DOCTOR, *and attendants.*]

    MACBETH.   Bring me no more reports. Let them fly all!
Till Birnam Wood remove to Dunsinane,
I cannot taint with fear. What's the boy Malcolm?
Was he not born of woman? The spirits that know
All mortal consequences have pronounced me thus:
"Fear not, Macbeth. No man that's born of woman
Shall e'er have power upon thee." Then fly, false thanes,
And mingle with the English epicures.
The mind I sway by and the heart I bear
Shall never sag with doubt nor shake with fear.   10

[*Enter* SERVANT.]
The devil damn thee black, thou cream-faced loon!
Where got'st thou that goose look?

    SERVANT.   There is ten thousand—

MACBETH.   Geese, villain?

SERVANT.   Soldiers, sir.

MACBETH.   Go prick thy face and over-red thy fear,
Thou lily-livered boy. What soldiers, patch?
Death of thy soul! Those linen cheeks of thine
Are counselors to fear. What soldiers, whey-face?

SERVANT.   The English force, so please you.

MACBETH.   Take thy face hence.

[*Exit* SERVANT.]

                                    Seyton!—I am sick at heart,
When I behold—Seyton, I say!—This push   20
Will cheer me ever, or disseat me now.
I have lived long enough. My way of life
Is fallen into the sere, the yellow leaf;
And that which should accompany old age,
As honor, love, obedience, troops of friends,
I must not look to have; but, in their stead,
Curses not loud but deep, mouth-honor, breath,
Which the poor heart would fain deny, and dare not.
Seyton!

[*Enter* SEYTON.]

SEYTON.   What's your gracious pleasure?

MACBETH.   What news more?   30

SEYTON.   All is confirmed, my lord, which was reported.

MACBETH.   I'll fight, till from my bones my flesh be hacked.
Give me my armor.

SEYTON.   'Tis not needed yet.

MACBETH.   I'll put it on.
Send out mo horses, skirr the country round;
Hang those that talk of fear. Give me mine armor.
How does your patient, doctor?

DOCTOR.   Not so sick, my lord,
As she is troubled with thick-coming fancies
That keep her from her rest.

MACBETH.   Cure her of that!   40
Canst thou not minister to a mind diseased,

Pluck from the memory a rooted sorrow,
Raze out the written troubles of the brain,
And with some sweet oblivious antidote
Cleanse the stuffed bosom of that perilous stuff
Which weighs upon the heart?

DOCTOR.   Therein the patient
Must minister to himself.

MACBETH.   Throw physic to the dogs, I'll none of it!—
Come, put mine armor on. Give me my staff.
Seyton, send out.—Doctor, the thanes fly from me.—
Come, sir, dispatch.—If thou couldst, doctor, cast   50
The water of my land, find her disease,
And purge it to a sound and pristine health,
I would applaud thee to the very echo,
That should applaud again.—Pull't off, I say.—
What rhubarb, cyme, or what purgative drug,
Would scour these English hence? Hear'st thou of them?

DOCTOR.   Ay, my good lord. Your royal preparation
Makes us hear something.

MACBETH.   Bring it after me!
I will not be afraid of death and bane
Till Birnam Forest come to Dunsinane.   60

DOCTOR [*Aside*].   Were I from Dunsinane away and clear,
Profit again should hardly draw me here. [*Exeunt.*]

SCENE IV: *Country near Birnam Wood*

[*Drum and colors. Enter* MALCOLM, SIWARD, MACDUFF,
SIWARD'S SON, MENTEITH, CAITHNESS, ANGUS, LENNOX, ROSS,
and soldiers, marching.]

MALCOLM.   Cousins, I hope the days are near at hand
That chambers will be safe.

MENTEITH.   We doubt it nothing.

SIWARD.   What wood is this before us?

MENTEITH.   The wood of Birnam.

MALCOLM.   Let every solder hew him down a bough
And bear't before him. Thereby shall we shadow

The numbers of our host and make discovery
Err in report of us.

    SOLDIERS.   It shall be done.

    SIWARD.   We learn no other but the confident tyrant
Keeps still in Dunsinane and will endure
Our setting down before't.

    MALCOLM.   'Tis his main hope;   10
For where there is advantage to be given,
Both more and less have given him the revolt;
And none serve with him but constrained things,
Whose hearts are absent too.

    MACDUFF.   Let our just censures
Attend the true event, and put we on
Industrious soldiership.

    SIWARD.   The time approaches
That will with due decision make us know
What we shall say we have, and what we owe.
Thoughts speculative their unsure hopes relate,
But certain issue strokes must arbitrate;   20
Towards which advance the war. [*Exeunt, marching.*]

    SCENE V: *Dunsinane. Within the castle*

[*Enter* MACBETH, SEYTON, *and soldiers, with drum and colors.*]

    MACBETH.   Hang out our banners on the outward walls.
The cry is still, "They come!" Our castle's strength
Will laugh a siege to scorn. Here let them lie
Till famine and the ague eat them up.
Were they not forced with those that should be ours,
We might have met them dareful, beard to beard,
And beat them backward home.

    [*A cry within of women.*]

                    What is that noise?

    SEYTON.   It is the cry of women, my good lord. [*Exit.*]

    MACBETH.   I have almost forgot the taste of fears.
The time has been, my senses would have cooled   10
To hear a night-shriek, and my fell of hair

Would at a dismal treatise rouse and stir
As life were in't. I have supped full with horrors.
Direness, familiar to my slaughterous thoughts,
Cannot once start me.

[*Re-enter* SEYTON.]

      Wherefore was that cry?

SEYTON. The Queen, my lord, is dead.

MACBETH. She should have died hereafter;
There would have been a time for such a word.
Tomorrow, and tomorrow, and tomorrow
Creeps in this petty pace from day to day   20
To the last syllable of recorded time;
And all our yesterdays have lighted fools
The way to dusty death. Out, out, brief candle!
Life's but a walking shadow, a poor player,
That struts and frets his hour upon the stage
And then is heard no more. It is a tale
Told by an idiot, full of sound and fury,
Signifying nothing.

[*Enter a* MESSENGER.]

Thou com'st to use thy tongue. Thy story quickly!

MESSENGER. Gracious my lord,   30
I should report that which I say I saw,
But know not how to do't.

MACBETH.   Well, say, sir!

MESSENGER. As I did stand my watch upon the hill,
I looked toward Birnam, and anon methought
The wood began to move.

MACBETH.   Liar and slave!

MESSENGER. Let me endure your wrath if't be not so.
Within this three mile may you see it coming;
I say, a moving grove.

MACBETH.   If thou speak'st false,
Upon the next tree shalt thou hang alive,
Till famine cling thee. If thy speech be sooth,   40
I care not if thou dost for me as much.

I pull in resolution, and begin
To doubt the equivocation of the fiend,
That lies like truth. "Fear not, till Birnam Wood
Do come to Dunsinane!" and now a wood
Comes toward Dunsinane. Arm, arm, and out!
If this which he avouches does appear,
There is nor flying hence nor tarrying here.
I 'gin to be aweary of the sun,
And wish the estate o' the world were now undone.   50
Ring the alarum bell! Blow wind, come wrack,
At least we'll die with harness on our back! [*Exeunt.*]

SCENE VI: *Dunsinane. Before the castle*

[*Drum and colors. Enter* MALCOLM, SIWARD, MACDUFF, *and their army, with boughs.*]

MALCOLM.   Now near enough. Your leavy screens throw down
And show like those you are. You, worthy uncle,
Shall with my cousin, your right noble son,
Lead our first battle. Worthy Macduff and we
Shall take upon's what else remains to do,
According to our order.

SIWARD.   Fare you well.
Do we but find the tyrant's power tonight,
Let us be beaten if we cannot fight.

MACDUFF.   Make all our trumpets speak, give them all breath,
Those clamorous harbingers of blood and death.   10

[*Exeunt. Alarums continued.*]

SCENE VII: *Another part of the field*

[*Enter* MACBETH.]

MACBETH.   They have tied me to a stake. I cannot fly,
But bearlike I must fight the course. What's he
That was not born of a woman? Such a one
Am I to fear, or none.

[*Enter* YOUNG SIWARD.]

YOUNG SIWARD.   What is thy name?

MACBETH. Thou'lt be afraid to hear it.

YOUNG SIWARD. No; though thou call'st thyself a hotter name
Than any is in hell.

MACBETH. My name's Macbeth.

YOUNG SIWARD. The devil himself could not pronounce a title
More hateful to mine ear.

MACBETH. No, nor more fearful.

YOUNG SIWARD. Thou liest, abhorred tyrant! With my sword   10
I'll prove the lie thou speak'st.

[*Fight, and* YOUNG SIWARD *slain.*]

MACBETH. Thou wast born of woman.
But swords I smile at, weapons laugh to scorn,
Brandished by man that's of a woman born. [*Exit.*]

[*Alarums. Enter* MACDUFF.]

MACDUFF. That way the noise is. Tyrant, show thy face!
If thou beest slain and with no stroke of mine,
My wife and children's ghosts will haunt me still.
I cannot strike at wretched kerns, whose arms
Are hired to bear their staves. Either thou, Macbeth,
Or else my sword with an unbattered edge
I sheathe again undeeded. There thou shouldst be.   20
By this great clatter one of greatest note
Seems bruited. Let me find him, Fortune!
And more I beg not. [*Exit. Alarums.*]

[*Enter* MALCOLM *and* SIWARD.]

SIWARD. This way, my lord. The castle's gently rendered:
The tyrant's people on both sides do fight;
The noble thanes do bravely in the war;
The day almost itself professes yours,
And little is to do.

MALCOLM. We have met with foes
That strike beside us.

SIWARD. Enter, sir, the castle.

[*Exeunt. Alarum.*]

SCENE VIII: *Another part of the field*

[*Enter* MACBETH.]

MACBETH.   Why should I play the Roman fool and die
On mine own sword? Whiles I see lives, the gashes
Do better upon them.

[*Enter* MACDUFF.]

MACDUFF.   Turn, hellhound, turn!

MACBETH.   Of all men else I have avoided thee.
But get thee back! My soul is too much charged
With blood of thine already.

MACDUFF.   I have no words;
My voice is in my sword, thou bloodier villain
Than terms can give thee out!

[*Fight. Alarum.*]

MACBETH.   Thou losest labor.
As easy mayst thou the intrenchant air
With thy keen sword impress as make me bleed.   10
Let fall thy blade on vulnerable crests.
I bear a charmed life, which must not yield
To one of woman born.

MACDUFF.   Despair thy charm!
And let the angel whom thou still hast served
Tell thee, Macduff was from his mother's womb
Untimely ripped.

MACBETH.   Accursed be that tongue that tells me so,
For it hath cowed my better part of man!
And be these juggling fiends no more believed,
That palter with us in a double sense,   20
That keep the word of promise to our ear
And break it to our hope! I'll not fight with thee!

MACDUFF.   Then yield thee, coward,
And live to be the show and gaze o' the time!
We'll have thee, as our rarer monsters are,
Painted upon a pole, and underwrit
"Here may you see the tyrant."

MACBETH.   I will not yield,
To kiss the ground before young Malcolm's feet
And to be baited with the rabble's curse.
Though Birnam Wood be come to Dunsinane,   30
And thou opposed, being of no woman born,
Yet I will try the last. Before my body
I throw my warlike shield. Lay on, Macduff,
And damned be him that first cries "Hold, enough!"

[*Exeunt fighting. Alarums.*]

[*Retreat and flourish. Enter, with drum and colors,* MALCOLM,
SIWARD, ROSS, *thanes, and soldiers.*]

MALCOLM.   I would the friends we miss were safe arrived.

SIWARD.   Some must go off; and yet, by these I see,
So great a day as this is cheaply bought.

MALCOLM.   Macduff is missing, and your noble son.

ROSS.   Your son, my lord, has paid a soldier's debt.
He only lived but till he was a man,   40
The which no sooner had his prowess confirmed
In the unshrinking station where he fought
But like a man he died.

SIWARD.   Then he is dead?

ROSS.   Ay, and brought off the field. Your cause of sorrow
Must not be measured by his worth, for then
It hath no end.

SIWARD.   Had he his hurts before?

ROSS.   Ay, on the front.

SIWARD.   Why then, God's soldier be he!
Had I as many sons as I have hairs,
I would not wish them to a fairer death.
And so his knell is knolled.

MALCOLM.   He's worth more sorrow,   50
And that I'll spend for him.

SIWARD.   He's worth no more.
They say he parted well and paid his score,
And so, God be with him! Here comes newer comfort.

[*Enter* MACDUFF, *with* MACBETH'S *head.*]

MACDUFF.   Hail, King! for so thou art. Behold where stands
The usurper's cursed head. The time is free.
I see thee compassed with thy kingdom's pearl,
That speak my salutation in their minds;
Whose voices I desire aloud with mine—
Hail, King of Scotland!

    ALL.   Hail, King of Scotland!

    [*Flourish.*]

    MALCOLM.   We shall not spend a large expense of time   60
Before we reckon with your several loves
And make us even with you. My Thanes and kinsmen,
Henceforth be Earls, the first that ever Scotland
In such an honor named. What's more to do
Which would be planted newly with the time—
As calling home our exiled friends abroad
That fled the snares of watchful tyranny,
Producing forth the cruel ministers
Of this dead butcher and his fiendlike queen,
Who (as 'tis thought) by self and violent hands   70
Took off her life—this, and what needful else
That calls upon us, by the grace of Grace
We will perform in measure, time, and place.
So thanks to all at once and to each one,
Whom we invite to see us crowned at Scone.

    [*Flourish. Exeunt omnes.*]

COMMENTARY

1   *Plays*

Plays are more difficult to read than stories or poems. The explanation of why this should be so may begin with some consideration of the fundamental differences between the literary forms. A
Shakespearean play is even more difficult to read than a modern
play, but this topic we will take up later.

A poem or story is constructed in the mind of its author and
transmitted more or less directly, by means of print (less often, the
spoken voice), to the mind of the reader. We can only say "more or

less" directly, because the transmission is never complete: no reader ever understands any poem or story *completely*—the reason for this being that it is quite impossible to set arbitrary bounds to the area of suggestiveness of any good poem or story. Two other problems arise at once, resulting from inadequacies in this brief formulation. An author does not exactly make up his poem or story, in its entirety, and then write it down. Sometimes this happens, but not always; more often, in fact, the work in part creates itself, altering as it grows, becoming perhaps quite different in the end from what the author intended—even if, in the beginning, he intended anything at all definite and foreseen, as authors sometimes do not. It is by no means mystical, then, to speak of a work of literary art as having an independent existence, independent (to some degree) of its author; so that the communication is partly just between the poem or story and the reader. Our formulation did not allow for this. Second, because of these facts of the imperfection of the author's control over many excellent poems and stories, and the independent communication between work and reader, a good reader may legitimately find things in a work that its author did not know were there. We had better put the word "know" in quotation marks, meaning that he did not *consciously* know they were there, though of course he put them there, or his unconscious mind did. A great part of artistic creation is unconscious. This is a subject to which we will be returning later, but it already serves to explain what we meant by "the imperfection of the author's control"; it is part of an author's *job* to let his unconscious mind work, and what it works on is partly the unconscious mind of the reader. Thus art is inevitably, to some extent, mysterious. Of course we are speaking here only of things the reader finds which are really there. An ingenious—one might say an unscrupulous —reader can find things in any work of art that are *not* there, things that are coincidental or irrelevant or simply imagined by the reader; and we call this bad reading.

You see the matter is by no means simple, even with respect to a poem or story. Still, with the reservations noted, our generalization was on the whole correct: in a poem or story, the mind of the writer speaks directly to the mind of the reader, and the communication takes place in private.

Now in a play everything is different and far more complex. We may put the difference first in terms of *freedom*. The poet or story-writer can, if you like, say anything he wants; he is closeted with the reader and has him directly listening. The playwright can say *nothing* directly. All he can do is write speeches for actors, who then speak them in the presence of an audience. The dramatist has no immediate contact with the audience at all. It is true that there are special modern cases like G. B. Shaw, who wrote elaborate stage directions, in his own person, and endless prefaces and explanations of his plays; but these were written for readers, not for audiences. By its nature a play is intended not to be read but to be performed and witnessed and listened to ("closet drama" [1] is the term applied to the very special kind of play meant only to be read, and we will not be considering these plays here). There are other sorts of freedom which the playwright lacks also, and we shall be treating several of these presently; but this primary inability to address the hearer directly is fundamental.

A second difference is just the opposite, so to speak. A poem or story is words on a page, at most a voice (as from a phonograph record of an author reading his work). A play is, after a trip to a theatre, lights, color, sound, costumes, men and women moving, human beings apparently suffering and exulting—a version of *reality* such as no poem or story can physically offer. All this is essentially what the playwright gets for the heavy cost, to him, of not being allowed to deal with his audience directly. Naturally it is only a *version* of reality. We know that these men and women are not the characters they are impersonating, we know that this is not twilight falling, that no one will *die* in this battle, and so on. But to the power of the physical impression made on a spectator in a theatre (at a good performance, needless to say) we must add something: the peculiar tension and excitement of being part of an audience responding as one. Nothing, for the reader of a poem or story, corresponds to this.

We can see now, in terms of two basic differences between poems-stories and the drama, why plays are difficult to read. *Neither* does the author speak to you directly *nor* have you the compensating physical version of reality and the strongly participatory audience-sense. The reader has to imagine for himself both the voices and the action, at the same time that he (as it were) generalizes himself into a whole audience. The effort of imagination is not easy for some readers to make. One might ask, indeed, why the effort should be made. Plays were written to be performed: why read them? One answer to this question is very simple, and can be suggested by imagining an analogous question: of the several billion persons living on earth during a man's early lifetime, it is improbable that he will meet the woman most exactly suited to him; so why marry? Yet men do marry and some are happy. A startling proportion of the world's greatest literature is dramatic; much of it the ordinary man will never see performed properly, or at all, and in order not to be shut off from it entirely, he reads.

A second answer is that, in spite of what we have been saying, reading is not a bad way of making acquaintance with drama. One loses something, as against the experience of a spectator at a performance, but one gains something. One gains so much, in certain cases, that certain Shakespearean critics have insisted that some of his masterpieces are *best* approached by reading. *King Lear,* they say, is too titanic for anything resembling adequate performance; it is best appreciated in the study. One important aspect of *Macbeth* may appear to make it a similar case. But before saying what this is, we ought to investigate the general question of how it is that a play can be thought more satisfying to read than to see produced.

We said, a little while back, that a play performed offers us a version of reality. But this is not quite true. People go in and out of rooms, and say "Yes" and "No," on the stage, much as people do in ordinary life. But clearly no *close* version of reality is even aimed at, much less achieved, in most fine plays. What is aimed at is a version of an *enhanced* reality; and this is what matters in a play, not its realism. The realistic elements aim only at making the version *persuasive,* at creating and maintaining illusion, so that what is *un*real can have its effect. This general truth about drama applies *a fortiori* to poetic drama, drama written in verse (which men do not talk in ordinary life) as much of Shakespeare's is. Several things follow here. First, the apparent physical reality offered by a performance is not what really matters in drama, so that if we dispense with it, in reading, and only imagine it sufficiently to bring us with force to the passions and the presentment of a super-real life which *are* what really matters, we may not be merely losing. Second, a performance must follow one line of interpretation and one only, whereas a reader is not so tied: he is freer to respond to the variety and complexity of the dramatist's suggestiveness. An example would be the character of Shylock in *The Merchant of Venice,* which obviously contains elements both comic and tragic that the reader is in a better position to respond to than the actor is to present, since the actor needs broad and consistent effects. Another would be Ophelia in *Hamlet,* who is treated as a creature of pathos on the British and American stage but as a coarse slut on the German stage. The reader of a Shakespearean play certainly has a great deal of work to do, but he does not have to decide for one line of interpretation only. Moreover—this is really a third point, and returns

us to the position adopted by some critics with regard to *King Lear*
—the very concreteness of the presentation necessary on a stage may
find itself seriously at odds with the vastness of *Lear* or the mysteri-
ousness of *Macbeth,* so far as the spectators are concerned. The
imagination is superior to the eyes. Some of Macbeth's speeches are
so mysterious that they seem to proceed from a sort of underworld,
not from a man; yet here is this actor, six feet and one inch tall, with
a certain kind of nose—can he be thinking or saying such things?
For a reader's imagined Macbeth, this sort of obstacle does not
arise.

In some ways, then, the reader is not merely less at a disadvantage than we might have thought, in not being able to see the play,
but he has definite advantages. One of the most important of these
is the ability to choose his own pace and *to study the language* as
an audience cannot, chained to the actors' gait. A Shakespearean
play—any play—should be read first rapidly, at one sitting, without much more pause for reflection than would be allowed in the
theatre. After that, the process of understanding begins.

A dramatist is unfree, we saw, in comparison to other kinds of
authors. Shakespeare was specially unfree, writing as he did for a
particular company (in which he was also an actor) and a repertory
company at that. If he wanted a certain kind of character in a
play, and no such actor was available, he could not have that character. Further, the company was called—when he wrote *Macbeth*—
the King's men, and its plays had to please not only the London
public audiences, the audiences of nobles who would occasionally
command a performance, the witty young lawyers of the Inns of
Court, and the provincial audiences the company played for when
they went on tour in the summer, but the Court and the King himself.

It is certain that in *Macbeth* Shakespeare made an extreme effort both to interest and please King James. The play is very short,
for one thing; the King tended to sleep during long plays, and his
taste was well known. For another, the play is laid in James's country
—he had succeeded to the English throne only two years before, in
1603. It is elaborately attentive to certain of his special interests,
such as witchcraft (on which he had written a book); and its major
spectacle—the procession of the Scots kings at IV:i:111—is addressed directly to James's vanity and pride of family: these are the
King's actual ancestors. Among all these limitations upon the dramatist's freedom—some imposed, some voluntary—it may seem that
an artist could not do his own work at all. Yet scarcely any work in
world literature strikes one as more characteristic or freer than *Macbeth.* This freedom is above all a freedom of *language.* It is through

his incomparable language, more than any other feature of the work, that Shakespeare communicates his vision. This is also the feature that a spectator cannot study at all—he can only feel it and only feel part of it correctly: thus, when he hears

> violent sorrow seem[s]
> A modern ecstasy

it is hard to know what he will think, but he will not be very likely to know that "modern" meant for Shakespeare and his actor and his audience, not "up-to-date" with admiring connotations, but "ordinary, commonplace" with bored and (here) despairing connotations. It is the reader who can study the language, and in the sketch that is possible here of some of the play's salient qualities and meanings, this is the topic we take first.

II *Language*

As soon as the charm is wound up, in the Witches' scene that begins Act IV (Hecate's little speech and the extra witches and their song were very probably added to the play after Shakespeare's death), one of the Witches says:

> By the pricking of my thumbs,
> Something wicked this way comes.

There is an allusion here to the ancient superstition "that all sudden pains of the body, which could not naturally be accounted for, were presages of somewhat that was shortly to happen." But she might also have said: "It is suggested to me, by a sensation of prickling in my thumbs, that an evil man is on his way here." What is the difference between Shakespeare's intense two lines and our rather general, unconcentrated alternative?

A first difference is in the quality of the sound, as there is a difference between what you hear at the beginning of Beethoven's Piano Sonata Opus 111 and what you hear from a juke-box. The word "wicked" keeps the sound of "pricking" going; the reader's experience of the pricking of the Witch's thumbs intensifies. In other ways, too, the two lines are built very closely into each other: "*Something*" half-rhymes with "thumbs," and the four short-*i* sounds that measuredly follow (-thing, wick-, -id, this) carry on the two short-*i* sounds of "pricking" as well as they convey powerfully the sense of movement, something coming, marching. There is an unusually intimate association between the lines, and perhaps we ought to understand the word "By" has quite a different sense from the way we first took it (By means of this sensation, I know, etc.): In accordance with the pricking of my thumbs, something is on its way here, obedient or at any rate *consonant* to my sign. One gets an impression of a fated *assignation* entirely lacking from our paraphrase of the Witch's couplet. This sense is greatly strengthened by the alliteration in the second line: "*w*icked this *w*ay"—as if there were something very natural about the wicked man's coming the Witches' way, as indeed there is. One thinks of the two Ways, of good and of evil, of the Sermon on the Mount (Matthew 7:13–14); and one does not think of them by accident, for the Porter in II:iii winds up his Hell-discourse with "I had thought to have let in some of all professions that go the primrose *way* to the everlasting bonfire." This play is certainly about Good and Evil, and we learn so partly from the aural organization of this couplet.

We have been talking about the couplet just in itself, and we have not done with that either. But a second difference takes us outside—as indeed the word "way" has taken us already. The combination of the concept "thumb," in this Witch-context, and of the particular rhyme that binds the couplet, reminds us irresistibly, if we are careful readers, of four lines back in Act I (I:iii:28–31):

> FIRST WITCH.   Here I have a pilot's thumb,
> Wracked as homeward he did come.
> THIRD WITCH.   A drum, a drum!
> Macbeth doth come.

The same rhyme (here thrice repeated) heralds each of his interviews with the Weird Sisters, and each time there is a thumb. Now this pilot is the second of the adventuring figures (the first being the sleepless sailor) in whom the dramatist is foreshadowing the fate of his hero: Macbeth, for *his* wife's greed, is to suffer from lack of sleep, and he is to be wrecked as he comes home, both in the literal sense home (where he will do the murder) and in the metaphorical sense (as he achieves the crown, what he aims at, home). The calling up, in Act IV, of this foreshadowing passage, deepens the drama of the couplet, making present, for its suggestiveness, the moral wreckage that had been foreshadowed. But in addition to this general usefulness, there are two or three specific points that claim our attention. It is not possible to be certain about the first one, because we do not know how clearly Shakespeare differentiated his Witches in his mind or whether his speech-prefixes [2] for them have been faithfully preserved. According to those we have, it is the First Witch who has a pilot's thumb and the Second whose thumbs prick; but in the light of the fact that presently Macbeth is going to be saying "Had I three ears, I'd hear thee"—a striking speech that will interest us

again later in our discussion—there is an eerie chance that Shakespeare was thinking of *three* thumbs pricking, one of them not joined
to its body. But here we are working speculatively, at the outer
edges of suggestion. The other points are definite.

Macbeth is announced, at his first coming, by a military drum; it
is open, public; he is a hero, a man with a name. At his second coming he is announced by the pricking of a witch's thumbs; his resort
is secret, and he comes not as a hero but as a tyrant; we must imagine
as suggested also a terrible diminishment, from the booming of a
drum to a slight physical manifestation, corresponding to a removal
of the real scene from the objective world to the subjective. But this
is not all, nor even the main thing. It is as "Macbeth" that he first
comes, to be saluted by three prophetic titles. It is *with* his three
titles that he next comes, but not called by them, nor even described
as a man, but only as "Something wicked." His nature has changed—
not his characteristics merely, but his essential nature. He has become,
perhaps, a demon; and the form, and sound, and allusive value of
the couplet help to suggest this as no paraphrase could do.

A modern critic speaks of the exquisite line about wintry trees,
in Shakespeare's Sonnet 73,

> Bare ruin'd choirs, where late the sweet
>   birds sang,

as suggesting marvelously, in a second meaning, the devastated
monasteries and chantries of post-Reformation England, where the
choirs of monks had sung for centuries. If a line in a short lyric
poem can give, in addition to doing superbly its practical, literal
work, this sort of perspective, it need not seem surprising that the
analysis of a couplet in a play takes us into complex problems of
characterization and theme. Macbeth himself opens the question that
leads at last to "Something wicked" when he says to his wife (I:vii:
46–47),

> I dare do all that may become a man.
> Who dares do more is none.

This is variously glossed by the commentators as "superhuman,"
"subhuman," "devilish"; but the meaning is clear: that there is a
possibility other than the human for Macbeth—the demonic. His
next formulation of this subject, at III:iv:59–60, is a little different.
"Are you a man?" she asks him as he stands appalled at the Ghost
of Banquo:

> Ay, and a bold one, that dare look on that
> Which might appal the Devil.

The daring here has expanded, is "more"; and the claim that he is still a man does not convince. Then we hear "Something wicked this way comes" and we know where we are. Later the non-human diabolic terms applied to Macbeth, "hellkite," "hellhound," confirm our sense, and one's impression of his standing, or boiling, outside human life is crowned by his horrifying expression,

Whiles I see lives,

not men but *lives,* as if he had not one himself or only one so different that for human lives he could just say "lives" (like targets merely for his sword) and aim at destroying them (V:viii:2).

III   *Terms*

Dramatic criticism—the understanding, analysis, and assessment of plays—is very old, at least as old as Aristotle. Unfortunately his critical method and terms apply much less well to some Greek plays, such as Euripides's *Bacchae,* than to others such as Sophocles's *Oedipus the King;* and to Elizabethan tragedies they apply less well still. Elizabethan tragedies are not only much longer and more various in their materials than Greek tragedies but also complete in themselves (each Greek tragedy was part of a trilogy, or tetralogy with the satyr-play) and much less intimately associated with religious and folk ritual than Greek drama. So that we will only be employing certain of Aristotle's terms and certain others; and even so, it has to be recognized that most of both kinds lend themselves better to description than to definition. The terms are: melodrama, tragedy, action, motivation, catastrophe, denouement, pathos, scene, and tempo. (Several others, like dialogue—cf. p. 444 —will be more conveniently treated later in the commentary.) Many other relevant terms, like dramatic or tragic irony, have been treated, of course, in the earlier parts of the book, and others will come up in the exercise on Chekhov's play.

It is important, first, to distinguish between tragedy and melodrama. For "melodrama" [3] a dictionary gives us: "a kind of romantic and sensational drama, crude, sentimental, and conventional, with strict attention to poetic justice and happy endings." This is admittedly rather vague and does not contrast very effectively with the same dictionary's even vaguer definition of "tragedy" [4]—"a species of drama in which the action and language are elevated, and the catastrophe usually sad." But if we take a really fine description of what happens in Shakespearean tragedy, A. C. Bradley's, the contrast with melodrama becomes clearer. "We see a number of human beings," Bradley writes, "placed in certain circumstances;

and we see, arising from the co-operation of their characters in these circumstances, certain actions. These actions beget others, and these others beget others again, until this series of inter-connected deeds leads by an apparently inevitable sequence to a catastrophe. The effect of such a series on imagination is to make us regard the sufferings which accompany it, and the catastrophe in which it ends, not only or chiefly as something which happens to the persons concerned, but equally as something which is caused by them. This at least may be said of the principal persons, and, among them, of the hero, who always contributes in some measure to the disaster in which he perishes. . . . The 'story' or 'action' of a Shakespearean tragedy does not consist, of course, solely of human actions or deeds; but the deeds are the predominant factor. And these deeds are, for the most part, actions in the full sense of the word; not things done ' 'tween asleep and wake,' but acts or omissions thoroughly expressive of the doer,—characteristic deeds. The centre of the tragedy, therefore, may be said with equal truth to lie in action issuing from character, or in character issuing in action" (*Shakespearean Tragedy*, pp. 11–12). If the reader will now look again, having Macbeth in mind and Bradley's words, at the definition of melodrama just quoted, the contrast will appear very great. It is not, indeed, complete, for Shakespearean tragedy is romantic, and there is even a sense in which it may be claimed that *Macbeth* ends happily; but it is decisive.

The other terms may be handled in more summary fashion. "Motive" appears in melodrama as well as in tragedy, but the word "motivation" [5] we will hardly use except for tragedy, referring as it does to a more systematic, as well as more complex, treatment of why the characters do things. So with "catastrophe" [6] ("an overturning: a final event: the climax of the action of the plot in play or novel") and "denouement" [7] ("the unraveling of a plot or story: the issue, event, or outcome")—terms not, by the way, very easy to distinguish. If we use them for melodrama, we will not use them with quite the same bearing as for tragedy, what leads to the catastrophe or denouement being in melodrama merely sequential (one thing after another) whereas in tragedy it is *con*sequential (coming in necessary connection after).

For "pathos" [8] the dictionary is not very helpful: "the quality that raises pity." But anyhow, of the two emotions that Aristotle thought proper to tragedy, pity and terror, the first is much less important in *Macbeth* than the second. Shakespeare's other greatest tragedies depend far more upon the pathetic than *Macbeth*. Its pace,

or "tempo" [9] also differs from theirs: it moves decidedly faster—
even Macbeth's deliberations, and the one quiet scene (that in England), hardly slow its headlong flight toward doom.

The word "scene," [10] finally, is used in quite a different way
in dramatic criticism from the way we use it in everyday life, where
it tends to connote something high-pitched or "dramatic." In the
various national dramatic literatures, it is employed in various
ways. In Shakespeare it refers to a series of speeches, or even a
single speech, after which the stage is cleared of actors.

IV *Plot*

As our study of the language of Shakespeare will have made
clear, a separation of the critical elements, in our investigation of
Macbeth, into plot, characterization, imagery, and theme is highly
artificial. All are interwoven; the play is a tissue of suggestion. The
reason for this is that man's nature is complex. The *ambiguity* of
Macbeth's nature is perhaps the play's major subject. This is the
shortest of Shakespeare's tragedies; it is barely half the length of
Hamlet. It follows that the intellectual and artistic work that is being
done in the play is being done, even more than is the case in the
other tragedies, in terms not of statement but of suggestiveness.

At the same time, it is useful to describe the essential action,
because it is that to which everything else contributes, and on which
everything else depends. The action is extremely simple. A man is
tempted, falls, suffers, his nature changes, and he is killed. Such a
statement does not tell us very much about the play. But it does suggest to us at once the fundamental difference between *Macbeth* and
a mystery novel. Here there is no question of suspense about who
has done the deed; the suspense is about how *Fate* will work itself
out. And of course Macbeth is not the only person in the play.

Elizabethan Englishmen, including King James, did not feel as
we do about the supernatural. They regarded it as a serious topic—
just as the American philosopher William James did, for that matter,
three hundred years later. The Witches are fundamental to the play.
Technically, they form an enveloping action,[11] oracular in nature. But
the element they represent, the supernatural (the presiding, we might
say, except that this term raises problems that we can only touch
later), reaches and operates inside the action also; so that our description of the plot can hardly leave it out.

In fact we must begin with it. Act I consists of: an initial statement about the fundamental ambiguity of Nature ("Fair is foul, and
foul is fair") by the Witches; an external war which turns out also

to be a civil war, owing to the treachery of the Thane of Cawdor; a prediction to Macbeth, the hero of this war, that he will inherit the (sinister) thaneship of Cawdor, and then become actually King; a debate within himself, like the civil war, conducted on progressive levels—first silently, as he stands enthralled with the Cawdor news of the Scottish lords, next in soliloquy (I:vii:1ff; the dialogue with his wife at the end of I:v shows him so taciturn that it is best grouped with the silence and asides of the heath), then in controversy with his wife, winding up first in a declaration that he will *not* go on, then in a statement of their plan. You will have noticed already the alternation of outer and inner struggle. And the feast, or supper, for Duncan, as victorious and kindly King, as kinsman (first cousin to Macbeth), and as guest, in a society where the relation of host to guest was a grave ethical matter—during which the debate between the murdering couple takes place—already symbolizes the concord of the State which is to be wrecked.

The ironic and terrible concord of murderer and victim is symbolized by the Banquet in Act III (where the chaos of the State is openly dramatized). These are the fruits. Meanwhile, the uncertain weather of Act I (moral weather for the Witches, made physical weather by Macbeth in his first line, "So foul and fair a day I have not seen") has settled for *night* in Act II, which is about the deed. It begins with Banquo's ambitious, troubled dreams about the Three Sisters, and its supernatural phenomena are the apparitions of the Dagger, and the Voice—one leading to the deed, the other forecasting its consequences.

In the murder scene several points need emphasis. The succession of short, nervous questions exchanged between husband and wife, directly following the murder, suggests the uncertainty of the new world they have just entered by committing the murder. But this is only the most tense passage of this sort; critics have remarked on the fact that no other play of Shakespeare's is so *full* of questions—of doubt, of mystery. Then the terror of the offstage deed needs expressive outlet somehow, and gets it in Macbeth's terrible, crescendoing speeches about the Voice. *This* is the new single certainty: that sleep is gone. Macbeth clearly is hysterical in these speeches (reaction after murder), and the tone lifts so high that relief is necessary. It is provided at once in the Hell-soliloquy of the porter. But this is not merely comic relief, of course; it is very rare in Shakespeare to find anything that serves one purpose only; and what is probably the most famous essay in all Shakespearian criticism is devoted to a study of this passage, Thomas De Quincey's "On the Knocking at the

Gate in *Macbeth*." The *noise,* after the terrible silence, like a re-
entry into the play of the real world, suspended during the murder,
is staggering in the theatre; but a good reader will hear it also for himself in "Knock, knock, knock!" And Lady Macbeth's confident "A
little water clears us of this deed" is succeeded by "the primrose
way to the everlasting bonfire." The essential irony of the passage is
simple: the porter thinks that he is just joking about "hell-gate" and
"this place is too cold for hell," whereas the audience sees that with
Macbeth's deed Hell has been let into the world.

With Act III we see Macbeth seated in power, and learn at once
his sense that he has accomplished nothing at all:

> To be thus is nothing,
> But to be *safely* thus.

He sets at once to his new purpose, the murder of Banquo and
Fleance. Note that he does *not* employ, or even fully confide in, Lady
Macbeth, and that he sets a third murderer to watch his original
two. These are the beginnings (or continuations, for already Malcolm
and Donalbain have stolen away) of the situation of universal distrust which come to a climax in the scene in England in Act IV and
the denudation of Macbeth in Act V. After Duncan has been murdered by Macbeth, who can trust anyone? Macbeth is now fully in
alliance with the powers of darkness, and fully at the mercy of his
own nerves. The very strange tone created for him by the poet in this
Act partly accounts for one cardinal mystery of this most demonic
of tragedies: that he does not lose the audience's or reader's sympathy.

> O, full of scorpions is my mind, dear wife!

he says, and "be thou jocund," and

> Be innocent of the knowledge, dearest chuck,
> Till thou applaud the deed.

This combination of the domestic with the terrible is unbelievably
sinister, and grotesque. But it is also pathetic, when we hear it in
connection with his fierce suffering and hopeless longing:

> Better be with the dead,
> Whom we, to gain our peace, have sent to peace,
> Than on the torture of the mind to lie
> In restless ecstasy.

His strangeness, then, and his suffering, and also the fact that he is
not *profiting* from his crimes, help to explain the fact that he does
not alienate us. But we will have more to say about this in Section V.

It remains to be noticed that the feast of Act I has moved onstage to become the banquet of Act III, so that we now *see* the atrocious linkage made by Macbeth between hospitality and murder. The fact also that it is Banquo murdered, who was declaring "In the great hand of God I stand," is striking: God seems altogether remote here in the central Act—a place of the Witches, the tyrant, the murderers, the Ghost.

Act IV is much lower in key than any of the first three Acts, as is usual in Shakespearean tragedy. Such tension cannot and ought not to be sustained. First there is the Witches' spectacle, hard only on the nerves of Macbeth, an ironic or sycophantic pleasure to its first audience; then the short pathetic scene of the killings at Fife; then the long—very long—scene in England of the tempting of Macduff. Clearly there is nothing high here. But the scenes are not unrelated: the first ruins Macbeth's dynastic hopes, the second completes the ruin of his moral claims, the third looks to the ruin of his security. The essential subject, then, is still Macbeth. About the long third scene certain points are worth notice. Its length—how *long* it takes for Malcolm to become assured of Macduff's sincerity—is itself a profound instruction in how deeply trust has been corrupted under Macbeth; as Macduff's sturdiness under Malcolm's progressive "revelations" tells us how low hopes have sunk under the tyrant. It is hard, now, for men to believe each other, and they expect little or nothing; the realm is chaos. Against this chaos in the North is set a realm in concord, England, such concord that the King, instead of being himself a thing of evil, is able to cure evil by "touching" (IV: iii:140ff)—as James I had in fact been doing. This manifestation of a *benevolent* supernatural force is set by the dramatist against all the supernatural evil that has preceded it; critics who take the passage as a gratuitous compliment to King James have hardly done it justice. It looks forward, too, to the discrediting of the Witches' guarantees (about the wood moving and "no man *born*") which takes place in the final Act.

After this long respite—if it is one—from the Scottish horrors, we are returned in Act V *not* to Macbeth directly but to his wife, in the most ghastly scene of all, where truth, after all the deception and pretense, emerges in the delirium of the sleep-walking scene. Except for this deep inward look, and several magnificent speeches, Act V is huddled, exhausted, and external—evil has worn itself out; the great final gestures of Hamlet, Othello, Lear, are not possible here, and Macbeth can only die in a warlike parody of himself as the fighting hero we first met him as.

v   *Character*

Most of us never get to know many other human beings very well—even our closest friends, even our husbands and wives, above all our children, even ourselves. Our experience of them is discontinuous, our attention uneven, our judgment and understanding uncertain. Let us mark off at once, then, certain advantages and disadvantages, as against the experience of character in life, enjoyed and suffered by the dramatist in creating character. He has no face or body to work with, only two or three hours to work in—less, because plays are about several people; but our experience of his people is much less discontinuous than our experience of others generally is in life, our attention is acute, and we have *his* understanding and judgment to go by, as well as our own. In one very important respect the means available to him are similar to what happens in life: we know people, perhaps, chiefly by their *voices*—their individual, indescribable, unmistakable voices—and the creation of an individual *tone* for each of his major characters is of course one of the clearest signs of a good playwright. In this particular strength Shakespeare is agreed to be peerless. But the playwright has also two immense advantages over life—"clumsy life," as Henry James put it, "about its stupid work." Even when someone *wants* to reveal himself to another person, he is usually not very good at it, and probably most people spend most of their lives in self-concealment; but self-revelation [12] is a large part of the creation of dramatic character. Moreover, in life we seldom enjoy really informed, highly focused comment by others *on* the person who interests us; and this in drama is the rest of the essence—unless we add that *significant* action plays at least as striking a role in the revelation of character in drama as it does in life, while *insignificant,* distracting action is excluded altogether, enforcing a kind of concentration very rare in ordinary experience.

But not much action, after all, occurs in plays—in *Macbeth* there is some fighting, some eating, no doubt some walking up and down. Plays consist of *talk*. The talk is not conversation. Conversation occurs when several people are talking. In a play, only one person is talking—the author—*through* his characters, *about* them, to the audience. Therefore there is, as there is not in conversation, one absolutely continuous subject, which is the characters and the action (it has been convenient, in our discussion, to distinguish between the characters and the action or plot, but really this is misleading: the actions of Macbeth are not more meaningful apart from his character than his character would be apart from them). Everything said, in short, is, ideally, functional—as very few things indeed are in life; so that the connotations of the word "dialogue" [13] are remote from those of the word "conversation." Even when a line of dialogue is so unstylized, or "natural," that it might occur in conversation, it is easy to show that the purpose it serves in its play is quite unlike the purposes of conversation. For instance, Olivia in *Twelfth Night* is the subject of a good deal of dialogue before we see or hear her: we learn that she is young, noble, wealthy, beautiful, and living secluded, in mourning—she is always spoken of, as it were, *upward,* with love, admiration, longing. Then she enters, and says brusquely, "Take the Fool away." The purpose of this unexpected remark is to naturalize, so to speak, the large and gracious image one has formed of her—to give it a voice different enough from expectation to show the audience that that image was only the *beginning* of our understanding of her, though not so inconsonant with the image as to contradict it, and to create for her a tone that convinces, makes an illusion of life. Elizabethan noblewomen no doubt said, from time to time, "Take the Fool away"— meaning nothing but "Take the Fool away."

We might approach the characters of Lady Macbeth and Macbeth through one of her observations about him in her soliloquy (I:v:21–22):

> What thou wouldst highly,
> That wouldst thou holily . . .

Here is a remark unlike any ever made by an actual human being since the beginning of speech—as unlike life as a great work of music is unlike anyone's humming. Its *subject* is life, but the means is high art, *just as* the means—the true means—of "Take the Fool away" was. What is Shakespeare telling us, through Lady Macbeth, about Macbeth and about herself? Macbeth is ambitious, but an idealist. Now Lady Macbeth is ambitious also, as the whole soliloquy sufficiently shows. But the tone of contempt in "holily"—extraordinary word!—tells us that she not only possesses no such double nature herself but complains of it in him. Lady Macbeth's character—about which so much has been written—is very simple. She is unscrupulous, but short-winded. No doubts beset her, except about the steadfastness of her accomplice. Singlenatured, she is even willing to lose the nature she has ("Unsex me here") in order to accomplish her purpose. But, nihilistic, she has no staying power. Macbeth stays the course. By Act III she has already ceased to matter, weary, plunging toward insanity and suicide. The nature was shallow from the beginning, with its confidence that "A little water clears us from this deed"; only ambition mobilizes it, and only the horror of guilt can deepen it. There are just enough touches of sensibility—her analysis of her husband, and "Had he not resembled / My father as he slept, I had done't"—to make her seem lifelike.

Lady Macbeth, in short, has no idea of what she is getting into. Now the reason she is conceived in this way, of course, is that she may throw a contrasting light on her husband, who is double-natured, heroic, uncertainly wicked, both loyal and faithless, meditative and violent, and *does* know what he is getting into. This knowledge of his is the real burden of the great soliloquy in I:vii:

> If it were done when 'tis done, then 'twere well
> It were done quickly.

The first "done" here means "finished," and the lines that follow show that what Macbeth has in mind is far deeper and more savage than any mere not-getting-away-with-the-murder, so to speak. Macbeth believes in "justice," and is afraid of teaching his own assassin (later) what to do; and he believes in eternal life, punishment, and would like to *skip* it ("jump the life to come"). He *believes;* his wife believes in nothing except her own ambition and her own guilt. He is also given to us as "brave," and "deserving" to be so called, and "worthy," and "frank," and he is full of scruples. But he has another nature. He is envious, ambitious, and hypocritical (the reasons he gives his wife, at I:vii:31ff, for not proceeding, are quite different from the reasons he has just given himself). Therefore he can be tempted. Shakespeare holds the balance exquisitely even between supernatural *solicitation* to evil (original) and supernatural *encouragement* to evil (secondary), as in Macbeth's line to the apparitional dagger:

> Thou marshall'st me the way that I was going.

Holding the balance even is really to ask: does it matter? Does it matter, that is, whether man falls in with temptation or just falls? The world is certainly full of temptations, whether created by nature or by the underworld of man's nature.

This duality of Macbeth is what makes the play possible; it also accounts for the ambiguity, the mystery, that characterizes the play throughout. But it only partly accounts—in a way to be taken up in the next Section—for his hold upon the audience's or reader's sympathy. This is primarily a response to the imagination with which his creator has endowed Macbeth. His imagination mediates between his two natures, expressing and accounting for both, and projecting itself also into the future, in a way inaccessible to Lady Macbeth. One minute before she is bleating about "A little water," he has said:

> Will all great Neptune's ocean wash this blood
> Clean from my hand? No; this my hand will rather
> The multitudinous seas incarnadine,
> Making the green one red.

His mysterious brooding has scarcely a parallel elsewhere even in Shakespeare's work. Increasingly, as the play advances, its antithetical subjects are cruelty and his own suffering; hand in hand these move, until the universe seems to consist of nothing else. There is nothing in *Macbeth* so intolerable as the last Act of *Othello,* but no other Shakespearian tragedy is so desolate, and this desolation is conveyed to us through the fantastic imagination of its hero.

The course of action adopted by Macbeth, however, changes his nature, as we saw in Section 2, and the celebrated description of life as meaningless (at V:v:19ff.)—which has been so often and foolishly taken for Shakespeare's own conviction—is that of a man who is sickening to his end, who has ceased to be a man, who has acted himself—so to speak—out of his beliefs.

Duncan's character is fundamental also to Macbeth's fate. His mark is generosity, trust—even to foolishness, as is made plain at once, when he says of Cawdor the traitor:

> He was a gentleman on whom I built
> An absolute trust . . .

Such trust, Shakespeare is suggesting, *invites* treachery; so that, in some degree, Macbeth is merely co-operating. Such foolish trust leads also to the necessity of the depth of morbid *distrust* Duncan's son Malcolm feels obliged to display in Act IV. A certain natural suspicion, we may generalize, is a reasonable attribute in a ruler.

VI *Imagery and Theme*

Every reader of *Macbeth* notices the word "blood." From "What bloody man is that?" (I:ii:1) to "thou bloodier villain / Than terms can give thee out" (V:viii:7) the noun and its derivatives darken the play. Critics have given statistics for it; all you have to do is count the number of occurrences in Bartlett's *Concordance to Shakespeare's Works*. But more important than statistics are: one way in particular in which it is used, and the fact that it is often suggested without being stated. In the Witches' dialogue (I:iii:1–2) we hear:

> Where hast thou been, sister?
> Killing swine.

Though the word does not even occur, the idea or *image* is present even to inundation, a flood of blood, such as spurts from a stuck pig. The same thing is true of Lady Macbeth's ghastly "yet who would have thought the old man to have had so much blood in him?" (V:i:45), and accounts—along with the coarse insolence of her reference to the King, guest, benefactor, as "old man"—for the power of this celebrated line. We have blood not only everywhere, then, but swarming. Moreover, in a number of other very powerful passages, the audience or reader is compelled to imagine blood for itself even more specifically than in the "swine" passage.

> It will have blood, they say: blood will have blood

Macbeth mutters to himself (III:iv:122). Here the mysterious "It" is explained immediately—murder cries out for retribution—and yet the force of its initial, dreadful vagueness is not dissipated by the explanation. The horrible suggestion is in fact made, by the explanation, that anything in the universe not at once identified as something else *is blood;* and iteration of the actual word thrice in one line assists the suggestion. As a man thinks of his wife not by name but as "she" and "her," so Macbeth thinks of *his* topic—blood, the murder—as "it": central, permanent, a point to which other things are referred. The implied picture of his mind makes one shudder. This is psychological. The physical counterpart we hear at V:ii:16–17, with Angus's

> Now does he feel
> His secret murders sticking on his hands. . . .

This can only be blood, as private as the floods of blood just discussed were public, blood ineradicable, intimate (and one thinks of Lady Macbeth's "A little water" and Macbeth's "This my hand will rather / The multitudinous seas incarnadine"); you notice that the verb is practically a pun—what sticks cannot be got rid of.

Now an ordinary play just tells its story, more or less efficiently. Clearly a Shakespearean play is concerned with something different as well: the presentment and enforcing, through imagery as well as through action and character, of a human experience complex and drenched, so to speak, as well as of a view of it similarly complex. Among the most brilliant results of twentieth-century Shakespearean criticism have been the studies of his imagery by Caroline Spurgeon, Msgr. F. C. Kolbe, Wolfgang Clemen, Edward A. Armstrong, and others. These studies have been little hampered by the fact that no satisfactory definition of "imagery" is really possible; thus also have modern astronomers been able to learn a good deal about a universe

which they are quite unable to define. We would *like* to take the word
to refer to any representation in language of that which makes its
appeal primarily to the *senses*. One *feels*, for instance, the word
"sticking" as one does not feel, say, the word "as," which is a purely
relational term. "Blood" is seen, smelled, felt, can even be tasted, as
the word "position," say, cannot. But language, representing or em-
bodying as it does the operations of the human mind, does not lend
itself easily to these pigeonholes. Take the word "sleep": is it abstract
or sensual? Shakespeare makes it, in *Macbeth,* sensual enough, and
we get an elaborate image-pattern. Worse still, a clear abstraction, like
the word or idea "confusion," can be treated so obsessively and dra-
matically, as it is in *Macbeth,* that one has an impression that one is
experiencing images. For example: "incarnadine" is plainly, or presents plainly, an image, visual, whereas "multitudinous" does not—
or does it? The sensing and reflecting aspects of the mind are not so
readily distinguished, except at their outer edges.

Just so, the reader responds both emotionally and intellectually
to the image-patterns. One both suffers and enjoys (understands) the
Blood image-pattern: one recoils emotionally, *and* sees its point—
that "blood will have blood," there is Nemesis, and this is satisfying,
in a world so terrifying and chaotic as the world of *Macbeth.*

But the Blood image-pattern is not of course given to us in isolation. There are other patterns, in the absence of which, indeed, the
Blood-pattern itself would have much less than its actual effectiveness
and meaning. One critic (Msgr. Kolbe, in *Shakespeare's Way,* London, 1930) connects the Blood-pattern with the Sleep-pattern, which
not only forms the burden of several overwhelming speeches by
Macbeth and of the Sleep-walking scene but receives heavy emphasis
in speeches by Banquo (II:i:4–10), the Witches (I:iii:19ff, etc.),
and others; and with these two patterns he associates what he calls a
Dark-pattern—one of the most striking things in the play, of which
the student will easily discover examples for himself. These he generalizes very simply as resulting from the nature of the crime: "Duncan's *blood* was shed during his *sleep* in the middle of the *night.*"
But all this is still preparatory.

Msgr. Kolbe has half a dozen pages of quotation showing that
Ambiguity, Confusion, *resulting* from this three-fold nature of the
crime, "is even more pervasive . . . than . . . Blood": "Fair is
foul . . . broil . . . his country's wrack . . ."

> Shakes so my single state of man, that function
> Is smother'd in surmise, and nothing is
> But what is not . . .

"Unsex me here"—these from Act I alone. He notes, of "Double, double toil and trouble," in Act IV, that "The ingredients of the cauldron form a hell-broth of chaotic incongruities." (The Cambridge editors' brilliant conjecture "and none," for the Folio's "and move" at IV:ii:22, accepted now by Dover Wilson and Peter Alexander, has really to be studied in this context of Msgr. Kolbe's:

> when we hold rumor
> From what we fear, yet know not what we fear,
> But float upon a wild and violent sea
> Each way, and none. . . .)

These three patterns are then explained by the critic as follows: ". . . in this story of a great Temptation issuing in a great Crime, resulting in a great Retribution, Shakespeare has intensely individualized the sinners and the sin, but has universalized the consequences of the sin." Is a framework discernible for the patterns so far discovered? Msgr. Kolbe finds one in the antithesis throughout between the forces of Sin (witches, demons, spells, damnation, curses, hell, falsehood, doom) and the forces of Grace (angels, mercy, pity, justice, prayer, blessing, providence, truth). Again the reader will want to follow the development of the antithesis for himself in the text. But at least two parallelisms ought to be noted briefly. Behind Macbeth stand the Witches, behind Malcolm the "gracious" (the word is from "grace" of course, which then itself occurs, IV:iii:189) King of England; and the expression "By the worst means, the worst" near the beginning is exactly balanced by the extraordinary phrase "by the grace of Grace" as almost the last words of the play (V:viii:72).

Clearly, the study of imagery emerges even more directly and rapidly into *theme* than does the study of plot or of character. The reason for this is that both plot and character tend to be more explicitly formulated in the artist's mind than either theme or imagery. In the case of a play like *Macbeth,* no formulation can ever hope to exhaust either theme or imagery. It will hardly be wrong, however, to suggest that one of the major themes of *Macbeth* is the exploration, in a very gifted and ambiguous and active man, of Man's possibilities downward. It is *our* lower nature, as well as our higher, to which we attend in Macbeth; hence our sympathy. One critic (the late Donald Stauffer) once remarked that the King-murder obviously symbolizes Macbeth's murder of his own higher faculties. He picks his line, for evil, and is thenceforward committed to it. How briefly evil flourishes, how rapidly it succumbs to exhaustion (leaving out of account altogether, here, the *narrative* element of its overthrow from outside), is one of the dramatist's cardinal points, even in the dark state of mind in which Shakespeare was when he wrote this play. (The evil which in his directly preceding tragedy, *King Lear,* is reserved to definite villains—Edmund, the elder sisters, Cornwall—is here incorporated with his hero and heroine; and his next work was one of almost universal disillusion, *Antony and Cleopatra.*) Macbeth has no emotion left even for the death of his wife (the contrast here is with Macduff's reception of *his* news). Evil dehumanizes and wears itself out.

Needless to say, the image-patterns we have glanced at here are not the only ones in the play. Others that have been particularly studied are the Clothes-pattern, the Animal-pattern, the Disease-pattern, the Discord-Concord-pattern. This last pattern is so closely associated with Msgr. Kolbe's Confusion-pattern that perhaps they ought to be identified. One theme in this pattern is worth special notice: the images of Milk. "I fear thy nature," Lady Macbeth says,

> It is too full o' the milk of human kindness
> To catch the nearest way.

Two minutes later:

> Come to my woman's breasts
> And take my milk for gall, you murd'ring ministers . . .

Malcolm, in his pretense to Macduff, says:

> Nay, had I pow'r, I should
> Pour the sweet milk of concord into hell . . .

Here we have a triple association of that which *nourishes* and is bound to the ideas of "kindness" and "concord," with the ideas "fear," "gall," "hell," producing, for the reader, a sense of chaos, of the unnatural, which is fundamental to the play. We begin, as human beings, with milk—we end, in this play, in blood—and the patterns are set against each other in such a way as to suggest that the whole spectrum of human possibilities is being explored, with dismay. Images of courtship, procreation, infancy, allied to the Milk-pattern, intensify the irony, as in Banquo's speech on arriving at Macbeth's castle: "wooingly . . . bed . . . procreant cradle" (I:vi:6–8)—the birthing, here, is to be a murder—and Macbeth's

> Pity, like a naked new-born babe,
> Striding the blast,

and Lady Macbeth's terrifying

> I have given suck, and know
> How tender 'tis to love the babe that milks me:
> I would, while it was smiling in my face,

Have plucked my nipple from his boneless gums,
And dashed the brains out, had I so sworn
As you have done to this.

Images—and ideas, as in this solemn undertaking of Macbeth's to do evil—which in nature are wholly separate and opposed, are joined by the dramatist. The interweaving of the consequent patterns is one of the aspects of the tragedy which the reader will want to explore further for himself.

TERMS AND PRINCIPLES

1. *Closet drama:* A play or plays intended to be read rather than acted.
2. *Speech-prefix:* The speaker's name prefixed to a speech.
3. *Melodrama:* Drama romantic and sensational, as a rule inadequately motivated and therefore crude; and sentimental, with strict attention to a conventionally conceived poetic justice and to a happy ending.
4. *Tragedy:* Drama in which the action and language are elevated, and the catastrophe usually sad. But see the text of the commentary.
5. *Motivation:* The systematic and concrete attribution of motive, by a dramatist, to his characters. Men's motives for what they do, in life, are regularly complex, and so in serious drama various motives are shown as woven into a strand that effectively simulates reality.
6. *Catastrophe:* An overturning: a final event; the climax of the action of the plot.
7. *Denouement:* The unraveling of a plot or story; the issue, event, or outcome. The word is used much as "catastrophe" is, but lacks the connotation of disaster which usually accompanies "catastrophe."
8. *Pathos:* In drama, the quality said to characterize the representation of what excites pity.
9. *Tempo:* Pace, the speed at which a play or a part of a play proceeds.
10. *Scene:* A division of a play marked off by the fall of the curtain or by the clearing of the stage of actors. This is the usual modern and Shakespearean sense, though exceptions will be found to it here and there; and the convention in Latin and French drama is quite different.
11. *Enveloping action:* An action which forms a surrounding context for the principal action.

12. *Self-revelation:* The device whereby characters explain directly (or almost directly) to the audience what is in their minds. The soliloquies of Macbeth and Lady Macbeth are the chief examples in this play, but her speeches in the sleep-walking scene may also be considered as self-revelation.

13. *Dialogue:* The conversation, usually formal or imaginary, of two or more persons. See the commentary for some suggested differences between dialogue and ordinary conversation.

ANTON CHEKHOV

A Marriage Proposal

A Joke in One Act

CHARACTERS

STEPAN STEPANOVICH CHUBUKOV, *a landowner, elderly, pompous but affable*

IVAN VASSILEVITCH LOMOV, *healthy, but a hypochondriac; nervous, suspicious. Also a landowner*

NATALIA STEPANOVNA, *Chubukov's daughter; twenty-five but still unmarried*

Chubukov's mansion—the living room

[LOMOV *enters, formally dressed in evening jacket, white gloves, top hat. He is nervous from the start.*]

CHUBUKOV [*Rising*].   Well, look who's here! Ivan Vassilevitch! [*Shakes his hand warmly.*] What a surprise, old man! How are you?

LOMOV.   Oh, not too bad. And you?

CHUBUKOV.   Oh, we manage, we manage. Do sit down, please. You know, you've been neglecting your neighbours, my dear fellow. It's been ages. Say, why the formal dress? Tails, gloves, and so forth. Where's the funeral, my boy? Where are you headed?

LOMOV.   Oh, nowhere. I mean, here; just to see you, my dear Stepan Stepanovitch.

CHUBUKOV.   Then why the full dress, old boy? It's not New Year's, and so forth.

LOMOV.   Well, you see, it's like this. I have come here, my dear Stepan Stepanovitch, to bother you with a request. More than once, or twice, or more than that, it has been my privilege to apply to you for assistance in things, and you've always, well, responded. I mean, well, you have. Yes. Excuse me, I'm getting all mixed up. May I have a glass of water, my dear Stepan Stepanovitch? [*Drinks.*]

CHUBUKOV [*Aside*].   Wants to borrow some money. Not a chance! [*Aloud.*] What can I do for you my dear friend?

LOMOV.   Well, you see, my dear Stepanitch . . . Excuse me, I mean Stepan my Dearovitch . . . No, I mean, I get all confused, as you can see. To make a long story short, you're the only one who can help me. Of course, I don't deserve it, and there's no reason why I should expect you to, and all that.

CHUBUKOV.   Stop beating around the bush! Out with it!

LOMOV.   In just a minute. I mean, now, right now. The truth is, I have come to ask the hand . . . I mean, your daughter, Natalia Stepanovna, I, I want to marry her!

CHUBUKOV [*Overjoyed*].   Great heavens! Ivan Vassilevitch! Say it again!

LOMOV.   I have come humbly to ask for the hand . . .

CHUBUKOV [*Interrupting*].   You're a prince! I'm overwhelmed, delighted, and so forth. Yes, indeed, and all that! [*Hugs and kisses* LOMOV.] This is just what I've been hoping for. It's my fondest dream come true. [*Sheds a tear.*] And, you know, I've always looked upon you, my boy, as if you were my own son. May God grant to both of you His Mercy and His Love, and so forth. Oh, I have been wishing for this . . . But why am I being so idiotic? It's just that I'm off my rocker with joy, my boy! Completely off my rocker! Oh, with all my soul I'm . . . I'll go get Natalia, and so forth.

LOMOV [*Deeply moved*].   Dear Stepan Stepanovitch, do you think she'll agree?

CHUBUKOV.   Why, of course, old friend. Great heavens! As if she wouldn't! Why she's crazy for you! Good God! Like a love-sick cat, and so forth. Be right back. [*Leaves.*]

LOMOV.   God, it's cold. I'm gooseflesh all over, as if I had to take a test. But the main thing is, to make up my mind, and keep it that way. I mean, if I take time out to think, or if I hesitate, or talk about it, or have ideals, or wait for real love, well, I'll just never get married! Brrrr, it's cold! Natalia Stepanovna is an excellent house-keeper. She's not too bad looking. She's had a good education. What more could I ask? Nothing. I'm so nervous, my ears are buzzing. [*Drinks*.] Besides, I've just got to get married. I'm thirty-five already. It's sort of a critical age. I've got to settle down and lead a regular life. I mean, I'm always getting palpitations, and I'm nervous, and I get upset so easy. Look, my lips are quivering, and my eyebrow's twitching. The worst thing is the night. Sleeping. I get into bed, doze off, and, suddenly, something inside me jumps. First my head snaps, and then my shoulder blade, and I roll out of bed like a lunatic and try to walk it off. Then I try to go back to sleep, but, as soon as I do, something jumps again! Twenty times a night, sometimes . . .

[NATALIA STEPANOVNA *enters*.]

NATALIA. Oh, it's only you. All Papa said was: "Go inside, there's a merchant come to collect his goods." How do you do, Ivan Vassilevitch?

LOMOV. How do you do, dear Natalia Stepanovna?

NATALIA. Excuse my apron, and not being dressed. We're shelling peas. You haven't been around lately. Oh, do sit down. [*They do*.] Would you like some lunch?

LOMOV. No thanks, I had some.

NATALIA. Well, then smoke if you want. [*He doesn't*.] The weather's nice today . . . but yesterday, it was so wet the workmen couldn't get a thing done. Have you got much hay in? I felt so greedy I had a whole field done, but now I'm not sure I was right. With the rain it could rot, couldn't it? I should have waited. But why are you so dressed up? Is there a dance or something? Of course, I must say you look splendid, but . . . Well, tell me, why are you so dressed up?

LOMOV [*Excited*]. Well, you see, my dear Natalia Stepanovna, the truth is, I made up my mind to ask you to . . . well, to, listen to me. Of course, it'll probably surprise you and even maybe make you angry, but . . . [*Aside*.] God, it's cold in here!

NATALIA. Why, what do you mean? [*A pause*.] Well?

LOMOV.   I'll try to get it over with. I mean, you know, my dear Natalia Stepanovna that I've known, since childhood, even, known, and had the privilege of knowing, your family. My late aunt, and her husband, who, as you know, left me my estate, they always had the greatest respect for your father, and your late mother. The Lomovs and the Chubukovs have always been very friendly, you might even say affectionate. And, of course, you know, our land borders on each other's. My Oxen Meadows touch your birch grove . . .

NATALIA.   I hate to interrupt you, my dear Ivan Vassilevitch, but you said: "my Oxen Meadows." Do you really think they're yours?

LOMOV.   Why of course they're mine.

NATALIA.   What do you mean? The Oxen Meadows are ours, not yours!

LOMOV.   Oh, no, my dear Natalia Stepanovna, they're mine.

NATALIA.   Well, this is the first I've heard about it! Where did you get that idea?

LOMOV.   Where? Why, I mean the Oxen Meadows that are wedged between your birches and the marsh.

NATALIA.   Yes, of course, they're ours.

LOMOV.   Oh, no, you're wrong, my dear Natalia Stepanovna, they're mine.

NATALIA.   Now, come, Ivan Vassilevitch! How long have they been yours?

LOMOV.   How long? Why, as long as I can remember!

NATALIA.   Well, really, you can't expect me to believe that!

LOMOV.   But, you can see for yourself in the deed, my dear Natalia Stepanovna. Of course, there was once a dispute about them, but everyone knows they're mine now. There's nothing to argue about. There was a time when my aunt's grandmother let your father's grandfather's peasants use the land, but they were supposed to bake bricks for her in return. Naturally, after a few years they began to act as if they owned it, but the real truth is . . .

NATALIA.   That has nothing to do with the case! Both my grandfather and my great-grandfather said that their land went as far as the marsh, which means that the Meadows are ours! There's nothing whatever to argue about. It's foolish.

LOMOV.   But I can show you the deed, Natalia Stepanovna.

NATALIA.   You're just making fun of me . . . Great Heavens! Here we have the land for hundreds of years, and suddenly you try to tell us it isn't ours. What's wrong with you, Ivan Vassilevitch? Those meadows aren't even fifteen acres, and they're not worth three hundred rubles, but I just can't stand unfairness! I just can't stand unfairness!

LOMOV.   But, you must listen to me. Your father's grandfather's peasants, as I've already tried to tell you, they were supposed to bake bricks for my aunt's grandmother. And my aunt's grandmother, why, she wanted to be nice to them . . .

NATALIA.   It's just nonsense, this whole business about aunts and grandfathers and grandmothers. The Meadows are ours! That's all there is to it!

LOMOV.   They're mine!

NATALIA.   Ours! You can go on talking for two days, and you can put on fifteen evening coats and twenty pairs of gloves, but I tell you they're ours, ours, ours!

LOMOV.   Natalia Stepanovna, I don't want the Meadows! I'm just acting on principle. If you want, I'll give them to you.

NATALIA.   I'll give them to *you!* Because they're ours! And that's all there is to it! And if I may say so, your behaviour, my dear Ivan Vassilevitch, is very strange. Until now, we've always considered you a good neighbour, even a friend. After all, last year we lent you our threshing machine, even though it meant putting off our own threshing until November. And here you are treating us like a pack of gypsies. Giving me my own land, indeed! Really! Why that's not being a good neighbour. It's sheer impudence, that's what it is . . .

LOMOV.   Oh, so you think I'm just a land-grabber? My dear lady, I've never grabbed anybody's land in my whole life, and no-one's going to accuse me of doing it now! [*Quickly walks over to the pitcher and drinks some more water.*] The Oxen Meadows are mine!

NATALIA.   That's a lie. They're ours!

LOMOV.   Mine!

NATALIA.   A lie! I'll prove it. I'll send my mowers out there today!

LOMOV.   What?

NATALIA.   My mowers will mow it today!

LOMOV.   I'll kick them out!

NATALIA.   You just dare!

LOMOV [*Clutching his heart*].   The Oxen Meadows are mine! Do you understand? Mine!

NATALIA.   Please don't shout! You can shout all you want in your own house, but here I must ask you to control yourself.

LOMOV.   If my heart wasn't palpitating the way it is, if my insides weren't jumping like mad, I wouldn't talk to you so calmly. [*Yelling.*] The Oxen Meadows are mine!

NATALIA.   Ours!

LOMOV.   Mine!

NATALIA.   Ours!

LOMOV.   Mine!

[*Enter* CHUBUKOV.]

CHUBUKOV.   What's going on? Why all the shouting?

NATALIA.   Papa, will you please inform this gentleman who owns the Oxen Meadows, he or we?

CHUBUKOV [*To* LOMOV].   Why, they're ours, old fellow.

LOMOV.   But how can they be yours, my dear Stepan Stepanovitch? Be fair. Perhaps my aunt's grandmother did let your grandfather's peasants work the land, and maybe they did get so used to it that they acted as if it was their own, but . . .

CHUBUKOV.   Oh, no, no . . . my dear boy. You forget something. The reason the peasants didn't pay your aunt's grandmother, and so forth, was that the land was disputed, even then. Since then it's been settled. Why, everyone knows it's ours.

LOMOV.   I can prove it's mine.

CHUBUKOV.   You can't prove a thing, old boy.

LOMOV.   Yes I can!

CHUBUKOV.   My dear lad, why yell like that? Yelling doesn't prove a thing. Look, I'm not after anything of yours, just as I don't intend to give up anything of mine. Why should I? Besides, if you're going to keep arguing about it, I'd just as soon give the land to the peasants, so there!

LOMOV. There nothing! Where do you get the right to give away someone else's property?

CHUBUKOV. I certainly ought to know if I have the right or not. And you had better realize it, because, my dear young man, I am not used to being spoken to in that tone of voice, and so forth. Besides which, my dear young man, I am twice as old as you are, and I ask you to speak to me without getting yourself into such a tizzy, and so forth!

LOMOV. Do you think I'm a fool? First you call my property yours, and then you expect me to keep calm and polite! Good neighbours don't act like that, my dear Stepan Stepanovitch. You're no neighbour, you're a land grabber!

CHUBUKOV. What was that? What did you say?

NATALIA. Papa, send the mowers out to the meadows at once!

CHUBUKOV. What did you say, sir?

NATALIA. The Oxen Meadows are ours, and we'll never give them up, never, never, never, never!

LOMOV. We'll see about that. I'll go to court. I'll show you!

CHUBUKOV. Go to court? Well, go to court, and so forth! I know you, just waiting for a chance to go to court, and so forth. You pettifogging shyster, you! All of your family is like that. The whole bunch of them!

LOMOV. You leave my family out of this! The Lomovs have always been honourable, upstanding people, and not a one of them was ever tried for embezzlement, like your grandfather was.

CHUBUKOV. The Lomovs are a pack of lunatics, the whole bunch of them!

NATALIA. The whole bunch!

CHUBUKOV. Your grandfather was a drunkard, and what about your other aunt, the one who ran away with the architect? And so forth.

NATALIA.   And so forth!

LOMOV.   Your mother was a hunch back! [*Clutches at his heart*.] Oh, I've got a stitch in my side . . . My head's whirling . . . Help! Water!

CHUBUKOV.   Your father was a rum-soaked gambler.

NATALIA.   And your aunt was queen of the scandalmongers!

LOMOV.   My left foot's paralyzed. You're a plotter . . . Oh, my heart. It's an open secret that in the last elections you brib . . . I'm seeing stars! Where's my hat?

NATALIA.   It's a low-mean, spiteful . . .

CHUBUKOV.   And you're a two-faced, malicious schemer!

LOMOV.   Here's my hat . . . Oh, my heart . . . Where's the door? How do I get out of here? . . . Oh, I think I'm going to die . . . My foot's numb. [*Goes*.]

CHUBUKOV [*Following him*].   And don't you ever set foot in my house again!

NATALIA.   Go to court, indeed! We'll see about that!

[LOMOV *staggers out*.]

CHUBUKOV.   The devil with him! [*Gets a drink, walks back and forth excited*.]

NATALIA.   What a rascal! How can you trust your neighbours after an incident like that?

CHUBUKOV.   The villain! The scarecrow!

NATALIA.   He's a monster! First he tries to steal our land, and then he has the nerve to yell at you.

CHUBUKOV.   Yes, and that turnip, that stupid rooster, has the gall to make a proposal. Some proposal!

NATALIA.   What proposal?

CHUBUKOV.   Why, he came to propose to you.

NATALIA.   To propose? To me? Why didn't you tell me before?

CHUBUKOV.   So he gets all dressed up in his formal clothes. That stuffed sausage, that dried up cabbage!

NATALIA.   To propose to me? Ohhhh! [*Falls into a chair and starts wailing*.] Bring him back! Back! Go get him! Bring him back! Ohhhh!

CHUBUKOV.   Bring who back?

NATALIA. Hurry up, hurry up! I'm sick. Get him! [*Complete hysterics.*]

CHUBUKOV. What for? [*To her.*] What's the matter with you? [*Clutches his head.*] Oh, what a fool I am! I'll shoot myself! I'll hang myself! I ruined her chances!

NATALIA. I'm dying. Get him!

CHUBUKOV. All right, all right, right away! Only don't yell! [*He runs out.*]

NATALIA. What are they doing to me? Get him! Bring him back! Bring him back!

[*A pause.* CHUBUKOV *runs in.*]

CHUBUKOV. He's coming, and so forth, the snake. Oof! You talk to him. I'm not in the mood.

NATALIA [*Wailing*]. Bring him back! Bring him back!

CHUBUKOV [*Yelling*]. I told you, he's coming! Oh Lord, what agony to be the father of a grown-up daughter. I'll cut my throat some day, I swear I will. [*To her.*] We cursed him, we insulted him, abused him, kicked him out, and now . . . because you, you . . .

NATALIA. Me? It was all your fault!

CHUBUKOV. My fault? What do you mean my fau——? [LOMOV *appears in the doorway.*] Talk to him yourself!

[*Goes out.* LOMOV *enters, exhausted.*]

LOMOV. What palpitations! My heart! And my foot's absolutely asleep. Something keeps giving me a stitch in the side . . .

NATALIA. You must forgive us, Ivan Vassilevitch. We all got too excited. I remember now. The Oxen Meadows are yours.

LOMOV. My heart's beating something awful. My Meadows. My eyebrows, they're both twitching!

NATALIA. Yes, the Meadows are all yours, yes, yours. Do sit down. [*They sit.*] We were wrong, of course.

LOMOV. I argued on principle. My land isn't worth so much to me, but the principle . . .

NATALIA. Oh, yes, of course, the principle, that's what counts. But let's change the subject.

LOMOV. Besides, I have evidence. You see, my aunt's grandmother let your father's grandfather's peasants use the land . . .

NATALIA.   Yes, yes, yes, but forget all that. [*Aside.*] I wish I knew how to get him going. [*Aloud.*] Are you going to start hunting soon?

LOMOV.   After the harvest I'll try for grouse. But oh, my dear Natalia Stepanovna, have you heard about the bad luck I've had? You know my dog, Guess? He's gone lame.

NATALIA.   What a pity. Why?

LOMOV.   I don't know. He must have twisted his leg, or got in a fight, or something. [*Sighs.*] My best dog, to say nothing of the cost. I paid Mironov 125 rubles for him.

NATALIA.   That was too high, Ivan Vassilevitch.

LOMOV.   I think it was quite cheap. He's a first class dog.

NATALIA.   Why Papa only paid 85 rubles for Squeezer, and he's much better than Guess.

LOMOV.   Squeezer better than Guess! What an idea! [*Laughs.*] Squeezer better than Guess!

NATALIA.   Of course he's better. He may still be too young but on points and pedigree, he's a better dog even than any Volchanetsky owns.

LOMOV.   Excuse me, Natalia Stepanovna, but you're forgetting he's overshot, and overshot dogs are bad hunters.

NATALIA.   Oh, so he's overshot, is he? Well, this is the first time I've heard about it.

LOMOV.   Believe me, his lower jaw is shorter than his upper.

NATALIA.   You've measured them?

LOMOV.   Yes. He's all right for pointing, but if you want him to retrieve . . .

NATALIA.   In the first place, our Squeezer is a thoroughbred, the son of Harness and Chisel, while your mutt doesn't even have a pedigree. He's as old and worn out as a pedlar's horse.

LOMOV.   He may be old, but I wouldn't take five Squeezers for him. How can you argue? Guess is a dog, Squeezer's a laugh. Anyone you can name has a dog like Squeezer hanging around somewhere. They're under every bush. If he only cost twenty-five rubles you got cheated.

NATALIA.   The devil is in you today, Ivan Vassilevitch! You want to contradict everything. First you pretend the Oxen Meadows are yours, and now you say Guess is better than Squeezer. People should say what they really mean, and you know Squeezer is a hundred times better than Guess. Why say he isn't?

LOMOV. So, you think I'm a fool or a blind man, Natalia Stepanovna! Once and for all, Squeezer is overshot!

NATALIA. He is not!

LOMOV. He is so!

NATALIA. He is not!

LOMOV. Why shout, my dear lady?

NATALIA. Why talk such nonsense? It's terrible. Your Guess is old enough to be buried, and you compare him with Squeezer!

LOMOV. I'm sorry, I can't go on. My heart . . . it's palpitating!

NATALIA. I've always noticed that the hunters who argue most don't know a thing.

LOMOV. Please! Be quiet a moment. My heart's falling apart . . . [*Shouts.*] Shut up!

NATALIA. I'm not going to shut up until you admit that Squeezer's a hundred times better than Guess.

LOMOV. A hundred times worse! His head . . . My eyes . . . shoulder . . .

NATALIA. Guess is half-dead already!

LOMOV [*Weeping*]. Shut up! My heart's exploding!

NATALIA. I won't shut up!

[CHUBUKOV *comes in.*]

CHUBUKOV. What's the trouble now?

NATALIA. Papa, will you please tell us which is the better dog, his Guess or our Squeezer?

LOMOV. Stepan Stepanovitch, I implore you to tell me just one thing; Is your Squeezer overshot or not? Yes or no?

CHUBUKOV. Well what if he is? He's still the best dog in the neighbourhood, and so forth.

LOMOV. Oh, but isn't my dog, Guess, better? Really?

CHUBUKOV. Don't get yourself so fraught up, old man. Of course, your dog has his good points—thoroughbred, firm on his feet, well sprung ribs, and so forth, But, my dear fellow, you've got to admit he has two defects; he's old and he's short in the muzzle.

LOMOV.   Short in the muzzle? Oh, my heart! Let's look at the facts! On the Marusinsky hunt my dog ran neck and neck with the Count's, while Squeezer was a mile behind them . . .

CHUBUKOV.   That's because the Count's groom hit him with a whip.

LOMOV.   And he was right, too! We were fox hunting; what was your dog chasing sheep for?

CHUBUKOV.   That's a lie! Look, I'm going to lose my temper . . . [*controlling himself*] my dear friend, so let's stop arguing, for that reason alone. You're only arguing because we're all jealous of somebody else's dog. Who can help it? As soon as you realize some dog is better than yours, in this case our dog, you start in with this and that, and the next thing you know—pure jealousy! I remember the whole business.

LOMOV.   I remember too!

CHUBUKOV [*Mimicking*].   "I remember too!" What do you remember?

LOMOV.   My heart . . . my foot's asleep . . . I can't . . .

NATALIA [*Mimicking*].   "My heart . . . my foot's asleep." What kind of a hunter are you? You should be hunting cockroaches in the kitchen, not foxes. "My heart!"

CHUBUKOV.   Yes, what kind of a hunter are you anyway? You should be sitting at home with your palpitations, not tracking down animals. You don't hunt anyhow. You just go out to argue with people and interfere with their dogs, and so forth. For God's sake, let's change the subject before I lose my temper. Anyway, you're just not a hunter.

LOMOV.   But you, you're a hunter? Ha! You only go hunting to get in good with the Count, and to plot, and intrigue, and scheme . . . Oh, my heart! You're a schemer, that's what!

CHUBUKOV.   What's that? Me a schemer? [*Shouting.*] Shut up!
LOMOV.   A schemer!
CHUBUKOV.   You infant! You puppy!
LOMOV.   You old rat! You Jesuit!
CHUBUKOV.   You shut up, or I'll shoot you down like a partridge! You idiot!

LOMOV. Everyone knows that—oh, my heart—that your wife used to beat you . . . Oh, my feet . . . my head . . . I'm seeing stars . . . I'm going to faint! [*He drops into an armchair.*] Quick, a doctor! [*Faints.*]

CHUBUKOV [*Going on, oblivious*]. Baby! Weakling! Idiot! I'm getting sick. [*Drinks water.*] Me! I'm sick!

NATALIA. What kind of a hunter are you? You can't even sit on a horse! [*To her father.*] Papa, what's the matter with him? Look, papa! [*Screaming.*] Ivan Vassilevitch! He's dead.

CHUBUKOV. I'm choking, I can't breathe . . . Give me air.

NATALIA. He's dead! [*Pulling* LOMOV'S *sleeve.*] Ivan Vassilevitch! Ivan Vassilevitch! What have you done to me? He's dead! [*She falls into an armchair. Screaming hysterically.*] A doctor! A doctor! A doctor!

CHUBUKOV. Ohhhh . . . What's the matter? What happened?

NATALIA [*Wailing*]. He's dead! He's dead!

CHUBUKOV. Who's dead? [*Looks at* LOMOV.] My God, he is! Quick! Water! A doctor! [*Puts glass to* LOMOV'S *lips.*] Here, drink this! Can't drink it—he must be dead, and so forth . . . Oh what a miserable life! Why don't I shoot myself! I should have cut my throat long ago! What am I waiting for? Give me a knife! Give me a pistol! [LOMOV *stirs.*] Look, he's coming to. Here, drink some water. That's it.

LOMOV. I'm seeing stars . . . misty . . . Where am I?

CHUBUKOV. Just you hurry up and get married, and then the devil with you! She accepts. [*Puts* LOMOV'S *hand in* NATALIA'S.] She accepts and so forth! I give you my blessing, and so forth! Only leave me in peace!

LOMOV [*Getting up*]. Huh? What? Who?

CHUBUKOV. She accepts! Well? Kiss her, damn you!

NATALIA. He's alive! Yes, yes, I accept.

CHUBUKOV. Kiss each other!

LOMOV. Huh? Kiss? Kiss who? [*They kiss.*] That's nice. I mean, excuse me, what happened? Oh, now I get it . . . my heart . . . those stars . . . I'm very happy, Natalia Stepanovna. [*Kisses her hand.*] My foot's asleep.

NATALIA. I . . . I'm happy too.

CHUBUKOV. What a load off my shoulders! Whew!

NATALIA. Well, now maybe you'll admit that Squeezer is better than Guess?

LOMOV. Worse!

NATALIA. Better!

CHUBUKOV. What a way to enter matrimonial bliss! Let's have some champagne!

LOMOV. He's worse!

NATALIA. Better! Better, better, better, better!

CHUBUKOV [*Trying to shout her down*]. Champagne! Bring some champagne! Champagne! Champagne!

Curtain

SOME QUESTIONS

1. Not all literary art is "serious." All of it is serious as it aims at a changing or moving or touching of men's minds or souls by technical means—that is, it aims seriously at this end—but the means it adopts are various. Among these means are comedy and farce. The definition for "farce" [1] given us is: "comedy of extravagant humor, buffoonery, and improbability"; which is not only very unsatisfactory in itself but depends upon our definition of "comedy." For this the dictionaries are even less satisfactory. "A dramatic work of a pleasant or humorous character," they say, and the best of them (for definition) says: "a story with a happy ending." Can you enumerate some elements of extravagance, buffoonery, and improbability, in this farce of Chekhov's?

2. Does it end happily? Or would you qualify this statement? How?

3. The term "climax" [2] is frequent in dramatic and literary criticism. Everyone knows what the word means in ordinary conversation; but all the dictionary tells us is: "the arranging of discourse in order of increasing strength: (*loosely*) the last term of the rhetorical arrangement: hence, a culmination." Here we have three possibilities. But some critics would say, of our play, that the climax comes with the daughter's wailing "Back! Bring him back!" How would you criticize both technical and colloquial definitions in terms of this difficulty?

4. Where would you locate the denouement?

5. In a work of "extravagant humor, buffoonery, and improb-

ability," one would not expect pathos. Is this a feature of Chekhov's farce? Where?

6. How would you describe the daughter's motivation? An executive type, opinionated and disillusioned (what passages would you choose to illustrate this last quality?) she twice nearly costs herself her marriage. What kind of connection would you make between this combination of characteristics in her and Lomov's hypochondria? Is the fact relevant that the great Russian author was also a physician?

7. Important authors have a tendency to disturb literary forms. Farce tends to be naive, ridiculous, implausible, physical, antipsychological, and we do not look to it for the criticism of life that is employed in high comedy.[3] Does, however, any criticism of life seem to you to be implied anywhere in this farce? If so, how would you express it?

8. Of the three characters, which seems to you to approach most nearly to the condition of comedy?

9. How does Chekhov vary the tempo of his dialogue?

TERMS AND PRINCIPLES

1. *Farce:* A species of humorous drama characterized by extravagance, buffoonery (often physical), and improbability.
2. *Climax:* The arranging of discourse in order of increasing strength; (loosely) the last term of the rhetorical arrangement; hence, a culmination.
3. *High comedy:* Comedy is more sophisticated than farce, and we use the term "high comedy" for the most sophisticated comedy of all—like Shakespeare's *Twelfth Night* or the plays of Congreve: polished, psychological, social, critical.

Glossary of Terms
and Principles

The page number following each of these terms is that of the page of text where the term originally appears. Each term is used in the Commentary or authors' Questions immediately preceding this page in the text, as noted under each term in the Index.

Many of these definitions employ terms that are themselves defined elsewhere in this Glossary; cross-referencing major terms in the definitions may be of help to the reader.

ACTION: The movements of *events* in a story, novel, or drama. A very limited term, compared to most of those we have been using. 224

In a poem or story or play, what happens in a narrative sense. 314

ACTION, ENVELOPING: An action which forms a surrounding context for the principal action. 452

ALLEGORY: A story in which the actions represent other actions and the characters other characters, or types. So there are at least two meanings, each sometimes even in a different series, for every incident. 297

ALLITERATION: The recurrence of the same initial sound in words in close succession. 235

AMBIGUITY: Inexactness about which one of several clear meanings the sentence, phrase, or word actually has. 131

Ambiguity is resolved by deciding which meaning to assign, or by making a separate statement for each meaning. 131

ANALOGY: A comparison of one thing with another in respect to some element which is identical, or alike, in both. Analogies may clarify or persuade; they are not proof. 12

A resemblance in certain respects between things otherwise different. 314

469

ANALYSIS: The truth or falsehood of factual matters cannot be decided by the use of logical analysis alone. It requires observation. Analysis can yield formal truth (as in tautology) and formal falsehood (as in self-contradiction). 103

ANAPEST: A foot consisting of three syllables, two unstressed syllables followed by a stressed one. 316

ANECDOTE: A short narrative of an incident of private life. 224

ASSERTION, THE PRINCIPLE OF SIGNIFICANT: A statement or phrase has meaning only if its contradictory has meaning. 71

ATMOSPHERE: The psychological "feel" of a story or its characters, the psychic medium in which the events occur. 235

BALLAD: A simple straightforward narrative poem in short stanzas. 329

CACOPHONOUS: Disagreeable, discordant, in sound. 316

CATASTROPHE: An overturning: a final event; the climax of the action of the plot. 452

CAUSE OF AN EVENT: Traditionally, the necessary *and* sufficient conditions for that event. 82

CHARACTERIZATION: The marking out by an author of his characters as distinct, by traits mentioned, description given, dialogue reported, etc. 225

    The speech or thought of a character in a play or work of fiction must not be treated as the belief of the author. 169

    The speech or thought of a character may not express what he himself means. The way to find out what he means is to relate it to the situation, the conduct of the character, and the whole work. 169

CHORIC: A chorus (from which "choral" and "choric") is a group talking or singing in unison. Greek tragedy developed from a religious chorus and always retained a chorus of some sort. The members are not distinguished from each other as individuals; they are just Theban elders or the townsmen of Corinth. They comment on the action or enter into it, but not as principals. 235

CIRCLE, ARGUING IN A: A logical fallacy. It occurs when we try to prove A and offer as evidence a statement that assumes the truth of A. Also known as begging the question. 104

CLASS OF OBJECTS: All objects referred to by the same word when it has a single meaning. 59

CLIMAX: What a sequence comes to its end in; culmination. 243

    The arranging of discourse in order of increasing strength; (loosely) the last term of the rhetorical arrangement; hence, a culmination. 467

COMEDY, HIGH: Comedy is more sophisticated than farce, and we use the term "high comedy" for the most sophisticated comedy of all—like Shakespeare's *Twelfth Night* or the plays of Congreve: polished, psychological, social, critical. 467

COMPLICATION: The name given in criticism to the entanglement of action, in most stories, which makes up the first part of the narrative (though frequently this is preceded by an *introduction*) and leads to the *resolution,* or second part, where the entanglement is straightened out or "resolved." This division of the parts of a story is artificial, of course; good stories seldom divide themselves so conveniently, the relations between their parts being organic. This term will be made clearer in the text; for the moment, it will be enough for you to ask yourself where your shoulder ends and your arm begins. 224

CONCEIT: Extended metaphor; a witty thought or analogy carried out far more elaborately than the usual simile or metaphor. 314

CONDITION, NECESSARY: Something in the absence of which an event does not occur. 82

When we try to learn whether A is a necessary condition for B, we must see whether or not B exists in the absence of A. (If it does, A is *not a necessary condition.*) We must make sure, if B has occurred in the presence of A and of other possibly related circumstances, that when we eliminate A to see if B, too, is eliminated, all of the other circumstances remain. 103–104

CONDITION, SUFFICIENT: Something, granted the necessary conditions, in the presence of which an event does occur. 82

CONNOTATION: To the logician, "connotation" is a synonym for "intension." To the grammarian it means the associations that cluster around a word, rather than its precise definition. 103

CONSISTENCY: The logical agreement of the parts of any statement, the absence of contradiction in a single argument, or at any one time. 12

CONTENT: *See* Form

CONTEXT, HISTORICAL: The meaning of statements uttered in other times and places can be discovered only by learning how the words were used then or there and by finding the assumptions and beliefs relevant to the passage that were common to the writer and his probable audience. 47–48

CONTEXT, TEXTUAL: Meaning is not entirely in isolated words but is provided by their context as well. 47

The statement, argument, and purpose of a sentence bears on the meaning of the words and phrases in it; the meaning of a sentence depends in part on the paragraph in which it occurs; and so on. 71

CONVENTION: A usage, in literature or painting, say, or for that matter in behavior (as hand-shaking) or thought, which is *agreed upon,* not experimental or idiosyncratic. The Commentary [on Marvell's "To His Coy Mistress"] will make the term clearer than any short notation can. 308

CORRELATIVE: A person or thing correspondingly related to another (person or thing). 314

COUNTERPOINT: The art of combining melodies, proceeding simultaneously. 316

COUPLET: Two successive lines of verse that rhyme with each other. 351

COUPLET, HEROIC: A couplet of which the meter is iambic pentameter. 351

DACTYL: A foot of three syllables, a stressed followed by two unstressed. 316

DEFINITION: The meaning of a word. 59

Definitions characterize classes. 59

A definition of a word properly includes all objects to which the word refers and excludes all others. 59

Defining characteristics are chosen because they are useful for some interest or purpose. 59

Defining characteristics are chosen from the totality of actual characteristics. 59

A definition may be substituted for the word it defines. The two are equivalent. 59

DEFINITION BY HYPOTHESIS: The use of a hypothesis about an event as though it were a definition of that event. 104

DENOTATION: To the grammarian, "denotation" is a synonym for "intension." To the logician, it is a synonym for "extension." One must make sure of the context—grammatical or logical—before deciding how it is used. 103

DENOUEMENT: The unraveling of a plot or story; the issue, event, or outcome. The word is used much as "catastrophe" is, but lacks the connotation of disaster which usually accompanies "catastrophe." 452

DEVICE: The way in which something is got done; contrivance. 250

The means by which something gets done; conveyance. 323

DIALOGUE: The conversation, usually formal or imaginary, of two or more persons. See the Commentary [on Shakespeare's *The Tragedy of Macbeth*] for some suggested differences between dialogue and ordinary conversation. 453

DICTION: Choice of words or language (as whether to use, depending on the context, "car" or "automobile"). In this sense, the word has nothing whatever to do with speaking or accent. 335

DRAMA, CLOSET: A play or plays intended to be read rather than acted. 452

ENTHYMEME, RHETORICAL: An argument of probability only, which is given the air, however, of logic, of demonstration, of certainty. An enthymeme is a syllogism with one of its three parts unstated, but assumed. Thus the syllogism, "All men are mortal, Socrates is a man, therefore Socrates is mortal," becomes an enthymeme when stated as, "All men are mortal, so Socrates is mortal," or "Socrates is a man, so Socrates is mortal."

A *rhetorical* enthymeme is intended to persuade rather than to demonstrate. Leaving out one step in the implied syllogism makes it easier to overlook any reference to proof. 308

EPIC: Here, larger than life size, heroic. 287

EPIGRAPH: A motto or citation at the beginning of a literary work. 350

EXTENSION: The meaning of a word in the sense of the things it refers to, or stands for; the *members* of a class, not the class itself. 103

FARCE: A species of humorous drama characterized by extravagance, buffoonery (often physical), and improbability. 467

FORM: The systematic and structural pattern, and unity, in a literary work. 225

The content of a work of art is not fully separable from the form of the work. And the form, of course, has no actual existence apart from its content. 169

FOOT: A division of a line of poetry. 316

FRAMEWORK, FRAME-ACTION: The action or dialogue which encloses, in some stories, the body of the story. 225

GLOSSING: Explaining a word or expression. 329

HYPERBOLE: Extravagant exaggeration. 308

HYPOTHESIS: One should not express a belief or hypothesis about the conditions under which an event takes place as if it were a definition, or part of a definition, of that type of event. (This does occur sometimes in science, but it is safe only when the hypothesis has been validated over and over by rigorous scientific methods.) 88

Whenever two or more hypotheses account equally well for all the known facts, find out whether one will account better for facts not now at hand. If so, choose that one throughout. If the hypotheses are interpretations of a passage, read on and see which interpretation best suits the sentences that follow. 12

IAMB: A foot of two syllables, an unstressed followed by a stressed. 316

IDEA, AS IDEAL: The idea of anything (thought of as a definition) is also the ideal of that thing, for the idea is a *conception* of a class or type, and so does not include the blemishes in any of its individual members. 82

IDEAS, LOGICAL NOVELTY IN: Meaning in a statement that was not contained in immediately prior statements or arguments. 150

IDEAS, PSYCHOLOGICAL NOVELTY IN: Discovery of the meaning of a conclusion that was already contained in its premises, but not recognized. 150

IDENTIFICATION: The tendency of a reader to identify himself with a character or characters in an imaginative literary work, or even with the author of it. 224

IMAGERY, IMAGE: The term applied to whatever, in a literary work, makes its appeal to the reader's *senses,* as of sight, hearing, taste, touch, smell. 225

Anything in a literary work which makes its appeal primarily to the senses, as of hearing, seeing, taste, touch. 335

IMPLICATION (or IMPLY): Logicians use this term to mean whatever follows deductively, or by reason alone, from a statement. Grammarians often use the word to mean whatever we associate with a word, its connotations (in their sense). 103

INTENSION: The meaning or definition of a word, in the dictionary sense. It characterizes a class, not a particular object. 103

IRONY: Briefly, conveyance of meaning by words, or events, whose intended meaning is different from their literal meaning, sometimes indeed the opposite. There is invariably some hidden force involved. 225

We have described *irony* as "speaking two ways" [in the Commentary on Ransome's "The Equilibrists"]. Here the poet says the lovers are "ruined," but yet they achieve a secret moral victory. The irony is *tragic* because the victory is won at the price of their destruction. 335

ITERATION: Repetition. 287

JARGON: Unnecessary technical language. It hides thought and gives a false impression of profundity. It is to be avoided. When jargon is encountered by the reader, he should try to translate it into ordinary English. 22

LEGITIMATE: A word of many meanings, most of them in the area of:— making its appeal to one's best judgment, or to standards of authenticity, or to the permanent. The opposite adjective always has a connotation of underhandedness, which is denied in "legitimate." 250

LYRICAL: Songlike (used here [in the Commentary on Eliot's "The Love Song of J. Alfred Prufrock"] ironically, of course). 351

MATERIAL: What goes into a literary work, the separate elements as they (or some of them) may have existed in the author's mind before composition. 225

MEANING, SECONDARY: Many expressions used in imaginative literature—poetry, fiction, drama—must be regarded as having two or more meanings, of which it is convenient to regard one as primary, the literal, and the others, depending as they do more on suggestion than statement, as secondary, tertiary, and so on. 324

MEANINGS, DISTINCTIONS IN: Distinctions between meanings should be made when, and only when, there is a real difference in the things meant. 12

MELODRAMA: Drama romantic and sensational, as a rule inadequately motivated and therefore crude; and sentimental, with strict attention to a conventionally conceived poetic justice and to a happy ending. 452

METAPHOR: Usually understood as a comparison without the use of "like" or "as," it normally applies terms from one context to things in another. This clarifies the meaning of relationships. 145

A figure of speech by which something is spoken of as *being* what it only *resembles*. 335.

MOCK-HEROIC: Burlesquing the heroic style. 287

MODE: Manner of existing; mood. 323

MOTIVATION: The systematic and concrete attribution of motive, by a dramatist, to his characters. Men's motives for what they do, in life, are regularly complex, and so in serious drama various motives are shown as woven into a strand that effectively stimulates reality. 452

NARRATIVE: A continued account of any series of occurrences; story. 224

NARRATOR, EFFACED: The author appearing in the story as little as possible, but without using a narrator inside the story. The method is usually scenic (see Point of view)—short views predominate. 226

NARRATOR, FIRST PERSON: The author telling the story through one of its characters, or by putting himself into the story. 226

NARRATOR, OMNISCIENT: The author telling the story in the third person, knowing everything. 226

NORM: Pattern, rule. 316

PACE: Rate of speed, as an element of style in a literary work or a part of it. 225

PARABLE: A short fictitious story from which a moral is to be drawn. 297

PARADOX: (1) A statement which seems to be self-contradictory, but turns out on analysis not to be; (2) a statement whose logical implication seems to contradict it, but actually does not. 15

A seemingly self-contradictory statement or situation; that which seems absurd but is or may be true. 314

Paradoxes may be resolved by specifying exactly what is meant. 15

PATHOS: In drama, the quality said to characterize the representation of what excites pity. 452

PENTAMETER: A verse (line) of five feet—in the case of iambic pentameter, all iambs of course, *in theory,* though as is pointed out in the text very few lines of poetry are perfectly regular. The *norm* will be iambic, however. 316

POEM, NARRATIVE: A poem that tells a story. 329

POINT OF VIEW: Two rather different technical ways of looking at fiction are comprehended under this awkwardly elastic term. The first concerns the different kinds of narrators that are possible: the omniscient, the first person, and the effaced (*see under* Narrator). The second concerns something more like long shots and close-ups in a film. The long view gives us panoramas, summaries; the short view gives us *scenes,* incidents. Instead of just telling *about,* looking off at, it dramatizes. Of course these two ways of understanding point of view overlap. 226

POST HOC ERGO PROPTER HOC (after this, therefore because of this): The fallacy of assuming that A caused B just because A preceded B. 74

PRESUPPOSITION: An unstated assumption. Its truth gives our argument logical validity. If it is false, our conclusion *may* yet be true, but that is accidental and not the result of the argument's logic. 73–74

PROBLEMS, VERBAL, AND REAL PROBLEMS: A verbal problem is actually a problem about the meaning of a question or proposition, although it often seems, erroneously, to be a question of truth. A real problem is a question of truth, and cannot be resolved, as a verbal problem can, by stating clearly what is meant. 88

PROPOSITION: There are three kinds of proposition:

(a) ANALYTIC: Their truth-value (truth or falsehood) depends on whether they are tautologies or self-contradictions. In either event, no evidence outside the propositions is relevant. Analysis of meaning is all that counts.

(b) EMPIRICAL: Their truth-value is determined in the end by reference to observation. Evidence comes ultimately from outside the propositions.

(c) NORMATIVE: These are judgments of value, moral and aesthetic. They assert that something is good or bad, beautiful or ugly, better or worse. 47

QUATRAIN: A stanza of four lines. 316

REALISM: A word with many meanings and ambiguous banners; here [in the Exercise on Lewis's "Song"] the meaning is "the taking a practical view in human problems." 323

REDUCTIVE: Beginning with something from which one then takes away. 351

RHETORIC: The theory and practice of eloquence: the use of all the arts of language to persuade or delight. 314

ROMANTIC: Another mysterious word; here [in the Exercise on Lewis's "Song"] the meaning is extravagant, fictitious (both are common dictionary meanings). 323

SACRIFICE: This is almost a technical word, so important is it in modern literature, perhaps in all literature. It comes, the notion of sacrifice, from primitive religion: an offering to a feared deity: something important has to be given up, voluntarily, in order that some fate may be escaped. From Homer to Henry James the idea has obsessed the creative mind, and it is one of the keys to "The Open Boat," as to Tolstoy's story "Master and Man" and other masterpieces. 288

SCAN: Analyze metrically (metrics is the science of versification). 316

SCENE: A division of a play marked off by the fall of the curtain or by the clearing of the stage of actors. This is the usual modern and Shakespearean sense, though exceptions will be found to it here and there; and the convention in Latin and French drama is quite different. 452

SELF-CONTRADICTION: A proposition whose subject and predicate contradict each other. All self-contradictions are logically false. 47

SELF-REVELATION: The device whereby characters explain directly (or almost directly) to the audience what is in their minds. The soliloquies of Macbeth and Lady Macbeth are the chief examples in this play, but her speeches in the sleep-walking scene may also be considered as self-revelation. 453

SEMI-PERSONIFICATION: An incomplete attribution of human traits to an abstract quality. 335

SENTENCE, PERIODIC: A sentence whose structure is opposed to that of a "loose" sentence, which will allow the insertion of a period, bringing it to an end as a grammatical whole, at some point *before* its end. 356

SENTIMENTALITY: Excess or affectation of feeling, or self-indulgence in it, generally with connotations of lack of genuineness and steadiness, qualities we associate with "sentiment." ("Connotation" we use here in the grammarian's sense, *see* Connotation.) We are referring to a word's secondary suggestions or associations, rather than to its intension. 250–251

SETTING: The place in which the action of a story, play, or poem goes on. But it also gives the physical characteristics of the action, and these provide some of the atmosphere. 235

SIMILE: An explicit likening of one thing to another. 225

A likening of one thing to another, made explicitly. 314

SONG: The melody to which something is sung. 316

SPECIFICATION, WEAK: The introduction of irrelevant or unnecessary details. 335

SPEECH: That which is spoken. 316

SPEECH-PREFIX: The speaker's name prefixed to a speech. 452

SPONDEE: A foot consisting of two syllables, both stressed. 316

STANZA: A group of lines of verse forming a definite pattern. 316

A group of lines of verse forming a definite pattern. 324

STATEMENTS: Analytic statements are certain because they are tautological. But they give no new knowledge, and no knowledge about fact. 150

Empirical statements can only be probable. But they do give new knowledge, and knowledge about fact. 150

If one statement implies a second, then if the first is true the second is true, but if the second is false, the first is false. 169

STRUCTURE: Arrangement of parts; manner of organization. 325

STYLE: The mode of expressing thought in language, distinctive to a particular author or a particular work. 224

SUBJECT: The stuff of the story, what is in it. But this term is to be distinguished sharply from the notion of *action* or what happens in the story. In Babel's story the subject is identified as "the qualities and responsibilities proper to a King, discoursed on by age for youth." 224

What a piece of writing is *about*. See Babel Commentary, p. 206. 325

SUBSTANCE: What underlies the subject, what it bears on, and how. This might be considered as the broad, permanent thought—or way of taking life—of the author, the "subject" being the particular instance embodied in the story in question. But the term shades forward into "theme" and the Commentary [on Babel's "In Odessa"] should be studied for the distinction. 224–225

SYMBOL: The word "symbol" is used differently in philosophy and in literary criticism. In the former it means either anything that functions as a sign, i.e. refers to something else, or a conventional sign (words, flags, traffic lights) rather than a natural one (dark clouds, which mean rain). In literary criticism, a "symbol" is usually a term whose meaning goes beyond the immediate story or event (as one says "home" in a context which reminds the reader of the idea that the soul's home is heaven). 235–236

Words themselves are conventional symbols. 59

TAUTOLOGY: A proposition the meaning of whose predicate is contained in the meaning of its subject. All tautologies are logically true. 47

TEMPO: Pace, the speed at which a play or a part of a play proceeds. 452

TETRAMETER: A verse-line of four feet. 316

THEME: A term which generalizes the activity, and outcome, of the substance; *why* the subject and substance are what they are. Theme comprehends the ideal, and the imaginative, more distinctly than the preceding terms. 225

TONE: A term originally musical, now used for the prevailing character or spirit in a literary work or anywhere in it, analogous to the tone of an individual human speaking or singing voice, not practically definable but to the acquainted ear unmistakable. 225–226

The prevailing *voice* (tint, shade, temper, mood) of a literary work, comparable to the individual speaking voice of a man or woman. 314

TONE, COLLOQUIAL: Tone of ordinary speech. 335

TRAGEDY: Drama in which the action and language are elevated, and the catastrophe usually sad. But see the text of the Commentary [on Shakespeare's *The Tragedy of Macbeth*]. 452

TRAGICOMIC: A term in which emphasis is to be laid on the first of its two components. There are no tragic authors whose view of life is essentially comic; the term is reserved for apparently comic authors whose views are at least in part essentially tragic. 225

TROCHEE: A foot of two syllables, the first stressed, the second not. 316

TRUTH, ANALYTIC: All propositions that are true analytically are themselves tautologies, or are part of an argument or a system that is formally or logically true. When a conclusion is derived logically from premises, its meaning is contained in those premises. The conclusion is true if the premises are, and is said to be analytic of the premises. 47

UNDERSTATEMENT: One understates when he says less than the literal truth. In imaginative literature, understatement can make the full, unrevealed truth stronger than if stated. 243.

UNITY, AESTHETIC: As the text explains, it is only by analogy that we speak of a work of art's having organic form, for it is not alive. But if we contrast the notion of the *mechanical* in bad art with the notion of the *organic* in good art, we can see that there is a sense in which it is useful to say that a poem or statue *is* alive: all of its parts grow from and supplement each other in an aesthetic unity which is entirely different from the mere piecemeal perfection of a machine. 308

UNIVERSE OF DISCOURSE: A context that includes everything meant by a given term and its contradictory. So the universe of color is the context including everything meant by "red" and "non-red" (which amounts to all colors). A universe of discourse contains some terms that are literally applicable only to the things in that context. The term "criminal," for example, applies literally to actions only in a legal and political context; "sin" in a religious and moral one. 145

VAGUENESS: Inexactness of meaning of a sentence, phrase, or word. 131
    Vagueness is often the result of using ideas that have their meanings only in a relation to other ideas, without including a statement of that relation. So if we use a comparative form without specification, we are vague. "That hill is higher" makes sense only if we have been talking of another hill, or some object. Otherwise it is hopelessly vague. 131
    Vagueness can be resolved by specifying the relations that have been omitted, or by qualifying a vague word or phrase. 131

VEHICLE: A means of conveyance, a medium. 314

VERBIAGE, EXCESS: Excess verbiage hides thought. It is to be avoided. 22

VERSE, BLANK: Unrhymed iambic pentameter. 351

VERSE, FREE: Verse in which the laws obeyed are different from, and have not been so acceptably formulated as, those obeyed by traditional verse; both as of foot-structure, and rhyme. 351

VERSIFICATION: The making of verse, or the analyzing of it. 316

WISDOM LITERATURE: A term applied to certain books of the Old Testament—which is Christian as well as Hebrew—which aim at an explanation of how human life should be conducted. 225

WIT, METAPHYSICAL: A term quite impossible to define; see the text [of the Commentary on Marvell's "To His Coy Mistress"]. The term comes from a celebrated passage in Samuel Johnson's *Life of Cowley* where the addiction of Donne and Cowley and other poets of the seventeenth century to farfetched conceits (for this word see the Commentary on Donne) was noticed and criticized. 308

WORD: A word should be used in one and the same sense throughout any single argument or statement. 15

WORTH, JUDGMENT OF: Our preferences and likes do not determine even our own judgment of the worth of works of art. We often like what we acknowledge as mediocre and dislike what we acknowledge as great. 169

Index

481